THE BOOK OF THE ACTS OF GOD

THE BOOK
OF THE ACTS
OF GOD

Contemporary Scholarship Interprets
the Bible

BY
G. ERNEST WRIGHT
AND
REGINALD H. FULLER

ANCHOR BOOKS
DOUBLEDAY & COMPANY, INC.
GARDEN CITY, NEW YORK

TYPOGRAPHY BY SUSAN SIEN

The Book of the Acts of God was originally published in a hardbound edition by Doubleday & Company, Inc. in 1957.

Anchor Books edition: 1960

FOREWORD

This book was written primarily for laymen. Its purpose is to introduce the Bible to the reader in something of the manner in which two scholars of the contemporary church present it to their students who are preparing for the Christian ministry. To be sure, many technical matters are omitted. The usual biblical introduction must concern itself in a technical way with the history, the text, and the canon of the Old and New Testaments. While these matters are here not ignored, they are nevertheless touched lightly, in order that the space may be used to depict the movement of biblical theology, the thoughts of believing men who sought to understand the ways of God and to proclaim those ways to their fellow men. Each writer treats his subject in an individual way, but on the whole they reflect the tendency of modern biblical scholarship to present the unity of the whole Bible in a somewhat different manner from that of the teachers on whose shoulders they stand.

The Prologue and Parts I and II were written by G. Ernest Wright. He would here publicly express his gratitude to the Reverend Edward F. Campbell, who has been of great service in the revision of the manuscript after it came from the hands of the typist, and but for whom its publication would have been delayed by the author's absence from this country. Some of the material used in Part I was taken from Sunday-school lessons written by the author and his wife and published in *Crossroads* and *The Westminster Teacher,* October–December, 1952 (Copyright 1952 by W. L. Jenkins). It is here used by permission.

Parts III and IV and the Epilogue were written by Reginald H. Fuller, who here would express his gratitude to his wife for detecting many typing errors and infelicities of expression.

Harvard Divinity School G. ERNEST WRIGHT
Cambridge, Massachusetts

Seabury-Western Theological
    Seminary REGINALD H. FULLER
Evanston, Illinois

G. ERNEST WRIGHT, Parkman Professor of Divinity at the Harvard Divinity School, is, in addition to being an Old Testament scholar, an archaeologist—one of the world's leading experts on the dating of artifacts—and has supervised major excavations in the Middle East. He is the author of several books, among them, *God Who Acts,* and *Biblical Archaeology.*

REGINALD H. FULLER is an English scholar who recently came to the United States and now teaches at the Seabury-Western Theological Seminary in Evanston. His teaching and lecturing have taken him to colleges and seminaries in England, Wales, Germany, and Switzerland. He is the translator of the works of Bonhoeffer and Bultmann, as well as being the author of *The Mission and Achievement of Jesus.*

A SUGGESTION TO THE READER OF THIS BOOK

The authors would advise the person who is thinking of using this book to read it straight through in order to see the sweep of the whole Bible before he begins to study the books of the Bible separately.

There is nothing so vitiating to interesting and productive Bible study as the continual focusing on individual verses or passages without relating them to their context in the work of a particular author, and without relating the author to his time, and both him and his time to the movement of the whole.

The Bible is a "historical" literature in which God is proclaimed as the chief actor in history who alone gives history its meaning. To study the Bible in such a way as to make abstractions of its spiritual or moral teachings, divorced from the real context of their setting in time, is to turn the Bible into a book of aphorisms, full of nice sayings which the devil himself could believe and never find himself particularly handicapped either by the knowledge of them or by their repetition.

CONTENTS

PROLOGUE: Introducing the Bible   1
  CHAPTER I: The Biblical Point of View   3
  CHAPTER II: The Knowledge of God   17
  CHAPTER III: How the Bible Came to Be Written   31
    A. The Old Testament   31
    B. The New Testament   39
    C. Many Volumes, One Book   42

PART I: The Histories of Israel   45
  CHAPTER I: The Priestly History   47
    A. The Introduction (*Chapters 1–11*)   48
      1. The Creation Stories (*Genesis 1–2*)   49
      2. The "Fall" of Man (*Genesis 3*)   54
      3. The Story of Civilization (*Genesis 4–11*)   59
    B. God Chooses a People: The Stories of the
      Patriarchs (*Genesis 12–50*)   61
    C. The Exodus: God Delivers the People from
      Slavery (*Exodus 1–18*)   73
    D. God Makes the People a Nation: The Covenant
      (*Exodus 19–Numbers 36*)   84
  CHAPTER II: The Deuteronomic History of Israel
      in Her Land   99
    A. God's Gift of a Land (*Joshua–Judges*)   102
    B. The Problem of Government: The Monarchy
      (*I–II Samuel*)   112
    C. God's Controversy with the Kings (*I–II Kings*)   121
      1. Solomon   123

2. Ahab and Jezebel 127
3. The Fall of Northern Israel and
Its Sequel in Judah 131
4. The Last Days of Judah and Jerusalem 132
CHAPTER III: The Chronicler's History of Judah
(I–II Chronicles, Ezra, and Nehemiah) 137

PART II: The Prophetic, Devotional, and
Wisdom Literature 147
CHAPTER I: The Prophets 149
A. The Prophets of the Eighth Century B.C. 151
B. The Prophets of the Seventh Century B.C. 163
C. The Last of the Old Testament Prophets 170
CHAPTER II: The Devotional and Wisdom Literature 183
A. The Psalms 183
B. The Wisdom Literature 190
CHAPTER III: The Close of the Old Testament 207

PART III: Between the Old and New Testaments 215
CHAPTER I: Historical Background—From the
Maccabees to Jesus 217
CHAPTER II: The Jewish Community 223
CHAPTER III: The Jewish Religion 227
A. Pharisaism and Rabbinic Judaism 228
B. Apocalyptic 231
1. The Testament of the Twelve Patriarchs 233
2. I Enoch 234
C. Palestinian Sects 235
D. The Damascus Covenanters 236
E. The Qumran Community 237
F. John the Baptist and Jesus of Nazareth 241
G. Hellenistic Judaism 243
H. Josephus 251

PART IV: The New Testament 253
CHAPTER I: In the Beginning Was the Word 255
CHAPTER II: Jesus 261
A. Introductory 261
B. The Proclamation of Jesus 266

C. The Demand of Radical Obedience 270
D. Jesus' Teaching about God 271
E. The Works of Healing 272
F. The Cross 275
G. The Person of Jesus 281
CHAPTER III: The Earliest Church 287
A. From Easter to Pentecost 287
B. The Life of the Earliest Church 292
C. Greek-Speaking Jewish Christianity 298
CHAPTER IV: Non-Pauline Hellenistic Christianity 301
A. Introductory 301
B. Its Preaching 302
C. Its Sacramental Life 310
D. The Synoptic Gospels 314
   1. Mark 315
   2. Matthew 316
   3. Luke 317
CHAPTER V: St. Paul: The First Theologian 321
A. Critical Presuppositions 321
B. Paul the Theologian 323
C. Redemptive History 324
   1. Redemption 332
   2. Justification 334
   3. Reconciliation 335
   4. The Appropriation of Christ's
      Redeeming Work 336
   5. Victory 339
   6. Sacrifice 340
   7. The Resurrection 342
   8. The Spirit and the Church 343
   9. The Church 345
  10. The Sacraments 346
  11. The Person of Christ 350
  12. The Consummation 353
CHAPTER VI: After Paul 357
A. Ephesians 357
B. Hebrews 358
C. The Pastorals 365

D. James   366
E. I Peter   369
F. Jude   372
G. II Peter   373
CHAPTER VII: The Johannine Literature   375
A. The Apocalypse   375
B. The Fourth Gospel and the Johannine Epistles   379
    1. Authorship   380
    2. Affinities of Thought   382
    3. Literary and Oral Sources   385
    4. Authorship—Final Conclusion   386
    5. The Johannine Writings—An Interpretation   386
    6. The Farewell Discourses   398
    7. The Passion Narrative   402
    8. The Resurrection   403
CHAPTER VIII: Epilogue: The Unity of the
             New Testament   405
Index of Biblical References   407
Index of Names   417

INTRODUCING THE BIBLE

CHAPTER I

THE BIBLICAL POINT OF VIEW

Christianity has always held that the Bible is a very special book unlike any other book in the world. It is the most important of all books because in it, and in it alone, the true God has made himself known to man with clarity. The world is full of sacred literatures and it is full of gods. But in the vast confusion the one source which can be relied upon for the truth is the Bible. There we are told about the events which brought the Church into being, and the purpose for its being. There we encounter the answer to the meaning of our own lives and of the history in which we live. There the frightening gulf between our weak, ignorant, and mortal lives and the infinity of power and space in our universe is really bridged. There we discover our duty defined and our God revealed. The many segments of the Christian Church have said all this in a great variety of ways with a variety of emphases; but all have agreed that the Bible has been the fountain from which have come the Church and its faith. It is the common starting point to which we must constantly return for guidance and stimulation.

Yet how is a modern man to receive and believe the Bible? When it speaks about the world being created in six days, while the seventh is to be a day of rest because on it God rested from his labors of creation, what does it mean? Was there ever a Garden of Eden, and did a serpent actually speak within it? To many people today the Bible, while possessing beautiful sayings and fine ideas, is nevertheless basically a collection of myths and stories which no one can really take seriously. The American commentator, H. L. Mencken, once wrote:

> Christianity, as religions run in the world, is scarcely to be described as belonging to the first rank. It is full of vestiges of the barbaric cults that entered into it, and some of them are shocking to common sense, as to common decency. . . . It is full of lush and lovely poetry. The Bible is unquestionably the most beautiful book in the world. Allow everything you please for the barbaric history in the Old Testament and the silly Little Bethel theology in the New, and there remains a series of poems so overwhelmingly voluptuous and disarming that no other literature, old or new, can offer a match for it. . . . No other religion is so beautiful in its very substance—none other can show anything to match the great strophes of flaming poetry which enter into every Christian gesture of ceremonial and give an august inner dignity to Christian sacred music. Nor does any other, not even the parent Judaism, rest upon so noble a mythology. The story of Jesus . . . is, indeed, the most lovely story that the human fancy has ever devised, and the fact that large parts of it cannot be accepted as true surely does no violence to its effectiveness, for it is of the very essence of poetry that it is not true: its aim is not to record facts but to conjure up entrancing impossibilities. . . . Moreover, it has the power, like all truly great myths, of throwing off lesser ones, apparently in an endless stream.[1]

The typical "bible" of the world is filled with a great variety of spiritual, moral, and cultic teachings, whence the popular saying "Confucius say this" or "Confucius say that." The Christian Bible has teachings, too, but they are a part of a larger whole—a history of a people that starts with the creation of the world, then passes through Abraham, Moses, David, etc., and ends with Paul and the early Church. Somehow we are

[1] H. L. Mencken, "The Poetry of Christianity," *The World's Best* (New York, The Dial Press, 1950), pp. 148–150. Originally published in a volume of Mencken's essays by Alfred A. Knopf, Inc. and used by permission.

supposed to be taught religiously from that story. When the missionary goes to other lands and seeks to convert people to Christianity, he begins with the elements of this Bible story. Small groups of Christians gather in their weekly meetings, studying the Bible, seeking first a knowledge of the great story. Christianity has always taught that in a real history of what once happened in the ancient world God came and revealed himself. Hence the Bible presents factual history, in which is seen the work of the living God. Jesus Christ is thus a real personage, not simply a beautiful piece of imaginative poetry, because he is related to the work of the sovereign God, who has sent him into history with a mission to perform.

Yet it may well appear to an intelligent critic that I as a Christian want to base my faith on a series of stories a man simply cannot believe any longer. I open the Bible and begin to read, and soon encounter an explanation of the existence of woman as being built out of a rib of a man, about a snake that speaks, about a world in which God and his angels are heard in daily life communicating with various personages and with one another, about waters dividing and people crossing through, about water turning into wine, etc. How is any man to believe these things? Are they anything other than a kind of poetry, beautiful in its essence, crude in its externals? And if one does not believe one part of it, how can he take any of it seriously?

Among the many curious episodes of modern times none is more strange than the so-called "controversy" over the Dead Sea Scrolls. The first scholarly reports of this remarkable discovery were published in 1948 in journals of the American Schools of Oriental Research, edited by W. F. Albright and the writer. They did not come to popular attention, however, until Mr. Edmund Wilson published a lengthy account of the find in *The New Yorker* magazine.[2] With that article the "controversy" may be said to have begun. Of course, as was to be expected, a scholarly debate had been going on for some time

[2] The issue for May 14, 1955. Wilson subsequently published his story in book form, *The Scrolls from the Dead Sea* (New York, 1955).

regarding the date of the manuscripts, their interpretation, and their significance. During the course of this, as with all such debates, a great deal of nonsense was written. Yet on the scholarly level major issues of this sort can gradually be resolved, as they have been in the case of the scrolls by more information and deeper study. The "controversy" over the scrolls, however, was on a different level. It arose from the suggestion that somehow the new discovery was a threat to the Christian faith, because Jesus and the New Testament writers will now be seen to have a historical background. One will no longer have to make elaborate claims concerning the supernatural character of New Testament events. Jesus can be studied, not as a being of miracle, known only by dogma and divine revelation, but as a human being in history, with a background for his teachings and the interpretation of his mission in the world. In other words, the divinity of Christ can now no longer be believed; he was not let down out of heaven; he is just another of history's great men.

Leading biblical scholars the world over, whether Protestant or Roman Catholic, looked on in amazement, not to say amusement, at this rather artificially contrived "controversy," carried on by those who were little acquainted with modern biblical or theological scholarship. What is so important theologically about the Dead Sea Scrolls? After all, it has always been understood that Christianity arose from a Jewish background. Part of the significance of the scrolls is that now we can say more in detail about that background. But is the theological understanding of Jesus Christ in any way affected by the discovery of more information about his background? What, after all, is the Bible? Is it simply a series of tales about supernatural doings which only the gullible can accept and then only on "faith"? Or is it an interpretation of the meaning of earthly happenings at a certain time and place and with a given background of faith and experience? Is revelation a series of dogmas from heaven, or the actions of God which give meaning to history? And if the biblical events that are understood to be the acts of God are seen to be continuous with and interpreted by events that a historian can study on a "secular level," does this mean that the theological understanding of them is automatically wrong? On earth a meteor is a piece of rock, but does that mean it did not come from the heavens? Behind these queries is the question as to whether the Bible itself has a particular religious point of view that we today do not readily comprehend. What is the relation between fact and faith in the Bible? What are the acts of God? Let us attempt to give a brief answer to these questions.

A. Christianity, historians have said, is a historical religion. In one sense this means that it has a history like all other religions. In that context it is one of the world's religions. Yet in another sense it must be affirmed that Christianity among the religions seems to be the only one that takes history seriously, for it assumes that the knowledge of God is associated with events that really happened in human life. For illustration let us take the period of the prophets in the Old Testament, between the ninth and the fifth centuries B.C. This is the first great age of empire building in world history. The time was dominated by the great imperialistic wars, with one great empire succeeding another. The biblical historian and the prophet affirmed that God's attitude toward his people, his intention, and his purpose were revealed in those very events. The Assyrians, the Babylonians, and the Persians were God's instruments in effecting his historical purpose. The biblical eye of faith was not focused internally, in the belief that religion is primarily an internal experience, nor was it focused sacramentally in various great forms of religious expression, though of these it had a great number. The eye instead was focused on the great external events of world history during that age. Of course, there were people present in the nation of Israel who wanted to turn the whole religion into a more comfortable sacramentalism, but there was something deep within the faith which rebelled and always has rebelled against such a conversion of the faith into that which it is not. People were called to look at themselves in their current society in Palestine. They were asked by the prophets to measure what they saw against certain standards which had been revealed to them. In the light of what was going on in the international politics of the day, what do these things mean? Simply this, said the prophets: God intends the destruction of the Israelite and Judean states.

In making this affirmation, every major segment of ancient Israelite life was saying that the standards already given by which current life was to be measured are to be found in the Mosaic period, in the early days of Israel's history as a nation before her entrance into Palestine. They are to be found in the ancient Sinai covenant. The biblical historian and prophet further said that the destruction which was at hand was not the end of the nation. Early in their history, God had made wonderful promises to this people. Hence they affirm there will be a future, and with it a resolution of their problem and the problem of the whole world. That future is God's kingdom when his rule will be acknowledged throughout the world. In the centuries just past the most remarkable characteristic of God's action toward them had been his love and his grace. It had been his undeserved loyalty to his promises, a loyalty first seen in the fact that they were delivered from slavery in Egypt, in the fact that they were given a land, in the fact that they were given a fine government under David.

In this point of view we note that the rootage of the faith seems to be found in the following: (1) The Israelite patriarchs, whose stories are preserved in the book of Genesis, had received certain promises, and the history of the nation of Israel was interpreted as a fulfillment of those promises. (2) The exodus from Egypt was interpreted as God's freeing of a people from slavery. It was a setting free and it was interpreted by the historian as a fulfillment of the promise. (3) A special and unique experience had taken place in the wilderness after the people had left Egypt. It took place at Mount Sinai, where the understanding of society and of community obligation was somehow obtained in a law or a teaching regarding community duty. (4) The conquest of Canaan whereby Israel secured a land for itself, was interpreted as God's gift of an inheritance. The land was not interpreted as belonging to various individuals and families of Israel as a natural right, but was thought of as a gift of God. Thus there came about a special understanding of the meaning of property and of obligation in relation to it. Unless Israel was faithful to her assumed obligations in relation to God, the land, which was God's gift, would be taken away at a future time. (5) The conquests of David were regarded as the final fulfillment of the promise of land, and the Davidic government was regarded as the final fulfillment of the promise of security from enemies and from slavery.

There are, then, five "events" in the Old Testament in which the whole faith seems to center. These are the call of the fathers, the deliverance from slavery, the Sinai covenant, the conquest of Canaan, and the Davidic government. Of this group of "events," the call and promises to the fathers, the deliverance from slavery, and the gift of a land (the conquest) are known from liturgy and confessions to be the key elements of the whole story. When an Israelite confessed his faith, he simply gave an interpreted version of his national tradition. One of the oldest confessions in the Old Testament is contained in Deuteronomy 26:5–9. When a worshiper brought a basket of his first fruits to present at the central sanctuary, he was to repeat the following:

"A perishing Aramaean was my father; and he went down into Egypt, and sojourned there with a few, and there became a nation, great, mighty and populous. But the Egyptians treated us evilly, afflicted us, and laid upon us hard bondage. And when we cried unto the Lord God of our fathers, the Lord heard our voice . . . and the Lord brought us forth out of Egypt with a mighty hand . . . and he hath brought us into this place, and hath given us this land, even the land that floweth with milk and honey."

Clearly in this confession, which dates before the tenth century in all probability, the central events are the exodus and the conquest. If an Israelite wished to confess his faith in even shorter form, he might confine his attention to the exodus. Who is God? He is "the Lord thy God, who has brought thee out of the land of Egypt, out of the house of bondage" (Exodus

9

20:2). The 105th Psalm is a beautiful example of a longer confession written in a later period; there the whole story is told, beginning with the words "O give thanks unto the Lord . . . make known his deeds among the people" and ending with the words "praise ye the Lord." In other words, when biblical man confessed his faith, he did so by telling the story of his past, interpreted by his faith. He learned to present his faith in the forms of history.

B. In the five basic elements which stand in the background of all Old Testament writing and faith, what can be said to be factual? Modern historical and archaeological research make it highly probable that each one of the five rests on a real historical or factual footage. The patriarchal stories so reflect an atmosphere in the first half of the second millennium B.C., and the patriarchal movement itself is so closely related with great migratory movements that we know to have been going on in that time, that it is difficult to separate the narratives from the contemporary history. The whole background and color of the patriarchal age has been brought to life by modern research. There is undoubtedly a factual basis to the patriarchal stories. That there must once have been an exodus of a group of slaves from Egypt, slaves who had been put to work on public building projects in the Egyptian delta, also is undoubtedly historical. We can say as much, too, for some experience during the wilderness wanderings whereby this group of heterogeneous slaves was organized into a nation with one common faith. The conquest of Canaan, interpreted as God's gift of a land, is given eloquent testimony in the devastation visited upon a number of the Palestinian cities which are known from archaeology to have been destroyed during the second half of the thirteenth century (before Christ), a time to which all other indications also lead us as a date for the period of Joshua. When we come to David and the Davidic theology of government, we are in the firm light of history, with contemporary sources upon which to rest our investigation.

Yet other peoples have had events in their background which are not dissimilar. We in the U.S.A. have our founding fathers, our exodus from European oppression, our covenant in the Constitution and Bill of Rights, our conquest of America, and a succession of great men who have been the fathers of our country, beginning obviously with George Washington. In other words, the biblical event as event of history is not overly impressive as to its uniqueness. Historical research has shown it probable that an Abrahamic family did migrate from Mesopotamia in the first half of the second millennium. But is this particularly significant? The main point of the biblical story is not simply the migration, but the statement that God called Abraham and gave to him the wonderful promises. Is that fact and are those promises the empirical, objective, verifiable facts of history? Obviously they are not. Israel during the second half of the thirteenth century gave the old Canaanite city-states in Palestine a very severe drubbing. That seems to be a historical fact. But is it a fact in the same sense that God was the commander in chief of that war?

The point is, then, that real historical events are here involved, but in themselves they do not make the biblical event. In the Bible an important or signal happening is not an event unless it is also an event of revelation, that is, unless it is an event which has been interpreted so as to have meaning. Indeed, this is true for any fact. Unless it is given meaning in a certain context, it is meaningless and insignificant. Everything that is significant demands interpretation. In the Bible every historical event is always interpreted by the historian and the prophet, by those who were present at the time, and by the successive generations of religious worshipers in the community of faith. Thus every event had a context of meaning attached to it. No modern scholar can "prove" the Bible. Historical and archaeological research can uncover the factual background in ancient history. But the meaning, the interpretation, the faith which in the Bible is an integral part of the event itself—this no one can prove. Like all great convictions it is something which is shared and proclaimed. Nothing of basic or ultimate meaning in our world can ever be proved. One cannot prove the value of Mozart's music any more than he can prove the nature of space. With regard to the biblical viewpoint I either accept or I reject the general over-all conviction that these happenings in the history of the ancient Near East are indeed significant in that they convey a real knowledge of the true God. This is a conviction which is shared in a community of faith, which is given certainty through the experience of the Church through the centuries, together with the examination of rival views as to the meaning of life and history.

C. We have seen that the point of view of the Old Testament is that real events have been interpreted as God's purposed and planned activity, an activity in which a future is involved. In the atmosphere thus established the New Testament is firmly set. There the first four books describe a true human being, who was born under Herod the Great and died under Pontius Pilate. That was a real historical event. But as objective or factual history it means little until it is interpreted, until the whole context of meaning is given it. As previously suggested, every event in history, if important, will be interpreted by a particular context of meaning. In the New Testament, therefore, Jesus is interpreted as God's great act; he is not to be understood apart from the planned activity of God.

In the New Testament story the following appear to be the important events: (1) The real life and teaching of Jesus. (2) His death on a cross at the hands of the Romans. (3) His resurrection as head of the new community established in him, that is, the Church. There have been those in Christian history who would insist that the birth of Christ is also a primary event in the New Testament story. Yet the only places where his birth is mentioned in the New Testament are in the introductions to Matthew and Luke. It is never mentioned elsewhere in the literature of the first-century Church, insofar as it has been preserved for us. None of the early preachers ever allude to it. Hence it is questionable whether for the New Testament itself the birth stories are to be placed on the same level of importance as the three above mentioned. In any case, the purpose of these stories is to affirm that the birth of Christ is God's great act, that God has here come into our history in a dramatic fashion as a fulfillment of his promises of old.

D. It is clear then that not all of the contents of the Old and the New Testaments are on the same level of importance. The five Old Testament faith-events previously pointed out and the three central faith-events of the New Testament are those main events which carry in themselves for the biblical man the main significance of life and history. It is by these great events that all else is interpreted. It is also these same events which form the central content of confession and liturgy. Around them the whole Bible takes form.

Yet it is also true that not all of these events have behind them the same amount of factual evidence. The life of David, the life and teachings of Jesus, and the death of Jesus: for these three we have the most detailed and in general reliable information. The general picture of the exodus, the Mount Sinai or wilderness experience, and the conquest of Canaan can also be drawn, though perhaps somewhat more sketchily. Matters are different, however, with regard to the patriarchs in Genesis. Except for the Joseph story in Genesis 37–50 we do not have a connected narrative. The material is fragmentary, and provides only occasional glimpses of the life of this time. Although archaeological research has given us a historical basis for the narratives, nevertheless the material is near the level of saga. It has had a long history before it has reached the written form. Hence, we should add one new point to those previously mentioned: namely, that the Bible is a literature which takes history and *historical traditions* seriously. That is, the people of the faith interpreted the factual material which they had and the traditions of their people which had come down to them in the light of their faith.

This furnishes a clue to our understanding of the prehistoric material preserved in Genesis 1–11. These traditions go far back into the dim and unrecoverable history of Israel; they are the popular traditions of a people, traditions which in part go back to a pre-Canaanite and North Mesopotamian background. For this reason there is little question of objective history here. We are instead faced with the question of why the old traditions were written down. What was the purpose of the writers who preserved them for us? They were not simply writing down the traditions of their people for purposes of entertainment. The old folk stories with which all were familiar had a deep meaning, if understood in the light of God's work. What is significant in this prehistoric, legendary, and mythological material, therefore, is not simply the collection of factual statements concerning world origins which they contained. Those statements are certain to reflect the views of the universe which were then current. What is of importance here is the purpose which caused the writers to recast and reform the old traditions and to put them into writing.

Finally, what shall we say about the resurrection of Christ, as understood in the New Testament? This cannot be an objective fact of history in the same sense as was the crucifixion of Christ. The latter was a fact available to all men as a real happening, and pagan writers like Tacitus and Josephus can speak of it. But in the New Testament itself the Easter faith-event of the resurrection is perceived only by the people of the faith. Christ as risen was not seen by everyone, but only by the few. Easter was thus a reality for those in the inner circle of the disciples and apostles. That is not an arena where a historian can operate. Facts available to all men are the only data with which he can work, the facts available to the consciousness of a few are not objective history in the historian's sense.

Hence we have to view the resurrection in the New Testament as a faith-event, unlike other events, which is nevertheless real to the Christian community. It testifies to the knowledge that Christ is alive, not dead. The living Christ was known to be the head of the Church; and his power was real. The process, the how of Christ's transition from death to the living head of the new community, and the language used to describe that transition ("raised the third day," "ascension," "going up," "sitting on the right hand of God")—these are products of the situation. They are the temporal language of the first-century Christians. To us, they are symbols of deep truth and nothing more, though they are symbols that are difficult to translate.

E. Finally, if it be granted that the clue to the Bible is to be found in these events, understood as here we have attempted to suggest, we can return to the beginning and say that Christianity is a historical religion in the sense that real events and traditions are interpreted in such a way as to reveal the nature of God and of man. The biblical point of view was to take history and historical tradition seriously and through them to foresee a future. Faith is thus set within the forms of history.

In this perspective what are we to make of all the unbelievable things to which allusion was made above: the snake talking, water turning into wine, woman taken from the rib of man, etc.? These are all there, but somehow they are no longer so troublesome. They belong to the fringe of the central narrative for the most part, and neither their affirmation nor their denial can be used to negate the whole historical viewpoint either as fact or faith. They belong to the temporal features of the story. They show God's action in history as one which made use of people as they were, employing the outlook and the categories of mind and the traditions of the people as then they actually lived and felt. And, furthermore, they suggest to us that God who is still Lord, is using our minds, our culture, our science, our art, our limitations, our evil as the means by which his revelation is today to be comprehended. The Bible, the story of what God once did, provides us spectacles whereby we are made to see, whereby the otherwise confused notions of God and life are brought into focus around a central perspective. Archaeology and historical research are vitally important to us as we seek to understand the Bible, because they illumine the background and history of the time from which the Bible comes. The more we know about those times the more we shall be able to understand the data with which biblical man was working. His faith was centered in the realities of life, in the attempt to understand what they meant; he projected his faith deep within the realities of historical evil and saw in the backdrop of the world's darkness the brilliant light of God. The more we know, therefore, about biblical man's age, the more we shall be able to comprehend the reality of his faith.

CHAPTER II

THE KNOWLEDGE OF GOD

For biblical man the knowledge of God is inseparably associated with the understanding of history's meaning. He believed that he was existing in a unique history which possessed a special significance because God, through it, was shown to be in the process of redeeming all history. He learned to confess his faith in the forms of history by taking the events of his own people and the traditions of his past seriously, because these alone revealed the nature and the purpose of the true God. Jesus Christ was not simply another of the many religious teachers on earth. He had come as one sent especially from God at the fulfillment or climactic point of a special time, a time prepared through the centuries by God through his special work with this one people.

How had biblical man come to so unusual a point of view concerning the source of his knowledge of God? The explanation must lie in the historical experience of his people. It must rest far back in the beginning of their national existence when Israel as a group of slaves was a people whom the world's law and justice passed by. The great gods of the world at the time of Moses were gods who were particularly interested in the owners and providers of the great temples. These gods were the world's greatest aristocrats, and they were served by an elaborate political, economic, and ecclesiastical system. The whole religion about them was a support of the current status quo in society. But with Israel a most unusual thing had happened. A power greater than any known power in the universe, a power great enough to make both the heart of a recalcitrant

Pharaoh and all the powers of nature serve him, had rescued a depressed people from the hands of her oppressors.

This fact is the rootage of that peculiar viewpoint by which Israel is clearly to be differentiated from all other peoples of her time. Wherever one moves in the later society of Israel, whether in religious hymns or prophecies, whether in instructions for priests or teaching for children, whether in legal tradition or in pastoral or agricultural festival, the early encounter with deity in the events of a great deliverance is normative. God met the people while they were needy and delivered them from their oppression. From this point it was inevitable that the eye of the Israelite would be trained to give attention to the events which happened subsequently. The great Power which had saved him must have had a purpose in doing so. What was God about? The primary place for the Israelite to learn was in what was happening around him. The eye of faith was trained to take human events seriously because in them was to be learned more clearly than anywhere else what God willed and what he was doing. Consequently, in all that happened subsequent to the exodus the Israelite simply interpreted the meaning of events by recognizing and acknowledging in them the God who had formed the nation by the remarkable signs and wonders experienced at the exodus and in the wilderness. History, therefore, was always pointing forward to something. God's purpose and plan always was to be discerned ahead.

The purpose involved a vocation in history; it attracted the best from the Israelite follower. It was an external, independent purpose. It was always in conflict with the normal, national desires of the people. The nation had to follow, or suffer the consequences. During the great international wars in which Israel was soon enmeshed, like many other small nations of the ancient civilized world, the faith was never lost. The God of Israel did not die as the gods of the world died in the events which destroyed the political existence of the people. The Lord was one who was directing these wars toward his own ends, even though the conquering armies did not know or acknowledge it. God alone is in charge of history. As one who had met Israel in historical event he thus was recognized as the Lord of all events who was directing the whole course of history toward his own ends, for nothing happened in which his power was not acknowledged. For this reason the gospel stories present a picture of one who is not simply a fine rabbi; he is to be understood as vitally associated with God's historical purpose. He and the Church that exists in him are not to be understood in their humanity alone. They can only be comprehended in their relation to the purposive activity of the sovereign God. The Lord of history is the Lord of Jesus Christ; the latter has come to earth to do the former's work. Thus we, too, who are members of Christ's Church must find the clue to our own lives, not simply in devotional exercise, nor in the service of self, but in the service of him who placed us here. We become followers of him whose action in history has saved us from slavery.

This biblical viewpoint toward the source of our knowledge of God is not a common or usual one. The normal person seems to think of the knowledge of God as available from some other sphere than history. This was true in biblical times and it is still true today. The message of the great prophets of Israel met with disbelief on the part of many hearers, for example, who said in effect, "God does not see us, and he is not going to send these terrible punishments upon us" (e.g., Jeremiah 5:12; Zephaniah 1:12). That is, God is not the kind of a God the prophets said that he is. He is not a being with eyes that are always keeping watch over us. He is not a God who takes that much individual or personal interest in us. He is not one who pushes people and nations around like pieces on a chessboard. His is not a will that moves history and that ultimately alone can give the explanation of history. Whatever or whoever God is, he has too many other concerns for this sort of thing. In the Bible this was a typical kind of disbelief; it was the practical "atheism" of sinners who rejected a theology which in any way imposed a threat upon their way of life and demanded of them reformation.

Furthermore, it may be added that the bold affirmation of God's Lordship over history involves all sorts of problems which classical philosophies have always sought to avoid. If God is Lord, why is there so much evil and misery in the world? Why does God not prevent it? God is surely too good and too pure to be involved with the filth and muck of current human history. To be a religious man must surely mean to climb out of this historical arena into another which is truer, finer, more beautiful. The biblical answer is to affirm the truth as it appeared in history. We were slaves, but now are free, and that is no accident. It was the saving work of God. The mystery and the miracle of God is precisely that he has made himself known as a saving power in the bleakness of our existence. One cannot charge him with evil, even though he makes evil serve his ultimate purposes.

If the knowledge of God were not to be found in history, where would it be discovered? The most common answers seek the source in nature or in the human heart. The God of nature and the God within—these are the age-old gods of the natural man in our earth. The devotional leader of a vesper or a sunrise service in a summer conference on the edge of a lake is inclined to say: "God is the beauty of nature or the glory of the sun." But what kind of a god is this? An aesthetic feeling? The ancient polytheists of biblical times saw more clearly into nature's true being. They believed in many gods because Mother Nature does not speak with one voice only, but with many voices. The mother goddess and the god of healing depicted for the polytheist one side of nature. But the other side was more somber and awful, even while glorious. Baal and Enlil, the gods of the storm, were kings, the personification of nature's force, with hidden, uncontrollable, amoral (if not immoral) depths to their natures. Then there were Ishtar, Anath, and Ashtoreth, the goddesses who depicted all the beauty and wonder of love. These were also goddesses of war, because uncontrolled love for its own sake is closely allied in nature with blood and battle. And then there were the gods of death, pestilence, and disease. These are in nature too. The struggle among them for supremacy is almost constant. Indeed, Darwin's "survival of the fittest" may well give a more accurate portrayal of the observable heart of nature than do such descriptions as we force upon nature by giving it such attributes as "beauty," "health," "motherhood," etc. Can one, therefore, say that the primary knowledge of God is to be found in nature? Can nature be unified into a god? If the argument from nature is simply to prove that God exists, that there is a first cause, then perhaps the arguments of Professor Tillich must be considered when he says that to try to prove that God exists in this way is to deny him. God is not a thing among things. Existence and causation are elements of creation. Certainly God is no cause like other causes nor does he exist as a thing exists. He is above and beyond all such categories of the human mind.

As for the God within, all great mysticisms have emphasized the fact that God is revealed within the human soul. A Hindu would point within himself when asked where God is. He would say, "He is in here; this is where I know him." The categories of mysticism, spiritual experience, even prayer, as ways of *experiencing* God—when these are developed in and for themselves alone, are they not types of self-fulfillment, and therefore self-centered? Protestantism of our time has too frequently taught that the chief end of man is to have some sort of spiritual (meaning emotional and aesthetic) occurrence within the heart. The picture of the truly pious man has typically been the picture of a man on his knees, struggling to become aware of God and to "experience" him. The medieval saint was typically portrayed as an emaciated figure with a halo around his head, emaciated because of the severity of his spiritual self-discipline. The more dominant stream of influence from biblical faith, however, has been more objective. It affirms that God has placed us in history, not simply to "experience" him but to serve him by following a divinely-given vocation.

For clarification of this issue let us examine the great religious experiences of the Bible. What was their purpose? Was their aim that of obtaining a knowledge of God, or were they for the purpose of securing a knowledge of one's vocation? What is the central thing about the great experience of Moses as recounted in Exodus 3? Is it the burning bush? But that was simply to attract attention! Is it the words "Put off your shoes . . ."? No, it is "Moses, come now, I send you to Pharaoh that you may bring forth my people . . . out of Egypt" (Exodus 3:10). Or what of the great experience of Isaiah? Was it solely the prophet's feeling of God's holiness and his own sin? Are those scholars correct who try to derive Isaiah's theology, his whole knowledge of God, from this one great experience? Rather is it so that the center and climax of that sixth chapter of Isaiah is in the eighth verse: "And I heard the voice of the Lord saying: 'Whom shall I *send,* and who will *go* for us?' Then said I: 'Here am I! Send me.' And he said: 'Go . . .'" Similarly in the call of Jeremiah, the central words are: "I appointed you a prophet to the nations . . . to all to whom I *send* you, you shall *go*" (Jeremiah 1:5, 7). And finally, in the conversion experience of Paul on the Damascus road, the Lord's words were: "Rise and enter the city, and you will be told what you are to *do.*" And to Ananias the Lord said: "Go, for he [Paul] is a chosen instrument of mine to carry my name before the Gentiles and kings and the sons of Israel" (Acts 9:6, 15).

Note the frequent occurrence in these widely separated passages of the words, "send," "go," "do." The experience of God conveyed no complete theology, no statement of abstract doctrines, no precious feelings that were cherished for years hence. The experience was too awful to be sentimentalized, to be made either pretty or petty. It was rather God's way of turning a man around in his tracks and confronting him with his job. "Here is the way! Walk in it!" "Here is your work. Go, do it!"

It is clear that the knowledge of God gained through these experiences was not a static faith floating through a man's consciousness; it was something to be done. Knowledge and truth in the Bible involve things to do, not simply a belief in a God of nature nor an experience of the God within. God is too busy, too active, too dynamic to wait for us to experience him in the acts of worship we devise in our schedules. He is to be known by what he has done and said, by what he is now doing and saying; and he is known when we do what he commands us to do.

Yet the awareness of a calling, of being sent to do something, comes in and through a community of life. The knowledge of God is not formed in us in our solitariness. It is not a private or mysterious something which one treasures within. Knowledge is not conveyed or communicated apart from a social form or structure of thought and experience. In the Bible, that structure is the covenant society, and the knowledge of God is communicated in and through it. In Israel the universe was conceived of as a cosmic state, ruled by one divine will. The world is in rebellion against this great Lord, and he is in the midst of the struggle to make it his faithful kingdom. Meanwhile he has formed a new society in this earth as a foretaste of the goal.

In other words, God is presented to us primarily in the form of a ruler who is doing definite things. He is a *king in warfare* to make the world his kingdom. He is the *king as judge,* trying people and nations for their rebellions against his rule. He is the *king as lord,* shepherd, and father of his new community which he has formed and with which he struggles to the end that it may become his faithful steward or agent.

The new society also had a definite picture behind it which gave a structure of meaning to human existence. That picture was derived from the conception of covenant, a term borrowed from legal usage. Covenant was then and still is a treaty between two legal communities sealed by an oath or vow. The so-called suzerainty treaties of the second millennium B.C. furnish us with the particular pattern which undergirds the relationship between God and his people Israel. This pattern is described in detail in the section about the covenant (see pages 85–90). The major point to be noted is that God is known in his covenant as the great suzerain, whose prior acts of love and mercy call forth a response of love and service from his people. The pattern is what we might call a benevolent feudalism, with the whole society dependent upon a Lord who has proved over and over again his benevolence and trustworthiness.

These remarks, I realize, are to some extent cryptic. Yet the main point I am making here is that the knowledge of God in the Bible was communicated through a definite social form with its own particular language to describe the nature of God and the meaning of our human lives. In this structure of thinking the emphasis is not on some pious, private, or esoteric experience of the great King. One does not do that sort of thing with a king. Instead, our focus of attention is upon a knowledge of the Lord's will, on our attachment to him for what he has done, and on our loyalty to him in all that we do. The Lord has placed a vocation before his society and each member hears God's command addressed to him personally.

My description here has been drawn from the Old Testament, because it provides the key to the New. The essentials of this conception of the meaning of our lives under God have actually been fulfilled and realized in Christ. God has made Christ the head, the king, of this community, and to live in it is to live "in Christ," to love him and serve him loyally.

In other words, the knowledge of God in the Bible is first of all an acknowledgment that God is the sovereign, that he is the ruler who claims, and has right to claim, our obedience, because of all that he is and has done. God is not thought of as a being who has always existed and whose existence is to be argued about one way or another; he is known as the will who has a determined aim, who judges, who is gracious, who requires. Knowledge, then, is not of God's eternal being but of his claim upon us. It is the reverent acknowledgment of God's power, of his grace and requirement. Hence knowledge is not a private, inner possession of the knower. Man has knowledge only when he obeys, only when he acts in obedience. Knowledge involves the movement of the *will*, so that *not to know* is an error not correctable by more good ideas; it is a *guilt*, a rebellion. He who knows God is he who reverently acknowledges God's power and God's claim, a claim which leads him to practice brotherly love, justice, and righteousness.

This conception of knowledge is very different from that which we normally hold. To us knowledge is usually a coherent body of truth, an understanding of something which was always there awaiting our seeing and knowing. Yet in the Bible knowing is an event in the intercourse between two personalities. In the words of Professor Emil Brunner it is characteristic of the Bible that:

"This two-sided relation between God and man has not developed as doctrine but rather is set forth as happening in the story. The relationship between God and man and between man and God is not of such a kind that doctrine can adequately express it in abstract formulas. . . . It is not a timeless or static relation arising from the world of ideas—and only for such is doctrine an adequate form: rather the relation is an event, and hence narration is the proper form to describe it. The decisive word-form in the language of the Bible is not the substantive, as in Greek, but the verb, the word of action. . . . God 'steps' into the world, into relation with men. . . . He acts always in relation *to them,* and he always *acts.*

Similarly, men are . . . those who from the first are placed in a specific relation to God and then also place themselves in such a relation: either positive or negative, obedient or disobedient, true or false, conformable to God or impious. They too are always considered as those who act: and their action, whether expressing sin or faith, is always understood as action in relation to God."[1]

The language about God in such a presentation is going to be the type of language that pertains to narrative. It will be a language filled with pictures drawn from human experience and from human society, that is, a language filled with symbols. The apostle Paul in I Corinthians 2:12–13 contrasted the wisdom of the world and the wisdom of God in the gospel as revealed to us in the Church by the Holy Spirit. He says:

"Now we have received not the spirit of the world, but the Spirit which is from God, that we might understand the gifts bestowed on us by God. And we impart this in

[1] Emil Brunner, *The Divine-Human Encounter* (Philadelphia, 1943), pp. 47 f.

25

words not taught by human wisdom but taught by the Spirit, interpreting spiritual truths in spiritual language."

(*R.S.V. margin*)

The apostle Paul is probably the most abstract writer in the Bible. Yet, even so, his language still does not measure up to the desires of many of the Greek-speaking peoples to whom he addressed his message. He goes as far as he can to meet them, but in the last analysis his message is based upon the New Testament story, which to many Greek intellectuals was surely naïve. The language of the gospel is a special language, and the Christian faith can be presented in the last analysis in no other way than by means of this narrative type of discourse. As the passage quoted above clearly indicates, the gospel for Paul must be imparted not in the words of human wisdom as it is currently conceived but by the special language required by the Spirit. Paul is conscious then of the special character of the language which he uses.

Thomas Aquinas once asked whether the Holy Scripture should use metaphors. He said that people object to this because divine truths should not and cannot be put forward by comparing them to things of the earth. Man is not God. But, he says, "I answer that . . . it is natural to man to attain to intellectual truths through sensible objects, because all our knowledge originates from sense. Hence in Holy Writ spiritual truths are fittingly taught under the likeness of material things. . . . Then it is clear that these things are not literal descriptions of divine truths . . . because this is more befitting the knowledge of God that we have in this life."[2] In other words the special language of the Bible, says Thomas, is not a literal description, but it is nevertheless a language in which the truth of God is truly conveyed. It is a language that uses pictures to speak about hidden things, a language in which the truth is revealed in symbolic form. But what is a symbol? Concerning this there has been some difference of definition. Ordinarily, we think of it as a sign of something. In early Christianity, for

[2] Erich Frank, *Philosophical Understanding and Religious Truth*, pp. 101–2.

example, the fish was a symbol for Christ. It was a picture which related the knower to the real.

Today we suffer from the literalization of knowledge, of words, of language. We forget that what we know by the senses is only a fragment of experience. To live is to feel, to understand, to participate in memory which relates past and future, to connect the passing moment to an over-all unity, so that life is not fragmentary or aimless but meaningful. A fact is not a *significant* fact until it has meaning. We have no way of presenting or understanding the meaning of things except by symbols, by a picture language. In fact, in whatever realm of discourse or study we happen to be we shall find ourselves using a special language with its own series of symbols. If we think of science as being non-symbolic, then perhaps we may recall that no one really knows what an electron is like. Its movements can be described and inferences can be made on the basis of its movements. Yet it is not a *thing* in the sense that we would normally consider a concrete entity to be a thing. It has all the qualities of energy or motion, and yet it seems to be more than that. In fact, what it is in itself is by no means clear; it is a mystery. And yet scientists have developed a whole language of symbols by which the electron can be talked about in its relationships to other things. What it is in itself is not clear, but what it does, how it acts, and how it relates—these can be known and described by symbols. Similarly, algebra and higher mathematics would appear to be an elaborate system of symbols which relate us to the real, though they in themselves do not describe the real as it is in itself.

The God of biblical faith hides himself; he is mysterious in the sense that he is never seen by human eye. Occasional glimpses are caught of his glory, of the shining envelope that surrounds his being, of the effulgence of beauty or order that derive from him, but what he is in himself is the great mystery. As one prophet has written: "It is he who sits above the circle of the earth, and its inhabitants are like grasshoppers; who stretches out the heavens like a curtain, and spreads them like a tent to dwell in; who brings princes to nought, and makes the rulers of the earth as nothing. . . . To whom then will you compare me, that I should be like him? says the Holy One" (Isaiah 40:22–23, 25). The prophet is very conscious of the problem of language. No words are sufficient to describe the greatness of the power of the God who has made all things and before whom all things are as nothing. In a preceding verse he has suggested that normally people liken their gods to things of wood and stone; the impoverished man chooses wood that will not rot and seeks out a skillful craftsman to make an image of him. That is, the greatness of the living God is reduced to a material image, an idol which is made by hand. The Bible thinks of God in terms of the sovereign king or lord who is known in the form of a commander in chief of the armies, of judge, or of lord or father, though in themselves these picture-words do not confine him or convey all that is significantly to be known about him. What is important is what this great Lord has done. He is the concrete God, the Lord who led Israel from Egypt and the Father of Jesus Christ. He is not a principle; he is individual, personal, definite, all this without being an idol. As Professor Tillich has put it, he is independent of his nation, Israel, and he is also independent of his own individual nature as conveyed by the symbols. He is known, but not confined, by them.

Many people have used the term "symbol" and mean by it that since something is merely symbolic it need not be taken seriously. Yet we do not have in this life a choice between using a symbolic and non-symbolic language when it comes to matters that are vitally or ultimately important. A symbol or picture-word is the only way by which the ultimate and infinite is made real to us who are of limited minds and understandings. It always points beyond itself; it hints at reality without confining it; it relates us to the real while at the same time the real is opened for us to comprehend and to love. In other words, the religious symbol is a relationship word, and without it we would have no way of knowing God or anything that matters. Every religion has its system or structure of symbols which relate our lives to the meaning of the universe.

In Christian theology the Church through the centuries has made attempts in every generation to translate its message into the current idiom. It must always do this; its creeds are one means by which it has done it, while at the same time protecting its members from straying too far from the fold. Nevertheless the Church's theological and creedal attempts are always products of their situations. In the last analysis the Church must always go back to the Bible to discover the truths that lie behind all translation attempts. The whole biblical drama is actually our only means of presenting the Christian faith. For this reason the Bible is always at the center and must always be at the center of the Church's faith and proclamation.

Yet there is always the final lurking question: Is the Bible true? What is truth and what is just symbolic? Cannot I have anything that is absolutely certain? The answer must be that the symbol *is* the truth. We have no other truth. We know it is not literal truth, but we know that the biblical portrayal is the relationship between the unknown infinite and ourselves here and now. No precise dividing line can be drawn between the ultimately real and the poetic symbol, because God has not made us infinite. "Now I know in part, but then shall I know even as also I am known" (I Corinthians 13:12). If we are not content with this, then we are not content with our creaturely finitude. But whether content or not content, we will not get anything more than this. And it is the biblical proclamation that God has revealed himself in this history, and in so doing has given us all that we need for our salvation. The result is, as a marvelous biblical passage suggests (Deuteronomy 30:11–14), God's teaching is not so far off that it has to be wrested from the uttermost parts of the universe. It is not so high that it cannot be attained. "But the word is very near you; it is in your mouth and in your heart, *so that you can do it.*"

CHAPTER III

HOW THE BIBLE CAME TO BE WRITTEN

How did it happen that a particular group of books came to compose the Bible? In other words, how was the "canon" of scripture formed? The word "canon" is the technical name for the body of books which make up the Bible, to which nothing is to be added. Its literal meaning is "measuring rod"; this particular literature, then, is the measure of all else belonging to the faith.

The story of how the Bible came to be written is a very long and complex one. No one set out to prepare a scripture. A great variety of people and traditions is represented, most of them in one way or another related to the central story, but the time between the earliest and the latest writings is some 1300 years. Let us begin with the Old Testament.

A. THE OLD TESTAMENT

At the heart of the Old Testament is the simple story which furnishes the theme of the first six books, Genesis through Joshua. God the Creator, in order to redeem men from their sin of rebellion against him, chose Abraham and his posterity (that is, the people of Israel) that through this one people his blessing might be mediated to all peoples (Genesis). His greatest acts were the demonstration of his saving power in rescuing

Israel from Egyptian slavery, in forming them into a nation in covenant with himself at Mount Sinai (Exodus through Deuteronomy), and in giving them a land in which to dwell (Joshua).

We do not know when the essentials of this story were first committed to writing. Some of the earliest datable literature preserved are old poems, such as the Song of Deborah (Judges 5), the Blessing of Jacob (Genesis 49), the Song of Miriam (Exodus 15), the Prophecies of Balaam (Numbers 22–24), etc. The Old Testament does not tell us exactly what Moses himself wrote. Late Jewish tradition was to the effect that he wrote the whole Pentateuch (the first five books), but the contents themselves speak of Moses in the third person and give no hint to support the theory. That he prepared at least a collection of laws, known later as the Book of the Covenant, including the Ten Commandments in their original form, seems quite probable (cf. Exodus 24:7; 34:27). For the rest, all we can say is that while the substance of Israelite faith was Mosaic, the present *written* form of the literature is later in date. There is thus no more reason to accept the Jewish tradition regarding the Mosaic authorship of the Pentateuch than there is to accept other Jewish traditions regarding authorship of various books, including the one which held that Ezekiel was *not* responsible for the book which bears his name. Virtually all of the leading scholars of the Protestant wing of the World Church hold a more dynamic view of scriptural origins than Mosaic authorship permits. The Roman Catholic Church has recently stated officially that though the Pentateuch is substantially Mosaic, this does not mean that Moses was responsible for everything written in it, because it was supplemented during the course of the centuries.

It must be recalled that in Old Testament times writing did not play the role that it does today. For the most part it was the work of a specialist who made his living by it. He was the "scribe" who worked for commercial concerns and temples, making lists, drawing up formal documents and the like, and also was needed in the diplomatic and political affairs of a nation in order to assist in foreign affairs and in keeping the nation's life in order. Other than this all emphasis was placed upon the oral transmission of historical and literary works. Plato once said that the invention of writing was not necessarily the greatest of all good things in human culture. When writing was invented and widely used, it tended to "produce forgetfulness in the minds of those who learn to use it" so that "they will not practice memory." The biblical world was dominated by a genuine, living oral tradition, whereby everything worth while was known and transmitted orally. Writing was not considered an independent mode of expression. Literature and historical traditions, such as descriptions of legal practice (laws), were put down on leather or papyrus only when there was a crisis of confidence, when faith in the spoken word began to waver, when there was fear that all might be forgotten.

In the Old Testament, as we have already observed, there was a living oral tradition about what God had done by a series of mighty acts, beginning with Abraham and coming to a climax with Moses and Joshua, whereby the nation was brought into being. This tradition was nourished by the living community which was formed and conditioned by it, while at the same time the community was its bearer. There is increasing agreement among scholars today that the first edition of the early Israelite history was probably put into writing during the great age of the United Monarchy, perhaps during the reign of Solomon about 950 B.C. The unknown author is called the "Yahwist writer" (or simply "J") because he uses the proper name (Yahweh) for God from the very beginning of his work, while the other strata of the literature preserve the tradition that this name was first revealed to Moses. His work forms the core of our present books of Genesis, Exodus, and Numbers, but at what point it ended and whether or not it extended into Joshua is now no longer clear. It is a great work, as we shall see, full of joy, confidence, and faith. God's selection and his promises to Abraham are viewed by the J writer as fulfilled in three stages: the exodus and formation of the nation at Sinai, the gift of the land, and the granting of security and "rest" under David (during or just after whose time the author apparently lived).

As a backdrop to this portrayal of God's action toward one people and as an answer to the question, "Why?" he collected some of the old stories about prehistoric times which had circulated among his people. By the very manner in which he retells these hoary traditions he gives a penetrating analysis of the problem of man and his civilization. His story of a chosen nation, Israel, is then set over against this backdrop of human civilization, and, as we shall see, he appears to view the former as God's answer to the problem of the latter.

Why the Yahwist committed his work to writing when he did is not entirely certain. We may surmise that the reign of David, marking as it did the death of an old order and the beginning of a new one, brought with it a crisis of understanding. How did all of the old traditions make sense in the new day? In order that they might not be lost but might speak for the new order, it is not impossible that David himself encouraged someone in his court to write the stories down as the One Story. It was probably the official version of the national epic, encouraged by David and Solomon as they sought to make one nation out of a group of tribes. This is not to say that the central core or theme of that story, and even much of the detailed working out of it, had not been composed orally long before this time. But the more complete written version, with its reworking of the prehistoric materials, housed in the newly established political and religious capital, Jerusalem, must have provided a powerful sanction for the new order.

As we read through the early Old Testament books, however, it is quite apparent that a conglomerate of material has been heaped around the central narrative. This is a testimony to the fact that these books have had a history, in which various materials have been used to supplement the first edition. Scholars have long detected a second stratum of old material, very close to that of J (the Yahwist), in Genesis (first clearly noted in Chapter 15), Exodus, and Numbers. Theologically it is much more conscious of the problems of obedience and loyalty to God against idolatry, of the way God reveals himself to man, of the role of the prophet, etc. It is generally felt that this source may have been a connected oral or written edition of the national epic that circulated in North Israel. It is called the "Elohist" or "E" stratum and is perhaps to be dated to the ninth century, since during the controversies of that time the religious teachers of North Israel became much more conscious of certain special theological questions than had been the case a century before. Perhaps after the fall of North Israel to the Assyrians in 721 B.C., or at least sometime during the ninth or eighth centuries, certain parts of this document, if it was that, were used to supplement the work of the Yahwist. At a few places where it was more detailed it was even permitted to displace the Yahwist's story. The resultant written document is called JE by scholars; it is simply a term for the oldest material in Genesis, Exodus, and Numbers, material far older certainly than the written stage of its transmission.

It was probably during the exile in the sixth century B.C., after the fall of Jerusalem and the destruction of the Jerusalem temple, that a circle of priests from that temple decided to edit JE and to make extensive additions to it from sources which they had saved out of the archives of the destroyed temple. For example, they added the detailed description of the wilderness tent-shrine (tabernacle) which is found in the second part of Exodus; they also contributed all of Leviticus, mainly old orders and rules relating to worship and priesthood, and quite a variety of heterogeneous fragments in Numbers. The Jerusalem priesthood was vitally concerned that material of such central importance to them and to the temple be preserved. Central to it was their theology of the God whose presence was so graciously "tabernacling" in the midst of his people, the God who had revealed the manner by which he might be served and worshiped. The present final form of the first four books, Genesis through Numbers, was thus probably fixed by the Jerusalem priests during the course of the sixth or early fifth centuries B.C., and was used as the normative guide to the newly established community following the return from exile.

Meanwhile other bodies of literature had been written or

were in process of formation. An old book found in the temple in 622 B.C. (II Kings 22) had caused a great religious revival and had so inspired one great soul that, by using it as the basis for his writing, he prepared the remarkable history of Israel in Palestine which we have in the books of Joshua through II Kings. The old book was evidently the core of our present Book of Deuteronomy. The history based upon it was finished sometime between about 600 and 550 B.C., as we know from the last events recorded in it. The author wrote in the light of the covenant faith, interpreting to Israel the meaning of all that had happened.

In the Book of Deuteronomy he had at hand an exposition of the relation between the faith and the land. Here were the Lord God's terms, what he required of his people if they were to be permitted to keep the land. Using this as the introduction to his great work, the historian proceeded to the story of the people in the Promised Land, giving an interpretation which furnishes the reasons why the land was lost.

Finally, the Chronicler, working from older sources, prepared the history of Judah which we have in the Books of I and II Chronicles, Ezra, and Nehemiah. He completed it, probably during the early part of the fourth century B.C., for the small Jewish community which was struggling to reconstitute itself after the exile. We have then the three great documents which compose the historical part of the Old Testament: the priestly edition of the early history (JE) from the creation through the covenant at Sinai (Genesis–Numbers); the Deuteronomic history of Israel in Palestine (Deuteronomy–II Kings); and the Chronicler's history of Judah (I Chronicles–Nehemiah). Nehemiah 8:1–8 tells us of a great ceremony led by Ezra for the renewal of the covenant. Before the taking of the vows, he read from "the book of the law of Moses." This was probably either JE described above or a priestly collection of older material which we have in Exodus, Leviticus, and Numbers. In any event, it was the occasion for the public presentation of a collection of covenant laws gathered together by the priests in exile, which Ezra brought with him back to

Palestine (Ezra 7:14, 25) and used as a basis for religious reform.

The prophetic books, in four large scrolls (Isaiah, Jeremiah, Ezekiel, and the Twelve), are collections of sermons largely gathered together by disciples of the prophets; they were completed in their present form at least by the fourth century B.C. The collections of Psalms and Proverbs were also finished by the same period. The latest books in the canon to be written were Daniel, Esther, and Ecclesiastes. The first was composed about 165 B.C. but the other two are earlier, probably not later than the third century B.C. Between the fourth and first centuries B.C., however, many other books were written, and as the conception of a canon of sacred writings took form there was considerable discussion as to which of these books should be admitted and which left out. Ecclesiastes and the Song of Songs, for example, were long debated, and final decision regarding certain of these marginal books seems not to have been made until the rabbinic Council of Jamnia about A.D. 90, long after the death of Christ. Certain of the disputed books, called the Apocrypha, are still included in Roman Catholic Bibles, following the Greek and Latin versions of the early Church. The Protestant Reformation excluded them from the canon, however, because they were not accepted by early Palestinian rabbis. Protestants generally regard them as valuable for instruction but not as a source of doctrine.

The study of the Dead Sea Scrolls will undoubtedly give us more information about the final stages of the fixing of the Old Testament text and canon. As is well known, the recovery of these scrolls, beginning in 1947, is one of the greatest archaeological events of modern times. They represent the fragmentary remains of a large library of a Jewish sect, one group of which lived in and near a community center on the northwestern edge of the Dead Sea. The ruins of this center are now called Khirbet Qumran. The library dates between about 200 B.C. and A.D. 68. Farther south other manuscripts from the end of the first and the early second centuries A.D. were found. The discoveries indicate that the period between the second century B.C. and the second century A.D. was one of great literary activity among the Jews. The sacred writings were studied intensively. Many commentaries were written, and a great variety of theological works were produced under the direct inspiration of scriptural study.

The biblical manuscripts can be identified quickly and distinguished from the rest of the material in these libraries by the special color and fine quality of the leather used and by the special book hand in which they were written. Portions of over a hundred scrolls of Old Testament books have been found, all but three or four in a very fragmentary condition, some of them consisting of no more than one or a few tiny fragments. By studying the evolution of the script in relation to all available knowledge on the subject, scholars have arranged the fragments in the approximate order in which they were written. All books of the Old Testament were present in the library, with the exception of Esther, which has not yet been identified. Deuteronomy, Isaiah, and the Psalms were represented by a dozen or more scrolls each. While scholars in the past have been inclined to date Ecclesiastes about 200 B.C., the presence at Qumran of a scroll of that work, dating from the mid-second century and written in the book hand and on the leather used for other biblical books, would suggest that it must have been originally composed before the second century. A period of time must have elapsed for it to have been set aside as special or sacred. Similarly some scholars have believed that the Book of Isaiah was not put into its final form much before 200 B.C., but the great Isaiah scroll from Cave 1 at Qumran, dating about 100 B.C., would lead one to conclude that the final arrangement of the chapters had been completed some time before the second century B.C. On the other hand, at least three different scrolls of Daniel were found at Qumran. One of them is said to date less than a century from 165 B.C. when the book was written. To get so close to the time of composition of an Old Testament book is something few had dared to hope for. Yet there seems to be evidence that these Daniel fragments were not yet considered sacred literature. Both the writing and the leather suggest to some of the international team of scholars working on the scrolls that they probably were not. If so, then within the Jewish sect at Qumran, Daniel's position as a canonical book was not yet decided.

When all the evidence is sorted and arranged, the most reasonable theory is that the conception of a "canon" of scripture and the decision as to just what should be included within it were products of the Jewish community of the fifth and fourth centuries B.C. Hence the basic Old Testament collections of historical writings, prophecy, psalms, and wisdom were probably completed during the fourth century B.C. After that, many, many religious treatises were written but few were admitted into the canon. The Palestinian Jews confined themselves to three, Ecclesiastes, Esther, and Daniel. In Egypt, judging from the Greek translation made there beginning in the early third century B.C., several additional books were included, and these were not omitted by the Jews generally until after the standardization of both canon and text at the end of the first century A.D.

B. THE NEW TESTAMENT

To the earliest Christians the scriptures were the writings of what later was to be called "the Old Testament," which is a poor translation through the Latin of "the Old Covenant." By their day the conception of a sacred literature, as distinct from all others, had already come into being. The Church inherited this distinction from Judaism and was most careful to preserve it because it was the Old Testament alone which set forth the preparation and the setting of God's work in Jesus Christ. Without it the meaning of God's action in the life, death, and resurrection of Christ could not be understood or proclaimed. With it one could understand that the new age, promised of old, was now at hand; God's messiah had actually come.

With the scriptures (that is, the Old Testament) at hand, the Church of the first century did not set out to replace them nor did it even plan to write the New Testament. The latter came into being more by what Christians would call the unseen direction of the Holy Spirit than by the conscious plan of man. At first Christian witnesses scattered gradually through the world, proclaiming the gospel and founding churches. The story of Jesus was told in sermons, and passed orally from one person to another. Various collections of Jesus' teachings were made and used in the teaching of catechumens and the baptized. But as the churches became many in number and widely scattered between Europe and Palestine, numerous problems began to arise. The apostle Paul attempted to solve many of these problems by writing letters to the churches he had founded, when he could not immediately get to them in person. So remarkable were these letters that they were repeatedly copied, treasured, and gradually distributed to churches other than those to which they were first sent. As finally collected together, they were not arranged in order of writing, with the earliest first, but chiefly in order of length, with the longest first. The letter to the Hebrews was put with them at the end, though the early Church was not certain as to its author. It differs so much in content and style from Paul's writings that scholars today believe it was written by an unknown person, a friend of Paul's disciple Timothy (Hebrews 13:23), to a Jewish Christian congregation.

Many other letters were written, of course, and it was long before the Church came to any agreement regarding which should be especially preserved and placed together with Paul's writings in a general collection of epistles. The seven finally agreed upon (James, I and II Peter, I, II, III John, and Jude) are called the Catholic Epistles because they were believed to have been addressed to the entire Church.

Meanwhile John Mark had collected and carefully edited the material for a connected story of Jesus' life and teachings. We do not know for certain when he wrote it, though the date most generally accepted is about A.D. 65. With the passage of time and the rapid spread of the Church it was necessary that the various traditions be edited and committed to writing before they were corrupted. In doing so Mark created a new form of writing, a gospel. It was not simply a biography of Jesus; it was primarily a testimony or proclamation to the saving work of God in the life, death, and resurrection of his Son. Subsequently, the gospels of Matthew and Luke were prepared. The writer of each used Mark as his basis, adding material from a collection of the sayings of Jesus which has not been preserved (scholars call it "Q"), as well as material which each author had available from his own individual sources. As was recognized by the fathers of the early Church, the gospel of John differs greatly from the other three gospels. It is more distinctly an *interpretation* of the life and person of Jesus, a setting forth of the doctrine of the office of Christ. The present written form of John, together with those of Matthew and Luke, probably dates from the last thirty years of the first century, after the fall of Jerusalem to the Romans in A.D. 70. An actual manuscript fragment of John, dating from the early part of the second century, has been found in Egypt. This warns against too late a date. But regardless of the date of the books as we now have them, their essential narrative content comes from Palestinian traditions, some oral and some written, from the period before A.D. 70. Luke's story of the Acts of the Apostles is a fitting supplement to the four gospels, for it is a history of what happened after Christ's death. It thus provides the setting in which we understand the nature of the epistles.

Finally, there is the Book of Revelation, from the very end of the first century, and very different in character from anything else in the New Testament. By the use of visions and symbols it portrays the future, the triumph of God, to a Church which was suffering persecution.

Only by a very gradual process did the churches agree, largely by usage, upon the particular books which should be set aside from others and circulated with the Old Testament. Certain books, particularly Hebrews and Revelation, were long in dispute. By the end of the second century seven books now included in the New Testament were still not generally recognized as canonical: Hebrews, James, II Peter, II and III John, Jude, and Revelation. It was only in the Easter letter of the church father, Athanasius (A.D. 367), that the present twenty-seven books and no others were first listed. Only by the end of the fourth century can we say that the New Testament canon had been fixed. It presents the "New Covenant" (Testament) which man has in Jesus Christ, and is thus to be placed beside the "Old Covenant" (Testament) on which it depends and which it fulfills.

C. MANY VOLUMES, ONE BOOK

One question which many people ask is this: Why is it necessary for us to depend solely upon these particular biblical books? Why not include certain other great classics within the Christian canon? It is true that within the canon there are certain marginal books which can be either kept in or left out without harming or marring the faith one way or another. In other words, the actual dividing line which includes Ecclesiastes and the Song of Songs, for example, but excludes such apocryphal books as Ecclesiasticus and the Wisdom of Solomon, is one that is drawn by fallible human decision. Yet a simple comparison of the biblical books with other competitors of that time shows without doubt their superiority. Furthermore, if we decide to include other books, what shall we include? On that few people could agree. The point is that the Bible as now constituted is the norm and judge of subsequent Christian literature, not the reverse. Consequently, Christians continually return to the Bible for fresh enlightenment, and not to the secondary literature which has been produced under the Bible's inspiration. In the final analysis, however, the Protestant believes that the truth and authority of the present canon of scripture is constantly confirmed by the work of God himself through his spirit of truth. If it is his word, he will sustain and confirm it. And it is the Christian witness throughout the centuries that the Bible confronts us with ourselves and with the true God as known from the witness of prophets and apostles, but especially in Jesus Christ, whereas other literature either does not contain such saving truth, or, if it does, the truth is but a reflection of the brilliant image of scripture.

A final problem which the study of the formation of scripture poses is that of the unity of the Bible. So many things are said in the Bible; there is such a great variety in type of literature and in content. Wherein does the unity lie? The peculiar fact is that the variety itself bears witness to the unity. People in all walks of life, with various interests in various periods of the history, have contributed their portion; yet all bear testimony to the God whose wondrous works are celebrated in song and story, in liturgy and prayer, in law and custom. The Bible's unity is certainly not to be found in the supposition that it presents a completely unified and systematic series of abstract dogmas. The Bible is not a static, but a living, book, in which the central figure is God and in which the central concern is to bear testimony to the story of what he has done to save man and to bring his kingdom into being on this earth. Central to the Bible is the history of a people, known by faith to be the story of the handiwork of God. There his determination is revealed to bring all men under his sovereignty. There he is shown to have reached down into our midst in order to show us what we are and to save us from our darkness. In so presenting God's action the Bible's goal, center, and climax is Jesus Christ, who died that his people might live and who now is the head of the Church. Such is the central proclamation which holds the variety of biblical literature together, which makes it one book, which continually throws out its challenge to us: "Choose you this day whether you will serve the idols of the nations, or the God who here has revealed himself!"

PART I

THE HISTORIES OF ISRAEL

If the reader has followed closely the descriptive summary in the third section of the Prologue, he will have noted that the historical narrative of Israel in the various books from Genesis through Nehemiah must be divided into three parts: (1) The Jerusalem priesthood's (P's) editing and supplementing of the older material in the first four books of the Old Testament (Genesis, Exodus, Leviticus, and Numbers); we may call this "The Priestly History," if we remember that the priests did not write it but simply added their material to the older account. (2) "The Deuteronomic History of Israel in the Promised Land"; the Book of Deuteronomy here serves as the preface to an interpretation of Israel's life from the entrance into her land until the time of her removal from it (Joshua, Judges, I–II Samuel and I–II Kings—originally one work). (3) "The Chronicler's History of Judah" from David to Nehemiah and Ezra (I–II Chronicles, Ezra, and Nehemiah). We shall now undertake an analysis of these three histories in order to comprehend their meaning and intent.

CHAPTER I

THE PRIESTLY HISTORY

During the exile from Palestine, probably in the sixth century
B.C., a priest or priests from Jerusalem reworked the older narrative materials (JE), and added a considerable amount of
data from documents preserved by the priests. In Genesis he
first added a fairly abstract account of creation in Chapter
1:1–2:3 and then gave the old history an outline by means of
an old genealogy which he had available. At stated intervals
he introduced fragments of the genealogy (for example, Chapter 5, part of Chapter 10, Chapter 11:10–27) and also inserted his outline headings, "These are the generations of . . ."
By means of the latter the book may be outlined: Chapter
2:4 (see R.S.V.) introduces the old Adam and Eve story;
Chapter 5:1 the generations between Adam and the flood;
Chapter 6:9 the story of Noah; Chapter 10:1 the separation
of the peoples of the earth; 11:10 the Semites, and 11:27,
from among the Semites, the family of Abraham. These headings serve until Abraham's death when new ones introduce his
sons, Ishmael and Isaac (25:12, 19) and the sons of Isaac,
Esau and Jacob (36:1; 37:2). In Exodus, Leviticus, and Numbers, as already noted, the editor's interest was to add a great
deal of information which the priests had saved about the
place of worship (Exodus 25–31; 35–40), the manner of worship (Leviticus), and a great variety of heterogeneous laws
and customs (in Numbers). The result is that the simple flow
of the story is interrupted time and again. This was done in
an age of crisis when the community had been destroyed and
when plans had to be drawn for a new one. To this end the

editor did his work. He to some extent spoiled the simple beauty of the old story, but he gave the new community of the fifth century something on which to stand. Let us turn to the history and look at it in more detail.

A. THE INTRODUCTION (CHAPTERS 1–11)

These first chapters of Genesis constitute the prologue to the great acts of God which begin with Abraham and together enunciate the unifying theme of the Bible. By means of this prologue the Church has learned and taught that God is the Creator, that man is made in God's image, and that man also is a sinner who has fallen away from God and whose civilization is in a sense a product, not of obedient service given to God, but of self-worship in defiance of God. These chapters reveal God's relation to us and to our world; he is our Maker and, therefore, our Lord. They also make clear the human problem because of which God's saving acts in history took place. Yet they have been the occasion for great argument in modern times because we are told that the evolution of the earth and of man make it impossible for us now to believe that there once was a Garden of Paradise, a flood that destroyed all life except what was saved in Noah's ark, and an Adam and Eve who were good until they ate some forbidden fruit.

As we take a close look at these chapters, we should remember that Israelite faith did not *start* at this point. The Israelites who wrote these stories were men of the faith. They knew God as Creator because he had already encountered them in their life as Lord and Savior. They understood the problem of man in the world because that was precisely their problem. They wanted to be God's loyal servants, but found themselves instead in a history of rebellion and disloyalty. The creation stories are a statement of the real meaning of a people's popular traditions about beginnings in the light of the God who had made them a people. The Lord of history was to them the Lord of the world and its Maker.

1. *The Creation Stories* (*Genesis 1–2*)

The creation story of Genesis remains unique among the many myths, legends, and scientific explanations provided by the ancient and modern worlds. The opening phrase sets the tone for the whole presentation: "In the beginning God . . ." God stands at the beginning of all things as their Creator. And this God is not a capricious deity or a blind force; he is not a mere "principle of order"; he is a person, who created a good and beautiful world which reveals his glory, his power, and his love. And in the center of this marvelous creation is man, the climax of God's work, set here as a steward, responsible to his Creator for all he does with the world over which he is given dominion.

We can readily see that Genesis gives us a unique version of creation when we compare this record with those to be found in ancient paganism. In Babylon and in Canaan, for example, creation was conceived of as the result of strife among the gods. These gods were the forces of nature; and as the forces were numerous, so were there a great number of gods. Some personify chaos; others represent powers in nature that work for order. The world was believed to have come into being through the triumph of the gods of order over the gods of chaos. In the Canaanite version of the story, creation and therefore order came when the power of the chaotic sea monster, Leviathan, was overcome by the king of all gods, Baal.

In Babylonian mythology there was in the beginning a primeval watery chaos represented by two deities, the god Apsu and the goddess Tiamat. After a passage of time during which several generations of lesser gods were born, this divine pair, feeling themselves threatened, planned to overthrow the newer gods. Apsu, however, was put to death by magic. Then a god named Marduk was chosen king by the younger gods, and, armed with a thunderbolt, he conquered Tiamat in a bloody struggle. Splitting her body in half, he made the firmament (heaven) and the earth out of the two halves. Then he divided the gods into two groups, placing one group in charge of the

49

heavenly regions and the other over the affairs of earth. But after a time the gods of the earth wearied of the work involved in irrigation, seedtime, and harvest. Consequently, man was created as the slave of the gods to perform the tasks that they found too burdensome.

In contrast to these pagan gods and goddesses stands the biblical God. He is no personified force of nature or the sum of nature's powers. As the Creator, his being is not identified with anything he has created. He stands above the world and is independent of it. He does not need it to exist. Consequently, the biblical writer could not think of creation as the product of a struggle among the powers in nature. It was instead the marvelous work of the one God, the Creator of the ends of the earth, the Lord of all he has made.

We have two accounts of the creation, one in Genesis 1:1–2:3 and the other in Chapter 2:4–25. The first gives the whole sweep of God's creative work; the second confines itself to what he made upon the earth.

Genesis 1:1–2:3. In this chapter God is seen fashioning order out of disorder by his word. He commands and it is done. The description is actually a radically demythologized version of the Babylonian conception of the creation.

The first act of creation is the separation of day from night after the formation of light. Note that in Chapter 1 God's creative acts are carefully organized within six days. The seventh is the day of rest, instituted and hallowed by God, and thus different from other days. It is clear, therefore, that the organization of human life within the pattern *of the week*, the last day of which is a holy day, is here presented as purposely ordained by God and reflects the world's first week in which the creative work was accomplished. Speculation that the author here had in mind a "day" of a thousand years or more, that is, an aeon of time, is thus excluded.

The view of the world that the chapter contains is the one conceived by all ancient people, and one held until comparatively modern times. To people of Bible times heaven was not a limitless space; it was a solid substance, a firmament, erected as a tent or dome over the earth. Without this solid dome, waters above the heavens would engulf and destroy the earth. It is important that this world view be kept in mind while reading the chapter; otherwise, the deeper dimensions of the author's faith will be missed. Every element of the universe owes its original *and* its continued existence to God. We are not to think of the world as so well governed by natural laws that it no longer needs God's sustaining and constant care. Without God's constant concern, the order of nature would be wiped out in a moment and would revert to the original chaos. The writer implies that without the "heavens'" being kept in place by God's decree, we would be destroyed.

Chapter 1:26–31. In these verses the climax of all God's creative work is described. Man enjoys a peculiar relationship to God; nothing like it exists between God and any other of his creatures. Man is set as king over the whole earthly dominion, though he is a kingly steward, serving *for* God. Note also that the "man" here is divided into male and female. Man and woman do not exist as isolated or completely separated beings. They are the two parts of the human species and exist in a close relationship of dependent being. Together they are to have dominion over the earth. For food they are to eat from earth's vegetation, as do the animals. The eating of meat is permitted only after man's fall from grace (Chapter 9:2–6). This reflects the biblical man's belief that there is something unnatural about the killing and destroying that goes on in a world in which everything is good. At creation there existed that perfect state of peace where nothing was killed or destroyed. This state, however, was lost in the fall of man, and it will once again come into being only in the new creation at the end of the age. At that time there will be no hurting or destroying, and all will exist together in perfect harmony (Isaiah 11:6–9; Amos 9:13–15).

The core of Genesis, beginning at Chapter 2:4, is an old document, probably written about the time of Solomon (tenth century B.C.). It is a compilation of the old traditions that had existed through the centuries, here presented with a profound theological perspective. Chapter 1 is the introduction of the Jerusalem priests to the older document. It is more abstract and detailed than the account in Chapter 2; but the latter was not omitted, because it forms the proper setting for the presentation of the problem of man on earth, described in Chapter 3. The accounts thus supplement each other in witnessing to God's work.

Chapter 2:4–25. A proper translation of verses 4–7 is as follows:

"These are the generations of the heavens and the earth when they were created. At the time when the Lord God made the earth and the heavens, there was as yet no shrub of the field on the earth and no plant of the field had yet sprouted, for the Lord God had not made it rain on the earth and there was no man to till the soil, although waters used to go up from the earth and water the whole surface of the ground. And the Lord God formed the man out of the dust from the ground, and breathed into his nostrils the breath of life; and the man became a living being."

It will be noted that the interest of this account is more confined than that of Chapter 1. The earth, not the universe, is the focus of attention. After it had been watered, man was formed out of its dust to till it. He is thus related to the earth, but God has given him the mysterious principle of life, here figuratively conceived of as breath. His abode is in Eden (Paradise); the whole of its goodness is for his enjoyment, except the fruit of one tree (verses 16, 17). But man was made for society; it was not good for him to be alone (verse 18). Consequently, the animals and the fowls were made and brought to him as their lord. Yet man was so different from the animals that they did not fill his need for companionship. So woman was formed as a helper, "meet" or corresponding to him. The incident of the rib should be understood as a colorful way of describing the close relation existing between man and woman, as verse 23 explicitly says. Since this intimate relationship does exist, the institution of monogamous marriage, in which a man and woman leave their respective homes and become "one flesh," that is, as one person, is to be understood as established by God at creation. It is the fundamental and basic institution of human society. It should be noted that this is the first time in the history of the world's literature that such a position has been so clearly affirmed. The knowledge of God as Creator of male and female has led the writer to a conclusion that for us remains unique and final.

A few further observations about the significance of these accounts may be made. (1) A common human tendency is to think of God in terms of some principle or process in the world, or in terms of our ideals of goodness and beauty. From the Bible, however, we infer that God is greater than any force or principle in nature, or than the ideals of society, because he created them. They reveal God's working, but in themselves they are not God. Man should not expect to discover God in test tube or telescope, because the thing made is not the Maker. God is the ultimate mystery beyond all things knowable; he is known only because, and in the manner that, he has revealed himself.

(2) Some philosophies both ancient and modern have a tendency to be pessimistic about the world, a pessimism that has assumed many forms. The earth may be full of evil spirits that must be appeased; or man is at the mercy of capricious deities, or lost in a purposeless universe, or fettered to material cares, when he should be free of all things earthly in order to achieve holiness. So, through the ages, there have developed all manner of cults whose only purpose is to "free" man from this evil world. As a result, men have marked their fellow men as "untouchables" and separated themselves to achieve their uncontaminated holiness. They have developed all sorts of "purification" ceremonies in order to rid themselves of this world's evil. They have mortified the flesh in order to glorify the soul. They have adopted all manner of asceticisms —and this by no means has been confined to pagans; it has appeared again and again in Christianity.

In contrast to all this is the biblical view of creation. This world and everything in it is *good*, fashioned by a wise Creator, who loves all things that he has made, so that not even a sparrow is forgotten by him (Luke 12:6). And the world as a good world is the proper setting for the "good" life, a life that is indeed possible here because God meant it to be so.

(3) The one statement that more than any other in the Bible summarizes its view of man is this one in Chapter 1:27: "In the image of God created he him." The Church accepts it as a noble, an exalted, view of man, but when we come to ask what it means, we are perplexed. The statement is hard to define because no one in the Bible ever attempts to clarify it for us. The word "image" means a statue made to look like someone else. Now how is man "in the image of God"? Is he a statue, a replica of God? In the Bible, we must remember, a person is not conceived of as made up of two separate parts, body and soul. He is a unity, a coherent, undivided being. In the Hebrew language, then, the phrase "in the image of God" would be the simplest way to express the thought that the total being of man bears a likeness to the total being of God. Man alone on this earth has this likeness; the animals do not possess it (though in paganism they did).

As a result of this divine likeness we see that man alone among the creatures of earth is dignified by God's direct address. He has the possibility of hearing, of communing, and of obeying. His dignity lies at this point: he has been chosen by God as the bearer of a responsibility and for that end he has been directly addressed as person to person. His dignity and power lie not simply in his bodily and mental structure, but in his *relationship* to his Maker and in his vocation given him by his Maker. As God is Lord of the universe, so man is lord of this created world; he is its king, crowned with glory and honor (Psalm 8). Why that is so is God's mystery for which the psalmist praises him. Man has freedom and power to rule, but as the following chapters point out his freedom is also his problem.

2. The "Fall" of Man (Genesis 3)

The writer of Genesis 2-3 has a wider interest than merely the presentation of the story of the first man and the first woman. This is quite clear not only from the manner in which he tells the story but also from the various names that have a symbolic significance. It is a mistake in translation to speak of Adam in these chapters (see R.S.V.). The word means "man" in the general sense of "mankind." It is never used as a proper name in the Old Testament, and in these chapters it has the article "the" before it. Consequently, the author is speaking about "the man" in the most general sense that the Hebrew language permits. The narrative also speaks only of "woman" or "the woman" until she is given a proper name, Eve, in Chapter 3:20. This name means "life" or "living" in the sense that Eve was "the mother of all living." "Eden" means "delight" or "pleasantness," and thus, properly, "paradise." The author had no clear picture of where it was; it was simply the place which the ancients believed to be the common source of the great rivers known to them. The "tree of life" and the "tree of knowledge of good and evil" are further evidence of the parabolic interest of the author. He is presenting a story that, to be sure, most people of his day knew and believed, but in doing so he exhibits a wider and more profound purpose than that which existed in the popular tradition. The history of the first man and the first woman to him is the history of all men, the history of every man and mankind as well. The Church has always understood the story in this way. As the words of an old couplet put it:

In Adam's fall
We sinned all.

In other words, the teaching intent in these chapters is so obvious as to make them unlike any other chapters in the Bible. The author's interest was not solely to present the *history* of sin's origin; it was to interpret the fact of sin through the old popular stories his people knew. Mythology and art in western Asia at that time also knew a paradise and a tree of life. The typical human being has always been concerned with death and has pondered about life, immortal life, without it. In the art of Syria, Palestine, and Mesopotamia the sacred tree plays an important role, and the Gilgamesh Epic, one of the most popular of the ancient stories, describes man's unsuccessful and disillusioning search for life in which there was no death. The fact that our author has *two* trees in his story indicates that in his background the tree of life once played an important role. Yet as he presents his material he says little about that tree which guarantees life without death. To him it is a simple fact that man is mortal, though it was perhaps not God's original intention that he be so. But the fact is that the tree of life is now denied him (Chapter 3:22–24). Why? It is this "why" which is our author's real concern. To deal with it he turns to a tree that has no parallel in ancient mythology, "the tree of the knowledge of good and evil." It is *this* tree, and not the question of how to get life without death, that for the author is the distinctive and all-important matter.

The manner of presentation is, at first glance, deceptive, and many Christians dismiss it as a primitive idea of the Hebrew people that has little importance for us. But let us not be deceived by the simple story form of presentation. The greatness of this story is its insight into the inner nature of man and the simple manner in which it presents that insight.

In Genesis 2 our author has presented the setting. Man was created by God and placed in Eden (Paradise) in a family relationship. He is the noble lord of all creatures, to which he gives names. By nature he is good; so is the garden with its trees; woman is good; the sexual relation is good; indeed, God is good. Yet a divine command is placed before man; the life of God's creatures is not one of such complete liberty that they can do as they please. The whole of Paradise is at man's disposal, except for one tree, "the tree of the knowledge of good and evil." Of that he must not, for his own good, eat, because in the midst of all life there is and must be a prohibition which the trained will obeys. Now what has happened to man? He no longer lives in Paradise. Instead, he seems to live in a world that has a curse upon it, one in which there is pain, toil, sweat, thorns, hardship. Chapter 3 presents the reason for this situation which stands in such contrast to man's original state.

Man's problem is that he has rebelled against his Creator. He has used the freedom that God has given him for the purpose of ruling over the earthly creation in order to assert his independence of God and to become like God. Refusing to accept his status as a creature dependent upon God, a dependence in which his true freedom is to be discovered, he attempts to put himself on equal footing with God. When he does so, however, he destroys the most precious thing he has— the free and natural communion that exists between himself and God. His assertion of independence is actually his separation from the source of all life and all blessing. He wants to enjoy God's blessing, but he also wants to be like God. The power given him by God to rule thus becomes the occasion for him to lust for more power. Yet this actually is something that cannot succeed, because it is an attempt to displace God as the *sole* Lord of the world. Such is the author's essential meaning in Chapter 3 when translated into less interesting and more abstract language than that which he uses.

The author begins by using the serpent as the instrument of temptation. In the ancient paganisms the snake was a god or goddess, having to do with life, fertility, and wisdom. Here it is simply one of the beasts of the field which God has made, but the pagan background survives in the statement that it "was more subtle than any beast." That is, it had a crafty, invidious cunning. It speaks to the woman, distorting God's command about not eating from the one tree, asking her whether it were not true that God had forbidden the eating of the fruit of any tree. This immediately puts the woman on the defensive. The serpent then suggests that the reason why God gave the command was a selfish one and not for the good of the human pair at all. So in verse 6, when the woman saw that the fruit was indeed attractive and also desirable to make one wise (like God), she ate and gave to her husband. Thus temptation was described in a manner true to life: by subtle argument a thing that in itself is evil becomes, or seems to become, a good. When that happens, man sins.

When the man and the woman ate of the forbidden fruit, it is said that their eyes were opened and that they knew that they were naked (verse 7). This seems to say that a new knowledge was indeed gained, but not the knowledge expected. As an illustration, the author singles out the example of sex. That which was perfectly natural and good now appears in another light, and the self-consciousness that arises

57

only from an awareness of something that is evil now appears. In other words, the evil use to which the good may be put is now evident. The "tree of the knowledge of good and evil" evidently refers to a knowledge of everything in a moral sense, and for man this means the ability to assert himself against God, to turn good into evil, and to bring upon himself a curse—fear and shame.

Next we note that when caught in their sin by God, they simply cannot make a clean confession. There is an infection in them that sullies their being. They are caught "red-handed," and yet they cannot confess their guilt. The man blames the woman, the woman blames the serpent, and disharmony now appears where once there was only harmony. There follows the divine curse or penalty. To our author this means first that enmity is placed between snakes and men (verses 14, 15), an enmity and a struggle that shall continue throughout subsequent generations. On the face of it this seems only to mean the simple fact that for the most part snakes have always been abhorrent to men. Yet the way verse 15 is phrased indicates that the author has a deeper meaning here, namely, that the life of man is to be a continual struggle with that which tempts him. There then follow the curse on woman (the pain of childbirth), the curse on the ground so that man is forced to toil in sorrow and eat his bread by the sweat of his face, and the expulsion from Paradise. Man has asserted his independence of God and would, if permitted, seize on immortality to become a god himself; and this God refuses to permit (Chapter 3:22–24). Here begins, then, that association of sin and death which plays such a prominent role, especially in the theology of the apostle Paul.

In Christian teaching this story has been known as the "fall" of man. That is, man has "fallen" from the grace of God in the sense that he now lives in sin and under the judgment of God. His rebellion against God's lordship has forced God to discipline him by punishment. This does not mean that the "image of God" in man has been destroyed; it is still there (Chapter 9:6). Nor does it mean that man shall know in the future nothing but the punishing judgment of God. The remainder of the Bible is the story of the loving and merciful acts of God in man's behalf. Yet it does mean that a deep, basic, and fundamental infection exists in the heart of man, with the result that wherever he moves he finds himself doing that which he knows to be wrong. Consequently, his life is a misery, and he comes to know the judgment of God in full measure with the love of God.

3. The Story of Civilization (Genesis 4–11)

The sequel to the "fall" and its effect on civilization is now described by a series of old stories and traditions in eloquent manner. The sin of the first man seems mild enough, but in the second generation there occurs the first murder, that of Abel by Cain, with the result that the murderer is cut off from human society. Yet several generations later we find the completely hardened character of Lamech (Chapter 4:23, 24), one whose vengeance knows no bounds and whose thoughts know nothing of the will of God. This, then, is the complete opposite of the intention of God as depicted in his creation of Paradise. What is God to do with this man whom he has created who now has so wantonly disregarded all the conditions of his creation by God?

The story of the flood in Chapters 6–9 presents one answer. Man must suffer the terrible judgment of God. To depict this judgment, an old tradition which all Israelites knew and which their fathers had probably brought with them in their migration from Mesopotamia is used: that of a great flood which once destroyed the greater part of the human race. In Babylon, where a similar story is known to have existed almost a thousand years before the time of the Hebrew patriarchs, the flood was a rash and irresponsible act of one of the gods, an act of which the god later repented. In Israel, however, it is given an utterly different setting—one that depicts God's just judgment on the human race. Yet the "anger" of God is always tempered by his mercy. God saves a remnant—the family of Noah, makes a covenant with him that from that time forth man might depend upon the orderly processes of nature (Chapters 8:22;

9:11–17). The sign of this covenant or solemn agreement is the rainbow. To the Israelite this became the sign of God's faithfulness in an orderly nature.

In this way, man gains a second chance. He does not deserve it; nevertheless God gives it to him. So the earth is repeopled and nations are established (Chapter 10). Yet man has not learned his lesson, for next is presented the story of the building of the great temple-tower (ziggurat) in Babylon. First erected sometime between 2400 and 1600 B.C., this high platform represented an old tradition in temple architecture along the Euphrates and Tigris rivers. Its erection in the dim past is remembered in the Hebrew story, but our early author uses it for his own purposes. He interprets it as a supreme example of human presumption. Men want to make themselves a name; thus they build a tower, the very top of which reaches to heaven (Chapter 11:4). Here again is man's ordering of his affairs in complete disregard of his Creator and Lord; he pays no attention whatsoever to what has happened before.

We should note another theme running through these chapters, however, one having to do with the interpretation of civilization. Man's civilized life advances by successive stages, and his progress in the arts of civilization corresponds with the increasing complexity of his sin. The first clothes (Chapter 3:7, 21) and the cultivation of the soil are associated with the fall of man from his created state. Cain the murderer is associated with Cain the builder of the first city (Chapter 4:17). Progress in the arts of nomadic life, metallurgy, and music culminate in the completely hardened and vengeful Lamech (verses 18–24). With the establishment of grape or vineyard culture we are presented the picture of a good man drunk (Chapter 9:20, 21). The growth and separation of nations and languages is associated with the story of the Tower of Babel (Chapter 11:1–9). In this interpretation, then, the growth of civilization is accompanied by a degeneration of the spirit of man, caused by the human refusal to accept all the conditions of creation.

The tenth-century author of most of the material, that is,

the basic narrative in Chapters 2–11, is first of all a compiler of the old traditions of his people. But he is much more than that; he is also a man of great faith and great understanding of the inner nature of man. He does not preach at us; he does not pause here and there to point out the moral of his stories. By the simple arrangement and narration of them he lets them speak their own lesson. Together they form a powerful and profound portrayal of the problem of universal man. That problem is sinful rebellion against the Creator and against man's created nature. And the sin is not primarily that of the "flesh." It has a much deeper rootage in the emotional and intellectual life of man. Man is in a fallen state, so deeply entrenched in his sin that he cannot pull himself from the mire by himself. The answer must come from God, the Lord and Creator.

Here then is the biblical preface. The remainder of the Bible presents the answer that God has provided to the problem there depicted. God's answer comes in two stages. The first is the choice of a people that through the one all may receive a blessing (Chapter 12:3). The second is the gift of his Son, Jesus Christ, who comes to save man from his sin and to reconcile him to God. "For since by man came death, by man came also the resurrection of the dead. For as in Adam all die, even so in Christ shall all be made alive" (I Corinthians 15:21–22, K.J.V.).

B.   GOD CHOOSES A PEOPLE: THE STORIES OF THE PATRIARCHS (GENESIS 12–50)

After leaving the last chapter of the preceding section about the prehistoric period, the interest of the biblical story has rapidly narrowed to one particular family among the Semites (the descendants of Shem). This family has migrated from Mesopotamia into "the land of Canaan" (Chapter 11:31), the old name for southern Syria and Palestine. In the stories which follow, the members of the family do not forget their old homeland in northern Mesopotamia at the city of Haran. Both Isaac and Jacob secured wives from the relatives who remained in that area. Hebrew tradition, then, preserved the memory of this migration from Mesopotamia. Deep within the Israelite consciousness was the sense of historical relatedness to a people whom they called the "Aramaeans."

Historical and archaeological research fixes the period of the Hebrew patriarchs approximately between 2000 and 1700 B.C. During that time and in the centuries just preceding it the whole of the ancient Near East had been inundated by fresh waves of people coming from the desert and settling in the cultivatable lands. The new invasions had brought to an end the great cultures of the first period of statecraft during the third millennium B.C. The great cities of Palestine that existed between 3000 and 2400 B.C., cities which possessed great fortifications and public buildings including temples, had all been destroyed. It was the first great age of civilization in the whole of the lands of the Bible from Persia to Egypt. It was succeeded, however, by a period of great disturbance, after the end of which we come to the patriarchal age when everywhere a new culture has been developed.

Abraham's migration to Palestine was probably one tiny part of this great movement of peoples. His name and that of his grandson, Jacob, together with a great many of the patriarchal names, were common personal names among the peoples of this period. Names of a few of his ancestors are also known as place names along the Upper Euphrates in the area of Haran whence he came. Several of the customs illustrated by the Genesis stories are known to belong to the common law of the Upper Euphrates region during the second millennium B.C. For example, Abraham is promised a son and a great posterity, but the story describes him as disturbed that his wife is unable to have children. In Chapter 15 he expresses concern in a prayer to God about the fact that his heir is to be one Eliezer of Damascus, and that he is apparently to go childless in spite of God's promises to him. This statement is illumined by our knowledge that during this time it was customary for elderly people who had no children of their own to adopt someone to be their "son." This adopted son would take care of the old folk during the remaining years of their lives and see to it that they received a proper burial. In return for this he inherited their property. Abraham and Sarah were elderly people and they evidently had adopted someone to take care of them and to be their heir. Then came a promise of a son, and the patriarch is asking God how this promise will be fulfilled.

In Chapters 29–31 the story of Jacob and his father-in-law Laban in Haran is recounted. It is the story of two crafty men, each trying to outdo the other within the context of ancient customary law. It, too, is illumined by the ancient custom of adoption. Jacob is evidently adopted as the son of Laban; he marries his daughters and works for his adopted father for a number of years. Laban had planned to get the better of the arrangement, but discovered that he in turn was being bested. Consequently, it seemed wise to Jacob to leave with his family for Canaan. Bad feelings ensued when Rachel stole from her father's house the household idols or "gods." The explanation of this act is that possession of these household or family idols was of great assistance in assuring one of inheritance rites in the family.

The various narrative materials about the patriarchs divide themselves up into three main sections: Chapters 12–25 deal for the most part with the family of Abraham; Chapters 26–36 for the most part with the family of Isaac; and Chapters 37–50 with the family of Jacob, especially with the story of his most illustrious son, Joseph. The last-mentioned story is a connected and beautifully polished narrative. Most of its elements had been collected together in their present form centuries before the narrative was set into writing as we now have it. The main thing to notice about the stories relating to the families of Abraham and Isaac is their episodic nature. That is, there is very little connected narrative but only a series of stories. Israel's traditions preserve only fragmentary memories of the founding fathers, a series of episodes in the lives of each one. Several have been preserved about Abraham, but very little was known about Isaac. It is amazing that these traditions so faithfully reflect the background color of their time, when one remembers that they are so fragmentary and that they come to us through such a long period of oral transmission. Since these stories had been told and retold for centuries before being written down, they are for the most part highly polished and are generally ranked among the finest examples of narration in short-story form to be found in the literature of the world, both ancient and modern. The eye of biblical man, having been trained to look at his history with particular care because there God revealed himself, was also trained, evidently, to be critical of narrative style. In any event, no people in history have ever surpassed these in the practiced art of simple, absorbing, and direct narration. On the other hand, we should also say that it is futile to inquire about the details of the stories, as to whether Abraham actually said precisely these words or actually did this or that thing. That a man named Abraham lived, that he was the ancestor of Israel, that he migrated from northern Mesopotamia into Palestine—these and many other things are most certainly historical fact. But archaeology and historical study can never penetrate into the spiritual life of the patriarchs. What we have here is later Israel's interpretation of the true *meaning* of the life of their ancestral fathers. This interpretation is a testament of faith, and it is with this faith that we are here concerned.

We must inquire, therefore, as to the theme or themes which bind this material together. We should not expect to find that every item of the narration contains some deep spiritual truth. The traditions have been preserved with various purposes in mind. Among them are early examples of tribal history, so that one cannot be sure whether the narrative about a patriarch means that it is to be taken as a tribal story with the patriarch standing for the tribe, or whether it is meant to be an episode about an individual. Nevertheless, throughout the whole it is very clear that the original editor of the tenth century B.C. (that is, the man who *wrote* the first edition of these old traditions) has conceived of the whole history of the fathers in a particular way and has cast the material in such a form as to let it speak his point. The tradition says that Abraham came from a family in Mesopotamia to the land of Canaan. It also says that the patriarch received marvelous promises from God, including the gift of the land to his posterity who would become in time a great nation. Thus, a conception of the meaning of the patriarchal age for Israel is presented in which the central theme is that of the promise of God. God has bound himself in promise to this particular family. That is why Abraham appeared in the land of Canaan, having left his home in Mesopotamia. Furthermore, this promise furnishes the clue to the relation between the story of Israel and the prehistoric traditions regarding the problem of man and his civilization in Chapters 1–11. This relation is depicted in Chapter 12:3, "by you all the families of the earth will bless themselves" (R.S.V.). These promises are repeated again and again to the successive patriarchs (Chapters 18:18; 22:18; 26:4; 28:14). Abraham is the father of Israel, and as such receives the promises for all Israel. What the phrase in Chapter 12:3 means, therefore, is that God has chosen Israel in order that through this one people all men may be brought to a saving knowledge of himself. God has chosen the one as the means whereby all may find their blessing. In this way God provides a saving answer to the problem of man and his civilization which the editor has previously described by the juxtaposition of the old traditions in the early chapters. Wherever and in whatever condition the patriarch may be, he is represented as never being away from the presence of God.

One old narrative about the patriarchs is used in three different instances by the different strata of material in order to teach this truth. This is the story about a patriarch in a foreign territory, concerned about his beautiful wife and afraid that he will be killed in order that the king of the territory may have her. Chapters 12, 20, and 26 are all variant treatments of this particular tradition. In them God is shown to be the faithful God who is guiding events to his own purposes and is rescuing his people in the distresses which they have brought upon themselves.

The Joseph story presents an eloquent treatment of the same theme, centering in family infidelity. Joseph's brothers sell him into slavery into Egypt, and in due time have themselves to go to Egypt for food in time of famine. Chapter 45:5 shows the central theological intent of the narrative. When Joseph identifies himself to his brethren who sold him into Egypt, he says: "And now do not be distressed, or angry with yourselves, because you sold me here; for God sent me before you to preserve life." God is the directing hand behind events, and he even uses the sin of man to further his providential purpose. The narrative does not dramatize the great quality of Joseph's personality, namely that he had the power to forgive, but instead focuses the attention upon the purposes of God who overrules the evil of the brothers for a greater good that is accomplished through the very events which put the lad Joseph into slavery.

Central through the whole narrative, and of great importance in biblical theology as a whole, is the manner in which the original editor of the stories presents the personality and character of Abraham. He is shown to be an extremely high-minded person. For example, in Chapter 13 the nomadic life of the patriarch is described. Because of trouble over watering places Abraham suggests to his nephew Lot that they separate. As the head of the family Abraham had the right to make such choices as he would. In this case, however, he allows Lot to choose what land he would prefer. At that time the Jordan Valley, both north and south of the Dead Sea, was thickly settled, as suggested both by the narrative and by archaeological discovery. The area of Sodom and Gomorrah, now covered by the waters of the southern part of the Dead Sea, was especially fertile, so Lot chose it, in spite of the fact that the people who lived in those cities were a very bad sort (Chapter 13:13). Lot's character is depicted here, and in Chapters 18 and 19, in vivid contrast to that of Abraham. Lot is a good man, but he is nevertheless very weak. He has not the strength of purpose to separate himself from evil associations. He is represented as an example of the danger of thinking exclusively about worldly comfort, the subtle temptation that always betrays the good man. In Chapter 14 the rescue of Lot from enemy invasion is presented. God's direction and guidance of Abraham is again made clear, as is also Abraham's disinterestedness, his independence and high-mindedness. After the victory, Abraham will accept nothing whatsoever for himself.

In Chapter 15:6 occurs the statement which appears to be the keynote of the whole Abrahamic cycle of material, and is so interpreted by the apostle Paul in the New Testament (Romans 4:3, 9, 22; Galatians 3:6). There we are told that Abraham "believed the Lord; and he reckoned it to him as righteousness." The very arrangement of the stories about Abraham furnishes a commentary on this text. In Chapter 12 the two halves of the chapter present two different stories about Abraham. In the first half Abraham is the recipient of these wonderful promises of God, as a result of which he leaves his home and country for the land of which he knows nothing. In the second half of the chapter Abraham, because of famine, is in Egypt and there is prepared to lie to the King of Egypt about his wife. He says that his wife is his sister, because he is afraid otherwise that he will be killed. Subsequently the Egyptian king discovers the lie and Abraham is severely reprimanded and sent away from the country. No attempt is made here to apologize for the patriarch. He has lied and no excuses can be made for him. He who has received the promise of God is unable to act as though the promise were true in a situation of crisis. In Chapters 16 and 17 the matter of a son and heir becomes critical. Sarah cannot take seriously God's promise that she, who is an old lady, will bear a son. To help matters along according to her common sense and the common law of her time, she gave Hagar to Abraham so that, as she said, "I shall obtain children by her." Hagar was her maidservant, and in contemporary law this was one way by which a childless woman could obtain an heir for the family. Yet this act promptly involved the family in a squabble, because Sarah soon thought that Hagar was acting in too superior a way. God himself is represented as having to solve the problem. Abraham and his wife are people of faith. Yet they are represented as sinning, not because they do not believe in God, but because in various situations they give way to fear and anxiety. Hence they simply cannot believe God's promises in every situation; they are unable to wait for God because of their anxiety. The substance of faith is here presented by means of illustration. Faith is simply believing what God has said, what God has promised; it is the knowledge that what he has said he will do. Faith is not a series of propositions which are either believed or not believed. It is instead that trust in God which leads one to follow him in whatever situation one may find himself, a trust which waits on the Lord even in times when one is fearful for his life. Conversely, sin is born of doubt and nourished by anxiety. It is a failure to believe God's promises. This led Abraham and his wife to assert their own wills and to plunge themselves deeper into trouble. Later in Exodus and Numbers the same theme is continued. In spite of everything, the people could not believe God's promises; they constantly murmured and attempted to take matters into their own hands. This served only to heighten their misery and resulted in the failure of their generation to secure the Promised Land. In other words, the perennial problem of even the good man who wants to believe is his fear and anxiety which prevent him from trusting God and waiting upon God. Against all appearances to the contrary, Abraham is portrayed as one who trusted God's word, and God accepted that trust as Abraham's "righteousness." Obeying moral rules without this faith is not true righteousness. The apostle Paul makes much of this verse in his argument for justification by faith instead of by works; that is, we are deemed right with God only when we possess the kind of faith that Abraham here typifies. The righteousness God wants is this kind of faithful commitment to the faithful God. Faith is primarily a relationship word which involves our commitment to the faithful One. A man can keep a great number of rules regarding right behavior and still not be a man of faith.

Chapter 15:7–21 repeats the promise of the land, and now God seals his promise by a solemn rite which Abraham could understand. Evidently one method by which people then ratified an agreement was to divide the bodies of certain animals, after which the two parties of the agreement passed between the separated parts. God offers to perform this rite with Abraham as an assurance to Abraham that he will keep his promises. The rite is called a covenant in verse 18; in it God binds himself purely by a gracious act to Abraham. In Chapter 17 the priestly editor of Genesis presents an additional and expanded version of this Abrahamic covenant. The sign of that covenant is the rite of circumcision, a rite that later became a fundamental institution of Judaism, marking a child's entrance into the household of faith. It was the outward sign of membership in the community of God, being replaced in the Christian Church by the rite of baptism. This promise or solemn oath in covenant by which God commits himself to Abraham is ever after remembered as the central meaning of the Abrahamic story. The great events which follow are understood as fulfillments of this promise.

Still another conception that informs and is central to the patriarchal narratives is that of the chosen nation. Israel is a special people whom God has chosen from the ends of the earth. For this reason Abraham was selected from among all the families of his world. A central theme of these chapters is the call of Abraham to a unique blessing and the separation of his family to a unique destiny. Indeed, this theme is one of the central affirmations of the Old Testament. Israel, the seed of Abraham, has been chosen by God out of all the families of the earth, and God has revealed himself to this people as to no other. The first appearance of this affirmation of faith is in the promises made to Abraham when he was called (Chapter 12:2–3). Theologians call this promise "the *election* of Israel."

This very claim of Israel to be a chosen people has been one of the chief sources of difficulty with the Old Testament ever since the time of the early Church. About a century after the death of the apostle Paul, a man named Celsus selected this claim as one of his arguments for the absurdity of Christianity. He said that the Jews and the Christians seemed to think that God made the whole universe for them in particular. Despising all others on this great earth, God takes up his abode among this people alone, "and ceases not his messages and inquiries as to how we may become his associates forever."

A God of love and justice, it was affirmed, could scarcely show such favoritism as that! The biblical answers to these objections are not difficult to discover. How did the people of Israel come to have such an idea? Nearly all scholars are agreed that the doctrine of special election arose in Israel during the time of the exodus from Egypt. Here was a poor, enslaved people whom the world's justice had passed by. They were made to work as slaves on public building projects in Egypt by a Pharaoh of that land, the greatest temporal power of the time. Yet suddenly they were free and were formed into a nation. How had it happened? They did not have the power in themselves; there was only one explanation available to them. That was the assumption that a great God had seen their afflictions, had taken pity on them, and had set them free. Thus when Israel claimed to be the chosen people, she was merely giving the one plausible explanation of the historical fact that whereas she had been in bondage, she was freed by the wonderful work of this one true God. He who had saved her from slavery must have had a purpose in doing so. Yet if this belief in special election began during the exodus, why do we find it the central theme in Genesis? The answer is that as the later Israelite men of faith told the story of their fathers, God's choice of Abraham and of each of the patriarchs was the only way by which the life of those patriarchs could be understood. How did Abraham happen to come to Palestine at all unless God had chosen and led him? The fact that he came is proof of God's call; the fact that Israel is chosen is the proof that God chose Abraham. But someone may ask: "Why did God choose Abraham and not some other person? Was not God 'playing favorites' in this choice?" We cannot answer these questions, and Israel did not know their answers either. Why God chose Abraham and not someone else, or why we individually are chosen for this or that task and not for another is one of the secrets of God to which he does not always give an answer. All that he asks of us is that we accept what he has done for us with grateful and humble hearts—this is the perspective of biblical faith. To the writers of Genesis the wonder of Abraham was that he did accept with no questions asked; he rearranged and ordered his life accordingly, leaving his home and kin for a land of which he knew nothing.

Was Abraham chosen because he was such a good man? Was Israel chosen because she was such a gifted people? Are righteousness and merit the bases of God's choice? The answer of Israel was an emphatic negative. Nothing whatsoever is said about the moral life of Abraham before his call. A later Israelite told his people most emphatically that they were not to think that God did what he did for them because they were so righteous (Deuteronomy 9:4–6). He continues by saying that they most certainly were not a good people but a "stiff-necked people." From the earliest days they had provoked God by their continual rebellion against him. To the wonderful things that God did for them, Israel had answered with the basest and the most wanton ingratitude. God does not choose sinless people for his work; he takes men as they are and makes even their sin praise him.

We must now ask: "What are the responsibilities involved in election?" Here in Genesis, God has revealed his purpose in choosing Abraham. It is to save the world, or so Chapter 12:3 implies. This suggests that the elect or chosen people have more than a passive role to play. Israel was a chosen people, but this gave them no liberty or license to do as they pleased. Instead it placed a terrible burden of responsibility upon them. The prophet Amos put the matter this way (Amos 3:2): "You only have I known of all the families of the earth; therefore I will visit upon you all your iniquities." In other words God had especially revealed himself to his chosen ones. Consequently the chosen have a great responsibility and are the more guilty and will be the more punished if they flout it. As a great scholar of the last century, William Robertson Smith, once wrote: "If Israel would not learn to know Jehovah in the good Land of Canaan, it must once more pass through the desert and enter the door of hope through the valley of tribulation." In the vast sea of ancient paganism, God did reveal himself to Israel, and from this nation the world has indeed come to know God—so the Christian Church has always affirmed. Yet the problem of Israel was the problem of sin and rebellion. The story of the Old Testament is God's revelation of the nature of the true life on this earth and of his dealings with his chosen people to the end that they might be faithful. But the story of Israel is a tragic tale, one in which God is forced so to punish his faithless elect that they suffer tragically and terribly. Election is not election to privilege but election to responsibility and that responsibility is truly enormous. Yet by means of gracious leading, unmerited love, and severe chastisement God did accomplish his purpose through Israel. In the fullness of time Jesus Christ was sent into the soil God had prepared for his coming. He came not to annul what God had done in Israel, but to fulfill it by dealing dramatically with the matter of sin. He came to save people from their sins.

In God's covenant with Abraham, described in Chapters 15 and 17, the emphasis is almost solely on God's part of the agreement. Therefore we may see in this particular covenant simply a sign and seal of God's election of Israel and the promises that went with it. The covenant is to be an everlasting one, valid for all generations to come. Nothing is said there about Israel's part of the agreement, except that the people must perform the rite of circumcision as the sign and seal of the covenant (Chapter 17). Not until the later covenant at Sinai (Exodus 19–24) would the nation's responsibilities be made clear. The Abrahamic covenant is one of promise, and it looks forward to its fulfillment. When and how was it fulfilled? Partly in the great work of God in and through Israel. Yet at the end of the Old Testament the chosen nation was still looking forward to the completion of the promise. The Christian Church understood that only in Christ was the covenant fulfilled. He is the fullness of Israel and the fulfillment of God's promises to his people.

Who is the true Israelite? Is he a racial descendant of Abraham? Is the everlasting covenant of God solely with one national entity? If Israel is the chosen people through whom salvation is to be mediated to the world, then would this not mean that God's promises come to us only as we become Jews by adoption? This was one of the first great problems of the early Christian Church (see Acts 15 and Galatians). Led by the apostle Paul, the Church answered as follows: Abraham was called, and he responded in faith; that is, he believed in God and obeyed (Genesis 15:6). The true Israelite, therefore, is not the man who merely happens to be a racial descendant of Abraham. He is the man who is Abraham's spiritual descendant, who likewise responds in faith and obeys as did Abraham. The Church in Christ, therefore, has considered itself the true Israel and the true heir of the promises in the covenant with Abraham. The early Church clearly assumed that Israel had violated her election. In other words God's choice of Israel to a vocation in the world could be and was annulled by her own act. Yet God was not defeated. Israel accomplished his purpose, and the Church as the New Israel carries the promises and looks forward to their fulfillment at the time when the whole earth shall be the kingdom of God and of his Christ. It was somewhat in this manner that the early Christians saw themselves in relation to that statement of faith which rests within the narratives of Genesis.

C. THE EXODUS: GOD DELIVERS THE PEOPLE FROM SLAVERY (EXODUS 1–18)

At the end of the Book of Genesis we find the family of Jacob (the grandson of Abraham) living in Egypt, where they had gone because of a famine in Canaan. Exodus begins with a brief review of the situation and then tells how the Hebrews were made slaves by a Pharaoh "who knew not Joseph." This is followed by the story of their remarkable deliverance from that slavery.

This deliverance was always conceived of as the most important event in the history of Israel. A people had been put into bondage, but a great God had seen their affliction, had taken pity on them, and by remarkable demonstrations of power had set them free! A weak, dispirited people whom the justice of the world had passed by, a people for whom there was no protecting law, a people oppressed by Pharaoh, who was the greatest temporal power of his day—these were the people whom God, mightier than the gods of the nations and mightier than Pharaoh, saw, pitied, and saved. Why had he done that? The popular gods of the human race show much more respect and consideration for the strong, the wealthy, and the powerful than they do for the weak. It is only the strong and the wealthy who can provide them with magnificent temples and magnanimous gifts. Yet here was a God who chose to combat the strong in behalf of the weak, for whom the world and the gods of the world cared nothing.

It is small wonder, therefore, that at the center of Israel's faith was this supreme act of divine love and grace. The very existence of the nation was due solely to this act; the beginning of Israel's history as a nation was traced to this miraculous happening. In confessions of faith it is the central affirmation. (Note such confessions in Deuteronomy 6:20–25; 26:5–10.) Who is God? For Israel it was unnecessary to elaborate abstract terms and phrases as we do in our confessions. It was only necessary to say that he is the "God, who brought thee out of the land of Egypt, out of the house of bondage" (Exodus 20:2). What more was needed to identify or to describe God than that? His complete control over nature and man is adequately implied in the statement; his purposive action in history in fighting the injustice of the strong and making even their sin to serve and praise him is also directly implied; so also is his redemptive love, which saves and uses the weak of the world to accomplish his purpose even among the strong.

The psalmists continually sang praises to God for what he did here, and the prophets repeatedly warned the people of their ingratitude. "When Israel was a child, then I loved him, and called my son out of Egypt. . . . I drew them with cords of a man, with bands of love; and I was to them as they that lift up the yoke on their jaws . . . And my people are bent on backsliding from me" (Hosea 11:1–7). It was the exodus, then, that kept Israel firm in the knowledge of God's love, even when they were experiencing his punishment. Furthermore, it was the knowledge of God derived from this event that became the original basis of the conception of his righteousness which is distinctive to the Old Testament. God's purpose is a saving purpose, and his righteousness is especially concerned with the weak, the dispossessed, and the outcast of the earth. Those for whom the world provides no justice are the very ones who shall know God's righteousness as a saving power. On the other hand, the Bible is extremely suspicious of those who have power and wealth in the midst of weakness. They, like Pharaoh, shall also know of God's righteousness, but it will be a righteousness that will judge and punish them. God demands humility, not pride; he demands stewardship, not self-assertion; he wants dependence upon himself, not self-sufficiency. Consequently, the righteousness of God in the Bible is to be seen in two aspects: on the one hand, it is his saving love for those in need; on the other, it is his wrath for those who are the enemies of his redemptive purpose.

Furthermore the righteousness of God as seen in the exodus event colored the believer's whole point of view toward God and his neighbor. In a summary of the Israelite's responsibility in the light of what God has done, one passage (Deuteronomy 10:14–22) puts the matter very vividly. The passage begins with a statement that, though to God belong the whole realm of earth and heaven, yet he has set his heart in love upon the fathers of Israel and has chosen their descendants after them. And yet he is not a God among gods; he is a God of gods and Lord of lords, that is, he is the sovereign Lord of all, who is great and mighty, who cannot be influenced by bribery or favoritism, but sees to it that the weak of the earth get justice; he loves the sojourner, that is, the stranger who lives within the nation's gates. "Love the sojourner therefore; *for you were sojourners in the land of Egypt.* You shall fear the Lord your God . . . and cleave to him . . . He is your praise: he is your God, who has done for you these great and terrible things which your eyes have seen. Your fathers went down to Egypt seventy persons; and now the Lord your God has made you as the stars of heaven for a multitude." In other words, we are to love God and cleave to him because he has shown himself to us in such a marvelous and loving way. But the manner in which he has done this, when we were in our period of

75

weakness, sets the tone and direction of our response to him. As we were once slaves and sojourners, so now we are to be kind to the slaves and sojourners who are in our midst. God's command that we love our neighbor as ourselves (Leviticus 19:18) means in its original context that the whole of our economic and social life has as its central purpose the service of the neighbor, the assistance of those in need. Obedience to God involves this as the first and primary commandment, once our love of him has been established and affirmed (Deuteronomy 6:4–5). In the New Testament, when Jesus was asked as to the meaning of the two greatest commandments, those concerning the love of God and the neighbor, a questioner, trying to justify himself, asked the familiar question, "And who is my neighbor?" Jesus replied by telling the story of the good Samaritan. He meant by it that any person who is in need is the Christian's neighbor (Luke 10:25–37). Because of the exodus event, therefore, the righteousness of biblical man became something different from the normal righteousness seen on earth, with its careful calculation of each man's due. It is a saving and redemptive righteousness directed toward all who need help.

The time of the exodus is the early part of the thirteenth century B.C., when Egypt is at the height of her power, and when Palestine and Lower Syria are a portion of the Egyptian Empire. Archaeological information from Egypt informs us that it was not unusual for families and clans of bedouins from Palestine and Sinai to enter Egypt in hard times and live along the border. That Israel, or some portion of the later nation of Israel, had at one time been in Egypt is verified not only by the tradition of the slavery but also by the presence in the tradition beginning with the time of Moses of a number of Egyptian names. The name "Moses" is itself from an Egyptian name; it was a very common verbal element used by the Egyptians in names to suggest that such and such a god had borne or begotten the particular individual in question. In the case of Moses the god name has been omitted and only the verbal element remains, its meaning having been forgotten in the Israelite tradition. A number of other names of Egyptian origin were likewise preserved, particularly in the tribe of Levi, which became the tribe of the priests and teachers of the faith. Most important for fixing the date of the exodus is the knowledge derived from excavations in Palestine about the conquest of Canaan, on the one hand, and on the other hand the statement in Exodus 1:11 that the King of Egypt put the Israelites to work on two cities in the region of the Nile Delta. This brings us immediately to what is known as the Nineteenth Egyptian Dynasty, more specifically after about 1308 B.C. The reason is that the kings of Egypt before this time had used Thebes in Upper Egypt as their capital and had done very little construction work in the Delta. Beginning in the Nineteenth Dynasty, however, a great attempt was made to win back the empire in Asia which had been lost during the middle of the fourteenth century. Consequently the center of operations was moved into Lower Egypt near the Mediterranean where ready access to Palestine and Syria was at hand.

This means that we are a long way from the time of the patriarchs in Genesis. Indeed Exodus 12:40 tells us that the time the children of Israel dwelt in Egypt was 430 years. Long ages have passed, therefore, and only memories of the forefathers remain.

The exodus story is brief and terse. The first chapter quickly describes the situation. The narrative then turns to the description of what God did about it. In Chapters 2–4 we are told about the birth and upbringing of Moses, how he had to flee from Egypt, and how God called him as his chosen man to deliver his people from slavery. Moses objected strenuously because he was afraid the people would not believe him and would say that God had not appeared to him. The Lord, accommodating himself to the situation, then gave Moses magical tricks to perform. Moses still objected. He was not an eloquent speaker. Finally God in exasperation says that he will make use of Aaron, Moses' brother, who will be the orator for the occasion and speak the words which Moses wants him to. And in typical biblical fashion the first results of the joint work of Moses and Aaron are briefly stated: "And the people believed; and when they heard that the Lord had visited the people of Israel and that he had seen their affliction, they bowed their heads and worshiped" (Exodus 4:31).

Then begins the great contest between God and Pharaoh as described in Chapters 5–11. The magical tricks which God has given to Moses are unavailing before Pharaoh, because the Egyptian magicians are able to duplicate them. But there follows a succession of plagues, each worse than the last, until Pharaoh in fear lets the people go.

It will be noted that the greatest concentration of miracle stories in the Bible occurs at critical points in the history where the power of God is especially felt to be present. Such critical points are the exodus, the period of Elijah and Elisha during the ninth century, and the ministry of Jesus. Scholars have long since pointed out that the various plagues described in the exodus story are natural scourges which have long been known in Egypt, and here apparently occurred with particular severity and were used as proofs of the power of God. Such a view hardly accounts for all aspects of the narrative, as for example the death of the firstborn in Chapter 12:29. Furthermore it should be observed that the biblical man did not look upon a miracle quite as we do. He did not have such a word in his vocabulary. He spoke of "signs and wonders." Any unusual or spectacular happening that was a sign of the direct working of God—this was his miracle. If a modern man could have stood beside him and given a rational explanation of all the events through which he passed, he would not have been particularly impressed. His question would always have been, "Well, why did they happen at exactly this time in this way and secure this result?" To us the major focus of attention in the matter of miracle is to explain how it could have happened without setting aside natural law. With him the point was rather what was happening, what was going on, what result God achieved through the unusual.

In Exodus 12–13 editors of the material have inserted a complete description of the Passover celebration as it was later known in Israel. The reason they did so was that they traced its foundation to this final plague, when God saved his people. The festival thus became the central one in Israel's life, and celebrated God's great deliverance. The climax of the story comes, however, in Chapters 14–15—two different versions of the miraculous events that happened when Israel left Egypt. Chapter 14 is prose and Chapter 15:1–18 tells the same story in poetry—an old poem, the original of which must date not far from the events described. By an act of God a terrific storm of some sort parted the waters, allowing Israel to pass through them (Chapters 14:21; 15:8). In one passage "strong east wind" is specifically mentioned; in the other the wind is figuratively called the "blast of thy nostrils." As a result of the wind, the waters, presumably rather shallow, were driven back; but when the Egyptians tried to follow, their chariot wheels floundered in the mud (Chapter 14:25), and they were trapped when the waters returned.

Two themes are woven together in these two chapters and those which precede and follow. One is the repeated assertion that God is in charge of the events, and therefore Israel need not fear. The other is the murmuring and lack of faith on the part of the people. Here again we have the contrast between God's promise and the human inability to believe it; it is the same contrast as that observed in the story of Abraham in Genesis. The first theme is the power of God to do what he has set out to do; the key verse in the first theme is Chapter 14:14: "The Lord will fight for you, and you shall hold your peace." There are times when matters seem completely out of human hand; there is nothing else man can do. Israel beside the sea, with Pharaoh's chariots behind, was in such a position. Had the hard-won release from Egypt been in vain? Would God fail Israel now after his promises of salvation? To Moses this was inconceivable.

God, in delivering his people, has determined that the deliverance shall be an act that shall lead all men to honor and respect him (Chapters 14:4, 18; 15:14–18). So confident of this are the Israelite writers that they go so far as to say that God actually hardened Pharaoh's heart to make the victory the greater. Elsewhere, however, it is said that Pharaoh hardened his own heart (for example, Chapter 8:15). The Israelite would have seen no inconsistency in this, though it appears to be one to us. To him God's foreknowledge is such that he does his work while still allowing for human freedom. God is at work there; yet it is in such a way that Pharaoh's moral responsibility is not annulled. It is a colorful way of affirming that God uses man's sin for his own glorification and to achieve his own end.

The second theme, which is in contrast to the promise of God and the faith of Moses, is the murmuring of the people (Chapters 14:10–12; 15:23–26; see also Chapters 16:3; 17:2, 3; Numbers 11; 12). All the old doubts and fears come to the surface, not only before the sea, but in every subsequent crisis. No matter what God has done in the past, every new danger brings on the murmuring that at times reaches the proportions of a rebellion. The people believed in God, but they were afraid to trust him, particularly when they found themselves in a crisis. It is remarkable that Israel should preserve the story of its past in such form. The truth is told; and their life is explained as one of infidelity to the kindness of God. It is very evident that in the exodus event something happened to Israel of such a nature as to make it impossible for the people to interpret their life apart from it. Because of what God did here, a special relationship was created between God and Israel. A disparate group of families and clans were now made into a people who thought of themselves as "the people of God." No attempt was made or could have been made to understand the meaning of Israel's peoplehood apart from this event and from the relationship which it established. And because of the way the relationship was formed, the biblical view of the nature of God as known from his work in history, and also of man's obligation to God, was utterly different and unique.

Of the many relationships which individuals and groups have with one another we may perhaps single out two which are of basic importance. One is a relationship which involves mutual obligation. Marriage is an example of this type of covenant or relationship. Solemn vows are taken and mutual duties are required. Another type of relationship exists in my job. My employer and I possess an agreement: he promises to do certain things for me and I in turn promise to do certain things for him. If either one of us fails in the fulfillment of these obligations, the relationship will probably be severed. In Genesis 30:31 Jacob and Laban enter into an agreement whereby Jacob becomes Laban's son and servant. The mutual obligations are closely defined. In I Kings 5 Hiram, King of Tyre, and Solomon, King of Israel, have a joint covenant or trade treaty. Hiram promises to supply materials for the temple Solomon desires to build in Jerusalem, and Solomon promises to deliver in exchange a certain amount of wheat and olive oil, though in the end Solomon had a trade deficit and had to cede to Hiram some twenty cities of Israelite territory in Galilee (I Kings 9:11). In such cases acts of giving and receiving are involved in a context of mutual duty. We live and move and have our being amid relationships of this type.

There is another type of relationship which exists between individuals and between groups. If the relationship began through some undeserved act of kindness, an act which sought no reward, nor did it require any reciprocal action; if someone goes out of his way to do something for me, particularly at a time when I am in need of help; if any of these happen, a special relationship is established between me and that person. I cannot pay him back. To reduce this act of kindness into a matter of bookkeeping so that I could easily repay what has been done is to annul the relationship. Nothing that I have done deserves what I have received. I am thus tied to the person in question by a bond that is stronger than any mutual agreement involving mutual obligations. I am grateful to him; and my gratitude means that I am somehow emotionally attached to him. And if the opportunity arises I will, out of this love that has thus been created, do a kindness to him in return. Such acts of mutual kindness have no obligation behind them. One is not a payment for the other. One's attachment to a parent, for example, is often on a far deeper basis than one of formal family tie or "blood" relationship. The parents' continual acts of kindness beyond any call of duty have pulled from the child a response of love and affection. He cannot repay his parents, but a close relationship has been established and he in turn will show deeds of kindness to them on whatever occasions it is possible for him to do so. In I Samuel 18:1–3 we are told about a relationship that was established between Jonathan, son of King Saul, and the young man David. Jonathan was a prince of Israel; he owed nothing whatsoever to David. Yet we are told that his soul "was knit to the soul of David, and Jonathan loved him as his own soul. . . . Then Jonathan made a covenant with David, because he loved him as his own soul." Later when Jonathan's father sought to kill David, this close relationship persisted, and Jonathan saved David's life. When David became King of all Israel, one of his early acts was to find out if there was anyone left of the house of Saul, in order that he might show them kindness "for Jonathan's sake." He found a son of Jonathan and provided for him during the rest of his life. This was an act of kindness which David did not have to do; nor did Jonathan need to have made the covenant with David in the first place. The relationship was closer than any made in the framework of law or custom. It rested upon an inner union of the soul, so to speak. No legal duties were required as a result of it. In such a relationship deeds are done, but they are done out of love and kindness. And if I am the recipient of one of these deeds of kindness, I want to reciprocate in love, for otherwise I will feel ungrateful. To break a relationship established out of undeserved goodness is far worse than to break a contractual relationship. One's deepest feelings of guilt and infidelity are involved in any betrayal of love.

A close relationship between God and Israel was established in the exodus event, but it was a relationship of the latter type rather than of the former. God did not save Israel from slavery because she was better than other people, and therefore worthy to be saved. Indeed Chapter 9 of Deuteronomy makes a special point of this: God did not give the people their land because they were more righteous than those being dispossessed. God had another reason and it was basically one of love. The people are to remember, however, that they have been sinners and rebels from the earliest days. God's act is one of undeserved kindness and the close tie that exists between him and his people is the result of that kindness. He has sought out, not those whom the peoples of the earth might call the deserving ones, but those whom no one would claim to be deserving. Israel's relation to God was one originally established in grace, not in law. It is only because God first loved his people that they love him in return, and they obey him primarily because they love him for what he has done. Indeed, they are to love their neighbors because he first loved them. Psalm 136 is a magnificent hymn of praise to God, centering precisely in these undeserved acts of kindness; "O give thanks to the Lord, for he is good, for his steadfast love [his undeserved deeds of kindness] endures for ever." Conversely, wrongdoing is interpreted with deep emotional overtones as ingratitude and infidelity. For example, Psalm 106:7–13: "Our fathers, when they were in Egypt, did not consider thy wonderful works; they did not remember the abundance of thy steadfast love, but rebelled . . . Yet he saved them for his name's sake . . . Then they believed his words; they sang his praise. But they soon forgot his works; they did not wait for his counsel."

The tie between God and Israel was thus of the closest possible kind. It was established in what to the Israelites was the history of their past. It meant that central to Israelite faith from this time forth was to be a conception of relationship. This new community belongs to God, and to God it must cleave. Whatever may happen, whatever dark valley of the shadow is encountered, he is their rock and their fortress. In whatever tragedy, he is good and just and righteous. The King of kings and the Lord of lords, the almighty power among all the powers of the world—this God is good and his goodness shall endure forever. It is central to his nature to love, to save, to redeem, to restore; he did this at the exodus, and subsequent history, when properly understood, is further testimony to that goodness. The story of the exodus is thus at the very heart and core of the faith.

D. GOD MAKES THE PEOPLE A NATION: THE COVENANT (EXODUS 19–NUMBERS 36)

An over-all title for the period which extends from the exodus from Egypt to the time of Joshua and the conquest of Palestine might be "In the Wilderness." It was in this time that certain experiences took place at the holy mountain (Mount Sinai or, as it is sometimes called, Mount Horeb) which formed the people into a nation. There followed, however, a long period of wandering in the wilderness, especially in the area of Kadesh-Barnea in southernmost Palestine, followed by a trek through Trans-Jordan and finally the conquest of Trans-Jordan as described in Numbers 20–21. The wandering in the wilderness is referred to in various ways by later writers. For example, in Joshua 24:8–10 it is mentioned as a scene of great deeds of salvation on God's part for his people. On the other hand, Jeremiah 2:2 speaks of the people's devotion in their youth, when they followed God in the wilderness, when the bond between them was very close. Then, too, there is the theme as expressed in Psalm 106:13–33; it is the story of the rebellions in the wilderness. These were Israel's responses to the goodness and the fidelity of God. Salvation, devotion, and rebellion—these were three different ways in which the wilderness wandering of Israel could be and was interpreted.

Yet if the wilderness wandering is the theme of this large collection of material, we must admit that here we encounter greater difficulty in comprehending what we are reading than at almost any other point in the Old Testament. The narrative here is by no means continuous. It is continually interrupted by a vast amount of heterogeneous material from a variety of sources. Exodus 19–24 describes God's covenant with Israel at Mount Sinai (Horeb). This is followed in Chapters 25–40 with a detailed description of the tabernacle, the shrine which was the center of the community in this age, the description of which reveals the center of the theology of the priestly writers. That theology was concerned with the tabernacling God whose presence in the midst of the people alone made them a people. In this section with its detailed prescriptions, Chapters 32–34 preserve some older narrative material about the people's rebellion and their desire to have a God to worship whom they can see or visualize. The Book of Leviticus has very little narration in it. It begins with the manual of public worship, which describes the various sacrifices or services of offering at the tabernacle. Following this manual of instructions there appears also a variety of matters relating to the priests, to the proper foods which shall be eaten, etc. Chapters 17–26, however, preserve a fragmentary collection of old laws as they have been preserved in the Jerusalem temple, laws dealing with all phases of the people's life. Among them we find in Chapter 19:18 the famous words, "Thou shalt love thy neighbor as thyself." This is a summary of the whole economic life of the people. The whole purpose of their economic and social life is that they shall love their neighbor, particularly the poor and the unfortunate, by assisting him according to his need. In the Book of Numbers, Israel leaves Sinai, spends a generation in the area of Kadesh because of a problem in morale which is interpreted as the judgment of God, and finally succeeds in the conquest of Trans-Jordan. This narrative is contained in Chapters 11–14, 20–25. And it concludes with the marvelous story about Balaam. The King of Moab, frightened by Israel and afraid to fight, instead sends to far-off Mesopotamia and hires a famous magician named Balaam. The latter does his best to conjure up a curse against Israel, but he is an honest practitioner who recognizes failure when his procedures do not come out right. The King of Moab is described as getting exceedingly angry with the magician, even refusing to pay him his fee! The Israelite writer of the narrative obviously enjoys the telling of it, and sees the whole event in a highly humorous light. To him it is the height of absurdity that the pagan arts of magic could in any way influence the course of action decided upon by the God of Israel! In fact, God uses the magician's art to serve his own purposes, rather than those either of the magician or of the king who hired him.

Around this essential story of the Book of Numbers there is a great variety of priestly material preserved in Chapters 1–10, 15–19, and 26–36. In them the Jerusalem priesthood has preserved a considerable amount of archaic materials, but their arrangement suggests considerable haste in the editing for reasons which are no longer clear.

Since the successive editors heaped so much traditional matter around the original story, we must assume that to them this period in the wilderness was a pivotal time in Israel's life. The central event of the period was considered to be God's covenant with Israel which was celebrated at the sacred mountain. From this covenant the Old Testament received its name; here was made the old covenant, as distinct from the new covenant in Jesus Christ. It is described in Exodus 19–24. Since it is so central to the Israelites' understanding of the meaning of society and history, we must pause to describe it in some detail.

The ancient world was a world full of covenants; man lived and moved throughout his life in an interlocking series of covenants. When two parties are bound together in an agreement or a treaty, sealed by a vow, but in which no means of enforcement are available, there we have a covenant. To this day international treaties have the form of covenant: they are agreements between two parties sealed by vows, but no means of enforcement are available other than those contained in the vows. In the ancient world the witnesses of the human covenants were the God or gods of the respective parties. They were called upon as the witnesses who would keep the covenant in case one or both of the human participants broke it. A good example of this type of parity treaty, or agreement between equals, is to be found in Genesis 31, the covenant between Jacob and Laban. Indeed, the Mizpah benediction, so often used in young people's groups today, had its original setting in that treaty. Jacob and Laban prayed to God that he would keep the covenant if either of them had a tendency to break it when they had left one another: "May the Lord watch

between me and thee while we are absent one from another."
These words do not mean that God will kindly keep us from
getting into danger after our meeting has broken up! They are
rather a part of a covenant: we have made our mutual vows,
but we are human and sinful. Our agreement is in danger if
we are left to our own devices. We beseech God, therefore,
to be the guard of our solemn vows to the end that they are
kept, when we are no longer present with one another to look
after each other in our weakness.

It is very clear that the conception of covenant, borrowed
from the social and political law of the day, was used to depict
the relationship of God and people. This relationship was one
which had been formed in the exodus when God had chosen
this people for himself and his own purposes. Covenant was a
way of making a picture out of the relationship, so that the
people would understand what it meant. In Exodus 19:5-6
God is represented as saying: "If you will obey my voice and
keep my covenant, you shall be my own possession among all
peoples; for all the earth is mine, and you shall be to me a
kingdom of priests and a holy nation." We note that in this
case the promise begins with a condition; there is now a covenant which must be kept. Before this we have noticed the concentration upon the grace of God, upon his undeserved acts
of goodness. The good news of God's marvelous and saving
activity has been related with joy, but here now we encounter
the divine requirement. Law is added to grace, and the good
news (gospel) from this point on in the Bible is associated
with a requirement God places upon his people. From this
point on gospel and law become a dominant biblical theme,
and their relationship one to another becomes something difficult to describe in simple words. The substance of the covenant is described in Chapter 20; it is the Ten Commandments.
This is followed in Chapter 20:23-23:33 by the oldest collection of legal practices which the Old Testament possesses, one
which the scholars call "the book of the covenant" (Exodus
24:7). In other words, God is here represented as a king who
is giving a law to the people, and the people are the subjects
of the king and are required to keep his law. In God's cove-

nant with Abraham (Genesis 15, 17) the whole emphasis is upon God's promise to the patriarch. There God commits himself, and Abraham is the one who receives the promises and acts upon them in faith. Here at Mount Sinai the people vowed to obey the king. One very common summary of the covenant which appears again and again in the Old Testament is the expression, "I will be your God and you shall be my people." The continuing lordship of God, as a result of the Sinai covenant, is dependent upon the loyalty of the people. The words express a close relationship, and it is the relationship pictured in a king bearing rule over his subjects. The nation of Israel understood itself, therefore, by means of a picture drawn from political life.

The particular type of political covenant that originally lay behind the biblical doctrine of society has only recently been discovered by Professor George E. Mendenhall of the University of Michigan.[1] It is to be found in certain treaties of the second millennium B.C. in western Asia. These treaties were of two types. One was a parity treaty between equals. The other was between a suzerain and a vassal. It should be understood that a suzerain is not a king among other kings, but a ruler who believed himself to be the king of kings and lord of lords, one who rules over many kings. He is the great king who offers his covenant to his vassal. In the typical suzerainty treaty he speaks to his vassal in the first person and begins by describing all his benevolent acts to the vassal in past years. By this means he hopes to get the vassal to obey him, not simply because of legal necessity, but because the great king has been so good to him. Then follow the stipulations of the covenant. These vary greatly in the various treaties, but one common prohibition opposes the vassal's having any relations with other powers. Furthermore the vassal is expected to keep the king's peace; there should be no internal civil war. There is also a provision for depositing the treaty in the sanctuary of the vassal, for reading it publicly periodically, a lengthy invocation to

[1] *Law and Covenant in Israel and the Ancient Near East,* The Biblical Colloquium, Pittsburgh 5, Pennsylvania, 1955.

the deities of heaven and earth who are the witnesses to the covenant, and finally the curses that will come to the vassal if he breaks the covenant and the blessings which will accrue to him if he keeps it. The treaty was binding only in the lifetime of the parties involved, and it had to be made again with each successive generation or dynasty.

When this type of political treaty is examined carefully side by side with the Mosaic covenant in the Old Testament, as Professor Mendenhall has done, it becomes necessary to conclude that a relationship in form exists between the two. Israel pictured her relationship to God in the form of some such treaty or covenant. In Exodus 20 God introduced the new relationship by identifying himself: "I am the Lord your God who brought you out of the land of Egypt, out of the house of bondage." The covenant begins by identifying him who gives it as one who is entitled to do so by his benevolent acts. This means, as Deuteronomy 6:5 has observed, that legal requirement is not the center of the relationship between God and his people. Rather the relationship is one of love and grace; as God has loved us, so we should love him with all our heart and soul and strength, for obedience must be rooted in love. As in the suzerainty treaties the first stipulation of the Decalogue is the prohibition against foreign relations: that is, God's people are to worship no one but himself. This meaning of the first commandment is made clear in Exodus 34:14 where the words, "You shall worship no other god," actually explain the true intent of the commandment. In the second part of the Decalogue the concern is with the inner wholesomeness and peace of the society: no murder, adultery, stealing, false witness, or coveting. These commandments were put within the ark, which was a portable box. As a result, it was called "the ark of the testimony" (Exodus 25:16) or "the ark of the covenant" (I Samuel 4:4). The ark, therefore, became the symbol of the covenant, and in later times the Ten Commandments could be called God's covenant (Deuteronomy 4:13). Hence the covenant, like the suzerainty treaty, was always kept in the central sanctuary of the people. There is also evidence that in the early days of Israel, before the time of the monarchy, there was a periodic celebration of the covenant in Israel, similar to the one periodically required of the vassal in the international treaties of the second millennium B.C.

Space does not permit a more detailed analysis of the relationship between the international treaty formulae and the covenant between God and people in the time of Moses. Enough has been said, however, to indicate that it originally provided the picture, the form or structure, through which the knowledge of God was communicated in the Bible. God was then known as the great suzerain whose benevolent acts toward his newly created community were to lead his people to serve him through love. No other divine powers could be honored, for these would weaken the central commitment. And the service was one of freedom. The general obligations were cast in the form of absolutes; within the framework they provided that the vassal was free to order his own life. The Ten Commandments have sometimes been objected to because most of them are negatively phrased: "Thou shalt not." Yet, as Professor Mendenhall has pointed out, the negative is the only truly universal form of law. A prohibition forbids action in one area, while leaving all other areas free. A positive law, "Thou shalt," limits all action to the one area prescribed, thus preventing freedom of decision and action unless the law is so general that it provides nothing more than a frame of reference.

One of the great struggles in both the Old and New Testaments is with the attempt to interpret the detailed positive law of the legal community as the constitutional law of the divine suzerain—something which happened in Judaism. In this sense, therefore, the Ten Commandments, that is, the Mosaic covenant, is a charter of freedom. Religious obligation is established, but the Israelite was not told precisely in what manner these laws were to be kept in the various phases of his life and history. In what manner was God to be worshiped? How was the Sabbath to be observed? How were one's parents to be honored? The Decalogue provides only the framework of life. The covenant community is responsible for working out for itself the detailed manner in which God shall be served in daily life. This Israel did in her various codes of law. As previously mentioned, the oldest one is in Exodus 21–23; the Holiness Code in Leviticus 17–26 and the Deuteronomic Code in Deuteronomy 12–26 are the two other collections of old laws in the Old Testament and contain also considerable exposition of their meaning. These laws describe how Israel served her Lord. They were descriptions of legal practice, but originally they were not compiled as constitutional law in the modern sense; there was at that time in the ancient world neither the vocabulary nor the mentality which would permit or compel the judge to decide a legal case on the basis of the "constitution." In Mesopotamia, for example, an earlier code dating from about 1700 B.C. is that compiled by the famous King Hammurabi. In that country there is no extant example of a judge rendering a decision by referring to that code, though there are many decisions contrary to the provisions in it. "Law" meant "teaching, instruction," and the codes were prepared at various times and occasions as descriptions of legal practice in various areas, but no judge felt any compulsion to be bound by them. The Judaism which arose in the post-exilic period was a comparatively new phenomenon in that it made these old detailed prescriptions of legal practice into constitutional law, and freedom of decision and action was limited by the host of positive commands. The Jews in the time of Ezra during the fifth century B.C. wished to obey God, and to do so they collected every law that they could find in the older codes and interpreted them as their constitution. They were God's will which could be written down.

The New Testament, of course, has no patience whatever with the compulsory nature of Israel's common law. It aligns itself with the pre-exilic prophets in the attempt to revive the old society envisioned in ideal in the original Israelite covenant. It was an order of freedom in which responsible people under God were called upon to make decisions in his behalf within a general frame of reference.

The picture of God as King of kings and Lord of lords, as the ruler who sought his vassal's love and obedience—this is what gave to the Israelite self-understanding and the understanding of himself in relation to his people. To be a people meant to be servants of the ruler, and love of God was alone what made possible the love of one's neighbor. That is, loyalty to the great king meant the preserving of the internal harmony and peace. Furthermore, while God bound the people in covenant, each member of the community heard the law addressed to him personally, *"Thou* shalt." The divine ruler dignified each one with his personal address. Man the individual was pulled out of the mass and honored with God's personal and individual command. He was a member of his people and that alone gave him meaning for his life; but since as a member of his people *he* had received God's command, this meant that he could be no slave to social pressure. He was an individual, with individual decisions to make in response to the divine will; by this means the individual in Israel received far more dignity than he did in any other nation of the time. In fact, the whole biblical teaching about the dignity of man probably originated in its earliest form as a clearly felt implication of God's covenant with Israel. Genesis 1:26, "man in the image of God," is undoubtedly based upon a reflection concerning the nature of man, as the Israelite understood himself and his true role under God in the covenant. Then, too, it can be affirmed that in this picture the true relation of the individual and the community is portrayed. There is no individual apart from a community, and there is no individual without a separateness, a uniqueness which is not submerged in the group. In Israel's covenant both things are clearly affirmed.

Since God as "lord," or "ruler," is the central figure in the Old Testament, the language of the faith was inevitably anthropomorphic, that is, filled with human words to describe the deity. This was because the context in which God was known was a context of relationship. It was a relationship between the individual or the people and the Lord. Hence the categories of personality are openly applied to God. God is conceived of as a great man. The biblical writers speak frankly about his voice, his hand, his back, his feet, etc. Yet this language is not a luxury or a primitivism which later stages of the faith outgrew. It was and is a necessity of the faith. The relationship of God to people and of people to God can be depicted in no other way, when the covenant as the framework of understanding is central in the faith.

If God is conceived of in terms of king or lord, then man would be spoken of as his *servant*. Before there can be worship or any kind of religious life, man must acknowledge God's lordship and his own position as a servant. Consequently, at the center of biblical morality is a necessity for humility before God and submission to his rule. To be religious is frequently expressed by the words "to hearken, to be obedient, to serve." Righteousness is maintaining the covenant, which means fulfillment of our vows to obey God. Sin is the violation of covenant and rebellion against God's personal lordship. It is more than an aberration or a failure which added knowledge can correct. It is a violation of relationship, a betrayal of trust. In the covenant man is bound to God in a close relationship that is centered in the realm of communion and will. In its light we live in a totalitarian universe, one in which God is king and demands our unqualified obedience. There can be no watering or weakening of this conception; otherwise the whole basis of biblical faith would be destroyed. It does mean, however, that totalitarianism is lifted from the earthly to the heavenly spheres; there can be no such thing as a self-sufficient, self-worshiping totalitarian government on earth, because God alone is king and lord of human life. It is small wonder, therefore, that when kings finally came to Israel, they were history's first constitutional monarchs. When they tried to be anything else, they usually had a rebellion on their hands.

Why did not Israel speak of God as father and of the people as children of the father, as the New Testament so frequently does? The father-son language to depict the relationship between God and his people is indeed used occasionally (for example, Hosea 11:1–7), but it is comparatively rare. Israel did not dare make much use of this term because of the crassly physical and literal conceptions of divine fatherhood current among her pagan neighbors at the time. Jeremiah 2:27 denounces pagans who say ". . . to the tree, 'You are my father,' and to the stone, 'You have borne me.'" Furthermore, we may say that the relations within a family do not involve a conception of government and society in as wide a sense as that involved in the original language of the covenant. In modern times our talk of God's fatherhood and of man's brotherhood is frequently so sentimentalized that the relationship between God and man loses any real power and content in the sense in which power and content were both present in biblical faith. The language suggesting a knowledge of God through the category of father needs always to be supported and strengthened by the conception of God's ruling power, his kingship. Otherwise the whole conception of the government of God in the world, of God's kingdom, and of God's purpose in history to establish that kingdom will be lost. In other words, the two terms need to be used together even as did Jesus in the Lord's Prayer ("Our Father . . . thy kingdom . . ."). In biblical faith it would appear that the relationship between God and man has as an irreducible minimum the depiction of God as the lord and the ruler and of his people as the servants who must be loyal and obedient. When this language becomes too cold, legalized, and formalized, it must be corrected by the use of other terms, as happened in the Bible itself. Not only is the expression of God's fatherhood very frequent, but even the marriage relation is used by the prophet Hosea. It was a vivid symbol used to portray the faithlessness of God's people to him. Hosea's wife was a faithless wife; similarly Israel's relation to God is that of a harlot. Sin can thus be described as harlotry, running after other lovers. This language was used occasionally over a period of some 200 years before it was finally dropped. The Song of Songs is a beautiful series of love poems: it was possible to preserve them in the canon by interpreting them allegorically. In the Church the two lovers were considered to be Christ and the people, and in the New Testament itself the Church as the bride of Christ is to be found (for example, II Corinthians 11:2; Revelation 19:7). This language indicates the closeness of the relationship between God or Christ and his people, but it has never been widely used because of the danger of sentimentality.

Not only did the language of the faith center in the covenant relationship, but further the covenant theology furnished Israel with the means of interpreting the meaning and course of her history. Her function was to be the faithful people that she had promised in the covenant to be. If the history of the covenant was a sad one, it was the story of a people's faithless violation of its covenant vows and God's demand that his chosen nation should be what it had promised to be. God is the lord of the nation's life, and he has given the nation its function in the world and its responsibility. If it will not fulfill that function and that responsibility, if it violates its solemn vows and commitments, then it has sinned against God and will experience the judgment of God. The history of the covenant becomes the history of Israel from this time forth; and it is a rather sad story. The difficulties of Israel in her promised land and her involvement in the wars between the nations in a corridor between Asia and Africa where lay the two centers of power presented a tragic picture. For this reason, the history of the covenant for the Christian has always led to Jesus Christ. To Israel, God revealed the manner and the nature of the true life of man and of society on this earth. But how is man to find that life when he so persistently sins, violates his vows, and chooses death rather than life? This fact about man's history together with God's warfare against it—all this constitutes the stuff of the world and the true meaning of the inner struggles of the world according to the Israelite writer. But is man forever to be caught in God's judgment? The New Testament opens precisely at this point. The revelation of God to Israel is true, but God has again intervened, as he did at the exodus, to provide man with salvation. In Jesus Christ the language of the exodus is used to suggest that God has rescued man from the "power" or the "bondage" or the "slavery" of sin, or of the "principalities" and "powers of darkness"; he has reconciled man to himself and given him a new chance. The warfare against evil is by no means over, but the victory is now assured.

What God has done in both Testaments, according to the biblical writers' viewpoint, is a great work of salvation, a deliverance, a redemption. Furthermore, in both Testaments, God's act of salvation is celebrated in a festival or a sacrament. In Israel that festival was called Passover and the descriptions for it are given in the story at the conclusion of the warfare between God and Pharaoh (Exodus 12–13). In the New Testament, the Lord's Supper was first instituted at the Passover time, and it commemorates our deliverance by Christ. Thus Christ is called "our Passover" (I Corinthians 5:7), the Passover lamb, slain in our behalf. Furthermore, the celebration of God's deliverance in Christ is directly connected with the conception of covenant in the Lord's Supper. Note that in Paul's record of the words of the institution of the Lord's Supper there are two parts of the service. The taking of the bread celebrates the new exodus, the work of Christ in our behalf. The drinking of the cup signifies the new covenant in Christ's blood (I Corinthians 11:23–26). This is the covenant of which Jeremiah spoke (Jeremiah 31:33–34), one that is written in the heart and is not centered in an outward written law. The seal of the new covenant in the New Testament is the blood of Christ, the fact of Christ's giving up his life in behalf of his people. The terminology "blood" derives from Exodus 24, where the old covenant was sealed in Moses' time. At Mount Sinai, Moses celebrated the covenant with a great sacrificial offering to God. The blood, which was conceived to be the life of the animals used in the sacrifice, was drained and put into basins. One half of the sacrificial blood was thrown against the altar, symbolizing God's portion. Moses then took "the book of the covenant" and read it before the people. On their part they took a solemn vow saying, in effect, "all the Lord has required of us we will do and we will be obedient." Then Moses took the remaining blood and sprinkled it on the people, saying, "Behold the blood of the covenant which the Lord has made with you in accordance with all these words." In this case the sacrificial blood in a solemn ceremony not only confirms the people in their vows, but it symbolizes the binding nature of the agreement because it portrays the close relationship with God. The same blood was thrown against the altar as was sprinkled upon the people.

We are now in a position to understand the importance of the wilderness period in Israel's life. At the beginning of this section three different ways in which the wanderings in the wilderness are used by later writers were summarized. Yet far more important than these, we have now observed, is the Israelite belief that in the wilderness their forefathers became a people. Later Israel had no way of understanding itself apart from that relationship to God, which depicted the meaning of their innermost life as involving a relationship, a relationship involving both grace and obligation. Grace to be seen in the undeserved acts of goodness on God's part, particularly in his saving work and in his desire to be the lord of his people; obligation in the people's understanding of themselves as servants of their ruler. Their nation was thus a small "kingdom" in which God was the true Lord, and the fortunes of this nation could be described in personal terms as involving matters of loyalty toward the Ruler. The conception of covenant, in other words, provided the whole setting for the language of the faith and for the people's understanding of themselves. Furthermore, the particular type of covenant that lies behind the Israelite understanding of society, namely the suzerainty treaty, was a proper one to depict the true relation between God and people as established in the exodus. It was a relation founded in the first instance not on legal obligation but out of an undeserved act of God in salvation. Legal obligation was always qualified, therefore, by a relationship involving love and affection, whereas sin became all the more a felt reality because it was a form of infidelity. The biblical community, as a result, was always more than an organization of people; it was an organism. And this portrayal of the true meaning of peoplehood under God is continued into the New Testament by a variety of languages, all depicting the same inner relationship, as it was re-established and renewed in a fresh way in Christ. We hear, for example, of "the family of Christ," "the household of faith," the "fellowship," the "body of Christ," the "little flock," "a vine with its branches," etc. Family, household, and fellowship all point to a community of people knit together not primarily by human structures of organization, but by an inner mutuality of spirit that came with the common worship and a common union with the Head of the community. In the case of the biological metaphors, the vine and the body, the inner vitality of the organism is still more vividly expressed; Christ is the life of the body or its head; he is the vine itself while the people are the branches. Branches are able to live only so long as they are related to the vine, while members of the body have meaning only so far as they are organically connected and receive their function from the body. The biblical community, therefore, was conceived of as an assembly in fellowship with God and with one another. It was a gathered people, a congregation before its Lord, one which existed in and by its Head. This is a conception, originally visualized in the early days of Israel under the idea of covenant, which distinguished Israel from all other people and was ultimately to make the Church such an unusual and unique institution in the world.

THE DEUTERONOMIC HISTORY OF ISRAEL IN HER LAND

As we open the Book of Deuteronomy we read the introduction to a remarkable history of Israel in Palestine extending through Joshua, Judges, I–II Samuel, and I–II Kings. This history was written under a unified plan and theological perspective in which the Book of Deuteronomy itself served as the introduction furnishing the theological viewpoint by which the history was written. The editor of this great work collected the various traditions, selected from them, edited and revised them in order to present a comprehensive and unified account of the history of his people from the final days of Moses and the gift of the land to the fall of Jerusalem. In the Book of Joshua the editor composed rather freely from old traditions, whereas in Judges and I–II Samuel he inserts large blocks of material which he has taken from older sources. In I–II Kings the historian has had to do much more free composition, though he is able to draw constantly from older sources now lost to us; indeed, he often refers the reader to them if they wish to have more information about this or that person. In other words, our editor is the author of a historical work which made use of various and sundry traditional materials according to a well-thought-out plan.

The clue to the author's plan is in the Book of Deuteronomy itself. This book is presented to us as a series of addresses by Moses, given to Israel on the other side of the Jordan shortly before his death. In earlier passages dealing with the covenant and with the law, God is represented as speaking directly to Moses or to the people, but in this book God is not speaking directly; Moses is speaking. As Deuteronomy 1:5 puts it, "Moses undertook to explain this law," meaning that this is a Mosaic exposition of the covenant faith. Furthermore, we are not to assume that the book contains a verbatim report of what Moses said. It is an interpretation and exposition of the Mosaic faith. Moses is represented as the teacher of Israel, who expounds the faith. Yet this is a liturgical and literary or teaching device. It was not meant to be taken as implying Mosaic *authorship* of the book itself. The material in the book originally arose, it now seems evident, in an old covenant renewal ceremony, celebrated year by year in the area of ancient Shechem in north-central Palestine. Its type of exposition was a means whereby the faith was taught in certain religious circles in north Israel. The core of the book, consisting probably of most of Chapters 5–28, may well have been rescued from the ruins of northern Israel after its destruction by the Assyrians in 721 B.C. It was stored in the Jerusalem temple, was found and evidently read to King Josiah in 622 B.C., with the resulting reform of the religious life of Judah (II Kings 22–23). For Josiah it was a marvelous restatement of the old covenant theology of early Israel, a theology that had largely been forgotten.

The first address is a historical summary of the exodus events in Chapters 1–3, and a statement of the implications for Israel's faith which can be drawn from these events (Chapter 4). These chapters may well have been appended to the book as an introduction to the whole history of Israel in Palestine. That is, they are more than an introduction to Deuteronomy; they are an introduction to the whole Deuteronomic history.

The older document began in Chapter 4:44 and continues in Chapter 5 with the statement of the covenant that God had made with Israel and the presentation of the Ten Commandments as a summary of God's requirements in the covenant. Chapters 6–11 then continue with a series of sermons on the meaning of the covenant, particularly of the first two commandments, for the life of the people. It may be noted in Chapter 5:22 and verse following that a clear distinction is made between the Decalogue and other laws which Israel knows. At the sacred mountain which is here called Horeb, but in other sources (J, P) may be called Sinai, it is affirmed that Israel heard God's voice. And the result of the hearing of the voice was the Ten Commandments: ". . . and he added no more." In other words, among the various laws which Israel has, only the Decalogue can be interpreted as being the primary will of God which he has directly revealed. All other laws are important perhaps for community life, but the primary will of God as expressed in the Decalogue has authority over them all. These commandments were taken over later by the Christian Church, and the latter has always considered them a valid summary of God's will for human worship and moral life.

Yet if one were to summarize the whole meaning of the covenant in even shorter form, what would he say? Chapter 6:4–5 presents such a summary. God is one, not many. Therefore, the people must not have a divided loyalty; the focus of their religious attention must be single. And they must love God with heart and soul and might. The heart was believed to be the seat of the mind and the will; the "soul" is actually the mysterious vitality that makes one alive and gives him vigor, according to biblical thought. Verse 5 maintains, then, that one must love God with his whole being—with mind and will, with vitality and strength. If one does this, then he will possess no divided loyalty and he will obey God because he loves him. This verse is repeatedly used in the New Testament, together with Leviticus 19:18, as the adequate summary of the will of God and of the teaching of Israel's law and prophets (Matthew 22:34–40).

One emphasis, then, in the theology of Deuteronomy is the intense and all-absorbing loyalty Israel owes to God. No easy tolerance is to be permitted, because Israel lives in the midst of a world filled with idol worship. Yet there is no god like the Lord of Israel; "There is no other besides him" (Chapter 4:35). The whole order of life in Israelite society rests upon the complete, unwavering, and unquestioning loyalty to him who has brought the nation into being.

Furthermore, the loyalty which Israel owes to God in the covenant furnishes the context in which her possession of the Promised Land is understood. Deuteronomy actually presents the conditions upon which Israel is to remain in possession of the land which she has been given. Repeatedly it is affirmed that a law must be kept in order that the land may not be defiled with sin and that there be no evil in the midst of the community. If land and covenant are violated, then it may be expected that, as God's punishment, it will furnish them difficulty and will ultimately be taken away. What God gave he can also take away. This conception is so central a Deuteronomic point of view that it becomes the presupposition of the whole history of Israel in her land. The order of life which Deuteronomy commands was thus presented as truly demanding a decision, one between life and death (Chapter 30:15 ff.). There is about the book, therefore, a somber and terrible earnestness, for the issues involved in this covenant theology are too great to be treated lightly. The land was God's marvelous and undeserved gift, but it was a holy gift which demanded a definite covenant decision and unqualified loyalty to the Giver. The books which follow in the Deuteronomic history present the story of what happened to Israel as evaluated in the light of this covenant theology.

A. GOD'S GIFT OF A LAND (JOSHUA–JUDGES)

The Books of Joshua and Judges present the story of how Israel obtained the land and what happened when the people settled in it. The Promised Land came into Israel's possession only after it was seized by force in hard fighting. Yet even after the conquest was over, the settlement of the land was a most difficult task because of the people who still remained in it as pockets of resistance and because of outside invaders who were always ready to move into areas of weakness. The two books before us give us not only the story but also a religious interpretation of its meaning.

Let us first examine the Book of Joshua with its description of the conquest. This book is divided into two main parts: (1) Chapters 1–12, the siege of Palestine, and (2) Chapters 13–22, the parceling out of the land to the various tribes. The final chapters (23–24) present sermonic material spoken supposedly by Joshua. In Chapter 23 the Deuteronomic historian who is responsible for this whole section of material uses the form of an address to summarize, as was done in the Book of Deuteronomy, the whole meaning of Israel's history. The land is God's conditional gift, contingent upon obedient loyalty to the covenant. In Chapter 24 there is preserved what was originally an older document. This describes a covenant ceremony which took place in central Palestine at the ancient town of Shechem, between the mountains of Ebal and Gerizim. The conquest was over and the tribes were gathered to renew the vows taken by their ancestors at Sinai. It is now commonly believed that on this occasion a number of the groups of people which had not participated in the deliverance from Egypt or in the original Sinai covenant under the leadership of Moses were accepted into the fellowship of the covenant society. In this manner the exodus and the Sinai traditions became the normative elements of the faith of all Israel. They played a very important role in uniting under one faith a people which by this time had a rather conglomerate background. In the Shechem ceremony Joshua recounts the history of the marvelous dealings with Israel up to that time, and in the solemn renewal of vows which followed he made very clear what the implications of the history were for the people's present and future life in their land.

It will be noted again how the historical confession which Joshua gives at the beginning of the covenant ceremony is centered around the three major events of Israel's national life: (1) God's election and guidance of the fathers of the nation and his promises to them; (2) his deliverance of the nation from slavery; and (3) his gift of "a land for which ye did not labor" (verse 13). Here as in other confessions in both the Old and New Testaments the references to the conquest of Canaan indicate that to biblical people it was considered to be one of the great acts of God's goodness. The two questions which we should now ask are these: first, what is the historical background of the events herein described? and second, how are they interpreted theologically, that is, how can a terrible war of conquest be considered a gracious deed of God?

Regarding the historical question, we may say that the Book of Joshua implies that in a series of campaigns by Joshua the whole land was completely subjugated and possessed by Israel. In Judges, Chapter 1, however, we discover that Israel is still fighting and that the fighting seems to be done by the various individual tribes who were attempting to possess their land. In attempting to harmonize these two seemingly conflicting bodies of material, we should say first that the complete subjugation of the country took a long time, probably over 300 years, since it was not completed until the reign of David in the early tenth century B.C. Nevertheless the work of archaeologists has indicated that a number of cities suffered severe destruction between 1250 and 1200 B.C., whereas between 1200 and about 1025 B.C. the ruins indicate one of the most disturbed periods in Palestinian history, when new towns were being founded all over the hill country and both they and the older cities were destroyed as many as four times within less than two centuries. We may reasonably infer, therefore, that there was a violent campaign of conquest on Joshua's part which took place during the second half of the thirteenth century and reduced the power of the Canaanite city-states so that there could no longer be organized opposition. Yet when the individual tribes and clans of Israel attempted to settle in the land there were still pockets of resistance, since there were still certain major cities left unconquered. Furthermore, outsiders continually attempted to press in and take what they could from an unorganized people. Thus while through the Books of Joshua and Judges we look back at the ancient events through the mists of tradition, we can nevertheless see that the tradition rests on solid historical fact.

The first time that the name "Israel" is mentioned in sources outside the Bible is in the annals of Pharaoh Merneptah, about 1220 B.C. He tells of the defeat of a number of cities in Asia, particularly in Palestine, and lists also the people of Israel among those defeated. The claim was undoubtedly exaggerated, but it does indicate that by his time Israel was a known people already established in their homeland. Furthermore, a large amount of information from archaeological work in Palestine points to the same conclusion. The peoples of Edom and Moab on the other side of the Jordan, around whom Israel had to go because permission to travel through their territories was denied, were not established in their cities until the thirteenth century B.C. This we know from the exploration of hundreds of ancient sites. Palestine proper was organized into a number of city-states, each of which was independent under its own king, though all gave nominal allegiance to the Egyptian kings. The particular number and situation of these city-states in the Book of Joshua points to the thirteenth century and not to an earlier period. Certain of the cities excavated in Palestine, for example, Bethel, twelve miles north of Jerusalem, Lachish and Debir in the lowlands of Judah, and the great city of Hazor, the capital of Galilee—these were all Canaanite city-states which Joshua destroyed; and their ruins as excavated present a vivid witness to the violence of the destruction. And the date in each case is in the middle or second half of the thirteenth century.

The biblical story begins with the conquest of Jericho and Ai (Chapters 6–8). Jericho is in the Jordan Valley, a site guarding the major pass leading up into the hill country just north of Jerusalem, whereas Ai is in the hills some twelve miles north of Jerusalem. In this way Israel secured a foothold in the central hill country without attempting to take Jerusalem, because that city was entirely too strong. Indeed, it was not taken until the time of David, who made it his capital. This initial phase of the conquest, however, causes historians some difficulty. The reason is that both Jericho and Ai were great mounds of ruins in the time of Joshua. Jericho probably had upon it a fort, that is, a small settlement with a small fortification. Ai, on the other hand, was a ruin (indeed, the name means "ruin") of a great city which existed there during the third millennium B.C. but was destroyed somewhere around 2400 B.C. We know from excavation, however, that the neighboring city of Bethel, which had replaced Ai as the major city of its area, was violently destroyed in Joshua's time, though it was immediately reoccupied by the Israelites. Consequently, we may assume that the great story of the conquest of Bethel was transferred later, as people told it from one generation to another, to the neighboring ruin. In the case of Jericho we do not have sufficient evidence to give explanation for the whole narrative regarding its capture. It was the oldest large village in Palestine, as far as we now know, first established and heavily fortified about 7000 B.C. Between 7000 and 5000 B.C., and again during the third millennium, it was a leading city of the country. Similarly, during the seventeenth and sixteenth centuries it was heavily occupied and fortified. It was then violently destroyed and only a small settlement existed on the site in the fourteenth century until sometime before or after 1300 B.C., precisely when is not clear.

The second phase of the conquest begins in Chapter 9, when a group of four cities (the Hivite cities), headed by Gibeon, secured a covenant with Joshua and were included in Israel without destruction. A coalition of five kings, headed by the King of Jerusalem, then attacked Gibeon because of that covenant. Joshua came to the rescue, defeated the coalition, and proceeded against one city after another along the Judean lowlands, after which Hebron in the center of Judah was easily taken. This campaign makes excellent geographical sense, and took place probably not far from the period around 1225–1220 B.C. The third phase of the conquest had to do with the successful Galilean campaign in the North (Chapter 11). None of the great cities was destroyed, however, except Hazor, a vast city of some 40,000 inhabitants we now know from recent excavations, indeed one of the greatest cities of western Asia, the capture of which by Joshua during the second half of the thirteenth century is to be inferred from the ruins of the city as recently excavated.

If one examines a map of Palestine, it will be noted that Joshua's campaign, as described above, says nothing about his having to conquer north-central Palestine, the area of which Shechem was the capital and in which Shiloh, where the tabernacle was erected, was situated. Yet in Joshua 24 all the tribes are gathered together in that territory for the covenant ceremony. Scholars infer from this that the Shechem area may already have been in the hands of a group of Hebrews with whom Joshua simply had to make an alliance since they were closely related. If this is the case, we can understand why it was that Joshua had to do no fighting in the area, and also why the great ceremony by which a united Israel came into being was instituted in this place. Indeed, the evidence that we have suggests that this ceremony was remembered and repeated at Shechem in yearly ceremonies thereafter, and it was from these ceremonies that much of the material in the present Book of Deuteronomy was derived in later times.

Israel interpreted the success of the conquest as a sign that the power of God was directing the events in Israel's behalf. A new land was not Israel's by natural right of possession. It was God's land, and he gave it to Israel as a gift that the people might have a place to live in security from slavery.

This point of view had extremely important consequences for the life of Israel. Since the land was God's, it was parceled out to the clans by lot. People at this time and later (see Acts 1:26) believed that the casting of lots was not a matter of mere chance: rather it was God who decided how the lot fell. Consequently, parceling out of the land by lot was actually believed to be God's decision as to which groups of people should live in what places on his land. The chief form of property and the means of production was the land. This being the case, God's concern was believed to be that every person should have equal access to the land. Consequently, God says in the law: "The land shall not be sold in perpetuity, for the land is mine" (Leviticus 25:23). That is, speculation in land and the taking advantage of the less able members of the community for the purpose of piling up large estates was believed to be sin. If a piece of land was to be sold for one reason or another, the clan was to have the right of redeeming it in order to keep it within the group. Every fiftieth year was (later at least) established as the jubilee year in which all land was to revert to the original families or clans (Leviticus 25:8–17). It is doubtful whether this legal provision was ever observed. Nevertheless, there was in Israel a deep and radical interest in the poor and the weak, and the whole effort in the economic life was to provide for their welfare. The weakness and the poverty of some, it was felt, should never be the occasion for profit on the part of the strong. No interest was to be charged on a loan because the poor man who needed help was to be aided in a neighborly way; his need was not to be made into an occasion for profit. The means of production were owned by God, and the people should use them as stewards in the service of one another. Later on in the prophets we shall hear it claimed that inasmuch as the people have not been good stewards in the use of the land, God is about to take it away from them.

The most severe problem with which the Book of Joshua faces us is the problem of God and war. The conquest of Canaan was believed by Israel to be conducted by God himself, and consequently the success of the war was credited solely to his power. God's purposive and powerful activity in history is here affirmed in a vivid way. Israel at the time of the conquest and throughout the period of the judges believed in such a thing as holy war. That was a special institution with special customs and laws governing the practice of it. In holy war God was believed to be the leader who would give the people the victory, provided that they followed him without any hesitation or lack of faith and with complete obedience to his will and law. The human leader was one whom God chose for the task, but the number of warriors was unimportant since God was the leader (see, for example, the story of Gideon in Judges 7). In holy war the booty of the enemy was the property of God; as regards the cities taken in the land of Canaan, no spoil was to be allowed; Israel was to gain nothing from the war except a place in which to live. The booty of the enemy was under the ban and was to be completely destroyed as a holocaust to God in order that the land might be purified and readied for new occupation. No human being was to enrich himself by keeping any enemy property in his own possession; the story of Achan in Joshua 7 is an illustration. The war was for God's ends and not for the benefit of any individual. Yet in the case of the conquest this ban against the taking of booty and the offering of all to God was extended to the pagan peoples in possession of the land. There were to be no captives whatsoever.

One of the age-old questions which people have had concerning the Book of Joshua is this: How is it possible to believe in the goodness of God and at the same time to affirm his role of commander in chief in the horrible blood bath of the conquest of Canaan? The Book of Deuteronomy contains a considerable amount of material that has been preserved from the old institution of holy war. The one passage in the Old Testament which attempts to deal with the question of God and war in this connection is Deuteronomy 9:1–6. There Israel is told that the conquest has been carried out by God, not because Israel is more righteous than anyone else. In fact, just the opposite is the case; Israel has been a stiff-necked and rebellious people since the time God first chose them. In the biblical point of view wars exist because of human sin, and God uses human agents to accomplish his purposes in history. When he does so, he does not add up the degrees of righteousness which his agent possesses. The agent is sinful, but nevertheless God uses it for his purpose. In Deuteronomy 6 it is affirmed that God is doing what he does in the conquest for two reasons: (1) because of the wickedness of the Canaanites and (2) because of his promises to the fathers of Israel. Now we know not only from the Bible but from many outside sources as well that the Canaanite civilization and religion was one of the weakest, most decadent, and most immoral cultures of the civilized world at that time. It is claimed, then, that Israel is God's agent of destruction against a sinful civilization, for in the moral order of God civilizations of such flagrant wickedness must be destroyed. On the other hand, God has a purpose in the choosing of Israel and in giving her a land, a purpose stated in the promises to the fathers of Israel in Genesis. All this does not mean that Israel as God's agent is free of her responsibility. Later on the prophets saw God using foreign agents as the instruments of his punishment for sinful

Israel; yet in time the agents also suffered judgment for their sin (see Isaiah 10:5 ff.). In other words, God has a purpose of universal redemption in the midst of and for a sinful world. He makes even the wars and fightings of men serve his end. In the case of Israel, his purpose as expressed in the patriarchal promises coincided at the moment of the conquest with the terrible iniquity of Canaan. It was a great thing for Israel that she got her land; it was also a sobering thing because with it went the great responsibility and the danger of judgment. It was likewise a great thing for the Canaanites in the long run. Between 1300 and 1100 B.C. Israel took away from them the hill country of Palestine, while the incoming Aramaeans took away the whole of eastern Syria. The remnant of the people was confined to the Syrian coast around Tyre and Sidon and further north. After 1100 B.C., they began to develop one of the most remarkable trading empires in the world (the Greeks called them Phoenicians). Their colonies were spread all over the Mediterranean world, much to the benefit of that world; and this was done, not by conquest, but solely by the peaceful means of trading.

But did God actually tell Joshua to carry on such terrible slaughter, involving even the defenseless elements of the population? It is rather difficult for a Christian to understand how God could be responsible for such a slaughter. From the biblical perspective we may perhaps frame an answer somewhat as follows: In the context of human sin wars and conflicts occur. But God has not withdrawn from the world to heaven. He is not defeated by human sin; even this he uses for his own ends. Unless he did we would have nothing in this earth for which to hope. Yet to say that God is in control, even of our wars and cruelty, does not mean that he is responsible for the way in which men carry them on. It is not God's fault that the Americans dropped an atomic bomb on Hiroshima. Yet no Christian can assume that God had no interest whatsoever in how the last war was to turn out. Two things must be held together in tension here: one is God's control and direction of history to his own ends, and the other is the terrible sin of man for which he is responsible. If we view the conquest in this light, then the Christian may say that God was "fighting for Israel," though his own purposes were larger than Israel understood at that moment. The sovereign goodness of God and the freedom of man must both be affirmed in a biblical understanding of theism. God is thus not responsible for man's atrocities.

The editor of the Book of Judges characterizes the twelfth and eleventh centuries as a time when there was no king in Israel and every man did that which was right in his own eyes (Chapter 21:25). Israel in possession of the land is now faced with the problem of settling down to a new mode of life. The great crises of the past are over; the people look forward to security. Yet the period of the judges is one of struggle, oppression by various enemy invaders, low moral and religious standards. Various groups of pagan peoples have been left in the land as a snare to Israel (Judges 2:3). In the attempt to possess the land and to hold it securely, battle after battle had to be fought in almost every part of the country. In such a situation spontaneous leadership rises out of the midst of the people to deal with the crises. This is the type of material with which the editor of Judges deals. His theological interpretation of the events of the age is clearly set forth in Chapter 2. In order to present his case clearly he has made the various wars and oppressions appear to have followed one another, whereas in point of fact many of them seem to have occurred simultaneously in the various parts of the country. Nevertheless, the editor makes his point forcefully, and the old hero tales of the pre-monarchial time are made to serve his purpose very well indeed.

To the editor the events of the time are a perfect illustration of a cycle which is repeated over and over: idolatry and punishment by an oppressor followed by repentance and salvation by a leader whom God raised up. To the editor the security of Israel lay solely in the covenant and in entire loyalty to her lord. Yet the pagan attractions were subtle and alluring. This was particularly true of the pagan gods who were so easily worshiped. The Canaanite gods especially promised so much, made so few demands, and were so conveniently followed, while allowing the people to indulge themselves largely as they pleased. That appears to be the way with the idols which man creates; they are projections of his own desires. Yet the more Israel turned to idols, the weaker became the covenant bond which held the people together. The Lord of the covenant made the people one; when they turned from him and from his covenant they were no longer a people but a group of tribes, each going its own way. Such a situation created an interior weakness in Israel, which made her easy prey to any invader or marauder. When she repented of her error, she was again drawn together by a leader whom God had chosen for the occasion. Idolatry was divisive and destructive, and the interior weakness which invited oppression became the subject of the historian's theology. The Book of Judges, then, presents the real problem of Israel: the problem of living within a covenant apart from which there is no security. It is also preparatory to the next event: the establishment of a king as an attempted answer to this problem.

B. THE PROBLEM OF GOVERNMENT: THE MONARCHY (I–II SAMUEL)

In Acts 13:16 and verses following the early Church has presented us with an account of the first recorded sermon of the apostle Paul, one which was given in a synagogue at Antioch in Pisidia (a region of Asia Minor). He begins as did the Israelites of old by making a public confession of the great acts of God in the history of his people. After making mention of the three chief events in the formation of the nation of Israel (the choice of the fathers, the deliverance from bondage, and the gift of the land), he speaks of the people desiring a king. Thereupon God gave them Saul as king for a time, he continues, but later removed him and raised up David, a man after God's own heart. From this point the apostle jumps immediately to Jesus (verse 23), saying that from the seed of David "God according to his promise raised unto Israel a Savior, Jesus." Both here and in the other sermons in Acts it is evident that the early Church understood the most important part of the history of the former times to be that from Abraham to David. Immediately thereafter the meaning of Jesus' life, death, and resurrection are described. The history between David and Jesus is considered notable only as a history of the people's sin in the midst of which God sent his words of judgment and of promise by his prophets. Jesus Christ is the direct continuation of the great acts of God from Abraham through David and the fulfillment of the promises made through the prophets. To understand how this point of view was achieved and what it meant, it is necessary to review something of the meaning of David and of the office of kingship which he held in Israel.

During the period of the judges the political organization of Israel differed radically from that of all other peoples around her. The latter were organized under a monarchy, the king having more or less absolute powers in ruling the people. Israel's king was God himself. In the covenant God ruled the people directly. During the period of the judges the tribes were bound together by a sacred compact around their central sanctuary at Shiloh where the ark of the covenant was kept. This sacred object symbolized the presence of God in the people's midst and the covenant compact in which they acknowledged him as their ruler. In time of trouble God would raise up a temporary leader (called a "judge") to deal with the situation. When peace was restored, the leader's job was finished. The covenant faith was that God would lead and protect his people provided that they obeyed him and kept their vows to do his will.

As we look back upon the situation, the faith of this people at that time is simply amazing. They had been taught, and the best among them wholeheartedly believed, that this type of political organization would succeed if only the people were faithful. God was their lord; he had said that he would lead and defend them, and they had no doubt whatsoever that he meant what he said. So they took him at his word. But there was the problem of sin, of faithlessness, and of covenant breaking. The result was insecurity, hardship, and anarchy, interpreted as the judgment of God upon their faithlessness. Meanwhile by the time of Samuel in the eleventh century B.C. one of their enemies, the Philistines, had become so strong as to threaten to make all of Palestine into a Philistine state. After the battle of Ebenezer in which Israel was soundly defeated and the ark captured (I Samuel 4), Philistine garrisons were stationed throughout the central hill country of Israel and a tight control was established over Israel's whole life. No Israelite was allowed to practice the trade of smith, for example, for fear the Hebrews might be able to make themselves swords and spear points for military rearmament. Instead each Israelite farmer had to take even his agricultural tools down to Philistine country along the southern coastal plain in order to get them sharpened and repaired—and he was charged exorbitant prices for the work! (I Samuel 13:19–21).

This was the situation in which the Hebrews found themselves by the second half of the eleventh century B.C. The elders of the people decided that the only solution to the problem was to reorganize their political life under a monarchy. Two accounts of the founding of the monarchy seem to have been preserved and placed together in Chapters 8 and 9 respectively. The latter is a simple story about Saul looking for some lost asses. Hearing about Samuel, he thinks that man of God may have some superhuman means of telling where the animals are. Meanwhile God has spoken to the prophet-priest, Samuel, about him and has indicated his plan to save Israel from her enemies by selecting a king.

The first account in Chapter 8 is not primarily a story, but a prophetic evaluation of the situation and of the meaning of Israel's desire to have a king. When Samuel warns the people concerning the nature of their future king in verses 11–17, he actually describes the nature of Solomon's reign. It is probable, therefore, that the writer of this chapter lived sometime after the reign of Solomon. That does not mean, however, that Samuel did not feel or say any of the things here expressed. It is not at all improbable, but indeed highly likely, that Samuel, together with a number of the more pious religious people of the country, felt that the institution of the monarchy was a dangerous innovation made in the stress of an emergency and in imitation of pagan customs. According to this view God grants the people's request for a king, but it is his concession to their weakness and his desire to give them still another chance to serve him faithfully. This chapter, then, though written later than the time of Samuel, is very probably an interpretation of the whole institution of the monarchy which was strongly held by a number of people in the nation both in the time of Samuel and later. In this view the Philistine menace brought a crisis in sovereignty. It was not Samuel whom the people were rejecting. In a deeper sense it was God himself. Samuel would continue as the spiritual leader of the nation, but the executive political functions would be taken over by a king. Yet how could a human being be king when God was king? That was the real religious issue. The people were faced with a desperate situation, and they simply felt that the old covenant organization was insufficient to cope with it. They saw as their only hope a new type of organization like that of the other peoples of the day. Samuel, on the other hand, saw the real issue as sin and faithlessness. In that condition no human king could permanently solve their problem. Nevertheless, God accommodated himself to the wishes of the people. His word to Samuel was to give them a king, though he warned them of the radical changes that would be made in their lives.

How was the new office to be filled and what was its function? God himself was believed to have elected the king, and the latter was inducted into his office by the sacred rite of anointing with oil. This rite was one used in worship by the priests. The oil was specially prepared according to a certain formula which was not to be imitated or used for any other purpose (Exodus 30:22–32). It was a specially consecrated holy oil. When poured upon the priests and the various objects used in worship, it rendered them "cleansed" and ready for the service of God (Exodus 40:9–15; Leviticus 8:10–13, 30). In our Protestant churches we no longer have anything like it. A similar conception still survives, however, in the holy water of Catholic and high Episcopal churches. This water has been consecrated; it is no longer like ordinary water; it has a special sacred function of cleansing.

This rite of anointing was used for the king. When the king was anointed, it meant that he was set apart from other people. His person was sacred. He had a special relationship with God. For this reason when Saul was attempting to capture David, David refused to harm a hair of his head when he had the opportunity to do so (see I Samuel 24:6, 10; 26:9–23). Consequently, while the ruler was simply called "the king" or "the King of Israel" in ordinary secular speech, he had another title in theological usage. That was "the anointed of the Lord." The Hebrew word for "anointed" is *messiah;* thus the King of Israel was God's Messiah (meaning simply his "anointed").

Hence the king was selected by God and especially consecrated for his office. The functions of his office were also fixed by God. They were to provide and to administer justice within the realm and to gain security from outward enemies. The king was to be God's executive officer on earth; indeed he could be called God's "son" (II Samuel 7:14; Psalm 2:7). Yet he could never have the absolute power over the people which other kings of the day had. God had given the law to the people as a whole. He had not given it to the king, and the latter could not take credit for it, as kings did in other countries. His job was only to administer the law. The government was thus a constitutional monarchy, and the basic freedoms of the people were protected by God against the encroachments of royal power (see Deuteronomy 17:14–20; note the incidents of David and Bathsheba in II Samuel 11–12, and of Ahab and Naboth in I Kings 21). The prophets, therefore, possessed a freedom of speech to denounce the king in the name of God, a freedom such as has existed in few places in history before modern times (note Nathan against David, Elijah against Ahab, Isaiah against Ahaz, Jeremiah against Jehoiakim and Zedekiah).

How did the institution of kingship work out? Did it provide the security and the justice which had been hoped for by the people? For a hundred years the answer must be generally affirmative. Saul had some fine political successes, but he seems to have possessed a certain instability of character. This instability was in strong contrast to the completely uncompromising and unbending character of Samuel. Consequently, the two soon broke off relations, and Saul was left an isolated figure without religious backing. His instability took the form of virtual insanity in his attitude toward David. He spent a large amount of his time trying to capture David until his hold upon political power was greatly weakened and he had lost the support of many of his people. He and his son Jonathan met their death in an unsuccessful battle with the Philistines, who were still hoping to gain control of the whole country.

David was a completely different figure. Attractive, engaging, brilliant, exceedingly clever, an adroit politician, he was an astute judge of men and kept himself surrounded with exceedingly able administrators even when he did not like them personally. A case in point is Joab, the general of the standing army. Time after time he rescued the kingdom from disaster and undid the errors of David. He was completely loyal to David, yet a blunt, direct man who either did not understand or did not always sympathize with David's adroit and often complex, occasionally underhanded, political maneuvering. David therefore seems to have come to dislike him, but for some reason he never got rid of him. This dislike occasioned one of the final and completely ungracious acts of David, when on his deathbed he told Solomon to put Joab to death (I Kings 2:5–6). Undoubtedly the reason lay in David's conservative religious nature. When he was attempting early in his career to unite the people under him, he indulged in some secret negotiations with Abner, the strong man in the northern section of the country. Joab considered Abner a dangerous blackguard and found opportunity to kill him. Yet David had evidently given Abner a sworn oath of safety, and from that time on David feared that a curse would fall upon his dynasty because of this betrayal of a solemn vow. He attempted to lay the blame on Joab (II Samuel 3:6 ff.), and finally tried to solve the case by having Joab killed. That course, he felt, would relieve his successors of the burden of the unexpiated shedding of innocent blood.

It is difficult to forgive David for many things that he did, not the least being the way in which he put Uriah to death in order to get Uriah's wife, Bathsheba (II Samuel 11–12). Yet David's life was open and well known to all his court. In spite of his failings in morality he was loved and followed as was no other man in Israel's history. A court biographer wrote the annals of his reign, a large part of which are preserved in II Samuel and I Kings 1–2. We know David better than any other person in the Old Testament because this biographer gives us so much detail. He was a devoted follower, and yet he presents a fairly objective picture of his hero so that we can see his strength and weaknesses. This above all else must be said about David: he sincerely wanted to rule responsibly as the anointed of the Lord; and when he committed a fault, he was in general ready to acknowledge it. Read the story in II Samuel 12. What other king in history would have had the grace and humility before God to take as he did the prophet's direct accusation: "Thou art the man!" Read also his lament over Saul and Jonathan in II Samuel 1:17 and verses following—a beautiful and moving poem which shows a depth of character in David which was part of the reason he was so beloved.

Thus David was "a man after God's own heart," not because he was sinless—he most certainly was not!—but because he was a pliable and at heart a sincere person. When in sin, he could repent deeply before God, accept his punishment without murmur, and secure God's forgiveness. He did not possess what the Israelites considered to be the root of all sin, a hard, proud, and rebellious heart. He sincerely wanted and tried to rule justly as God's servant and vicegerent on earth.

His success, for which he gave all praise to God, was phenomenal both in his military victories and in his organization of the realm. Vast changes in Israelite life took place during his reign, and at his death the nation was greatly altered from what it had been in the days of the judges. In the royal court of his time and later, the theology of the office of kingship was extended and deepened. A number of the psalms which mention the king are believed by scholars to have been composed as hymns for use in religious services in Jerusalem (such as the royal coronation, marriage, etc.), services in which the king was the central figure. Among others Psalms 2, 18, 45, 72, 89, 101, 110 are examples. The psalms, like our hymns of the Christian life, portray the ideal role which the king was to play in God's plan. He was to rule until all God's enemies were destroyed; he could be said to be seated at God's right hand, and in the day of God's kingdom over the whole earth he would be God's ruler to provide for safety, wisdom, and justice in the kingdom (see Psalms 2 and 110).

Unfortunately, few of the kings measured up to the standard set for the office. Solomon was very different from David. He was a lover of culture, wealth, and magnificence. He tried hard to put the small nation on the cultural map of the world. To do so meant a more radical limitation of individual freedom, the imposition of the draft for labor battalions, and heavy taxation. At his death the larger and more prosperous northern section of the country had had its fill, and split off from the jurisdiction of the Jerusalem king. Many sincere religious people, especially among the prophets, backed this move, because they felt that the Jerusalem king had become too strong and was threatening to violate completely the old covenant heritage.

In the Books of Kings the editor presents an interpretation of the whole history of the divided kingdoms as a story of God's controversy with the institution of kingship and with the people who followed it blindly. Every king of North Israel is said to have done evil in God's sight and to have flouted God's law. Most of the kings of Judah are deemed equally culpable. It was these evil kings who more than any other "made Israel to sin." Consequently, in seeking their own power after the manner of this world and not at all in keeping with the purpose of Israel's election, they were actually the enemies of God. Just as it had been revealed to Samuel at the beginning of the monarchy, kingship was actually to become an attempt to displace God as King.

What now of the promises of God? What of the people's

justice and security? Had God's plan and purpose for his anointed (Messiah) been completely frustrated? Certain of the prophets in Judah who were acquainted with the theology of kingship which had been kept alive by some circles in Jerusalem were sure that this was not the case. When God's new and final day dawned, the darkness of the world would be changed to light, and God would send his true anointed (Messiah) to sit upon the throne of David. Upon him the spirit of God would rest and he would be girded with God's power so that he could judge the earth in righteousness and rule all men in the fear of the Lord (Isaiah 9; 11; Jeremiah 23:6; 33:15–16; Ezekiel 37:21–28). Under him the chosen people would finally find safety and his dominion would be to the ends of the earth (Micah 5:4; Zechariah 9:10).

Yet in Old Testament times this king did not appear; God's intervention and the establishment of his universal rule did not come as soon as it was expected. Some, at the rebuilding of the temple in 520 B.C., thought that the ruler Zerubbabel was the Messiah, the shoot or branch from the root of David (Haggai 2:23; Zechariah 4), but it was not to be. In the New Testament it is Jesus who is seen to be the true anointed (the Greek word "Christ" means this and is a translation of the term "Messiah"). The Old Testament office of God's king is the dominant one used to explain the office of Christ in the plan of God. In his lifetime he was called the Christ, and after his death he was raised to "sit on the right hand of God" and to rule the world for God (Mark 16:19; Acts 2:33–36). Jesus Christ is the lord to whom all power has been given in heaven and earth; he is the hope of Israel, the mediator of the new covenant, of the new kingdom, of the new age.

Yet obviously Christ is not the king which Israel expected. He is not an earthly ruler with political power. His is a spiritual kingship from heaven. For this reason the Jews could not accept Jesus as the Christ. What had happened? Jesus had seen more deeply into the intent of God, and he reinterpreted the Old Testament faith in the coming Messiah by material in the Old Testament itself: namely, Isaiah 53. God's true king was the suffering redeemer who bore the griefs of all men. It is thus that Jesus was interpreted as David's true successor. He fulfilled the hope of Israel in its king and he became God's anointed with dominion over the whole earth.

C. GOD'S CONTROVERSY WITH THE KINGS (I–II KINGS)

Now that the system of government in Israel has been revolutionized with the introduction of the monarchy under the great personality of David, our historian proceeds to describe the procession of Israel's kings. His purpose is to interpret Israel's life under the monarchy, and his judgment is that the institution was a virtual failure. With king after king the historian affirms that he "did evil in the sight of the Lord" and led the people to do evil with the result that the purpose for which this people was given the land was annulled. Nearly 400 years of the nation's life are here summarized in brief, and the purpose is to show why the land was taken away from the people and why they were scattered among the nations. Because kings and people were unfaithful to their true ruler, God used the events of international history as a means of carrying on a controversy with the kings and people until finally they were swallowed by the empires. What is involved, then, is an attempt to understand the life of the chosen people in the midst of the international imperialisms. Why did God give the land and then take it away? We might say that inasmuch as Palestine is the bridge between Asia and Africa, between the two centers of political power, inevitably the country is going to be swallowed up by the dominant force of the moment. Yet to the Israelite historian this is by no means a sufficient explanation. God has made his promises and God does not lie. In Israel's involvement among the nations there must be observed a righteous and consistent plan of God. For our historian it was sufficient to point to the justice of God and affirm his righteousness even in the downfall of the monarchy. The great prophets whom we encounter in this age, beginning with Amos, Hosea, and Isaiah in the eighth century, continue to affirm the justice of God but go on to say that the end of the state is not the end of the people of God. Beyond the current tragedy lies the brilliant future, the end of all God's work, and the fulfillment of his promises. History's tragedies are not meaningless, even though while the darkness is at hand the future is difficult to envisage. Yet Israel must walk through the valley of deep shadow in order to enter the door of hope.

The historian's account of God's controversy with the kings, therefore, is a most remarkable document. God has chosen himself a people as his special servant in the world. Yet he allows his people to be destroyed and scattered among the nations. This history attempts to answer the question "why?" That the author succeeded in his endeavor is proved by the fact that a people of God survived the destruction and built anew, whereas similar destructions in the ancient world customarily meant both the end of a given people and the end of their gods also.

The central figures and events emphasized in the Books of Kings can be summarized as follows:

a. Solomon (I Kings 1–11)
    date: 961–922 B.C.
b. Ahab and Jezebel (I Kings 17–II Kings 11)
    date: about 876–840 B.C.
c. The fall of Northern Israel and its sequel in Judah (II Kings 15–20)
    date: about 746–700 B.C.
d. The last days of Judah and Jerusalem (II Kings 21–25)
    date: about 687–587 B.C.

In describing these various events the historian draws upon various sources, several of which he mentions, and some of which he does not mention. Through most of the period of the kings, after the division of the monarchy into two parts, North Israel and Judah, he interweaves the kings of the North and the kings of the South. At the beginning of each he makes a summary statement giving his evaluation of the particular king's reign. At the end of the story of each he gives further summary data about a king's death and burial, and then adds the words: "Now the rest of the acts of X, and all that he did, are they not written in the book of the chronicles of the kings of Judah?"—or—"in the book of the chronicles of the kings of Israel?" These two books are lost sources which evidently described in some detail the reigns of each king. The author here selects just that information which serves his evaluative purpose and then adds, in effect, "if you want to know more about the details, look up the original sources." Unfortunately, these sources are lost to us and we can only infer what was in them. Let us now examine the history in more detail.

1. *Solomon*

Solomon, David's son, reigned from about 961 to 922 B.C. He was not a military figure as David had been. The great aim of his reign was to consolidate David's conquests and make of Israel one of the great and respected nations of the ancient world, if not in size then at least in culture. The sources which our historian uses preserve as the dominant note in the reign of Solomon his desire to be considered glorious, "so that none like you has been before you and none like you shall arise after you" (I Kings 3:12). His ivory throne is said to have been so extraordinary that "the like of it was never made in any kingdom" (I Kings 10:20). The story of the Queen of Sheba in I Kings 10 gives special emphasis to the glory of Solomon's court. Without doubt this queen had arrived in Jerusalem to look after her trading interests, because trade with South Arabia was extremely lucrative for all concerned. Yet the story as we now have it serves to underscore the glory and honor accorded to Solomon. We are told that when the queen had heard all that Solomon had to say and had seen the splendor of his court and the luxury in which they lived, "There was no more spirit in her"—the Hebrew way of saying that her breath was taken away! She continues, "Your wisdom and prosperity surpass the report which I have heard."

Solomon's great effort was to place the nation of Israel on

the cultural map of the world. He was a great builder of marvelous buildings. He extended the old city of David northward in order to provide for an elaborate headquarters of government and for a temple to the Lord. He built an elaborate palace which took him thirteen years to complete, and to it he appended a smaller house for his queen, the daughter of Pharaoh of Egypt. Other governmental buildings were of unusual construction according to the latest fashions. Up to this time Israel had never specialized in the arts of material civilization. Consequently, Solomon had to go outside his kingdom for assistance. He hired specialists from Hiram, King of Tyre, and also made a commercial treaty with him so that he could obtain the required raw materials for his building project.

The most famous of his buildings was, of course, his temple. This structure was not as large as the palace and other governmental headquarters, but it undoubtedly represented some of the finest workmanship. It was built of carefully hewn stone and lined with cedarwood on the interior. The wood was carved and painted with elaborate Phoenician designs. In its innermost room, the holy of holies, there was no statue of the deity as in pagan temples. There were instead two olivewood cherubim, which were lions with human heads and with wings stretched out as though they were about to take flight. They were borrowed from a Phoenician art motif, and represented the sides and legs of the invisible throne of God. God was believed to be enthroned above the cherubim, and their outstretched wings evidently suggested to Israel God's omnipresence; that is, God was the living, active sovereign, and these mysterious beings were those which carried him rapidly from place to place.

Beautiful as the temple was, however, it raised theological questions in Israel. David had not been able to build a temple in Jerusalem because it was too radical a departure from old customs (II Samuel 7). The sanctuary of God had been a very simple tent (tabernacle). Yet simplicity was scarcely the characteristic of the new temple; it was built for Israel by pagans, and its symbolism was precisely that used in the temples of the gods. From this time forth there arose those in Israel who raised questions about the necessity of the temple. In I Kings 8 there is a long prayer which Solomon is represented as giving at the temple's dedication. In its present form this prayer evidently preserves the teaching of the school of thought to which our Deuteronomic historian belongs. Thus in verse 27 the question is raised: "But will God indeed dwell on earth? Behold, heaven and the highest heaven cannot contain thee; how much less this house which I have built!" In other words, how can the lord of heaven and earth live like human beings live in an earthly building? How can that structure which is called the "house of God" actually be God's dwelling place, when his dwelling place is not on earth but in heaven! The priests were to solve this problem by a sacramental symbolism and the use of a technical language in which it is said that God never really dwelt on earth. Yet it is a mark of his extraordinary grace that he has chosen to "tent" or "tabernacle" in the midst of his people. How God does this in relation to the temple is not stated; it is for the priest a mystery of God's grace. For the Deuteronomic school in I Kings 8, however, such a solution to the meaning of the temple in relation to God is unsatisfactory. A careful reading of that prayer of dedication will suggest the theology which they desire to have one accept: that is, that God in no sense dwells in the temple; this structure is simply the place where his name resides; it is a house of prayer. It is God's accommodation to human need, so that when prayer is directed toward this central symbol of God's presence among his people, then God who is in heaven will hear. In this way, our historian affirms the importance of the temple without in any way suggesting that God himself was housed in it or that he needed to be fed and served as did the pagan gods.

Solomon's business activities are quite as noteworthy as his architectural endeavors. He tried to establish himself as a great businessman, indeed a middleman in the trade between Africa and Asia. He became a purveyor of horses and chariots to the various kings of Syria. One of the cities which he rebuilt as a governmental headquarters was the city of Megiddo in northern Palestine. There archaeologists have discovered not only the palace of the local administrator but also stables for upward of 500 horses. Most of the structures date from the century after Solomon, but they probably rest on the foundations of tenth-century buildings. On the Red Sea there has been excavated a great refinery where Solomon, exploiting the copper and iron mines south of the Dead Sea, refined the metals for export.

Solomon also was a great lover of wisdom teaching. Wisdom teaching was characteristic of various religious cultures. Its form was a variety of short epigrammatic sayings which were easily memorized and taught. Its interest was not primarily theological, but practical and prudential. The Book of Proverbs in the Old Testament is a later collection of the type of thing that Solomon originally sponsored in his Jerusalem court. As David was considered to be the father of music and psalms, so Solomon was considered the father of the wisdom literature in Israel. As our historian sees him, he "excelled all the kings of the earth in riches and in wisdom. And the whole earth sought the presence of Solomon to hear his wisdom, which God had put into his mind" (I Kings 10:23). While the tradition admires Solomon's glorious reign, the evaluation given it is not favorable. For one thing, his fiscal policies laid such a heavy burden of taxation and forced labor for the state upon the populace that the freedom-loving peoples, particularly of the North, insisted that his son make a radical change in policy. When this change was not promised, the kingdom was split into two portions. In addition, Solomon's wives and concubines came in for censure. In order to maintain good relations with all of his neighbors the king seems to have made it a policy to marry the daughter of every king of western Asia, insofar as he was able. Indeed, he is said to have had 700 wives and 300 concubines! This tremendous harem obviously served for purposes of both politics and display. It added to his reputation for glory and splendor. Yet in order to keep his wives satisfied he had to import their religious cults into Jerusalem, and as head of the state he actually took formal part in the worship of these gods (I Kings 11). This type of easy, cultured tolerance was not in accord with Israelite traditions, and there were those in the state who would not put up with it without criticism. For this reason our historian gives his final summary of Solomon's reign: "So Solomon did what was evil in the sight of the Lord, and did not wholly follow the Lord as David his father had done" (I Kings 11:6). As a result, the outlying regions of the Solomonic empire began to secure their freedom sometime before his death, and a prophet of the Lord even encouraged one Jeroboam, Solomon's director of public works in North Israel, to revolt and divide the kingdom. The division of the kingdom at Solomon's death into two parts, a northern and a southern kingdom, is the first stage in the series of catastrophes which begin to fall upon the realm of David. It is interpreted as a judgment of God upon the policies of King Solomon.

2. Ahab and Jezebel

There are forty-seven chapters in the two Books of Kings as the material is now arranged. The first eleven of these chapters deal with the reign of Solomon, covering a forty-year period from about 961 to 922 B.C. Seventeen of the forty-seven chapters deal with a forty-year period from about 875 to 835 B.C. This is the story of Ahab and Jezebel, and of Elijah and Elisha, whose lives and times are described in I Kings 16:28–II Kings 11 with a story of a sequel to the North Israel events in Jerusalem described in II Kings 12. The amount of space given over to the events in this period of the ninth century is a testimony both to the wealth of material which survived from that age and to the importance with which it was regarded in the nation of Israel, or at least by our Deuteronomic historian.

The fifty-year period between the division of the kingdom after Solomon's death and the founding of the dynasty of Omri in North Israel is described as one of continual bickering and civil war between the two states of North Israel and Judah. Finally, to put an end to an impossible situation, the general of the army, a man named Omri, seized the throne of Israel about 876 B.C. and set about giving stability to his nation. He contracted a mutual assistance treaty with Judah. He purchased a new site and began the building of a marvelous new capital for the North Israelite kingdom at a place called Samaria. He oriented his nation toward Phoenicia, that is, the kingdom of Tyre and Sidon. The latter was the greatest international trading power in the world of the day. Omri cemented this relationship by marrying his son to a young princess of Tyre, a woman named Jezebel.

The findings of modern archaeologists in uncovering the ancient capital of North Israel at Samaria are a most eloquent testimony to the work of Omri and his son Ahab at that city. The city fortifications which they erected and the palace which they built for themselves are perhaps the finest examples of architecture surviving from ancient Israel. No fortification was built in ancient Palestine before the time of the Romans that excelled the work of these men. At this time we begin to hear of the Israelites from the royal inscriptions of the kings of Assyria. It is interesting to note that the Assyrian monarchs continued to speak of Samaria as the "House of Omri" and of Israel as the "Land of Omri" for a century after Omri's dynasty had been swept from the throne. In 853 B.C. a coalition of western kings headed by the kings of Damascus, Hamath, and Ahab of Israel met the Assyrian king in battle at a place called Qarqar in southern Syria. The Assyrian report of this battle says how many forces each king supplied to the total army opposing him. Ahab's contingent of 2000 chariots is more than all the chariots of all the other kings put together, though he has not introduced into Israel cavalry as a weapon of war, an item which the other kings are beginning to use. In any event this coalition appears to have been successful in preventing Shalmaneser's march into Damascus and into Israel at that time. These are indications of the strength and political acumen of the two main kings of this dynasty.

Our historian, however, is not sufficiently impressed with the political power of the Omri dynasty to pay very much attention to it. In the long run to him this is a most insignificant factor, one not worth mentioning. Most significant for him is the figure of Jezebel in whose hands Ahab seems very weak and pliable. Jezebel was a very forceful woman with a missionary spirit, determined to put this backwoods nation on the civilized map of the world. She evidently despised the religion of Israel as any good polytheist would have done, and she set about, without opposition from her husband, to displace it as the official religion of the state of Israel. The Lord God of Israel was no longer to be the national god; Jezebel was determined to substitute the gods of Tyre, particularly the god Baal and his female consort, as the heads of the state. To that end she imported, we are told, 850 "prophets" of this pagan religion and fed them in her own palace at the expense of the royal court. This large number of devotees to the religion of Tyre could have only one purpose in Israel and that was a missionary one (I Kings 18:19).

This, then, was a most critical time in the history of Israel. For what purpose had this people been called into the world and separated as a nation? For what purpose had they been given the land? Who was strong enough to oppose the policies of Jezebel, a woman able to use the whole power of the government to enforce her will? Indeed, we are told that there were only 7000 people in Israel who had not bowed the knee to Baal, the Canaanite god (I Kings 19:18).

There was only one man who became an effective force of opposition to the religious policies of the royal court. That man was Elijah, a prophet from a town across the Jordan. Elijah is a mysterious figure who was well known by few people in the scenes of civilization. He appeared and disappeared with startling suddenness, and no one knew where he would be at any one moment. Yet at every critical juncture he was at hand as the conscience of the nation. His work began in relation to a severe drought and famine, one which is also attested in Phoenician sources. Having prophesied the drought as an act of God's judgment, he was credited with having brought it on! Hence the first part of I Kings 18 describes how King Ahab had searched everywhere in order to find him. Suddenly he appeared and Ahab's first words to him were: "Is it you, you troubler of Israel?" (I Kings 18:17). Elijah's subsequent challenge to the priests of Baal for the great contest on Mount

Carmel furnishes the setting for as dramatic a story as is recorded in the pages of the Old Testament. What precisely happened we cannot now recover. Needless to say, something very dramatic occurred, with the result that Elijah won a resounding victory.

It is doubtful, however, whether a dynastic revolution could have been brought about by the prophet on religious grounds alone. The story about Naboth's vineyard, recounted in I Kings 21, undoubtedly is preserved in order to show how the common man in Israel became increasingly suspicious of the policies of the royal court. Law could not be set aside in Israel by the king as it could be set aside in the totalitarian Canaanite regime. Private property could not be claimed by a royal court simply because the court desired it. Ancestral law was hallowed and private right was respected in Israel. By disgraceful means Jezebel secured the vineyard for her husband. No sooner had the latter entered the vineyard to possess it, however, than he was met by Elijah. Ahab's first words to Elijah were: "Hast thou found me, O mine enemy?" And Elijah replied, "I have found thee!" The end of the story comes some years later after the death of Elijah and Ahab in the time of Elijah's successor, Elisha. Bitterness against the dynasty of Omri rises gradually to such a pitch that a revolt becomes possible. At the proper moment this is led at prophetic instigation by a general of the army, a man named Jehu. The bitterness of feeling may be gathered from the story of the revolt, which did not rest until every vestige of the Omri dynasty had been removed from Israel and Judah. The revolt was extremely bloody. It marks the first and only dynastic revolution sponsored by prophets for religious ends, while using the power of the army to effect these ends. The provocation, however, was severe and the whole issue of the meaning of Israel's existence was at stake. As a result, never again did any king or queen in Israel or in Judah attempt to use the power of the throne to displace the Lord of Israel from his position as the God of the people. This was a significant battle and all credit is due to Elijah for its outcome, even though a later prophet was to hear the Lord condemn the excessive bloodshed (Hosea 1:4).

3. *The Fall of Northern Israel and Its Sequel in Judah*

The Deuteronomic historian pauses to narrate in only four chapters the chief events between the Jehu revolution in 842 B.C. and the return with power of the Assyrian armies to the West one hundred years later. During the first half of the eighth century, strong kings lived in both Israel and Judah and great deeds were accomplished in both countries. In the time of great prosperity in Israel around 760 or 750 B.C. Amos prophesied in northern Israel, saying in effect that the current optimism was only a cloak for radical social dislocations in the nation and the day would soon come when the nation would be destroyed. In 745 B.C. a new Assyrian emperor came to the throne who again began the big push to take over Assyria and Palestine, preparatory to an attack on Egypt. Faced with this external pressure the political situation in North Israel deteriorated so sharply as to be a virtual anarchy. Finally, in 733 B.C. Israel became a subject nation to Assyria and, after a revolt, she was destroyed as a nation (724–721 B.C.). Those who remained were governed by Assyrians as a subject people. At this point the historian introduces in II Kings 17 a discussion of why this terrible destruction of the nation had taken place. The Assyrian is interpreted as God's agent of judgment against a sinful nation. God had warned his people constantly by every prophet, but they would not listen. The conditions which God had established whereby the people were entitled to keep the land had been violated, and now the land was taken away. Let Judah, therefore, the remaining nation, be warned and take heed.

II Kings 18–20 describes the reign of King Hezekiah (715–687 B.C.) in Judah. He is one of the few kings for whom the historian has little but praise. "There was none like him among all the kings of Judah after him, nor among those who were before him" (II Kings 18:5). He is considered the greatest king since David. Indeed, his ideal, now that the Northern

Kingdom had fallen, was to create a united Palestine under the Davidic dynasty. While he was a client king, paying yearly tribute to Assyria, he seems to have felt that this could be accomplished as a simple adjustment in the Assyrian empire. When his plans failed, he took advantage of the period of uncertainty following the coronation of a new king in Assyria in 705 B.C. to assert his independence. In 701 B.C. the Assyrians retaliated, besieged Judah and Jerusalem, saying in their own record that they shut up Hezekiah in his city "like a caged bird." While the fortifications of a number of Judean cities were broken down, the country was not devastated nor was Jerusalem destroyed. Hezekiah finally was able to buy his freedom as a client king by paying a very heavy tribute.

In the mind of our historian Judah had been warned, had almost succumbed as had Israel, but in the last minute had been saved by God. He seems to imply that if there had only been more good kings like Hezekiah, the story of Israel and Judah might have been different. Hezekiah's great contemporary was the prophet Isaiah, and the latter figures in the story in II Kings 19–20 as a close intimate of the king. For further information concerning the state of affairs in Judah and what Isaiah had been saying about them as well as about the international political situation, one must turn to a study of the Book of Isaiah.

4. The Last Days of Judah and Jerusalem

After the death of Hezekiah a period of reaction takes place under a poor king during the first part of the seventh century. The historian passes this period over quickly with a brief evaluation. In II Kings 22–23 the final major pause in the course of history is made to describe the reign of King Josiah. This man was an eight-year-old boy when he began to reign, and he reigned for thirty-one years before he was killed in battle. He is the second of the great kings of Judah to whom the historian accords the verdict of unqualified approval. "And he did what was right in the eyes of the Lord, and walked in all the way of David his father . . . Before him there was no king like him, who turned to the Lord with all his heart and with all his soul and with all his might, according to all the law of Moses."

By the time Josiah had come of age the power of the Assyrians had so weakened that their empire was beginning to crumble. Josiah gradually began to free himself from Assyrian domination, and accomplished what his great-grandfather Hezekiah had tried to do and failed. That was to reunite Palestine under the Davidic dynasty. His reign was thus the time of high hope, for independence had again been achieved and a united country had been gained. Yet Josiah well understood that his country would never be truly united unless the reformation came deep from within. Emulating his ancestor David, he insisted upon a thorough religious reformation which might turn the people's hearts back to God with the sincerity and wholeheartedness which characterized the reign of David, at least as it was now believed to have been in popular tradition. To that end Josiah began a thorough religious revolution. While repairing the temple, workmen found in its dusty archives an old scroll which was read before the king. So remarkable was this document that it shamed and humbled him. He called an assembly of the whole people and had the scroll read in their hearing, and the covenant vows were renewed. On the basis of this document a complete revolution in religious practice was brought about, every vestige of paganism was destroyed from the country as far as possible, and all sacrificial worship was confined to the central altar in Jerusalem. It is generally agreed, and has been for centuries, that this book which was found in the temple was some portion of the Book of Deuteronomy, if not in the present edition then in an earlier edition, lacking the introduction and the conclusion of the present book.

In 612 B.C. the capital of the Assyrian empire, Nineveh, was destroyed by the Babylonians and Medes from northern Iran. The remnant of the Assyrian army fell back on the provinces in northern Mesopotamia. In 609 B.C. the last great battle took place between the Babylonians and the Assyrians, the latter being annihilated in the battle of Haran. While this battle was brewing, Pharaoh Neco of Egypt had decided that the time was ripe for him to intervene. By seeming to support the Assyrian army and preventing its annihilation by the Babylonians, he could keep it as a buffer between himself and the Babylonians while recovering most of Syria and all of Palestine as a part of the Egyptian empire. King Josiah of Judah attempted to prevent the Pharaoh from joining forces with the Assyrians. He placed his Judean army across the pass at Megiddo in northern Palestine, forced the Egyptians to fight and so delayed them that they were unable to reach the Assyrians in time to help them. Josiah had achieved his goal, but he lost his life in the attempt. Pharaoh Neco now took control of Palestine and put a Judean on the throne who would obey him; thereupon a radical reaction set in against everything for which King Josiah had stood. During this time, the prophet Jeremiah utters some of his most remarkable prophecies, words that so angered the Judean king that the prophet had to spend no small part of his time in hiding. Jeremiah, like the Deuteronomic historian, understood that the last days of Judah were at hand. The international situation was now so clear that he could only infer that it was God's answer to a complete betrayal of trust. Judah was now to be destroyed and cast among the nations as Israel had been before her. In 605 B.C. a new international force appeared on the scene, the Babylonian Nebuchadnezzar. In a short time he had defeated the Egyptians, taken over Syria and Palestine, and forced Judah to become his client state. Twice within eleven years Judah rebelled. A newly found Babylonian historical document confirms the story, related in II Kings 24, of how Nebuchadnezzar sent his army against Judah and Jerusalem in the first revolt, forced them to submit, and took their young king and most of their leaders and men of substance off into exile in mid-March, 597 B.C. Less than a decade later, in opposition to the pleading of Jeremiah, Judah had rebelled again. In the summer of 587 B.C. Jerusalem was completely destroyed and the temple burned. Town after town in Judah was laid waste and the inhabitants killed, until the small country had become a virtual wilderness. It is improbable that any country has ever suffered a more horrible blood bath than did Judah. Two centuries went by before one could say that prosperity had begun to return to the land. The historian at the end of II Kings simply tells what happened without comment. The earlier chapters have made their own point. God's controversy with the kings of his people had come to an end with the destruction of monarchy, temple, and state. The history of Israel within her land had begun with hope and triumph and promise and conquest. It ends in sadness, bloodshed, and destruction. Yet even in the darkness, God's justice and goodness are assumed. With the gift of the land had come great responsibility. The responsibility had been betrayed and the land had been taken away. Will there now be a future? Will God's purposes as expressed in his promises to Abraham be fulfilled? Only the years to come after the Deuteronomic historian had completed his work would answer these questions.

CHAPTER III

THE CHRONICLER'S HISTORY OF JUDAH (I–II CHRONICLES, EZRA, AND NEHEMIAH)

The last and the latest of the collections of historical material in the Old Testament are the Books of I and II Chronicles, Ezra, and Nehemiah. It has long been agreed among scholars that these four books were produced by one man as one work. His name is unknown to us, but for convenience he is called the "chronicler." In the past he has been thought to have done his work sometime in the latter part of the fourth or during the third century. Today, most scholars are inclined to think that he wrote his history not long after 400 B.C., that is, shortly after the last events which he describes are over. His main importance for us is that he preserves the story of how a group of exiles were able to come back from their captivity in Babylon and begin life anew in and around the ruins of Jerusalem. With the completion of his work Old Testament history is completed. For information of what happened between about 400 B.C. and the time of Christ we must turn, almost exclusively, to sources outside the Bible which were not preserved in the biblical canon or authoritative list of books. Furthermore, as we shall see, by that time most of the literature of the Old Testament had been re-edited and completed in pretty much its present form.

Theologically, the chronicler adds little that is new or fresh. His value lies largely in his compilation of facts and traditions. In the first nine chapters of I Chronicles the author has preserved for us a large number of genealogies of varying types and from various circles of the Israelite population. They are very dull reading for the average person and are of importance solely for historical research. In the remainder of I Chronicles the story of David is related in which a considerable amount of material is quoted from the second book of Samuel. Nevertheless, the chronicler has a great deal of information of his own from various sources. For one thing, he is particularly interested in the new tabernacle which David built in his capital at Jerusalem and in the religious services and officials which he established in that tabernacle. His viewpoint is that the official worship in the later temple simply followed the procedures which David had established for the tabernacle during his reign. Of special note is the historian's interest in music and his description of the important role which music played in the official worship services held in the capital city. On the basis of the new information which the chronicler has here preserved, scholars have had a tendency to think that the chronicler must have been a member of the special tribe of Levi which was charged with the religious duties of the nation, and that in particular he might have been a temple musician. Such a supposition, however, can never be anything more than a guess; like most of the major compilers of material in the Old Testament the author and various editors remain unknown to us.

The thirty-six chapters of II Chronicles parallel, in the span of time covered, the two Books of Kings. The chronicler is largely dependent upon the latter work for his material. His own history continues the theme of God's controversy with the kings of Israel and Judah, but he confines his attention very largely to Judean matters. After the reign of Solomon is described (largely simply quoted from I Kings) he confines his attention primarily to Judah. He quotes from I and II Kings those portions pertaining to the Judean kings. With that as his core he then adds from a large variety of independent sources of information. He mentions a number of different works which are now lost to us, particularly chronicles of events written by various prophets [for example, "the chronicles of

Shemaiah the prophet and of Iddo the seer" (II Chronicles 12:15), "the chronicles of Jehu" (II Chronicles 20:34), and the history of the two greatest kings of the eighth century, Uzziah and Hezekiah, which was credited to the prophet Isaiah but of which we have no other information (II Chronicles 26:22; 32:32)]. As a result, the chronicler's history is filled with a great deal of important material which we otherwise would not have. On the other hand, scholars have been inclined to feel that with regard to various factual matters, like the transmission of numbers and dates, the chronicler is somewhat careless in his editing or copying. Nevertheless, we must be grateful to him for preserving as much as he did.

What was the purpose which the chronicler had in mind when he wrote his history of Judah? He, of course, had much material which no one had written down. But his real purpose was probably other than simply antiquarian or historical. In all probability he wrote as he did to assure the little community which was seeking to re-establish itself in the ruins of former Judah that it was the heir of all that had gone before. As we look at the history of Israel from the time of Abraham to the time of Christ, it seems to us a fairly continuous history. We must not forget, however, that it was not obviously so when it was being lived. What possible hope could a small group of survivors have, people who were desperately poor and hard-pressed, that they were the true heirs of the promises to Abraham? How could they believe that all was not lost, that God had not been defeated and had not forgotten them, but that he was still to accomplish his purposes and he would do so through them? It would appear, then, that the deeper purpose behind the chronicler's work was to join the pre-exilic history of Judah to that after the exile, so that the new community would be aware that it stood in a very special and close relationship to the history of its ancestry before the destruction of Jerusalem and its temple in 587 B.C. The chief value of the work of the chronicler is, therefore, that it emphasizes a continuity running into the period of darkness after the destruction.

The books now called Ezra and Nehemiah are of special

interest to the biblical student because of the information they preserve of the chief events which occurred during the first century and a half after a few of the exiles began to return home. The Persian empire had now replaced the Babylonian. It had one of the most enlightened governments the ancient world ever knew. For the first time the freedom and self-respect of local populations was fostered and not submerged. Captive peoples were encouraged to return to their former homes, if they wished to do so, and pursue their religious life as they saw fit. The permission for the Jewish exiles to return home was quite in line with official policy concerning all similar peoples. By 500 B.C. a small province with Jerusalem as its center had been re-established in Palestine and given the name Yehud, the Persian equivalent of the name otherwise familiar to us as Judah. It had a population of some 50,000 people, and a temple had been rebuilt on the foundations of that which Nebuchadnezzar had destroyed in 587 B.C. In 520 B.C. the Persian government had appointed a man named Zerubbabel as the governor of the Judean province. He was the last of the family of David to be given so important a political office. With the encouragement of two prophets, Haggai and Zechariah, the temple was rebuilt, though not without considerable agitation among the people. In veiled but unmistakable language the prophets proclaimed amid certain disturbances currently at hand in the Persian empire that the day of the Lord was at hand when God would shake all nations and establish his kingdom among them. In that day, which they believed to be just at hand with the completion of the temple in Jerusalem, God would undoubtedly take Zerubbabel and make him the Messiah, his king who would rule the world for him. After 515 B.C. Zerubbabel suddenly disappears from the record and there is evidence of a rather deep disillusionment. It is not unlikely that the Persian government removed Zerubbabel. In any event, never again, to our knowledge, was a member of the Davidic house given such a political post. The day of the Lord did not come as was expected and Zerubbabel did not become the Messiah. Nevertheless, the temple had been built and the prophets were successful in their encouragement of it. Yet we must understand that not all people in the community believed that God desired the temple quite as much as the prophets Haggai and Zechariah seemed to infer. For example, an unknown contemporary at this time spoke these words: "Thus says the Lord: 'Heaven is my throne and earth is my footstool; what is the house which you would build for me, and what is the place of my rest?'" (Isaiah 66:1). Here it is claimed that, inasmuch as God owns the whole heaven and the whole earth, he has no need for this building being erected for him in Jerusalem. What God wants is humility and contrition of spirit, one who reverences him and obeys his word. In this manner alone will the Lord truly be glorified. Such a point of view, however, was very much a minority opinion at this time. The new community was led very largely by those who had had a vested interest in the former temple and now were deeply concerned that it be re-established. It was, therefore, very largely a priestly community. The great days of former prophecy were at an end, for in this new community prophets were no longer what was needed. The day of God's controversy with kings was over, and the day of obedience to God's law had begun.

The Ezra-Nehemiah story now skips to the second half of the fifth century B.C. In 445 B.C., a Jewish cupbearer to the Persian king is appointed governor of the province of Judah and given permission to rebuild the city's fortification walls. This man was Nehemiah. The chronicler quotes from this man's eloquent memoirs in Nehemiah 1–7, 12, 13. The governors of the surrounding provinces did not approve at all of Nehemiah or his plan to rebuild the walls of Jerusalem. As long as the city was nothing more than a religious center over which they had considerable control, they evidently did not mind. But to have a strong province with a strong capital city which would offer competition in political and economic affairs re-established in their midst was not to their liking. Consequently, they threatened Nehemiah repeatedly, attempted to frighten him and the people from their plan, and practiced every device they could in order to prevent the completion of his work. The story of Nehemiah is that of a selfless man who with single-minded devotion was entirely devoid of fear and pursued his course to its successful conclusion.

The story of Ezra is preserved in Ezra 7–10 and in Nehemiah 8–10. In other words, while ten chapters of the chronicler's Ezra-Nehemiah narrative have been subsequently separated and given the title "Ezra," actually the story about him is told half in one book and half in the other. For some time scholars have been debating the rather ambiguous evidence as to the date of Ezra. Traditionally it has been thought that he returned to Jerusalem with a fresh group of exiles in 458 B.C. Today a majority of scholars seem prepared to say that Ezra probably followed, rather than preceded, Nehemiah, and they would date him about 432, 428, or 398 B.C. The reasons for this are complex, and it would not serve our purpose to enter into them in this place.

Ezra is said to have been a scribe who was a scholar in the law of Moses. He evidently had been born and reared in a Jewish community in Babylonia and had become a Jewish scholar. He returned to Jerusalem as an appointee of the Persian king with power for the reorganization of Jewish religious affairs. A copy of the royal decree which granted to Ezra his commission is preserved in Ezra 7:12–26. In it Ezra is told to initiate his reform on the basis of the "law of your God which is in your hand." The evidence which we have from the Bible and also from a Jewish colony which lived in Upper Egypt, suggests that this was a time of conservatism in Jewish history and that the accomplishments of Ezra were undoubtedly of great importance.

In Ezra 7:6 we are told that he was a scribe who was very skillful in the law of Moses, meaning not only that he could write as a scribe but that he was a scholar who had given himself to a detailed study of the Mosaic teaching and law. Furthermore, he is taking with him to Jerusalem what is evidently a new and special edition of the law, something which represented his own work or that of others in the Jewish colony in Babylonia. Scholars believe that this is the completed edition of the present Pentateuch (the first five books of the Old Testament which the Jews call the Law or Torah) or some special edition of the laws which had been abstracted from the completed Pentateuch. On the basis of this edition, a reformation was instituted.

From this and other evidence we can make certain inferences regarding the theological problem of the age and the way in which it is being solved. Before this age the prophets had affirmed that though God's people would have to be punished and suffer for their violation of the covenant, beyond this dark night there would be a glorious day when all the frustrations and problems and evil of history would be overcome in the kingdom of God. Two prophets, as we have already noticed, had believed that the great day would dawn immediately upon the temple's erection and that the governor of that day would become God's Messiah. These hopes had not been fulfilled. A community had been restored, Jerusalem had been rebuilt, yet the problems of history and the evil of history still remained. The day of the Lord had been delayed. How did God mean his people to live in the meantime when the interval between the past and the future seemed greatly extended? The priests in Babylon appear to have given considerable thought to this problem. They evidently arrived at the conclusion that the one thing they could do was to obey the Lord in sincerity and in truth. The prophets had affirmed and the historians had shown that the nation had been destroyed for its infidelity. This would not happen again if, from now on, the people vowed to be obedient with all their hearts. But how could one be sure he was doing exactly what God wanted? Men like Ezra in Babylon had for years been studying the various legal passages in the early books of the Old Testament. It was now decided that this great variety of laws could serve as a written constitution, the law of God given in detailed form. If men but understood what each of these laws meant and would obey them all, then it would be impossible for them to go wrong in this world. The Mosaic covenant, therefore, was now interpreted more as the giving of a law than as the establishment of a relationship. The primary law in the covenant was the Ten Commandments, and this was the law which protected the interests of God while leaving man free within its structure to arrange his own life. The great variety of other laws which appear in Exodus, Leviticus, Numbers, and Deuteronomy were meant originally to be simply descriptions of legal practice. There was no thought originally of their being written down as constitutional law, for before the time of Ezra no one in the ancient Near East thought in terms of constitutions or conceived of the necessity to decide a case on the basis of a written constitution. Things were not done that way. But now in this day something new entered the scene of history. It was the idea of constitutional law, influenced greatly, no doubt, by the "law of the Medes and the Persians," that is, by the royal decrees as they were conceived in the Persian empire. However that may be, the great variety of legal material that had been heaped around the original covenant was now interpreted as positive constitutional law, and to disobey any portion of it was to disobey the whole; it was to break the constitution. What now was needed was a large number of scholars like Ezra who could interpret what the law meant and apply it to the various situations which people encountered in their lives. If this could be done, then the sincere man would have a constitution within which he could walk, if he knew it well enough. He would never be able to break the major commandments if he knew all the minor ones and sought zealously to keep them. Needless to say, this was not the attitude of a prophet like Jeremiah toward the law. For him the content of the original Mosaic covenant was the establishment of a close relationship wherein God was acknowledged as a lord to be obeyed by conscious acts of decision. God was to be followed and obeyed, but following a lord who has made himself known in specific ways in the past is very different from simply obeying a constitution. Needless to say Jesus and Paul are more in line with the intent of the original Mosaic covenant and with such a prophet as Jeremiah than they are with the scribe Ezra.

As for the outlook toward the future, prophecy of the classical type is displaced by what is called "apocalypticism." The great prophets before this time had always stood firmly within their history. They were expounding a relevant word of God for their particular time, and any visions of the future to which they gave utterance were projections from the known past and present situation. Apocalypticism, on the other hand, is very difficult to date because it has very little definite historical reference. It is characterized by the view that the current world is meaningless, evil, wicked. God has given it over to destruction and in due time he will intervene and bring in the end of this age while inaugurating his kingdom. The earlier prophet emphasized the significance of the "now," so that no matter how hopeless things may have been God was working a new thing and had called his prophet to meaningful work in that particular moment. No prophet ever gave up his interest in the present. Yet in apocalypticism the present is not a time when God is working a new thing; God is beyond the current history and will not intervene until its end is come. Meanwhile, the faithful should wait patiently and obediently for the coming of the Lord. The one thinks of the present as always significant, while the other has lost any sense of the meaningfulness and significance of current history.

Ezra has often been called "the father of Judaism." It is true that for the first time one is entitled to use the words "Jews" and "Judaism" at this stage in biblical history. When one thinks of a Jew he thinks of Judaism. The latter is a definite religion which has developed out of that which Ezra stood for and culminates later in the Talmud. Before this time there were too many currents in the life of Israel, and historically one should not simplify the classic faith of the Old Testament by calling it "Judaism." Judaism and Christianity are two different religions because they have developed out of the classic days of Israel in different directions, each emphasizing different currents in Israelite life. Ezra is obviously to be considered more the father of Judaism than he is of Christianity. Yet at the same time it is this community of Ezra, those who went before and those who came after, who rescued the literature of Israel from the fires of destruction and preserved the faith until the coming of a new era and a new reformation.

PART II

THE PROPHETIC,
DEVOTIONAL,
AND WISDOM LITERATURE

In Part I we have examined the fifteen books of Old Testament history; they divided themselves into three major collections, each with its own intent and purpose. We now turn to the other books of the Old Testament, fifteen of them from the circles of Old Testament prophecy, four containing collections of Israel's devotional and wisdom literature, and five which must be classed as miscellaneous. This literature is to be fitted into the foregoing history; it must be understood as a part of that history and it is needed to complete our understanding of Israel's faith in its whole range and complexity. At the same time it must be admitted that we encounter writing in these books that is the most difficult to understand in the Old Testament. The prophets were preachers who spoke to their people regarding matters in their own day. Their words are full of detailed historical allusions that demand considerable study. In addition, such books as Isaiah, the Psalms, and Job were written for the most part in a very highly sophisticated and beautiful poetry. As is very frequently the case, writing of this type demands study in order to understand it fully. The student of the Bible, therefore, is encouraged in these books especially to make use of detailed aids which will help him to understand what he is reading. The most important of these now available is perhaps *The Interpreter's Bible,* a commentary on all of the biblical books. It is in twelve volumes and, while somewhat uneven in quality, is perhaps the best over-all work that is now available. While this is too expensive to be in every home, an annotated Bible with introductions to the various books and footnotes to the text and a glossary of difficult theological words can be obtained from the Westminster Press; it is called *The Westminster Study Edition of the Holy Bible.* A Bible dictionary in which terms may be found and explained is also a very great help. The Bible is sufficiently simple that anyone can get its central meaning. Yet it also has its deeper ranges, and like anything else that is worth while these must be worked for if they are to be grasped.

CHAPTER I

THE PROPHETS

We turn first to a brief description of the Old Testament prophets. They were men who belonged to a particular and recognized office in Israelite society, and it is important that we understand what that office was. Kings, judges, and priests held high positions in the society, but the position of the prophet was like none of the others. If a person happened to be the eldest son of a royal father in Jerusalem, there was no doubt that he would be the next king. Judges and army officers and cabinet officials were all appointed. A priest had to belong to a particular clan of the priestly family, and the particular clan to which he belonged determined the type of priesthood he could follow. In Jerusalem the high priest was selected from among those who could trace their ancestry back to Aaron in the time of Moses. The prophet, on the other hand, did not have an hereditary office, nor was it an office determined by human choice or ancestry. He was believed to have been appointed by God, and his job was to speak directly for God. Kings, priests, and judges did what they did according to established rules and precedents. When God wanted to speak directly to his people in a manner that was not mediated through an office, he always chose a prophet. The prophet was the messenger of the divine sovereign. His main concern was to speak what he profoundly believed to be God's message for a particular current situation.

It will be remembered that during the period of the judges and before that God was believed to have ruled his people directly by spiritually empowering certain key individuals to perform various tasks. The introduction of the monarchy was interpreted by some as being a limitation upon the divine choice of leadership in politics. From this time forth a man would become king, not because God approved of him, but because he had the proper father. It is precisely at this juncture that we begin to hear about the first prophets. No matter how great the king's political power, the prophet as God's spokesman was always at hand to say "Thus saith the Lord" to any king or to the people as a whole when they went contrary to the conditions established in the old Mosaic covenant. As a result, there could be no real curb on freedom of speech in ancient Israel. Never in history has there been a more profound and searching analysis of the course of a people's life than that provided by the Old Testament prophets. This freedom, of course, was subject to misuse. By the time of Elijah in the ninth century we begin to see that the country was overrun with prophets, and few of them did the people any good. The problem of false prophecy, of knowing who among the various voices speaking for the Lord was actually speaking the truth, became a very serious one indeed. The great prophets whose works are preserved in the Old Testament are, for the most part, fairly isolated figures, dissociating themselves from the popular prophets who used their office in order to speak what the people wanted to hear. Furthermore, the few great men are generally associated with particular crises in the life of their people. The first of these, as we have already seen, came at the time of Ahab and Jezebel in the ninth century, when the latter was attempting to displace the God of Israel as the lord of the nation. The prophets Elijah and Elisha led the movement that brought this process to a dramatic halt. In the middle of the eighth century, however, there appeared a new group of prophets at the time when Palestine became involved in the great thrust for empire on the part of the Assyrians in Mesopotamia. The essential message of these prophets was a terrible one: they interpreted the international events as meaning that God was going to destroy the political states of Israel and Judah and scatter the people again among the nations. They predicted, however, that God would again restore them to Palestine and when that happened the new and glorious age of God's kingdom would begin on earth. This was the interpretation of the meaning of the international imperialism of the time in relation to the people of Israel. It is to be observed that both Israel and Judah were destroyed, that their peoples were scattered among the nations, and that without the words of the prophets they would probably not have survived the catastrophe.

A. THE PROPHETS OF THE EIGHTH CENTURY B.C.

Let us first examine briefly the prophets of the Assyrian period during the eighth century; they are Amos, Hosea, Isaiah, and Micah. The men are the first of the so-called "writing" prophets. That is, they are the first whose words have been preserved and collected into the books which bear their names. One of the most remarkable things about them is the style in which they chose to deliver their messages about the meaning of current events. That style is a very elevated, carefully composed, and often beautiful poetry. This combination of message and poetic style is a most unusual and interesting feature of the classical prophets of Israel. The inspiration which they received from God did not result in the type of ecstatic utterance that characterized so many of the false prophets of their day; instead the inspiration led them to speak more beautifully and intelligibly than they otherwise would have done. These poetic works are products of careful composition and, as a result, have a great power within them that speaks not only to the emotions but to the mind.

Amos is the earliest of the series. According to an editor's introductory note at the beginning of the book, he prophesied during the reign of Jeroboam II (about 786–746 B.C.). From the contents of the book and especially from Chapter 6:13 (see R.S.V.) he spoke at a time when a great victory had been won or was in the process of being won by Israel. This event is mentioned in II Kings 14:25, 28, and it is generally thought to have taken place between about 760 and 750 B.C. It was just before the Assyrian pressure began on Palestine at a time when the Northern Kingdom had won a great victory by restoring the Davidic border up into Syria, Damascus again becoming a subject territory. Amos himself was evidently a Judean, though all that we know about his life is contained in a bit of biography written in prose about him, evidently by a disciple who edited and perhaps also committed to writing the prophecies that we have in the book. This biography is in Chapter 7:10–17. Here we learn that Amos, a Judean, was delivering his prophecies at Bethel, twelve miles north of Jerusalem across the border in Israel. It was a place where the central sanctuary patronized by the King of Israel was situated. He is told by the priest of that sanctuary to go back home and say what he pleases there, but to keep his mouth shut at the royal sanctuary in Israel where he has no business to be. In defending himself Amos dissociates himself from the popular prophets of his day and says that the Lord has taken him from a humble life as a herdsman and a "dresser of sycamore trees." The latter is a reference to the care of sycamore figs. In ancient times the figs of this type of sycamore had to be punctured at a certain point in their development in order that they might develop large enough to become edible. This background does not necessarily mean that Amos was an uncouth or an uneducated backwoodsman. On the contrary, he shows himself to be a highly intelligent man who has a deeper insight into the meaning of international affairs than do his contemporaries.

For Amos the victory which has brought joy and pride to the Israelite nation is simply a prelude to the disaster which is shortly to follow. God, who had given this people a land and a life within the land, is about to take it away and to scatter them in exile at the hand of the Assyrians. One of the key passages in the book is Chapter 5:18: "Woe unto you that desire the day of the Lord! Wherefore would ye have the day of the Lord? It is darkness and not light." We gather from this verse that the people of Israel were well aware of the teaching that

God had chosen them from out of the nations of the world and had a great destiny for them. They believed, therefore, that God held in store for them a golden future and would accord them this future in his great day when he brought all the nations of the world under his sovereignty. What Amos is saying in the above quoted passage is this: Woe unto you people who have violated God's covenant, filled his land with all sorts of misdeeds, and violated every one of the solemn vows which once had been taken. Do such a people believe that they can have a golden future apart from judgment? On the contrary, the judgment of God that will fall upon the world will first be experienced by Israel.

It is characteristic of the optimism of the prosperous that they hope to obtain a future apart from punishment for sin, that they can be blessed while violating the most solemn of their sacred covenants. Amos for the first time turns the popular view of the future into a solemn warning of the judgment that will surely fall. By so doing he was preparing his people for the critical and terrible events that were shortly to happen when the Assyrian army arrived in Palestine, and he enabled them to see that these events were not in spite of God but indeed because of the very righteousness of God.

But why was God to act so drastically as to destroy the Israelite nation? A part of Amos' answer to that question is to be found in Chapter 5:21–27. It is to this effect: What God wanted of the people as he established the conditions for their life in their land was justice and righteousness. In the original Mosaic system there was great concern for the weak and the poor in the society, people who always have such difficulty in taking care of themselves. Such people are always easy prey to the strong, and at their expense the strong can become stronger and wealthier. Because Israel had once been a slave in Egypt, they understood that the righteousness of God directed toward salvation of them as slaves should also characterize their own conceptions of justice in their society. Hence, the whole aim of their economic life was the love of neighbor (Leviticus 19:18). This meant that the central concern of economic life was the service of one's neighbor, and that meant the one who was in need. Laws such as the one saying that no interest should be charged on loans of money were very deeply ingrained in Israelite society. Another man's need should not become the occasion for profit—such was the theory. As we read the Book of Amos we see that his central concern is with the violation of social order as it had been classically conceived in Israel. There is no concern for justice, but the strong are continually grinding the weak into the dust in order to make their profits and they corrupt the courts of law in order to preserve their strong position. Amos pleads with his people, "Seek good and not evil that ye may live; and so the Lord, the God of hosts, will be with you, as you say. Hate the evil, love the good, and establish justice in the gate" [i.e. the gate as the seat of the law court] (Chapter 5:14–15). At the same time the same people are thronging to the shrines of worship and multiplying their sacrifices and their offerings and their pious songs and prayers. In the Book of Leviticus, however, it is repeated over and over that the forms of worship are accepted by God as meaningful only when they are practiced by a people who are sincere and whose sins are unwitting sins. What Amos is implying is that the people of Israel are sinning with a high hand and a stiff neck. At the same time they believe that the splendor of their services of worship will hide their acts. Hence he exclaims in God's name: "I hate, I despise your feasts, and I take no delight in your solemn assemblies" (5:21). What God wants is not simply pious acts in church; he wants a righteous national life from his people. And anyone who thinks that worship can be used as a substitute or as a cover for social responsibility, or in modern terms that "religion can be used as an opiate" to hide the need for social justice, must understand that God hates this kind of worship and will have nothing to do with it. Because Israel has corrupted her common life and has violated every condition of her existence, God is now about to destroy her as a nation. And her destruction will be the first in a series of events which can be described as "the day of the Lord." That Amos should have said these words at a time of great national prosperity and triumph meant that his message was not received gladly.

Nevertheless, what he had to say was at least partially verified in Israel by the destruction of the Northern Kingdom within thirty or forty years after he uttered his prophecy.

The prophet Hosea was a North Israelite. A close inspection of his prophecy leads to the conclusion that most of his message as we have it preserved in the fourteen short chapters of his book was delivered at a time somewhat later than that of Amos. It is a time when the Assyrian pressure on Israel had begun and when the internal political situation had weakened to the point of chaos. This we know to have happened in the period between about 745 and 721 B.C. It seems safe to date most of the prophecy of Hosea, as it is preserved, in the decade between about 740 and 730 B.C. Essentially, his message is the same as that of Amos. In Chapter 4, for example, he begins the main part of his prophecy with the statement of God's "controversy," that is, his legal case against his people, because there is nothing but immoral chaos in the land, and this means that there is no true knowledge of God among the people. In verse 6 of that chapter he says, "My people are destroyed for lack of knowledge." Hosea means by knowledge that acknowledgment of God's claim upon his people which leads them to loyal and loving obedience to him. Whereas Amos stressed the violations of social justice in the society in a time of prosperity, Hosea in a time of political chaos and weakness is inclined to stress the religious idolatry which leads the people to foolish and absurd actions. The nation flits back and forth in her political adventuring between Egypt and Assyria, acting "like a silly dove without understanding" (Chapter 7:11). She is a cake half baked (7:8) and, having sown the wind, she will "reap the whirlwind" (8:7).

In describing Israel's problem, Hosea uses a new terminology. He speaks of Israel's sin quite frequently as "playing the harlot." That is, instead of remaining loyal to her true husband who is God himself, she has chosen to play the harlot by joining herself to idols (Chapter 4:11–19); indeed, the people of the territory of Ephraim have joined themselves to idols because the spirit of whoredom is within them and they do not know the Lord (4:17; 5:4). In other words, Hosea has chosen a new way to make clear to Israel the enormity of her offense against God, and this is the explanation of her present political difficulty. The relation which had been established between God and Israel in the days of Moses is now likened to a marriage contract in which Israel appears as the wife of the divine husband. But the wife has been unfaithful, and her infidelity is the source of her present woe. Because Israel has violated the conditions of the covenant, God will afflict her and send her into captivity.

In saying this, which is essentially what Amos before him had said, Hosea gives us more of a glimpse into his innermost feelings than was the case with the prophet Amos. Hosea is a very sensitive person, and the prophecy which he must give is heart-rending to him. In keeping with his use of the marriage bond as a symbol typifying the relation of God and people, the prophet also for the first time makes large use of the term "love," a word drawn from family relationships, as descriptive of God's concern and attitude toward Israel. So convinced is he of the love of God as shown by God's past actions toward his people, that he is sure that the disaster which is shortly to fall upon Israel will not be the end of the chosen people; the time will come when God will restore his beloved. He quotes God as saying, "I will heal their backsliding; I will love them freely" (14:4). The depths of the prophet's internal distress causes him to give expression to the struggling love of God for his people both as the love of a husband for a faithless wife and as the love of a father for a faithless child. The most profound and beautiful of these statements is in Chapter 11. Here the prophet describes God's past relation to Israel as one in which God has reared his child, and now finds it in its maturity to be "bent on backsliding from me." Yet the prophet hears God say, "How shall I give thee up, Ephraim? How shall I cast thee off, Israel? . . . I will not execute the fierceness of mine anger, I will not be turned to destroy Ephraim, for I am God and not man."

The new terminology which Hosea used evidently had its root in the prophet's own marriage. This is described in the first three chapters of his book, though the exact nature of these chapters is most difficult to interpret and scholars are by no means agreed on their meaning. The most popular view is that Hosea married a fine woman by the name of Gomer, and had three children by her. These children, whose names are given in Chapter 1, symbolized through their names three of the chief points of Hosea's message of doom for his people. Subsequently, his wife left him for a life of harlotry. Yet Hosea still loved her, and in Chapter 3 we are told how he bought her back. This was to him a symbol of God's relation to Israel in the past and in the future. Many scholars, however, are by no means sure that this is the precise history of Hosea's marriage to Gomer. In Chapter 1:2 Hosea hears God command him to "take unto thee a wife of whoredom and children of whoredom because the land doth commit great whoredom." They take these words quite literally and believe that Hosea literally married a harlot and used his marriage as a symbol of the relation between God and Israel—as dramatic and forceful a symbol as one could possibly devise. It was quite customary for prophets to make use of all sorts of dramatic actions to symbolize what they were saying. That Hosea married a harlot, sought to redeem her from her life, and continued to love her even in defection would scarcely have been a shocking thing to Israelites in that day. Indeed it would have been the strongest possible sign of his theological position and his interpretation of the meaning and destiny of Israel in the Assyrian crisis.

The greatest of the Old Testament prophets during the Assyrian period was Isaiah of Jerusalem. He is one of the three "major" prophets, as distinct from the twelve "minor" prophets. This does not mean in itself that he was a greater man than his compatriots, Amos and Micah. It means that the book which bears his name is a lengthy one. The three major prophets and the twelve minor at one time made four written rolls of about equal length. An idea of their size is obtained from the complete manuscript of Isaiah found among the Dead Sea Scrolls and dating about 100 B.C. This is the oldest complete book of the Old Testament which we have in manuscript form and its scroll is about twenty-four feet long. The first difficulty which we encounter, however, in studying Isaiah is the fact that the book which carries his name is a compilation of a variety of prophetic materials, evidently preserved and put together by a school of disciples long after the original prophecies were uttered. Of first importance is the fact that the book seems to divide at Chapter 40, so that the first thirty-nine chapters for the most part belong to Isaiah of Jerusalem in the eighth century, but Chapters 40–66 belong to a later period, for the most part in the second half of the sixth century. Scholars speak of First Isaiah and of Second Isaiah. A general rule which is useful in determining the age of prophetic materials is as follows: a prophecy is obviously earlier than the things it predicts, but inasmuch as the prophets were preachers to the people of their time a prophecy is obviously contemporary with or later than the conditions it presupposes. First Isaiah proclaims the judgment of God upon Judah in the current crisis brought about by the Assyrian armies in Palestine. In Chapters 40–66, Second Isaiah knows a Judah and Jerusalem that have already been devastated. Jerusalem is laid waste, the temple is destroyed, and people are scattered in Babylon, and the prophet proclaims the coming of the Lord to deliver and save his people and to lead them in a new exodus back to the Promised Land (cf. Chapter 44:26–28). Even in First Isaiah there are certain chapters that seem to belong to a later period. For example, Chapters 13–14 seem to refer to the fall of Babylon that occurred in 539 B.C. Chapters 24–27 contain a series of remarkable visions of the future without definite historical reference, but scholars in general have long believed that they belonged to a later period than that of First Isaiah. Chapters 34–35 are in the style of, and are believed by many to belong to Second Isaiah. Chapters 36–39 are a fragment of history repeated from II Kings 18–20; they narrate the story of Isaiah's relation with King Hezekiah in Jerusalem at the end of the eighth century when the Assyrian army was besieging Jerusalem. These narratives form a fitting close to the prophecies of Isaiah because they preserve the memory of Isaiah's assurances to the king and to his people that Jerusalem would not be destroyed but that God temporarily at least would save the city and the temple. The Book of Isaiah thus illustrates in an acute form the problem one has in studying Old Testament prophecy. It is improbable that any of the prophets wrote down his own message. The poetic compositions were remembered, sometimes as in the case of Jeremiah were dictated to a secretary, in all cases were preserved by circles of disciples before finally being committed to writing and arranged in the form in which we now have them. Thus, snatches of biography will occasionally be preserved (Isaiah 7, for example), whereas in Chapters 6 and 8 material that may once have been in poetic style has largely lost its poetic form in the course of its transmission to us. Then again disciples were sometimes forced to fill out certain prophecies in their own words as the original was remembered, and other compositions of unknown origin were occasionally included if they were not completely out of keeping with the great master's original proclamation, and if they were works of genuine merit.

The power of Isaiah lies not so much in new doctrines that he promulgated as in the forcefulness and beauty with which he applied the prophetic message to the conditions of his own times in Judah and Jerusalem. The story of his call in Chapter 6 preserves one of the pictures which dominates prophecy. In a vision the prophet sees God enthroned in his heavenly temple with his angelic host surrounding him. It is a heavenly courtroom scene in which a judicial case is being tried. In most prophecy God appears as the judge trying and directing the course of history and the actions of people in it. In this case the prophet sees before he hears and is immediately overwhelmed with his own sinfulness and that of his people. He then experiences the miracle of the divine forgiveness and his ears are opened. He hears God asking his heavenly court who shall be designated to carry to the people of Israel the message of what the court has just decided. At that point Isaiah answers, "Here am I, send me." It should be noted that the great religious experiences described in the Bible are mainly of this type: they are vocational; God by them is taking hold of a man and giving him a job to do. The concern is not so much with a religious experience as with a work which God wants to have done.

Chapter 1 of Isaiah, while coming toward the end of Isaiah's ministry, is placed at the beginning because it is a classic summary of God's indictment of his people. It, too, is in the form of a courtroom discussion wherein all the elements of the heaven and the earth are called to bear witness to the indictment of the people. As in Hosea the basic problem is that God's people have rebelled against him, they do not "know" him. For this reason their country is in turmoil and they are sick from head to foot. As in the case of Amos, however, the prophet sees the people flocking to their worship services and using their piety as a way of escape from social responsibility. God wants none of it; he has had enough of the rites of worship which are separated from social responsibility: "Wash you, make you clean; put away the evil of your doings from before mine eyes; cease to do evil, learn to do well; seek justice, relieve the oppressed; judge the fatherless, plead for the widow. . . . If ye be willing and obedient, ye shall eat the good of the land; but if ye refuse and rebel, ye shall be devoured with the sword; for the mouth of the Lord hath spoken it" (1:16–17; 19–20).

Like Amos prophesying to Israel, Isaiah foresees the Assyrian peril as an instrument of God's judgment and the first stage in a series of climactic events which shall lead to the establishment of God's kingdom. In Chapter 2:5–6 the prophet warns of the day of the Lord as did Amos before him. In an unforgettable series of woes (Chapters 5; 9:8–10:4) the prophet vividly portrays the wicked irresponsibility of a people interested only in themselves and in their possessions while entirely uninterested in the knowledge of God and of his will for his people. ". . . they regard not the work of the Lord, neither have they considered the work of his hands. . . . Woe unto them that call evil good, and good evil, that put darkness for light, and light for darkness . . . that are wise in their own eyes, and prudent in their own sight . . . that justify the wicked for a bribe, and take away the righteousness of the righteous from him . . . they have rejected the law of the Lord of Hosts and despised the word of the Holy One of Israel." In Chapter 10:5–6 the prophet describes in more detail his view of the historical situation. The Assyrian army is God's instrument of judgment, the rod of God's righteousness, to chastise his sinful people. This does not mean that the Assyrian is more righteous than Judah. Indeed, he has no idea that he is God's instrument; he believes he is doing this under his own power, that he himself is God. But "shall the ax boast itself against him that heweth therewith?" It is typical of the powerful that they deify themselves. And God, as soon as he has accomplished his purpose through them, will then punish them for their wickedness. The great battles for empire and the struggles for power in history are not meaningless. The hand of God is to be seen within them, but his righteous judgment is over all and no one force in history can ever deify itself, but must know it is under judgment in time. Idolatry will be destroyed.

Isaiah, however, does not leave the future in deep darkness. He sees the historical blackness of his time as a prelude to the glorious coming of the kingdom of God. The day of the Lord is at its onset darkness, as Amos has said. But beyond it is the light. One of Isaiah's sons bore the name Shear-jashub. The name means "a remnant shall return"; that is, some shall repent. At first Isaiah used that name as a threat against a prosperous people: only a remnant would return. Later in the course of his life it became also a prophecy of hope. The people would never be completely destroyed. A remnant would survive and with that remnant God would build anew.

Isaiah, of course, is best remembered as the first prophet to give vivid pictures of the coming Messiah, that is, of the king whom God would raise up to fulfill his promises to David, the king who would rule the earth in righteousness and justice, the perfect king who would be God's answer to the problem of war and justice in the earth. In the tragedies of the current history, said the prophet, "the people that walked in darkness have seen a great light." A child shall be born who, as he grows into manhood, shall take the government upon his shoulders and shall bear a name which describes the character of God as he was and would then be known: "Wonderful Counselor, Mighty Warrior, Everlasting Father, and Prince of Peace" (Chapter 9:2, 6). This king shall have the spirit of the Lord resting upon him, the spirit of wisdom and understanding which will enable him to administer justice righteously and equitably with particular consideration for the poor and the meek, while possessing the strength and the will to fight and control the wicked in the earth. When that comes to pass, a new day will have dawned on the earth, a day when warfare will have ceased, when "they shall not hurt nor destroy in all my holy mountain; for the earth shall be full of the knowledge of the Lord, as the waters cover the sea" (Chapter 11:1–9).

The prophet Micah was a contemporary of Isaiah, at least during the second part of his ministry. His message is essentially the same as that of Amos and Isaiah. He lays strong emphasis upon the social iniquity of the Judean society, prophesies that Jerusalem will be destroyed, and reiterates the thought of Amos and Isaiah about the iniquity of rites of worship which are unrelated to the common life. "He hath shewed thee, O man, what is good; and what doth the Lord require of thee but to do justly, and to love the doing of merciful deeds, and to walk humbly with thy God?" (Chapter 6:8).

It is interesting to observe that while in 721 B.C. the Northern Kingdom was completely destroyed by the Assyrians, Judah escaped complete destruction at the hand of the Assyrian army both then and in 701 B.C. when the Assyrian emperor, Sennacherib, attacked Jerusalem. In each case Judah became a subject nation, paying yearly tribute. In prophetic terms *this* was the judgment of God, and *this* was the day of the Lord. And yet, Jerusalem was not destroyed until over a century after Micah's time. In the time of none of the prophets, nor in the time of Jesus, nor yet in our time has the golden age of peace in the kingdom of God arrived. The prophets expected this to arrive soon, but people were to learn that God's time is not identical with our time. Nevertheless the prophetic predictions of the coming end of current history in time became something of an embarrassment and of wonder. Will God's kingdom come? When?

B. THE PROPHETS OF THE
SEVENTH CENTURY B.C.

The story of the prophets does not take up again until a hundred years after the time of Isaiah. After about 630 B.C. the Assyrian empire rapidly declined in power until in 612 B.C. Nineveh, the capital of that empire, was destroyed by the Medes and the Babylonians. A Hebrew prophet, Nahum by name, celebrated this event in three chapters of stirring poetry. He saw it as the judgment of God upon a cruel and wicked people which for centuries had been preying upon others and keeping them in subjection. Meanwhile in Palestine during the 620s the kingdom of Judah under the fine king Josiah had been busily asserting its independence and re-establishing its control over the whole of western Palestine.

At this time Zephaniah and Jeremiah began their prophetic careers. We know nothing about Zephaniah, except that he, like Jeremiah in the early days of the latter's ministry, did not believe that the downfall of Assyria meant the dawn of a new age of freedom for Judah or for the ancient world as a whole. He could not specify precisely what the future would bring, but he was certain that a new northern peril was already in existence which was shortly to overcome Palestine. To him the downfall of Assyria meant that the coming day of the Lord was at hand, "a day of wrath, a day of trouble and distress, a day of wasteness and desolation, a day of darkness and gloominess, a day of clouds and thick darkness." It was a time, then, not simply for exultation but for repentance: "Seek ye the Lord, all ye meek of the earth, that have kept his ordinances; seek righteousness, seek meekness. It may be ye will be hid in the day of the Lord's anger."

Jeremiah and Zephaniah were correct in their fears that Assyria would soon be replaced by another power. The Babylonians, after their defeat of the Egyptians in northern Syria in 605 B.C., rapidly took over the coastlands of Palestine and Syria. From this period come the meditations of a prophet named

Habakkuk. His is no typical prophecy; it is truly a meditation on the problem of evil. The country is being overrun by bands of Babylonians, men whose might is their god (Chapter 1:11). He knows that God is a God of justice and of righteousness, but he also knows that complete disorder prevails in his land and "justice goeth forth perverted." He therefore prays to God concerning the meaning of what is happening. Why does God hold his peace when "the wicked swalloweth up the man that is more righteous than he?" In the second chapter the answer comes to the prophet. It is to the effect that the question is a legitimate one, that it should be written large so that all men might read it. It is also true that there is an answer to the question, but the answer lies in God and at a particular moment in history it may not be immediately forthcoming. For this reason one must wait in trust, knowing that it will surely come in its own time. Meanwhile "the righteous shall live by his faith" (Chapter 2:4). This text is one of the most famous in the entire Bible; it was used by Paul against Judaism and by Martin Luther in his struggles against the Roman Catholic Church. In its original setting it means this: while all the answers to our questions concerning the justice of God and the meaning of suffering in history are not to be had at any one moment, God's faithful will live and continue to live patiently in their complete commitment to God and in their fidelity to what they know is right, to what they know from earlier times to be the will of God. The word "faith" here is the same as the word "faithfulness." The good man shall live by his faithfulness: that is, a faithfulness that is completely committed to the Faithful One, a commitment that involves trust and loyalty. In the Bible faith-faithfulness is a relationship concept; in it there is complete reliance and trust on the one hand and entire fidelity and faithfulness to vows on the other.

Jeremiah is the second of the "major" prophets; he received his call about 626 B.C. and is last heard prophesying against the idolatry of Judean exiles in Egypt around 585 B.C. We have more intimate knowledge of him than we do of any other personality in the Bible, except David and Jesus. The reason is that the prophet had a close friend and biographer who has preserved the story of his life. The first twenty-five chapters of the Book of Jeremiah are for the most part a fragmentary assemblage of the words of the prophet, delivered at various times during his life. Chapters 26–45 are for the most part narratives about Jeremiah, written by his biographer. Chapters 46–51 are prophecies against foreign nations, a section that is typical of the major prophets, because they saw that the judgment of God against his own people in Palestine was but one step along the way to the total destruction of the principalities and powers of the earth. The whole of the civilized world would be judged before God's kingdom would be established. The final chapter (52) of Jeremiah is a historical appendix, except for verses 28–30 taken verbatim from II Kings 24:18 and verses following.

Jeremiah was very much like the prophet Hosea in the Northern Kingdom. He was an extremely sensitive, shy person, who was called to say the unpopular thing and to take a firm and unbending stand against kings, against royal officials, against the priests, and against the people. Consequently, in the call of the prophet (Chapter 1) the emphasis is upon God's strengthening of the fearful young man. The visionary sacrament which Jeremiah experiences is not so much one of purification as it was in the case of Isaiah; it was rather an experience of being strengthened: "The Lord put forth his hand and touched my mouth; and the Lord said unto me, Behold I have put my words in thy mouth. . . . Thou, therefore, gird up thy loins, and arise, and speak unto them all that I command thee. Be not dismayed at them, lest I dismay thee before them. . . . They shall fight against thee; but they shall not prevail against thee, for I am with thee, saith the Lord, to deliver thee." It is not surprising then that Jeremiah more than any other prophet preserves a record of the internal struggles which he had with the commission which God had given him. Through most of his life he was forced to stand alone, hated and attacked on every hand, even by members of his own family. It is small wonder, then, that at times he wished that he had never been born: "Woe is me, my mother, that thou hast borne me a man of strife and a man of contention to the whole earth!" (Chapter 15:10). He prays to the Lord in his trouble: "Be not a terror unto me; thou art my refuge in the day of trouble" (Chapter 17:17). Perhaps the most vivid passage in this connection is Chapter 20:7 and verses following. There he exclaims that he knows that God has persuaded him, that God is stronger than he and has had his way with the prophet. The result, however, is that he has become a laughingstock; everybody makes fun of him. The reason is that every time he opens his mouth it is to cry out violence and destruction; the very word of the Lord which he has been sent to speak has become a means whereby people laugh at him. And yet when he says to himself that he will stop it, that he will no more talk in the name of the Lord, "Then there is in my heart as it were a burning fire shut up in my bones, and I am weary with forebearing, and I cannot contain it." Yet the weakness of the prophet within was hidden from all public gaze. He bore pain and hardship and loneliness and derision without outwardly flinching. He fulfilled the Lord's commission, and stood like a fortified wall against the popular prophets who spoke what the people wanted to hear, against the priests who offered their simplified slogans for salvation, against the wickedness of the last kings of Judah, and against the expediency of their royal officials. In one of his greatest texts he said: "Let not the wise man glory in his wisdom, neither let the mighty man glory in his might, let not the rich man glory in his riches, but let him that glorieth glory in this, that he hath understanding, and knoweth me, that I am the Lord who exerciseth loving kindness, justice, and righteousness in the earth; for in these things I delight, saith the Lord" (Chapter 9:23–24). As to the state of the nation, he chided the people with having changed their God for gods that were no gods: "my people have committed two evils: they have forsaken me, the fountain of living waters, and hewed them out cisterns, broken cisterns that can hold no water" (Chapter 2:11–13). The popular prophets have deceived the people and have continually spoken about peace, when to Jeremiah there was no peace. Said the prophet: "A wonderful and horrible thing is come to pass in the land. The prophets prophesy falsely and the priests bear rule at their direction, and my people love to have it so. What will ye do in the end thereof?" (Chapter 5:30–31.)

A number of Jeremiah's prophecies are dated, and most of these are gathered around certain critical periods in the history of Jerusalem shortly before it was finally destroyed by the Babylonians. The first of these dated sermons is the famous temple sermon, delivered by the prophet at a great festival when the temple courtyards were jammed with people. The narrative version is recounted in Chapter 26, whereas a fuller résumé of the sermon delivered on the occasion is to be found in Chapter 7. The great King Josiah had been killed the year before by the Egyptians (in 609 B.C.), and now they had taken over the country and put on the throne a son of Josiah who was pliable enough to do the Egyptians' bidding. At this critical juncture in Judah, when all dreams of freedom had been dashed and now the nation was again under the control of a foreign power, the priests had coined a new slogan: "The temple, the temple, rally around the temple that we may be saved." They evidently recalled to mind the time a hundred years before when the prophet Isaiah had proclaimed that God would not destroy the city of Jerusalem by the hand of the Assyrians. In the course of his remarks Jeremiah called this new slogan of the priests a lying word. What God wanted was obedience in the whole of the people's life; the critical state of affairs called for national repentance. The temple, on the other hand, was being made into a kind of a den or cave where robbers could hide out. God wanted no worship that was not based upon a deep-rooted repentance and desire to obey in all aspects of the common life. If the priests and people thought that simply rallying around the temple would keep them safe because God would not destroy his own house, let them remember how God had destroyed the old tabernacle at Shiloh in the days of Eli and Samuel during the eleventh century B.C. These remarks so angered the priests and popular prophets that they immediately sought to put Jeremiah to death. His life was saved only by the intervention of the royal officials and by certain wise laymen among the people who recalled that a hundred years before Micah had prophesied that Jerusalem would be destroyed and yet Hezekiah, King of Judah, had not put him to death. Instead he had entreated the favor of the Lord, had repented of sin, and the Lord had saved the city. Should not the same be done again?

As a result of his temple sermon Jeremiah evidently had to go into hiding for a period of time. We next hear of him after the battle of Carchemish in 605 B.C., when Nebuchadnezzar, King of Babylon, had defeated the Egyptians. This meant, of course, that the royal house of Judah would shortly have to change its allegiance, shifting it from Egypt to Babylon. At this juncture Jeremiah could no longer refrain from speaking. Yet he was forbidden to address any public assembly in the temple. As a result, according to the narrative related in Chapter 36, he dictated to his friend and confidant, Baruch, a digest of all his prophecies from the beginning until that moment. Baruch then took it into a great assembly in the temple area and read the scroll in the hearing of all who were gathered there. The words made a tremendous impression, particularly upon certain of the better men among the royal officials. They succeeded in getting an audience with the king and had the roll read before him. The latter cynically cut it in pieces, while it was being read to him, and burned it in a fire. Undaunted, Jeremiah dictated his prophecies to Baruch again, with much additional matter. It is not improbable that this second scroll was preserved; in any event, the story provides one illustration of how some of the prophecies may have been preserved.

Most dramatic of all were the adventures of the prophet during the final siege of Jerusalem in 588–587 B.C. To Jeremiah, Nebuchadnezzar was a servant of the Lord for the punishment of Judah, and he believed that it was God's will that the whole civilized earth should be for a season subjugated by the Babylonians. When the Judean royal officials, with promises of Egyptian aid, had decided again to rebel against Nebuchadnezzar, Jeremiah could not restrain himself. He had counseled against the foolhardiness of this course in the days before the first rebellion in 598 B.C. He worked hard to avoid a second rebellion about 594–593 B.C., when it seemed that one was planned (cf. Chapters 27–29). And now the second and final revolt appeared to Jeremiah as nothing short of complete rebellion against God and his leadership of the nation. And so it was that when the government officials had decided upon their course of action, the words of Jeremiah became exceedingly troublesome. When finally the city was put under siege by the Babylonian army the government decided it could no longer afford the luxury of Jeremiah's free speech and he was confined during a good part of the siege. At one time the Egyptian army did appear and the Babylonians had to break off temporarily from Jerusalem. Just before this Jeremiah had purchased a field from one of his family in the neighboring town of Anathoth. He did this, not because he wanted the field, but because he wished to suggest to his people that though Jerusalem would be destroyed, this was not the end of the nation. They would again sow and plant; they would again want and need their fields. When the siege was lifted he attempted to leave the city to claim his field, but he was immediately arrested and accused of deserting to the Babylonians (Chapter 37:11 ff.).

One of the most interesting sections in the narrative about Jeremiah is his relation to the King of Judah, Zedekiah. We read in Chapter 38 that the king will not permit his royal officials to put the prophet to death. Surreptitiously he visits Jeremiah to ask for the word of the Lord while a siege is in progress. The narrative suggests that the king had made this inquiry repeatedly (cf. Chapter 21), but each time Jeremiah gives the same answer. If Jerusalem is to be saved it must surrender promptly to the Babylonians and cease its fruitless rebellion. If King Zedekiah would save his life, then he must immediately go forth to the officials of the King of Babylon (Chapter 38:14 ff.). The king expresses fear that he will be given over to those Judeans who have already fallen away to the Babylonians; but Jeremiah swears to him that this will not happen, that it is not the intention of the Lord so to do. It is an interesting fact that the king had a great respect for the prophet and seems to have realized that he was speaking the truth. Yet he did not have the strength of character to act upon what he knew to be right. He was a captive of his government and of the policies previously established. The result was that the siege ground on to its bitter close with the complete destruction of the city.

After the conclusion of the siege, Jeremiah was given permission by the Babylonian officials either to go into exile or to stay in Palestine. He chose the latter, but after the murder of the official whom the Babylonians had left in charge, a sizable group of the remaining Judeans fled for safety to Egypt and dragged the protesting prophet with them. There, it seems evident, he must have died, though not without protesting profusely against the idolatrous practices of other Judean exiles whom he found in Egypt when he arrived there. This was a prophet who suffered with and died for his people, an intermediary between them and God, a lonely man who had given up all for the sake of his prophetic calling.

C. THE LAST OF THE OLD TESTAMENT PROPHETS

The prophet Ezekiel was a priest who had been taken into exile to Babylon in March 597 B.C., at the conclusion of the Babylonians' first siege of Jerusalem. His prophecies have been very neatly arranged and carefully dated by a group of disciples, the dates being given by the years of the captivity of the young King Jehoiachin who had been taken into captivity with the other exiles in 597 B.C. Chapters 1–3 represent the prophet's call and commission. Chapters 4–24 come from the period before the final fall of Jerusalem in 587 B.C.; in them he desperately attempts to convict his people of their sin and to make them understand that Jerusalem shall indeed fall and that there is no escape from the punishment. Chapters 25–32 are prophecies against the nations surrounding Palestine. Chapters 33–37 were delivered after the fall of Jerusalem and their dominant note is one of hope for God's restoration of his people in the land. Chapters 38–39 appear to be a symbolic picture of a final war before the establishment of God's kingdom on earth, a war with the unrepentant and barbarian hosts of darkness from the distant reaches of the North. Following that the prophet gives a picture of the new Jerusalem and the new Palestine in Chapters 40–48.

One of the first things we note about the prophet Ezekiel is his psychological peculiarity. He is an extremely visionary man who makes use of many symbols because he seems to see each thing around him as capable of possessing symbolic meaning. He begins his prophecy with the vision of God enthroned upon his heavenly chariot; God visits him and calls him to be his prophet. Unlike Isaiah and Jeremiah in their inaugural visions, Ezekiel becomes so absorbed in the vision of the chariot which he sees that he must describe it in considerable detail. There is also a reference to the prophet's dumbness; God made his tongue cleave to the roof of his mouth so that he was not able to speak, except at those times when God spoke to him and opened his mouth (Chapter 3:26–27). We read that he was told to lie upon his left side for 390 days in order to symbolize the captivity of the Northern Kingdom of Israel, and then to lie on his right side for forty days in order to symbolize the captivity of Judah.

A number of people have attempted to psychoanalyze Ezekiel, with spectacular results. It is very much to be doubted that any of these attempts can be said to be successful. On the other hand, it is probable that Ezekiel was not perfectly normal and well-integrated. He was most evidently a peculiar person, but he could speak with power and in so doing employ the most vivid and powerful images. The people in exile evidently listened to him with great respect and his words were carefully preserved, even though there may have been such a long space of time between their original proclamation and their subsequent written form that some of the power of the personality has disappeared. One thing seems certain, however, that Ezekiel was a very straightforward, abrupt, and peremptory person. He understood his calling to be that of Israel's watchman (Chapter 3:17). Whether the people heard or whether they would not hear, he was to speak the warning.

He hears God say to him: "Behold, I have made thy face hard against their faces and thy forehead hard against their foreheads" (3:8). A suggestion of the same abruptness is to be seen in a refrain repeated throughout the Book of Ezekiel. It is to the effect that whatever happens, happens so that the people of Judah or the world may know that God is God: "Ye shall know that I am the Lord"; "And they shall know that I am the Lord; and I have not said in vain that I would do this evil unto them" (Chapter 6:7, 10).

There are also many suggestions of Ezekiel's priestly training. The central tenet of the theology of the Jerusalem priests was that God had graciously consented in the time of Moses to tabernacle in the midst of his people, and that as long as he did so the people would remain a people. In Chapters 9–10 Ezekiel portrays the fall of Jerusalem, not as a battle in which the Babylonian army is victorious, but as a purposive work of God, carried out by his angelic messengers. At the conclusion when the marking out of the city for burning is at an end, Ezekiel sees God's chariot and God himself, surrounded by a glorious light (the "glory" of God), ascend from the temple and leave the city. For a Jerusalem priest there would be no more powerful symbol of God's determination to destroy his people than to portray his departure from their midst. It is equally to be expected that in the new Jerusalem, which God will restore, the "glory" of God should be seen re-entering the temple; that was a sign that the restored people would again become the people of God (Chapter 44:4 ff.). It is also characteristic of the priest that he should be mainly concerned with proper religious arrangements in the new temple in Jerusalem, and less concerned about God's redemptive love working for the salvation of all men.

In Ezekiel's view of history the fall of Jerusalem was the first of God's just acts of judgment against current civilization which was alienated from him, its lord and master. God was first going to destroy and scatter his people. After that he would turn upon all the nations of the civilized world; there is nothing permanent or final in any of them; all of them are in sin and all of them will be judged before the new day will dawn. But after the day of judgment will come the beginnings of the new era. At this time God will restore his people to Palestine and give to them a new heart and a new spirit whereby they can live as his people obediently and loyally. Ezekiel has no faith that mankind can gradually evolve into that state of goodness whereby it can live happily and purely in the earth. In Chapters 36–37, which are among the most beautiful chapters in the book, the restoration of Israel is accompanied by the creation of a new humanity, a new heart, and a new spirit. When that happens the people will remember their former way of life; they will see that it was not good; they will loathe it and have no desire whatsoever to return to it. Yet, says the prophet, the people should realize that they have done nothing whatsoever to merit this act of God. God does it for his own sake so that all men in the earth may know that it is God who has built the ruling places and replanted them, that it is God who has cleansed them and given them what they have, so that all praise must be given to him rather than to any earthly power or merit. Ezekiel's contemporary, Jeremiah, was saying a similar thing in a very different way, when he spoke about the new covenant which God was about to make with the house of Israel. It was not an outward covenant, an external treaty which could be broken as was the covenant of Moses. It was to be a new covenant, a law written within the heart so that all men will know the Lord, and religious education will no longer be needed; "for they shall all know me, from the least of them unto the greatest of them, saith the Lord: for I will forgive their iniquity, and their sin will I remember no more" (Jeremiah 31:31–34). In Ezekiel 37 the restoration of Israel with the new heart and the new spirit is vividly pictured in terms of a valley of dry and scattered bones, which are reclothed with flesh and restored to life. This is God's miracle; they that were dead now live again. "And I will put my spirit in you, and ye shall live, and I will place you in your own land; and ye shall know that I, the Lord, have spoken it and performed it, saith the Lord" (Chapter 37:14). The central elements of this viewpoint are a basic part of the biblical hope for the future. The salvation of man is not within himself or within his current civilization. Man's ultimate hope lies within God himself and in the miracle of God's gift of life. As God once created life, so he will re-create it with a new heart and a new spirit. When that happens, man will be enabled to live in God's good earth in peace and security, in love and in loyalty, using the good things of earth to the glory of God and the benefit of all men.

Old Testament prophecy reaches its height in the marvelous prophetic poems of Second Isaiah. This work begins in Chapter 40 of the Book of Isaiah and has as its central concern God's restoration of a scattered people, the first step in God's creation of a new heaven and a new earth. Nearly all scholars are agreed that Chapters 40–55 of Isaiah belong to this unknown and unnamed prophet whose work is appended to that of the earlier Isaiah of Jerusalem. The chapters appear to date from about 540 B.C., just as the Persian King Cyrus is about to take over the whole of the Babylonian empire. The question uppermost in the minds of the people of that day is what is going on and what does it all mean. It is with that question that the prophet begins his prophecy. The source of Chapters 56–66 is not so clear. While some scholars in the past have spoken of a third Isaiah, there is more of a tendency today to think of these chapters as belonging in the school of Second Isaiah. Some of this material was written by him and the rest is an elaboration of his words by his disciples. The whole comes from the period after the restoration of the people from exile between about 539 and 500 B.C.

When the newly returned Jews were desperately trying to rebuild their temple, under the promise that if the temple were once rebuilt God would bless them wholly, the school of prophecy belonging to Second Isaiah remained unconvinced. Instead they heard the word of the Lord saying: "Heaven is my throne, and the earth is my footstool; what manner of house will ye build for me? And what place shall be my rest? For all these things hath my hand made, and so all these things came to be, saith the Lord. But it is to this man that I will look, even to him that is poor and of a contrite spirit, and that trembleth at my word" (Chapter 66:1–2). These words are certainly in the spirit of a First Isaiah and a Jeremiah. The Lord of the world is not in need of temples made with hands (cf. Psalm 50 and Acts 17:24–25); he is much more concerned with humble and contrite people who will serve him faithfully.

Second Isaiah begins in Chapter 40:1–11 with his call and commission by God. The prophet first hears God speaking to his heavenly assembly, commanding them to go and comfort his people Israel. In verse 3 a heavenly voice makes the proclamation: "Prepare ye in the wilderness the highway of the Lord." Then a second voice is heard, saying: "Cry" (i.e., "make the prophetic proclamation"). And the prophet replies (40:6 R.S.V.), "What shall I cry?" The answer has to do first with the transitoriness of all things earthly in contrast to the enduring stability of the word of God. That word now proclaims good tidings to Jerusalem; the return of the Lord is at hand, and he will treat his scattered flock like a good shepherd, gathering the lambs in his arm.

In Chapter 40:12 and following verses, the prophet pauses for meditation upon the nature of God. He does so because Israel, God's people, is a weak, dispirited, and scattered people with no hope left in them. They say, "My way is hid from the Lord, and the justice due me is passed away from my God" (verse 27). The prophet replies, "Hast thou not known? Hast thou not heard? The everlasting God, the Lord, the Creator of the end of the earth, fainteth not, neither is weary; there is no searching of his understanding." Recall the Creator of the world, who measured the heavens and the seas and before whom the nations are as a drop in a bucket. What is there in heaven and in earth to which he can be compared? The thing made is not the maker; the thing ruled is not the ruler. To whom or to what can this great one be compared? There is nothing in heaven or in earth that is his equal or equivalent. This is the God who now is at hand. He alone is the one who can give power to the faint. They who wait on him shall renew their strength and mount up with wings as eagles.

At this point the prophet begins his prophecy; that is, God begins to speak through him. Here God is portrayed as calling a great assembly of all the nations in order to decide what is the meaning of the coming of Cyrus. The nations are represented as vastly worried over the events, as indeed they were, and industriously preparing their idols who are supposed to give answers to their problems. Meanwhile God speaks to Israel in order to encourage her, to assure her that she is indeed his chosen one, that he has chosen her to be his witness in the current crisis, that he has not forsaken her, that he has not cast her off. Israel is not to fear, for God is with her; she is not to be dismayed for he will strengthen her. The council of the nations is then represented as gathering and the question thrown at them as to the meaning of Cyrus. The idols of the world are then told to produce their case and to explain the meaning of the current events. There is silence followed by the exclamation that they should do *something* whether good or bad, *anything* so that people may know that they are gods! Then in disgust the prophet exclaims: "Behold, ye are nothing, and your work is nothing; an abomination is he that chooseth you!" (Chapter 41:24). This, of course, is a very vivid bit of comparative religion. The gods of the world are here attacked at their weakest point. They were never devised or conceived as deities responsible for history. To the biblical man the God who had revealed himself to him was the sole God in charge of the world because he alone could control it, because he alone was the sovereign of history. Therefore God exclaims through the prophet that he alone is the one who has raised up Cyrus, that he alone has declared the meaning of history from the very beginning, and that of the peoples of the world it is only God's prophet in Jerusalem who actually understands the meaning of events.

To Second Isaiah, Cyrus the Persian is God's instrument to inaugurate the new age. He will break down all the walls and barriers and secret places, and in this respect will actually serve as God's Messiah (Chapter 45:1 ff.). Before the world can be drawn to God the centers of world power and pride must be shattered. This, according to the prophet, God is doing through Cyrus. On the other hand, a saving mission to the world has been given by God to his servant, Israel. God is about to restore Israel to Palestine, but for what reason? God says to the prophet: "It is too light a thing that the energies of the servant should be expended solely on restoring the people of Israel to Palestine." God has a far more important mission for the servant than that: "I will also give thee for a light to the Gentiles that thou mayest be my salvation unto the end of the earth" (Chapter 49:6). God's servant, Israel, or the ideal Israel, was not brought into being nor is it being restored simply for its own good. It has a mission to the world; it is to be God's agent of justice, so that blind eyes can be opened and prisoners set free and all those that sit in darkness (Chapter 42:1–7). God's servant is not to be the light of the world through the use of power and of force. Its work is to be accomplished peacefully, as a teacher and a prophet and as one who bears the bruises of the world in his own body. The needed force and power will be applied by Cyrus. In this way Second Isaiah solves in a most remarkable way the old problem of the Israelite theology of the Messiah. How is the Messiah as the leader of Israel to be a savior and a destroyer at the same time? The prophet splits the two aspects apart, and applies the title "Messiah" solely to the Persian emperor, Cyrus. God's servant as the instrument of his salvation for the Gentiles cannot effect its mission except by being willing to suffer and to die in order to effect it.

The best known of the servant passages is Chapter 53. The speakers are presumably the kings of the nations who now explain what previously they had not known (Chapter 52:15). To them this servant was an ugly, despised, and rejected person, filled with disease and sickness. They thought he was simply another of the world's afflicted people whom God for some reason was chastising. But now they have discovered that the servant was wounded for their transgressions and with his stripes they are healed. They confess, "All we like sheep have gone astray; we have turned everyone to his own way; and the Lord hath laid on him the iniquity of us all." The interpretation of this passage has been much disputed, and questions have always been asked concerning it (cf. Acts 8:34). Who is the servant—is he Israel or is he an individual? The prophet is by no means clear, and perhaps purposely leaves the question unanswered. His figure of the servant at one moment will be the whole people of Israel, at another moment the ideal Israel, and at still another a figure who in himself personifies the true role which Israel should assume in this world. The prophet explains to Israel in these various ways the meaning of her sufferings in the world. As the redemptive servant she must also understand that she is the vicarious sufferer for the sins of the world.

Jewish scholarship has always read these passages with a collective meaning. The figure of the servant is a personification of themselves and an interpretation of their past life of suffering in the world. The Christian, on the other hand, has always read Chapter 53 in relation to Jesus Christ, because it seemed such a perfect description of the meaning of Christ's life and death. Second Isaiah's figure of the servant has thus played a more prominent role in Christian theology than it has in the theology of Judaism. The reason is probably to be found in Jesus himself. It seems evident that both he and the early Church interpreted the role of the Messiah as one of being the suffering servant. For this reason Christ died, bearing in his body the sins of the world. And yet afterwards God highly exalted him so that his kingship was not exercised from a throne in this world. From the standpoint of the Bible as a whole Second Isaiah is the one Old Testament figure who gives the most eloquent interpretation of the redemptive work of God in the world and of the meaning of God's choice of a people who are to be his servant. In doing so he has also given the most glowing and triumphant portrayals of the power and the love of God which are to be found in the surviving literature of Israel.

The history of Israelite prophecy now draws rapidly to a close. Sometime in the sixth or early fifth century Arab invasions brought an end to the kingdom of Edom. The prophet Obadiah saw this event approaching and interpreted it as the judgment of God upon Edom because of its pride and because of the part which it played in the destruction of Judah in 587 B.C. Edom had taken over large portions of territory from the former Judah and had taken advantage of her weakened condition. Haggai and Zechariah are two prophets who together were instrumental in getting the temple rebuilt in Jerusalem between 520 and 515 B.C. In so doing, however, they made certain suggestions which later proved embarrassing. They seem to imply that once the temple was built, the troubles of Judah would be over and the glorious day of the Lord would arrive. Zerubbabel, the Judean governor of the province, it will be remembered, was expected to fill the role of the Messiah. This was a revival of older views which disregarded almost entirely the fresh interpretations of Second Isaiah. Immediately after the temple was rebuilt the whole subject was dropped and nothing is heard from it again. Zerubbabel did not become the Messiah, and the prophets who said that he would be would undoubtedly have been forgotten had it not been for their encouragement of the rebuilding of the temple. About the same time, or during the following century, a prophet named Joel proclaimed that the day of the Lord was at hand when a terrible locust plague visited his country. His words too would probably have been forgotten and not preserved in the canon had it not been for two beautiful passages about repentance and about the coming day when the spirit of the Lord will be poured out on all flesh (Joel 2:12–14, 28–29).

Two prophecies in which the spirit of pre-exilic prophecy survived are those of Malachi and Jonah in the fifth century. Malachi directs his words against the priesthood of his time, men who are not taking their duties seriously, who are disgracing their offices and are causing many people to "stumble in the law." Furthermore, they are engaging in wholesale divorces, violating the solemn covenant which they made with the wives of their youth, and this is the type of thing which the Lord hates. The day is coming when all such wickedness will be radically purged, though "unto you that fear my name shall the sun of righteousness arise with healing in its wings" (Chapter 4:2).

Jonah is a most eloquent book. It differs from other prophecies in that it is the story about a prophet rather than a collection of the words of the prophet. The prophet chosen for the

179

story is mentioned in II Kings 14:25 as a popular prophet who predicted the great victory for Israel in the reign of Jeroboam II. He was a contemporary of Amos, the latter seeing in the same events predicted by Jonah a warning of future doom. The language of the book is much later, however, than the eighth century, and most scholars date the book in the fifth century. It was written at a time when nationalistic exclusivism on the part of the Jerusalem priesthood had become very strong. It sought, therefore, to remind the new community of the restored exiles what Second Isaiah had previously reminded them of, namely that the love of God was broader than they were conceiving it, that he did not choose Israel in order to play favorites among the peoples of the earth, but that he chose her and his prophets to be instruments of his saving power in the earth. The true prophet is, therefore, the author of the book, rather than the man about whom the story is told. The book serves as a kind of parable. Jonah is portrayed as a prophet in Palestine who hears the command of the Lord to become an instrument of mercy to the city which was the worst enemy of his people, Nineveh, the capital of Assyria. Refusing to carry out the Lord's command, he flees in the opposite direction by boat as fast as he can go. But the Lord will not let him get away. He hurls a great storm into the sea, the sailors discover by a means typical of the day that the culprit is Jonah, and they are forced to throw him into the sea. God has him swallowed by a big fish who vomits him up again on the shore of Palestine, where he is once again commanded to go to Nineveh.

Many people, when they read the story of the big fish which swallowed Jonah, never get any further because they bog down in speculation about whether or not such a thing could actually happen. One can be certain that if the author of the book had only known the trouble this fish was to cause the minds of men, he would have been perfectly willing to substitute some other device. His concern is simply to show that one cannot run away from God; the fish is simply a device in the story whereby Jonah is returned and faced again with his duty. This time the prophet obeys, and in a remarkable

way his proclamation gets results; the city of Nineveh wholeheartedly repents, so that God does not have to punish it by
destruction. Yet this is precisely what disgusts the prophet
Jonah exceedingly. He quotes one of the great confessions of
God's love in the Old Testament, namely that God is merciful
and gracious and slow to anger and full of mercy, and uses
that as precisely his excuse for his anger. The mercy of God
is a fine thing when it was directed to his own people, but a
disgusting thing when directed toward his enemies. Hence the
prophet exclaims that he would prefer to die rather than to
live. He goes outside the city and builds a booth there in order
to see what will happen. A heat wave arrives, but a plant
which has grown up over the hut protects it from the sun.
During the night the plant withers and dies because of a worm
that attacks it, and again Jonah wishes in his heart that he
might die. And now gently God asks whether Jonah has a
right to be angry, and Jonah in great disgust affirms his right
to be angry even unto death. Then God replies even more
gently that inasmuch as he, Jonah, has had such great concern
for a plant which was simply a child of the night, should not
he, God, have concern for a great city wherein there are 120,-
000 people who cannot tell their right hand from their left?
And as though that were not sufficient, he makes a final humorous appeal to the prophet's common sense by suggesting
"and also much cattle"—that is, it would be a shame to destroy
so many excellent animals!

The Book of Jonah was obviously written by a great spirit
who was struggling against the narrowing of the faith within
the confines of the tiny province of Judah during the period
after the exile. Yet the book stands at the very end of the
prophetic movement. From this time forth the community of
Judah seems unable longer to listen to prophets. Priests and
lawyers in the law are those who are most needed in the developing Judaism, whereas prophets only create embarrass-
ments. The belief that God was about to do the new thing in
each succeeding crisis faded, and its place was taken by what
was known as apocalypticism. That is a view which interprets
current history as being a dark and terrible time which is con-

stantly getting darker and more terrible until it will finally be brought to a halt by the intervention of God and the coming of the Messiah. In this viewpoint the "now" loses a great deal of its dramatic significance; it becomes a time only for watchful waiting and for obedience as one understands obedience to the Lord. The period of excitement and urgency is gone. Indeed, it would seem that those who framed the canon of scripture were quite right in leaving the centuries between Ezra and John the Baptist very largely a blank. Only with the opening of the New Testament is the spirit of Old Testament prophecy again revived and the Lord who is about to do the new thing is again known, this time in Jesus Christ.

CHAPTER II

THE DEVOTIONAL AND WISDOM LITERATURE

We now turn to three major collections of poetry in the Bible. These are the Psalms, Proverbs, and Job. We shall first have a brief discussion of the Psalms as a manual of public worship, and then treat Proverbs and Job together as a part of the story of Israel's wise men. To complete that story we must add the third of the wisdom books in the Old Testament; that is, the small prose Book of Ecclesiastes.

A. THE PSALMS

The Book of Psalms has been the most widely read book in the Old Testament. Among Christians as well as Jews it has been the primary source for hymns and liturgical expressions. If the Bible as a whole can be said to be a book about what God has done, the Psalms may be said to be a volume of devotional testimony, composed in the light of God's gracious activity. Hymns of praise and thanksgiving, meditations, liturgy for special occasions, the outpouring of souls in a great variety of difficulties—all these are included and many more. While the individual psalms differ greatly in their quality of utterance, even those unlearned in biblical lore cannot fail to be impressed and inspired by the depth of feeling and sheer lyric beauty of many of the psalms, a depth and beauty that appear even in translation. Israel was among the poorest of ancient peoples; yet in literature she surpassed all her contemporaries of western Asia. This is surely not an accident. There was something about the people's faith in God which had an extremely purifying effect both upon the soul and upon the way in which the thoughts of the soul were expressed. As a result the successors of biblical faith have been able to use most of the psalms, almost without change, for over twenty centuries.

The Psalms as we now have them are divided into five books: book one, Psalms 1–41; two, Psalms 42–72; three, Psalms 73–89; four, Psalms 90–106; five, 107–50. Each of the first four books ends with a special doxology. For example, Psalm 41:13: "Blessed be the Lord God of Israel from everlasting, and to everlasting. Amen, and Amen." These words are not a part of Psalm 41, but are a conclusion to the first book of the Psalms. Psalm 150 forms a doxology to book five and to the whole Psalter. It is a final call for everything that has breath to praise the Lord to the accompaniment of a great symphony played by the temple orchestra. It should be noted that the psalms were not written to be used as for the most part we use them today. They were composed as hymns to be sung in worship at the Jerusalem temple. Many of them still have musical notations appended to them, but unfortunately we know nothing about ancient music and, therefore, we do not know what these notations mean. For example, Psalm 22 has a note at the beginning, "To the chief musician upon Aijeleth Shahar." We presume that this is a reference to a type of music or tune to which this psalm was sung, but we do not know for sure. It is important, however, to realize that this great manual of public devotion was undoubtedly the hymnbook of the Jerusalem temple during the fifth and fourth centuries B.C.

Who wrote the psalms and when were they written? These are questions which cannot be answered. The psalms represent every phase of Israelite life between at least the tenth century B.C. and the time of Nehemiah and Ezra. It is not probable that any psalms are preserved in the Psalter which were written after the fifth century B.C. On the other hand, it is certainly possible, if not probable, that there are psalms or at least passages in the psalms which date long before the tenth century. This is because Israelite musicians occasionally borrowed poetic compositions from their pagan neighbors, changing the wording as necessary to fit the worship of the Lord of Israel. Psalm 29, for example, was certainly a hymn to the Canaanite god Baal before it was borrowed by Israel and adapted for worship in the Jerusalem temple. All but about fifty of the psalms are ascribed to various people. Three fourths of these or nearly half of all the psalms are entitled, "A Psalm of David." This has traditionally been taken to mean that David wrote the psalms that bear his name. Such a view was believed even by the Jewish scribes who edited the present Book of Psalms long before the time of Christ. As a result they tried, on occasion, to find a proper setting in the life of David when the psalm might well have been composed. For example, Psalm 3 has the scribal notation, "A Psalm of David, when he fled from Absalom his son." Psalm 18 has a much longer note, suggesting that David spoke the words of this psalm at a time when the Lord had delivered him from all his enemies, particularly from the hand of King Saul. Scholars today do not find these notes a very satisfactory explanation of the contents of the psalms, nor of the facts about them as we now know these facts. David was very interested in music, and according to I Chronicles it was David who established the various services of worship which were later taken over into the service of the Solomonic temple. As one who was very interested in music, David even went so far, evidently, as to hire foreign musicians to assist Israelite musicians in creating a beautiful musical setting for the worship in Jerusalem. Liturgical music and psalmody, therefore, owe their origin in Israel to David. This should not be interpreted to mean that David wrote all the music himself, nor that he composed the psalms which were used as the text to be sung. It means rather that he was the patron of religious music. Thus when nearly half of the psalms bear the heading, "A Psalm of David," we should no longer think in terms of Davidic authorship. Psalm 29, for example, bears this heading, though as already observed we now know that it was a Canaanite psalm borrowed and adapted for the worship of Israel. David may have adapted it, but he did not write it. Instead, the title simply means that such and such a psalm belonged to the Davidic or royal collection, a group of psalms of which he was the patron, which he sponsored for use in the Jerusalem temple. It means that the particular psalm in question once belonged to "The Davidic Psalter," that is, to "His Majesty's Hymnbook." This does not mean that all of the psalms which bear the Davidic title were originally composed in David's time or before. It means that David, having established a royal psalter, provided the temple with a royally sponsored hymnal, to which additions were subsequently made. Other psalms were taken from other sources. Hence we may say that the present Book of Psalms is a collection derived from previous collections.

There is one note in several of the psalms that often bothers the Christian conscience. That is the outcries of particular psalmists against their enemies, prayers that God will take vengeance upon the wicked. Psalms 35, 41, and 109 are vivid examples. Almost instinctively we feel that the deepest note in prayer is to be found in the words of Jesus: "Father forgive them, for they know not what they do." This word of defense, however, should be said for the biblical psalmist. It must be remembered that he lived in a time very different from our own, when security in society was a comparatively rare thing. It was not uncommon for a man literally to be surrounded by enemies, and to suffer constantly therefrom. If he were a loyal and pious man, he could not but see that his enemies cared little for the Lord of Israel or for his worship and law. It is customary for the psalmist, therefore, to link his own predicament with that of God's just and righteous work in the world as a whole. He understands himself to be a member of God's people, wherever they may be, a people which knows the Lord, acknowledges his claim, and loves and obeys him. He also knows that the world is full of people who care nothing for the Lord. Thus the trouble in which the psalmist finds himself becomes in a measure a part of the whole trouble with the world. It was against the law of the Lord for a man to take vengeance in his own hands. Vengeance belonged to God himself. Thus the psalmist in praying to God could not but ask God to defeat the plans of his enemies and to take vengeance upon them. Yet he knew that when the word "vengeance" was applied to God it did not mean "getting even." God's vengeance was simply his righteous determination that wickedness in the world would not go unchecked and unpunished, while righteousness in the end would triumph.

As an example of Israelite psalms, let us pause for a moment on the most familiar of them all, Psalm 23. Israelite poetry is distinguished, not by its rhyme, but by its rhythm. The typical poetic line has two parts, more rarely three, each part distinguished by a certain number of beats. Each beat falls on a stressed syllable in the most important word, and around it may be one to four unstressed syllables. The most common Hebrew line is one with two parts, each having three beats. For example,

Psalm 29:1:

> *Give* unto *the Lord,* O ye *mighty,*
> give unto *the Lord* glory and *strength.*

The Twenty-third Psalm is arranged in English in six verses. The original Hebrew has nine poetic lines. If we would understand the detailed meaning of the original poet, it is of course necessary for us to recover the original poetic form. The following is a fairly literal attempt to indicate that form, though it is often impossible to fit the Hebrew into the same number of English words.

> The Lord's my shepherd, I'll not want;
>> In green pastures he beds me;
> By waters of restfulness he leads me;
>> My life he revives.
> He leadeth me in paths of safety
>> For the sake of his name.
> E'en though I walk in a valley of deep danger
>> I'll fear no harm,
> For thou art with me;

187

Thy rod and thy staff
> They comfort me.
Thou preparest before me a table
> In front of mine enemies.
Thou anointest my head with oil;
> My cup full!
Surely goodness and mercy shall follow me
> All the days of my life,
And I shall dwell in the household of the Lord
> To the end of days.

The psalm begins with four lines of three beats in the first part and two beats in the second. The last four lines are of the same nature. In the middle there is a longer line of three parts, each with two beats. Such is the very carefully arranged form of the poem.

As to meaning, the psalmist is simply saying that God is good, that he is trustworthy. Yet as a good poet he does not want to use abstractions; he wishes to make his point very vivid so that it will be felt as well as known, and for this reason he uses vivid images. His first image is that of the good shepherd. If we would enter into the emotional intensity of the psalm, we must in the first instance become sheep! In Palestine because of the heat and the scarcity of water the sheep are very dependent upon their shepherd. Green grass is as rare as water, except for a month or two in the spring. Hence the psalmist pictures the ways of the Lord as those of a good shepherd taking care of his sheep in the difficult land of Palestine. His general theme is that I as a sheep will lack nothing. The psalmist then specifies why that is so: at night the shepherd beds me down in a grassy meadow where there is plenty of wonderful grazing. He leadeth me to restful and refreshing waters after a long, hot day. The familiar words, "He restoreth my soul," actually mean that he revives my life! After the heat and weariness of the day, I am revived. Because he is the good shepherd he naturally leads me in safe paths. The shepherd's "name" is actually himself in biblical language. He does what he does for his name's sake, simply because he is the good shepherd and he will do no other. Consequently, even though I walk through a valley of deep darkness and danger I need not fear that any harm will befall me. Then comes the summarizing line: I need not fear "for Thou art with me. Thy rod and Thy staff, they comfort me." The shepherd's rod is his club, by which he protects his sheep from predatory enemies. His staff is the shepherd's crook, whereby he guides and assists the sheep in difficult places. The club and the staff are vivid symbols, then, of the two sides of the working both of the shepherd and of God. The power of God as protection and salvation is the ground for one's confidence.

In the second part of the psalm the picture changes to a bedouin encampment in the desert. Arab hospitality is proverbial, and the protection that it affords is here used as a symbol of the goodness of God. The "I" of the psalm is now a lone fugitive in the desert, where a person without a people is in real danger. Through the day he has been running from his enemies but now has been accepted by the wonderful host within the latter's encampment or household. Now he observes all the wonderful things being done for him, which of course he does not deserve. The host spreads out before him a table with plenty of food from which he can eat in perfect safety, though his enemies who have been chasing him are watching with greedy eyes just beyond the encampment. In a land where water is scarce, washing with perfumed oil was much appreciated, hence the anointing of the head with oil. The psalmist's cup is always full, a welcome thing after a hot, dry day. At this point the psalmist breaks off the description of God's encampment and exclaims: "Instead of enemies pursuing me, goodness and mercy pursue me, and that will be so all the days of my life. Consequently I have determined to make a choice; I shall now take up my abode in God's household to the end of my days." We know indeed that God is good. Yet when a psalmist pictures the goodness of God by means of these powerful symbols, and does so in a beautifully constructed poetic form, the result is a composition of great simplicity, but also of great power. One understands God's goodness intellectually, but much more one comes to *know* it in the biblical sense of that word "know."

The Twenty-third Psalm is a specially beautiful product of the Israelite psalmist. Yet it does not stand alone, because all of the psalms when studied in this fashion speak to the whole being of man with a power possessed equally by no other devotional literature in the Bible.[1]

B. THE WISDOM LITERATURE

The prophet Jeremiah in one place tells us that all of the intellectual classes of Israel were angry with him because he had condemned them (Chapter 18:18). These classes were the priests who were in charge of the law and of religious instruction as a whole, the prophets to whom the word of the Lord came, meaning the interpretation of current life by direct inspiration, and the wise who were responsible for counsel. Neither history nor prophecy tell us very much about this class of intellectuals known as the wise men, nor do we know under what occasions their advice and counsel was given. Jeremiah, however, classes them with the priests and the prophets among the important circles of leadership in Jerusalem and has condemned them as unable to save the people by their counsel. As David was the patron of psalms and music in Israel, so Solomon was the traditional founder of the wisdom movement. He was not a theologian nor a particularly pious man. As pointed out in the description of his reign, he was a man of culture who was intensely interested in becoming a leader in the main stream of the world's cultural movements during his day. Thus, as I Kings 4:29–34 describes it, he cultivated wisdom and in so doing had close dealings with all of the wise men of the countries round about, particularly of the neighboring Canaanites, the Arabs in the desert, and the wise

[1] For an excellent and more detailed study of the Psalter see Samuel Terrien, *The Psalms and Their Meaning for Today*, New York, Bobbs-Merrill Co., 1952.

men of Egypt. He is said to have uttered "three thousand proverbs, and his songs were a thousand and five." There can be no doubt, therefore, that the wise men as an intellectual class were first encouraged and sponsored as a movement during the reign of Solomon. For this reason, the product of the movement bears his name as its sponsor.

We now know from the literatures of Egypt and Mesopotamia, as uncovered by the archaeologists, that nearly every people of the biblical world had a great interest in the particular type of wisdom with which the wise men of the day were concerned. It is a wisdom of the world, a use of insight and common sense to discern how the world works and how we can best get along in it. Fundamentally, it is a character education movement, and, as we have discovered in our own time, this concentration on prudential ethics is able to flourish in a great variety of theological contexts. Thus Solomon could discuss ethics or matters of "wisdom" with an Egyptian or Canaanite, and not allow the theological differences between them to bother very much. The wise men were simply not deeply interested in theology in the way that Israel's historians and prophets and psalmists were.

It is the Book of Proverbs in the Old Testament which preserves a portion of the Israelite's wisdom. Like the Book of Psalms it is a collection made from previous collections. The heart of the book is in Chapter 10–22:16. The section is provided with a heading, "The Proverbs of Solomon." Chapters 25–29 are also said to be the proverbs of Solomon, but they represent a collection "which the men of Hezekiah King of Judah copied out." Chapters 30–31 are proverbs from unknown men, presumably non-Israelite, "the words of Agur" and "the words of King Lemuel." As in the case of the psalms we are not to think that a psalm or a proverb bearing the name of David or Solomon necessarily means that he himself wrote or composed it. The ascription simply means that the works quoted are from a royal collection begun, sponsored, and supported by one of the kings in question. One of these collections was made at the end of the eighth century by the men of Hezekiah. We have no knowledge of when the other collections were made, nor do we know when they were first committed into writing. The present Book of Proverbs probably did not reach its final form much before the fifth century B.C.

When we learn more about the writing of the wise men in the ancient Near East, the dependence of the Israelites upon their neighbors will be more apparent. Scholars have long believed that the collection of proverbs in Chapters 22:17–24:22 is very close to a collection of proverbs in Egypt known as the "Wisdom of Amenemope." If the archaeologists ever find a collection of Canaanite proverbs, we shall undoubtedly find a number of closer resemblances. Both Egyptian and Israelite wisdom sayings are in the form of a large variety of short, epigrammatic, poetic lines that are sharp, to the point, and easily memorized. Furthermore, the form in which they are given is the speech of an old man to a young man, the former sharing his wisdom with the latter. It is impossible to give a close outline of the proverbs; there are hundreds of them, one rapidly following the other, each with its own point to make. For example:

23:13–14 Withhold not correction from the child,
    For if thou beatest him with the rod, he shall not
      die.
    Thou shalt beat him with the rod,
    And shalt deliver his soul from hell.

24:28–29 Be not a witness against thy neighbor without
    cause,
    And deceive not with thy lips.
    Say not, I will do so to him as he hath done to me;
    I will render to the man according to his work.

15:20   A wise son maketh a glad father,
    But a foolish man despiseth his mother.

16:8   Better is a little with righteousness,
    Than great revenues without right.

10:12   Hatred stirreth up strifes,
        But love covereth [i.e., maketh atonement for]
        all sins.

17:1   Better is a dry morsel, and quietness therewith,
        Than a house full of sacrifices with strife.

18:7   A fool's mouth is his destruction,
        And his lips are the snare of his soul.

19:6   Many will entreat the favor of the prince,
        And every man is a friend to him that giveth
        gifts.

The above few examples are sufficient to indicate the dominant interest of the compilers of the Book of Proverbs. These men were not interested in the great themes of Israel's history, such as the deliverance from Egyptian slavery, the gift of a land, the Sinai covenant, the covenant with David, God's use of the Assyrians and the Babylonians to punish his people Israel, nor in their restoration, nor in the great new age to come at the end of the current history, nor in the belief that Israel was a special people chosen by God with a mission to perform in the world. These great affirmations which so characterize the center of Israel's faith are completely absent from the interest of the wise men. Instead the concentration of attention is upon the best way for an individual to live in society; the wisdom is a series of prudential teachings, often beautifully phrased, frequently with profound insight into the ways of human nature. The teaching represents the distillation of ethical thought for the individual from among some of the finest people of the ancient world. Israel did not make up all of these aphorisms, but when she borrowed them from other sources such as Egypt, while contributing her own, she was forced to make certain theological changes in the setting in which proverbs were understood. In Egypt that setting was polytheistic, with the whole emphasis being upon preserving world order. The good man was thus the silent, obedient person who did nothing to disturb the order of society but kept it going its integrated way. The evil man was the passionate, willful person who was always acting in such a way as to disturb the current order. In Israel the motto of the wisdom movement was the fear of the Lord. Reverence for God was believed to be the beginning of wisdom. The good man was then the righteous man in God's sight, while the bad man was the wicked or the fool who did not know the proper way of life or had forsaken the fear of the Lord. For the most part this is the sum of the theological doctrine to be gained from the Book of Proverbs, with two exceptions. It is typical of character education movements that at some time or another certain members of the movement begin to make large claims for their ethical insights, thinking that by them the world is to be explained. In so doing they erect their own theological system which can become a rival to that in which the movement has its particular setting. In Chapter 8 of the Book of Proverbs, for example, it is asserted that wisdom is the fundamental principle of the universe, by which alone it is to be understood. Wisdom is there spoken of as if it were a person and as old as creation. Yea, even before God created the world wisdom existed, and by wisdom God brought forth the heaven and the earth. Such a bold assertion would undoubtedly cause theological difficulty to men like Jeremiah in Israel, a difficulty overcome only when the wisdom of the wise, the word of the prophet, and the law or teaching of the priest were equated. This was what was to happen in the years to come, so that it is not improbable that the words in Proverbs 8:22 and verses following may have been influential in the composition of the prologue to the gospel of John.

A second theological factor which was to give difficulty in the wisdom movement is one that is not so clearly stated as it is implied. That is that God runs the world in accordance with the principles of prudential ethics. If you obey all the wise men's aphorisms, choose the median way, never get out on anybody's limb, then God will reward you and you will be prosperous. If you do not do these things, then you will not be rewarded and God will punish you. Everything is just that simple. Whether the best of the wise men would have stated things this baldly is not at all probable. Yet it was the general tenor and implication of the wise men's teaching, and one cannot help comparing the life of Jesus, and even that of the prophets and apostles, who were willing to throw away their lives for the sake of the Lord, taking no careful and calculated account of how best to win friends and influence people. Nevertheless the Book of Proverbs was kept within the canon of scripture, in spite of the theological difficulties which it raised. In everyday life there is always an important place for prudential ethics, and ancient Jews and Christians both interpreted the various teachings of the wise men as part of God's ethical instruction of his people.

There are two more books in the Old Testament which belong to that portion of the wisdom literature which has been preserved in our present Bibles. These are Job and Ecclesiastes. Yet these books can only be understood as products of theological controversy with some of the issues which the wisdom movement had been asserting. Job was written to explode the common notion of the wise men, and for that matter of most pagan peoples of the time, that deity rules the world in a moralistic way, so that one can assess his goodness in the sight of God on the basis of his prosperity. The author of Ecclesiastes is inclined to doubt nearly everything that the wise men have stood for. He claims that the pursuit of wisdom, like the pursuit of wealth, is vanity, and he fails to observe in the world any proof that the wise man is always happier and more prosperous than the man who is a fool or wicked. Neither of these books employs any of the central themes of Israel's faith regarding the Lord of history, his righteous purposes which will be fulfilled in a kingdom that is soon to come, and a chosen people with a mission in the world at this moment. The authors of both books stand within the narrow limits of wisdom's theological platform, and then proceed to show its inadequacy.

The Book of Job is usually considered one of the great classics of all literature, a profound inquiry into the ways of God with men. The first two chapters form a prose introduction, and the last eleven verses of Chapter 42 form a prose conclusion. The intervening portion of the book is in poetry that is so elevated in style and so sophisticated in language and vocabulary that an accurate translation of the whole is today impossible. One can follow the general trend of the argument, but in many places one cannot trust the translation in detail, simply because a modern translator must often surmise or guess in difficult places. Job is the most difficult book in the Old Testament to translate, and that is surely a testimony to the high caliber of the author of the poetic sections.

The book comes to us after a long history. The central figure, Job, is represented as a bedouin chieftain of the patriarchal type. His name and that of his friends belong to the class of names that were very common in the second millennium B.C., but they are not names which are typical of the first millennium B.C. We shall have occasion to point out that the prose introduction and conclusion in the present book are probably not by the same hand as the poetic section. Indeed the figure of Satan in the first two chapters leads us to a time not before the sixth century B.C. for the present form of the prose introduction. The figure of Satan does not appear in literature before that date, and it should be noted that even here he is not conceived in the same way as he is to be in New Testament times. He is a lawyer in good standing in the heavenly court of God, whose job it is to try and test the motives of men, indeed, always to present matters in their worst light. Opposite him in the heavenly court was another angel whose function was to be the lawyer in the plaintiff's behalf, defending him against false accusations (cf. Zechariah, Chapter 3). Scholars also believe that the Hebrew of the poetic sections is not earlier than the time between the seventh and the fourth centuries B.C. Even this has had a history, however, so that Chapter 28, which is a remarkable poem on wisdom, and the Elihu speeches in Chapters 32–38 are insertions. Elihu is represented as a young man who has been listening to the conversations between Job and his friends and has become very disgusted that the friends are not able to set Job right. Consequently he delivers an address to answer and to solve the whole problem. Yet a close study of what he has to say indicates that the author who has devised his speeches is on a distinctly lower level than the author of the poetic dialogue as a whole, and he has very little to say that either has not been said before or that is not going to be said in the chapters which follow. The Elihu speeches are thus a contribution to the Job literature, but they do not represent its finest part. In other words, the essential story is a very old one going back into the second millennium. Indeed, the prophet Ezekiel mentions Job as one of the great righteous and wise men of bygone ages (Chapter 14:14, 20), indicating that the story about him is a very old one. Yet the present written form is much later, and appears to be a compilation which uses fragments from at least two or three different editions of the story.

The prose introduction begins with the statement that Job was a "perfect and upright" man, "one that feared God and eschewed evil." This is the basic presupposition on which the book rests. Job is assumed to be the ideal man, the finest type of man that the human race is capable of producing. The word "perfect" in the biblical original does not mean precisely what we mean by the same word. It does not mean that Job as a mortal man is not subject to sin; it means rather that he is a person of integrity, that he has a wholeness and wholesomeness about him, that he is the type of man whom God loves. In Job's final defense of himself in Chapter 31, the author presents one of the finest summaries of what a good man is that the Old Testament contains. The goodness of Job is a basic assumption of the book; as the best man one can imagine, he gets into trouble, and the author vividly shows how inept are the answers of the wise men to such a person when he finds himself in distress.

In alternate scenes in the heavenly court and on earth the introduction quickly presents the problem. God allows Satan to test Job's integrity. Satan strips him of his possessions, his family, and finally of his health, leaving him a miserable outcast. Yet through it all "Job did not sin with his lips" (Chapter 2:10). The general theme of the book is therefore set forth: it is the suffering of the good man in earth. It will be noted further that the prose introduction already has within itself the answer to this problem. The good man suffers in this life because God is allowing his faith to be tested. If he stands firm, we presumably infer that he will come through the period of testing with strengthened faith. This is a common biblical theme, but it does not reach the depths of insight presented by the poetic sections to follow. If the prose introduction were all that we had, we would say that the theme of Job is "God's testing of a righteous man." Yet when we turn to the poetic sections we find a deeper level of discussion wherein the central problem soon comes to be in Job's mind the sovereign goodness of God. In the midst of so much evil of earth where is God? How can one assume that he is good?

The poetic section is cast in the form of a dialogue between Job and the friends who come from far away to comfort him. Note that they are not Israelites, that in the wisdom movement it is not necessary to be an adherent of Israelite faith in order to convey the counsel and comfort of the wisdom movement to a bereaved person. Job begins in Chapter 3 by setting forth his misery and devoutly wishing that he were dead or that he had never been born. Each of the friends then speaks to him, and after each Job makes a reply. Chapters 4–14 constitute the first cycle of speeches, Chapters 15–21 the second cycle, and Chapters 22–27 the third. Chapters 29–31 are Job's final summary of the case, Chapter 28 being a poem which an editor has inserted on the source of wisdom. In Chapters 26–27 some disruption of the material is apparent, and the third speech of the third friend, Zophar, seems to have become mixed with the words of Job.

The first of the friends, Eliphaz, is represented as the kindest and wisest of the three. He begins very gently and suggests that God has always acted righteously in the earth, that the innocent have never perished, that no mortal man can be righteous before God, all men are sinners. The only thing that a person can do is simply to accept whatever lot God gives him, blessing God even for his reproving and chastening because in the end God will heal. In reply Job again quietly states his lament and asks for death. Then in Chapter 7 his misery so overcomes him that he begins to address God directly. He wants to know why God picks on him all the time: "What is so important about me that God pays so much at-

tention to me!" "What is man, that thou shouldst magnify him
. . . that thou shouldst visit him every morning and try him
every moment?" God does not let him alone long enough to
allow him to swallow his spittle! The second of the friends,
Bildad, takes offense at these words and asks whether God
actually perverts justice. How can Job disregard the whole
knowledge of God which has come from the past experience
of the human race, particularly as filtered through the wisdom
movement? Job in Chapters 9–10 replies by throwing off all
restraint. Of course he knows that God is all-powerful; there
is no question about that because that is precisely the problem. He is so powerful that Job cannot even make a reply or
a defense of his own case. He is so powerful that he is even
irresponsible! Those who say that history is full of the righteousness of God simply disregard the fact that "the earth is
given into the hand of the wicked." In fact, God seemingly
destroys the blameless with the wicked and makes no distinction between them. At that point he ceases talking to his
friends and turns directly to God and seeks answer from him
directly. In Chapter 10:8 he voices the basic contradiction
which his own predicament brings to the fore: God has made
him, but now has turned about and is destroying him. He ends
in complete despair, asking again why God brought him forth
from the womb.

The third friend is Zophar. He is the most violent and hot-
headed of the three, and in great sarcasm he replies in effect
that Job is setting himself over against God and is committing
blasphemy. Job, he says, is like a foolish man who will get
understanding just about as soon as a colt of a wild ass is born
of a human being, and no sooner! He tells Job to put away his
sin, and when he can lift up his face without blemish, then he
can be sure that all will be well with him. He thus accuses Job
of gross sin; if he had not been a terrible sinner, he would not
be in the predicament that he is in! This accusation has been
implicit in the preceding speeches of the friends, but this is
the first time it is directly made. In the theology of the friends,
the author of the poetic sections of the book has the wisdom
movement attempting to explain individual human suffering.

The stock answers are given: God chastens and tests people; all human beings are subject to what Christian theologians have called "original sin," that is, as human beings in an earthly society they cannot be perfect; further, history shows that God always blesses the righteous and punishes the wicked. To these common answers the very predicament of Job is its own answer. Job is the ideal good man. It is true that he is a human being, and therefore subject to sin after the manner of men. But that does not explain why now he is having to suffer more than other men. It only raises the question as to whether God is just. Indeed, when the wise friends try to make continual defense of God by their old patterns of thought, they are actually telling lies for God (Chapter 13:4) and are only succeeding in proving that God is unrighteous. This point has now become one of the central issues in the debate. The power of God is not questioned; it is rather the seemingly unrighteous use of that power, God's coldness and refusal to give answer to Job when he calls upon him.

In his extremity Job turns on his friends in bitter sarcasm: they, of course, are the people who have all wisdom, and then when they die there will be no more wisdom! In fact, it is characteristic of those who are comfortable and at ease to look down from their lofty heights in contempt at the poor person who is in misfortune (Chapter 12:2, 5). The friends, he says, are worthless physicians who are incapable of looking at facts honestly, and for that God in his time will surely rebuke them (Chapter 13:2–12)! Job then turns directly to God and casts his case in the form of a legal brief which can be used for his defense. Yet the trouble is that God will not answer him and will not allow him his day in court. He begs God not to terrify him, to answer him, to make known his fault; but there is no answer, so Job in Chapter 14 can think only of man's hopelessness. By contrast there is hope for a tree, which when cut down can sprout again from the root. But not so man. He is much more like the water in a lake or a river which, when it is gone, leaves nothing but dryness. If it were only true, that when a man dies he would live again, that would be something to wait for; that would be one's hope. Yet no sooner has Job expressed this intimation of a future than he sinks back into his despair.

This brief summary of the first cycle of the debate by no means exhausts its depth, but at least the main issues are here presented. It is in this vein that the debate continues in the other cycles, with little that is basically new being added. It must be remembered that the author of the book is a poet who is not interested in arguing his question in a logical manner to a logical conclusion. As a poet he rather is examining the problem from every side, stating and restating it with all the vigor at his command, until both the problem and the inadequacy of the current wisdom movement to answer it are not only intellectually understood, but also deeply felt. Increasingly as the poem proceeds Job turns his attention directly to God, at one moment boldly appealing to him and at the next meditating within himself about his problem in relation to God. A climax is reached in Chapter 19:25 when Job utters the words, "For I know that my Redeemer liveth." Unfortunately this passage stands in a context which cannot be clearly translated because the Hebrew is corrupt. The general tenor of it, however, is clear. Job is asserting his certainty that in the future in the heavenly court an angelic witness (cf. 16:19), a legal savior, will arise and take up his case and defend it in the heavenly court. He has hope for his future legal vindication. The Christian Church has always seen in this great affirmation of faith the figure of Christ, who is indeed precisely this: the witness in our behalf, our redeemer, mediator, and friend.

Meanwhile the arguments of the friends become more and more traditional and less and less fresh, until it would appear that they have nothing more to say. In Chapters 29–31 Job makes the final summary of his case and at that point we await the conclusion, which is the expected appearance of God. The course of the poem is interrupted, however, by the insertion of the Elihu speeches referred to above. Finally in Chapters 38–41 the Lord is represented as appearing and speaking directly to Job. At first glance the tenor and content of the speeches are a disappointment. The author does not present an answer to Job's problem. He rather presents a marvelous picture of the providence of God as shown in his control of nature. Most vivid of all is the picture of Leviathan in Chapter 41. From recent archaeological discovery of Canaanite religious literature in Syria we know that Leviathan was considered to be a dragon who lived in the sea, a seven-headed snake who could even be called Sea. In Canaanite mythology he was the personification of chaos, everything in the universe which was opposed to world order. In pagan theology the major problem was indeed the problem of order against disorder. The king of the gods had fought the dragon at the beginning of creation and annihilated him, thus bringing about world order. Yet this order is something that needs to be struggled for constantly. Thus while the battle was once fought and won, it needs to be refought and rewon every year. To the pagan the most important festival of the year was the spring festival in which this divine battle was depicted in a magical ritual so that security in nature could be assured for the coming year. In various poetic sections in the Old Testament we find allusions to this chaos-dragon myth, and it is poetically affirmed that the God of Israel was he who annihilated the dragon. The dragon represents the disorderly elements of the universe, and these are most clearly observed or symbolized in the unruly masses of water in the sea which can easily overcome the sailor. Who can control such a chaotic waste? What man can catch Leviathan on a fishhook and control him so that he does not break out in destructive furor? God is the only one who keeps Leviathan in control, and apart from that sovereign providential control we infer that Leviathan would rage and destroy, and man would be indeed hopeless.

The author has now made his main point. It is that the wisdom movement cannot answer the deepest problems of life. God does not always act in accordance with the moralistic dictums of the wise. The formula of the wisdom movement cannot explain all suffering. The reason is that there is a mystery in God's dealing with man, and in the last analysis no human formula is capable of resolving that mystery completely. Those who attempt falsely to defend God on the basis of the wisdom formula are simply putting one in a position where he must deny the justice of God. Hence the friends are roundly condemned and with them the whole wisdom movement in its basic theological affirmations. Yet at the same time Job's rashness in denying the goodness of God on the basis of his own individual suffering is also seen to be wrong. In Chapter 42:1–6 Job replies to God in effect that he has been speaking about things that he really knew nothing about. He was, like so many people, one who had only heard of the Lord by the hearing of the ear, but "now mine eye sees thee." One cannot use his individual sufferings to deny the manifold evidence in God's world of his goodness. Without the goodness of God in creating and sustaining the world, man indeed could have no hope. Finally, the very fact that God chose to appear before Job is an act of grace. Job is comforted, not because he has an intellectual understanding of a problem which is hidden in the mystery of God, but because his own eyes have seen God and he can trust even where he cannot understand.

The Book of Ecclesiastes is the most skeptical literature in the whole Bible. It is represented as the words of Solomon when he was an old man, having learned all there was to learn about life. Scholars generally date it, however, somewhat later than the Book of Job in its present form, perhaps about 300 B.C. Like the Book of Job its content can only be understood as a part of the controversy brought about by the theological affirmations of the wisdom movement. The central word in the author's vocabulary is "vanity," a translation of a Hebrew word "nothing" or "nothingness." The author means by the use of it everything that is foolish, absurd, unprofitable. He begins by speaking about the weariness of life, of how everything repeats itself and there is nothing new. As a king in Jerusalem he searched after wisdom with all his heart and found that the whole thing is a vanity and a striving after wind. He sought out a life of pleasure and found that that was vanity. The same is the case with wealth and great possessions. It is true that wisdom excels folly as light excels darkness (Chapter 2:13), and yet it must be remembered that one thing happens to every man, whether he is wise or whether he is a fool: that is that he dies. As for the assertion that God punishes the wicked and rewards the righteous and that suffering is caused by God's testing of men to give them humility, the author notes that in every place of justice there is wickedness and he also notes that death is the great leveler of all men. The fate of a man, whether he is righteous or wicked, is the same as the fate of an animal. All die; all go to one place; all come from the dust and all return again to the dust. As for certain new notions about immortality that are coming upon the scene, the author further says, "Who knows about the spirit of man that the human spirit ascends up into heaven at death while the spirit of an animal goes down into the earth?" (Chapter 3:16–21.) In fact when one sees all the oppression under the sun, one could well argue that the dead are much more fortunate than the living who are now alive!

The author of Ecclesiastes is not a disbeliever in God. He believes, but he does not have much use for theology, certainly not for the type which the leaders of the wisdom movement have espoused. It is useless to try to talk about God's moral government of the world, or to penetrate into the secrets of life in relation to God. Whenever you try to figure things out, all you discover is vanity and foolishness. Nothing very much really makes sense. So what is one to do? Why, the one solid thing that a person has is his present life and the work and destiny which God has given him to fulfill at this moment. Therefore, there is nothing better for a man than that "he should eat and drink and find enjoyment in his toil." The author does not mean by this a seeking after irresponsible pleasure. God has made everything, yet not in such a manner that the mind of man can penetrate what God has been doing since the beginning of time. Man's lot is simply to enjoy the simple things of life which he has before him. Life's simplicities and the work which man is given to do—these are God's gifts and everyone should eat and drink and take pleasure in them (Chapter 3:11–14). Do not try to penetrate the theological secrets of the universe. Simply accept the lot which God has given you and learn how to enjoy it in all simplicity. Let this advice be especially observed by the young. Watch out for your life and remember that God holds you responsible for what you do. Take life cheerfully as you find it and put away vexation and pain before old age begins to come upon you and it is impossible to have joy in anything! (Chapter 11:9 ff.)

The author of Ecclesiastes is far more skeptical than is the author of the poetical portions of Job, but at the same time he has no depth to him. It is interesting that books like these are preserved within the canon of scripture. They are to be understood as rising within the wisdom movement, and pointing to the folly of human endeavor to explain all life on a moralistic basis. This does not mean that the ethical teaching of the wise men was wrong, but it does mean that prudential ethics and a dominant interest in how to win friends and influence people is no real clue to the meaning of God, history, and human life. The canon of scripture has included the best literature of the wisdom movement, and then included the Books of Job and Ecclesiastes as its corrective. It is interesting to observe that though the teaching of the wise men continued and though later collections of their teachings are to be found in the inter-Testamental Books of Ecclesiasticus and the Wisdom of Solomon, there was never a need for men like the authors of Job and Ecclesiastes to write again. They had made their point, and they did not establish skeptical schools which perpetuated and elaborated their point of view.

CHAPTER III

THE CLOSE OF THE OLD TESTAMENT

In the preceding survey we have mentioned all of the books of the Old Testament except a few which appear among the last group of writings in the Hebrew Bible. The little Book of Ruth is a charming story about the great-grandfather and the great-grandmother of King David. It could well serve as a gentle reminder that David's great-grandmother was not an Israelite but a foreigner. It is believed to have been edited about the fifth century and put in its present form, though the story is a very old one. It was placed in its present position as an appendage to the Book of Judges in the Greek translation of the Old Testament.

The Book of Lamentations is a series of poetical laments of great beauty and power about the destruction of Jerusalem in 587 B.C. They were in time appended to the Book of Jeremiah and some later Jewish rabbis even thought Jeremiah wrote them, though modern scholarship does not think this is very likely.

The Song of Songs is a marvelous collection of love poetry. Very close parallels to it have recently been found in Egypt. It was preserved, probably because it was very early allegorized. That is, it was interpreted not simply as human love between man and woman but as divine love between God and people. The Christian Church, for example, interpreted it as the love of Christ for his Church and the love of the Church for Christ. Most scholars typical of those working in this field do not believe that the original authors and collectors of the poetry had any such allegory in mind. They presented a beautiful portrayal of human love at its best, and as such the book is today welcomed within the canon of sacred literature. The book is felt to be a post-exilic edition of much earlier poems, dating at least from the ninth century B.C. and perhaps earlier.

The Book of Esther, perhaps to be dated around 300 B.C., purports to record events which led up to the institution of a great festival, still celebrated among Jews as the Feast of Lots. The setting of the story is the time of the Persian King Xerxes (486–465 B.C.). The purpose of the book was evidently to provide a justification for the celebration of this festival which had no basis in the Old Testament otherwise and had no religious significance. The festival, according to the book, was to be understood as a commemoration of the great delivery of Jews in Persia from massacre. The story is marvelously told, though at the end of the book the Jews are said to have turned on their enemies and carried out against them the massacre which had been planned for the Jews. The fact that God is not even mentioned in the book and that it does end with this vindictive spirit suggests the reasons why this book had more difficulty in getting into the Old Testament canon than any other. At least one sect of the Jews, the Essenes, seem not to have had it among their writings, and it was almost entirely ignored by the early Christian fathers in their comments upon the Bible.

The last book of the Old Testament to be written was the Book of Daniel. Chapters 1–6 of that book present a series of very familiar stories about the adventures of Daniel and his companions in exile in Babylon during the early sixth century. Chapters 7–12 present four visions in which the history of the known world is portrayed in symbolical form from the time of the exile in Babylon to the final triumph of the saints of God. To understand this second section of the book it is necessary to make use of a commentary. The whole is very symbolic and cast in quite general terms until it comes into the Greek period of the third and early second centuries. At that time it becomes increasingly detailed, and the events are described with great care and accuracy, though in symbolic form, up until about 165 B.C. A close observation of the history of the time and of the point where the book ends have led scholars to date it about this period.

The story was written at a time when the King of Syria, a man named Antiochus Epiphanes (175–163 B.C.), had decided to stamp out Judaism in Palestine as a needless disturbance in an empire that was otherwise culturally and religiously united. Shortly before this time he had entered the temple and desecrated it, turning it into a temple for the pagan god Zeus. This happened in 168 B.C., whereas the king died in 163 B.C. The book was written, evidently before his death, as a source of encouragement to the Jews who were undergoing severe trials of faith. God is on the side of all martyrs for his cause, and all those who stand firm in this crisis will see their hopes ultimately confirmed. When the king died, the temple was purified, and a festival celebrating this event is still observed by the Jews around the Christian Christmas season; it is called "the Feast of Lights."

As is now well known, the oldest-known fragments of the Old Testament in Hebrew, and even a few in Greek, are the famous Dead Sea Scrolls. By the spring of 1956 some eleven caves in the cliffs by the northwestern corner of the Dead Sea had been found to yield manuscript material of great interest and importance for both the study of the Old and the New Testaments. The complete Book of Isaiah is excellently preserved in one complete scroll which dates about 100 B.C. In the fourth cave fragments of over 400 scrolls were discovered, one fourth of which were copies of biblical books. Most of these are readily distinguished because they are written on a much finer leather and are copied in a special book hand with more care than that given to other manuscripts. Every book of the Old Testament except Esther is represented in the discoveries. The oldest fragments are those of a manuscript of Samuel and another of Jeremiah dating from about 200 B.C. A fragment of Ecclesiastes dates from about 150 B.C. Several copies of the Book of Daniel have been found, one fragment dating less than 100 years from the time the book was written. Before the last decade it was never thought possible that we would get that close to the original manuscript of an Old Testament book. Most of the manuscripts date from the first century B.C. and the first century A.D. Other manuscripts from just before and after A.D. 100 have been found about twelve miles further south of the original find in caves of a valley called Wadi Murabba'at.

These texts, when they are completely studied, will prove of exceedingly great importance for the translation of the Old Testament. As a result of these discoveries and from other information previously known, it is now clear that the text of the Old Testament was carefully revised by rabbis and standardized at the end of the first and the early part of the second century A.D. One of the difficulties which translators of the Old Testament have had is how to get behind the standardized text which has survived through medieval into modern times, back into the days where variant readings in certain difficult passages still were preserved. When one has other choices of text to study, he can sometimes make out with more assurance what certain hard-to-understand passages may originally have been intended to say. The Dead Sea Scrolls, though mostly of a very fragmentary nature, introduce us to the period during and before the time of Jesus, when the Old Testament text at certain points was still somewhat fluid and not frozen into one pattern.

The people of the scrolls, known in ancient times as the Essenes, were a sect of Judaism founded in the second century before the birth of Christ. As previously mentioned, the one book of the Old Testament which has not yet been found in their library is the Book of Esther. This suggests that in the scripture of the Essenes the Book of Esther had not yet found a place, and was not to do so until the final decision of the rabbis at the end of the first century A.D. On the other hand the books of history, prophecy, and devotional and wisdom literature were all present, some in a number of copies. While Ecclesiastes and Daniel were known, it is not entirely clear that they were considered canonical. The scholars working on the scrolls as of this moment are not entirely sure about the matter. This means that the Essenes in the time of Jesus held to the same group of Old Testament books as do Protestant Christians today, with the exception of two or three marginal books whose position was subsequently to be decided. On the other hand, during the third and second centuries B.C., Jewish scholars in Egypt made a translation of the Old Testament into Greek for Jews who spoke Greek in their everyday life. These translators in Egypt included, among the books of the Old Testament which were considered especially sacred, a small group of literature which we call the Apocrypha. In other words, there seems to have been some disagreement between Palestinian and Egyptian Jews as to which of these marginal books at the end of the Old Testament period should be included among the sacred literature. When the Christian Church needed a Greek Bible it simply took over the Egyptian translation of the Old Testament (known as the Septuagint). To this day the Roman Catholic and Greek Orthodox churches retain these marginal volumes in their Bibles, while the Protestants at the time of the Reformation went back to the list of sacred books as they were established by Palestinian rabbis, thus omitting the Apocrypha.

The list of sacred books which are separated from other literatures and considered especially sacred is called the canon, as indicated in the Prologue. The very idea of a canon of sacred literature is something new under the sun, and it is this idea which was responsible for the preservation of the Bible. The conception of a canon was apparently established in Judaism during the post-exilic period, when the Jews in Babylonian exile and in Palestine were industriously collecting their sacred literature, editing it, and seeking to live by it. Between the sixth and the fourth century, then, prophets were no longer as much needed in the popular conception as scholars in the scriptures. Ezra, it will be remembered, was typical of that development. This was the beginning of that intensive study of scripture which has been carried on by every generation among Jews and Christians from that time until this. The people of the Dead Sea Scrolls before and during the time of Jesus were ardent students of the Old Testament scripture, and many scrolls in the fragmentary portion of their library which has been recovered were commentaries on various of the sacred books.

It is often asked why we today do not include other books in the canon. If, however, the argument of the Prologue and of the pages which follow has been considered closely, it will be observed that the Bible is first of all an interpretation of the life of the people in a particular age, an interpretation which explains this life as a special working of God. The Bible is not a series of abstract religious teachings. These events happened at this time and no other, and they will never be repeated in just this way. Nevertheless the knowledge of God here presented is of basic significance because it illumines subsequent history. On the other hand, it is true that the decision as to which of the marginal books at the end of the Old Testament period should be included and which should be omitted is a matter for human councils. The Book of Esther, for example, could be omitted from the canon and I–II Maccabees, describing the independence struggle of the Jews during the second and early first centuries B.C., could be included, and nothing would be particularly changed. The classic forms of the faith as found in the history, the prophets, and the psalms remain the same. It is they which judge the marginal books and not the latter which judge the former.

We must also observe at this point that the problem of the marginal books in the period between the Old and New Testaments suggests that the great period of Israel is over. Little of creative significance is now happening. Yet how is a people to live by means of the old faith? The Old Testament ends with a number of unsolved problems, the chief of which is this one. We thus, as it were, are in a period of waiting, a time when various experiments may be expected, when various sects will arise, each with its answer as to how best to understand the relevance of the old faith. The Old Testament in itself is incomplete. How will it be completed, or, as the Christian would say it, how will it be fulfilled so that its expectations point to something that is secure and by which we have life? Nearly all of the Jewish sects disappeared except the one which survived as dominant. That was rabbinic Judaism, which saw the Old Testament fulfilled and made relevant in the Talmud. For the Christian, however, Jesus Christ, as it were the "word" of God become flesh in human history, is the fulfillment of the Old Testament, the end to which it was moving, and the summary of what God meant by it. To the Christian, then, the Old Testament is not the Bible apart from the New Testament, just as the New Testament is not the Bible apart from the Old. It is the whole of scripture, and that alone, which enables one to understand the work of God in Christ.

PART III

BETWEEN THE OLD AND NEW TESTAMENTS

CHAPTER I

HISTORICAL BACKGROUND— FROM THE MACCABEES TO JESUS

Throughout recorded history Palestine has succeeded in maintaining her independence only during those brief periods when her more powerful neighbors were preoccupied elsewhere or undergoing a temporary eclipse. Only twice during the biblical period did that happen—during the time of David and his immediate successors, and again during the period of the Hasmonaean dynasty (143–63 B.C.) founded as a result of the Maccabean revolt. Like the earlier period, the second was one of transition. The Greco-Macedonian regime under the successors of Alexander the Great was in decline, but the Romans had not yet come on the scene. Hence there was a real though short-lived chance of independence and national resurgence.

Our chief source of information for this period is I Maccabees in the Apocrypha, occasionally supplemented by II Maccabees.

I Maccabees, after a brief summary of Alexander the Great's conquests (1:1–9) and the subsequent division of his realms among his successors in the three kingdoms of Macedonia, Syria, and Egypt, relates the early phases of the Maccabean revolt in 1:10–2:70. The next main section (3:1–9:22) brings the story down to the death of Judas Maccabaeus, the leader of the rebellion. Chapters 9:23–12 deal with the career of his brother Jonathan, who succeeded him as leader, and the last section, Chapters 13–16, give an account of Simon, the last of the three brothers.

II Maccabees covers part of the same ground (the years 176–66 B.C.) from a different point of view. The author of the first book wrote from a national and patriotic point of view, with very little intrusion of the supernatural or even the theological, though his outlook is by no means secularist. He does believe that the Jews are God's chosen people, but the prophetic note is missing: the woes of Israel are laid at the door of her oppressors, never attributed to her own sins. II Maccabees however is theological first and foremost: it relates history in order to show that Israel's woes are caused by her own sins and are God's judgment upon them. The two works are clearly independent, and the historical discrepancies have long exercised the minds of scholars. Nowadays it is generally recognized that I Maccabees, while not infallible, is closer to history, while II Maccabees may be used occasionally to supplement the evidence of the first book on matters of factual detail.

It was the third of the Maccabees, Simon, who first succeeded in establishing a really independent rule (143–135 B.C.), not as king, however, but as high priest. True, he did not belong to the legitimate high priestly line. But, during the troubles, the last survivor of that line had escaped to Egypt to set up a temple (despite the Deuteronomic law of the central sanctuary) at Leontopolis, and had ended his days in a drunken brawl. The title of high priest was then conferred on Simon as an act of national gratitude for liberation, a natural enough procedure when one recalls that the only "rulers" with any semblance of power that the Jews had known since the exile were the high priests.

Simon died a violent death in 135 B.C. and was succeeded by his son, John Hyrcanus. Here I Maccabees fails us (see I Maccabees 16:23 f.) and we are thrown back upon Josephus' *Antiquities* and *Jewish War* (see below). Hyrcanus' long rule (135–104 B.C.) was notable for three developments. The first was his own gradual advance from high priesthood to monarchy, the second the territorial expansion of the Jewish realm to include Samaria and Idumea (thus bringing in the territory which was to produce the Herods of the New Testament period), and the third the breakup of the old revolutionary party, the "Chasidim." The main section of this party, which developed into the Pharisees of the New Testament, dissociated themselves from the Hasmonaeans (as the new dynasty was called) because of their increasing worldliness and disloyalty to the original religious motivation of the revolution. The group which remained loyal to the ruling dynasty was the Sadducees, the priestly party, conservative in religion but liberal in culture, and not averse to the comforts of Hellenistic civilization.

At his death, Hyrcanus was succeeded by his son Aristobulus, whose brief reign (104–103 B.C.) was notable because he was the first Hasmonaean to take the title of "king" and because he added Galilee to his domains. Aristobulus, in turn, was succeeded by his brother Jannaeus (Hebrew, Jonathan), who also married his brother's widow, Salome or Alexandra. He reigned from 103 to 76 B.C. His military ambitions intensified the estrangement of the Pharisees from the ruling dynasty, as did also his growing partiality for the Greek way of life. If Alexander Jannaeus is to be identified with the "wicked priest" of the sectarian documents discovered in the Qumran cave, it would seem that the secession of the "covenanters" occurred during his reign. They seceded from the mainstream of the national life because they were equally dissatisfied with the ruling dynasty and with the Pharisaic protest against it. Neither of the existing parties was loyal to ideals of the revolution!

When Jannaeus died, Alexandra, twice widowed, became queen regnant in his stead. As a woman she could not combine the office of high priest with the monarchy, like her predecessors, so the former devolved upon her son, the feeble-minded Hyrcanus II. Her reign was peaceful and prosperous, but marked the beginning of the end—the Romans by this time were approaching the scene.

In 63 B.C. the Romans, under Pompey, laid siege to Jerusalem and conquered the Jewish people amid scenes of terrible bloodshed. Pompey added insult to injury by entering the holy of holies itself, though he did refrain from interfering with the temple worship. Judea thus passed under Roman control and was shorn of the Hasmonaean conquests. Hyrcanus II added to his high priesthood the political title of ethnarch: the short-lived monarchy was abolished. But the power behind the throne was a certain Antipater, the first representative of the notorious Herod family who came from Idumea and soon established itself in place of the Hasmonaeans. A confused period followed, made even more so by the Roman civil war. During this period Antipater behaved very adroitly, changing sides from time to time, and always managing to keep on the winning side during the ebb and flow of the civil war. In the end his son Herod, the infamous Herod of the infancy narratives in the New Testament, was able to establish himself as ruler, a position which he strengthened by marrying Mariamne, a surviving princess of the Hasmonaean dynasty. His technical position was that of a *rex socius,* or allied king, governing his own territory independently, and subject to Rome only in foreign affairs. Herod once more enlarged the Jewish kingdom by annexing a number of Greek cities, though without forcing them to adopt the Jewish way of life. At the same time, despite his pro-Roman and Hellenizing proclivities, he allowed his Jewish subjects to practice their religion freely, and in fact rebuilt the ruined temple at Jerusalem. Even this tactful behavior, however, failed to arouse any enthusiasm for his rule among his Jewish subjects. At best they merely tolerated it as the better of two evils, better, that is, than direct Roman rule. The Psalms of Solomon, which are not in the Apocrypha, reflect the popular mood at this juncture. They clearly disapprove of Herod, while the later ones look forward to a renewal of the Davidic monarchy under a "messiah" or anointed king. This popular expectation provides part of the background to the gospels and on the whole represents a form of future hope which Jesus consistently rejected.

Herod's long reign, which was particularly troubled in his later years (the story of the massacre of the infants after the birth of Jesus is, if improbable on other grounds, at least in keeping with the character of his closing days), came to an end in 4 B.C. His kingdom was divided among his three sons, Archelaus taking Judea, Samaria and Idumea, Antipas receiving Galilee and Perea, and Philip being allotted Trachonitis and other parts. Of these, Archelaus was the least successful:

there was prolonged unrest, and Roman military intervention was necessary to bolster up his tottering throne. In the end, Roman patience was exhausted, for in A.D. 6 Archelaus was banished to Gaul and Judea placed under a procurator subordinate to the governor of Syria. Such then was the political situation in Palestine during the ministry of Jesus, when Pontius Pilate was procurator of Judea (A.D. 26–36) and Herod Antipas ruler of Galilee (see Luke 3:1).

CHAPTER II

THE JEWISH COMMUNITY

Jerusalem, first chosen in the time of David to be the capital city of his realm, had by the time of Jesus become an international religious center like Rome today for millions of Catholics of her obedience. That explains why, in Acts 2, we find people present in Jerusalem for the feast of Pentecost from all over the Mediterranean world. Since the captivity and exile in 586 B.C., people of Jewish origin had spread not only to Babylon, but to Egypt and then throughout the Mediterranean lands. Strabo's exaggeration was by no means unfounded:

> Jews are to be found in every city, and in the whole world it was not easy to find a place where they had not penetrated and which was not dominated by them.
>
> *Antiquities 14:115*

It is calculated that the Jews formed no less than 7 per cent of the population of the Roman Empire, and even allowing for their migrations and fertility, their expansion is a real problem and cannot be accounted for from these factors alone. Additional causes may be sought in the absorption of other Semitic people, in the action of Antiochus the Great in settling some two thousand Jewish families from Babylon in Phrygia and Lydia, in Pompey's transportation of Jewish prisoners of war to Rome, where after liberation they formed the nucleus of the Jewish community there. It was during this period, too, that the Jews took to trading and began to amass wealth, both factors leading to further settlements abroad. Lastly, we have to take into account the appeal of its religion, especially to women. This factor must not be exaggerated, however, for the number of people who were prepared to join the Jewish community by circumcision (or baptism in the case of women) was comparatively small, most interested Gentiles preferring to remain on the fringe as "God-fearers," attracted by the ethical monotheism of the Jewish religion but reluctant to submit to the more irksome restrictions of the ceremonial law.

Something should be said about the organization of the Jewish people. The temple, as already indicated, was their one proper center. Every Jew paid his temple tax. But the temple was no longer the real center of piety, except as a place of pilgrimage. The real center of their religious life lay in the local synagogue, so much so that the final destruction of the temple in A.D. 70, far from destroying the Jewish religion, inaugurated a new period of vitality.

As an institution the local synagogue (one could be founded wherever there were ten men) was fundamentally not a center of worship, but a school of instruction in the law. Apart from the formal worship of the temple, the family was the place of worship. The form of service in the synagogue was centered upon the reading of the law and its subsequent exposition, psalmody and prayer being incidental. The synagogue combined secular and religious functions, like the old Easter vestries in England, which not only appointed the church-wardens but also looked after highways and bridges! Their governing body consisted of elders (Hebrew, *zekanim*, which, translated into Greek as *presbyteros*, eventually gave us the English words "priest" and "presbyter"). The elders had power of excommunication. The worship of the synagogue was under the control of the "ruler of the synagogue," an official who figures in several places in the New Testament.

There was a similar body running the affairs of the worldwide Jewry at the center known as the "Great Sanhedrin," the "chief priests and elders and scribes" of the gospels. There has been much controversy as to whether they could inflict the death penalty at this period. Acts 7, the story of the stoning of Stephen, clearly implies that they had that power; John 18:31 expressly states that they had not. The best authorities seem to agree that they had in religious cases, and the point of John 18:31 will be that the Sanhedrin was determined to make the case of Jesus a political one. After A.D. 70 even this limited right to inflict capital punishment was taken away.

CHAPTER III

THE JEWISH RELIGION

One of the problems besetting the student of Judaism in New Testament times is that most of our direct evidence comes from a later date, from the "Mishnah," a collection of traditional teaching first written down toward the end of the second century and consisting largely of sayings of rabbis of earlier dates, back to the time of Herod the Great. This evidence must be used with caution, for in the second century there was undoubtedly a natural tendency to idealize Judaism as it used to be in the days before the destruction of Jerusalem in A.D. 70.

Our second source of evidence is the New Testament itself. Modern Jewish scholars suspect its picture of first-century Judaism of bias in the opposite direction—the early Christians naturally tended to be less than fair to their opponents. Yet the very writers most concerned with anti-Jewish polemic are the ones which were most familiar with it, namely, Matthew's special source, Paul, and the author of the fourth gospel. Moreover, the New Testament throughout emphatically insists that "salvation is of the Jews," and much in contemporary Judaism was valued and preserved in early Christianity.

Third, we have the two works of the Jewish historian, Josephus, his *Jewish War*, dealing with the revolt of A.D. 70, of which he had firsthand knowledge, and his *Antiquities*, covering the whole of Jewish history up to his own times and published in the last decade of the first century A.D. Josephus however is always concerned to present Judaism in as commendable a light as possible for his cultured Greco-Roman readers, and therefore tends to soften its asperities and to draw a discreet veil over its distinctive features.

A. PHARISAISM AND RABBINIC JUDAISM

We do however possess one work emanating directly from the scribal tradition in its early stage. This is the Wisdom of Jesus, Son of Sirach, or Ecclesiasticus. It was originally written in Hebrew at Jerusalem about 180 B.C. and consists of a collection of essays and maxims strung together in conscious imitation of the Book of Proverbs. It is striking that the author actually uses his own name and not a pseudonym like that appended to Proverbs before him and to the Wisdom of Solomon after him. His book is difficult to analyze because it is constructed on no definite plan; but he himself clearly divided it into two parts, Chapters 1–23 and 24–51, each part concluding with an acrostic poem. The original Hebrew was lost for many centuries, and the version in the King James Apocrypha was translated from a Greek rendering produced by the author's own grandson in Egypt about 130 B.C. Since 1896, however, some two thirds of the Hebrew text have been recovered.

As the author himself tells us in 51:23, he kept a sort of finishing school for young men, a *Beth ha-midrash,* or house of instruction, in which it was his practice to deliver lectures without charging fees (the later rabbis practiced a trade to avoid living by their teaching of the law), as he tells us in verse 25. The book is a reproduction of his lectures, which are partly the reapplication of the Mosaic law to the changed circumstances of contemporary life, and partly just the plain practical common sense of a shrewd observer of human life and manners. Much of it in fact reads very much like those handbooks for the "perfect gentleman" which were published in the eighteenth and nineteenth centuries. It may thus be said to mark the transition from the wisdom literature of the Book of Proverbs and the teachings of the early rabbis, a transition, as has been aptly remarked, "from the authority of inspiration to the authority of learning." Like Proverbs it is a Judaism less bound to the sacred history of God's redemptive acts and more concerned with the universal truths of piety and ethics. Yet, as the liturgical recital of 44:16–49:16 shows, this detachment from the redemptive history should not be exaggerated. In another respect, too, it marks a transition: here for the first time we find wisdom identified with Torah, which, having originally meant "instruction," came to mean the law of Moses, and was then further expanded to embrace the whole of God's self-communication to man—almost equivalent to "revelation."

The best-known passage in the Wisdom of Sirach is the hymn of praise which begins with "Let us now praise famous men" (44:1–15). There is also a remarkable description of the high priest officiating on the Day of the Atonement in Chapter 50.

The dominant concern of the Pharisaic movement was to preserve inviolate the Mosaic law and its way of life against the encroachments of alien cultures. Since that law had been given once for all through Moses there could be no new laws. Instead, the ancient laws, which had been intended for a more primitive society, had to be reapplied to later situations. In this reapplication there was no thought of introducing novelties: rather, the idea was to extract the real meaning of the law. The method adopted was that of casuistry.

The procedure of the rabbis was to repeat the interpretations of their predecessors and to add to them new ones of their own, covering further contingencies in daily life. The type of question they dealt with is indicated by the discussion about plucking ears of corn on the Sabbath day (Mark 2:23 ff.). There were lengthy discussions as to precisely what was and what was not involved by "work" on the Sabbath. There was little attempt to search for an underlying principle behind the numerous commands and prohibitions. The two great commandments, love of God and love of the neighbor, were of course part of the law, but even in combination they were not accorded that central and unifying position which they were given in the New Testament. All this naturally led to legalism and scrupulosity, to a belief in the saving value of good works, and the consequent sense of pride which a doctrine of merit inevitably entailed. Yet we should not belittle the achievements of rabbinic Judaism. It was precisely because they were such good men that they incurred the radical criticisms of Jesus and Paul:

> I bear them witness that they have a zeal for God, but it is not enlightened. For, being ignorant of the righteousness that comes from God, and seeking to establish their own, they did not submit to God's righteousness.
>
> *Romans 10:2 f. (R.S.V.)*

It is an exaggeration to say, as has recently been asserted, that the rabbis completely abandoned the idea of sacred history, of a history of God's mighty acts toward his people. They still looked back to the exodus as the decisive event of redemption by which Israel was constituted. They did not altogether ignore the crucial fact that the observance of the law was meant to be Israel's grateful response to the prior action of God. They still had the Pentateuch, which included gospel as well as law. They still observed the feasts, especially the Passover, as the memorial of that redemption. And they still looked forward to a future in which God would inaugurate his reign on earth, and this hope indeed took the strongly historical form of a restored realm under a new king of David's line as Messiah. And in this restoration the experiences of the exodus would be repeated. Yet these beliefs were peripheral. Their chief interest like that of the wisdom literature was in individual ethics.

Although the rabbis strove to maintain the purity of Judaism against the accretions of foreign culture, they unconsciously absorbed ideas from the alien world in which they had perforce to live. The influence of Hellenism was subtle and all-pervasive, and rabbinic Judaism assimilated ideas and even vocabulary from that suspect source. Sometimes this led to an enrichment of Jewish thought, sometimes to an obscuring of the authentic tradition of the Old Testament. Thus they came to hold the Greek doctrine of the soul, its metaphysical nature, its pre-existence and immortality. This doctrine they held rather awkwardly with the belief in the resurrection of the body, which had at an earlier date been adopted, perhaps, from Persian sources. But they never completely committed themselves to the Greek view of the duality of soul and body. In many ways the New Testament is the reassertion of the authentic Old Testament tradition over against the rabbinic distortion of it, for the New Testament reaffirmed the primacy of gospel over law, the basic importance of redemptive history, and the Hebraic doctrine of man.

B. APOCALYPTIC

Until recently it has been difficult to assign the apocalyptic writings to any distinct group within Judaism. They have generally been vaguely associated with Galilee. The Pharisees were uninterested in it, for their hopes for the future, as we have seen, took a purely historical, this-worldly form. But we now know that the Qumran community was interested in this type of literature, for fragments of it have turned up among their remains. True, their own literary products, while accepting some of the features of the apocalyptic world view, are not in themselves apocalypses. And it would be as fallacious to suppose that everything found in the Qumran caves was the product of the community itself as it would be to suppose that every volume in a university library is the work of members of that university! Nevertheless, the international team working on the scrolls, together with other scholars who are studying the material, are finding themselves increasingly drawn to the conclusion that the apocalyptists belonged to the same wider group as the Qumran covenanters, and that the wider group in question was the Essenes (see below). Almost all of these experts seem to agree that the Testament of the Twelve Patriarchs (see below), the Book of Jubilees, and the Book of Enoch (see below) are "Essene" documents. One of the strongest pieces of evidence for this position is that the

Qumran documents show that the community used the same calendar as Enoch and Jubilees. Undoubtedly, the Qumraners had affinities with the group that produced the apocalyptic writings.

The apocalyptic literature begins in the Old Testament with the Book of Daniel and blossoms into full flower in the "pseudepigraphic" literature such as the Book of Enoch, IV Esdras, and the Testaments of the Twelve Patriarchs. Unfortunately, these are not readily accessible to the general reader, for they are not included in the Apocrypha: but they will be found in English translation in R. H. Charles's monumental *Apocrypha and Pseudepigrapha*, Volume II.

With the help of ideas originally derived from Persian religion the apocalyptists made a significant advance on the prophetic interpretation of history by elevating it to cosmic dimensions. They believed in a cosmic dualism between the kingdom of God and the kingdom of evil. Unlike Persian dualism, however, which believed in a permanent opposition between these two principles, the apocalyptic dualism was only provisional. Here they were true to Old Testament insights. God was still the Creator of the universe: there was a time when evil was not and God was. The kingdom of evil was the result of a rebellion within the created order on the part of Satan and his angels. Moreover, this rebellion would last only as long as God permitted it to endure. Meanwhile, history was the scene of conflict between God and his angels and Satan and his. God was on the side of Israel, or at least of the faithful in Israel, while the devil employed as the instruments of his hostility towards God's people the succeeding world empires. History was hastening toward a final catastrophe in which the whole created order would collapse and a new heaven and new earth would be established by God on the ruins of the old, and the elect would be brought into everlasting bliss in his kingdom. The method of apocalyptic writers was to relate past history up to their own time in symbolic imagery, emphasizing the supernatural nature of the conflict behind the scenes. Then, as they reach the moment in history where they themselves are standing, they take a leap into the future. The conflict is intensified and spreads throughout the whole cosmic order. Sometimes an antichrist appears, the satanic counterpart of the agent of God's redemption. Then God himself intervenes, sometimes directly, sometimes, if our texts can be trusted (for they have been preserved by the Christian Church and are sometimes open to the suspicion of Christian interpolation), in the person of an agent of redemption called the "Son of man." He finally overthrows the last world empire and the powers of evil behind it, and establishes his reign throughout the universe.

The teachings of the apocalyptists are generally couched in the form of visions granted to great biblical worthies of the past, such as Enoch, Moses, Baruch, and Ezra. The reason for this device is that the period of revelation was thought to have closed with the law and the prophets, and the only way in which the new teaching could be put across as revealed truth was by pretending it was part of the original revelation. There is an element of truth in this for the apocalyptists are fundamentally true to the insights of the Old Testament. God is Creator and Lord of history, whose purpose is not just an abstract, eternal truth, but something to be realized at the end of history.

A brief account of some of the more important apocalypses follows.

1. The Testament of the Twelve Patriarchs

This was written in Hebrew in the latter part of the second century B.C. In its complete form it survives only in Greek translation, though fragments of some of its Aramaic sources have turned up at Qumran. As its title suggests, it is cast into the form of farewell discourses delivered by each of the twelve sons of Jacob. Each patriarch delivers a warning against the particular sin which marred his own life and exhorts his posterity to pursue the opposite virtue. Only Joseph and Issachar are exceptions who could point to their own virtues for imitation. To this advice is added, except in the case of Gad, a number of apocalyptic predictions.

This work is of importance for the study of the New Testament. Its ethical teaching anticipates in some respects the ethical teaching of Jesus and the exhortations of the New Testament epistles. Its dualistic language about light and darkness, truth and falsehood finds a striking echo, even verbally, in the Johannine writings.

2. I Enoch

This is a highly composite document whose various parts were composed over the period of a century (165–63 B.C.). Contemporary scholars believe that it was originally written, not in Hebrew, but Aramaic. It survives as a whole only in an Ethiopic translation of a Greek version, but much of the Greek version has been recovered in recent years.

After an introduction (Chapters 1–5) there follows a section (6–36) on the fate of the fallen angels of Genesis 6:1–4, whom Enoch visits in their subterranean prison. Then comes a section known as the Parables or Similitudes of Enoch (Chapters 37–71). Three parables are presented, each of them on the theme of the Last Judgment. This section is of particular importance to the New Testament scholar, for it is seemingly the earliest evidence we have in Judaism of the figure of the Son of man as the agent of God's judgment and redemption. If we could be sure that this section of Enoch is pre-Christian, it would be an important clue to Jesus' use of the term Son of man. But it is not at all certain that this part of Enoch is in fact pre-Christian, for none of it has as yet turned up among our considerable Greek fragments of the work.

After a section on astronomy (Chapters 78–82), there follow two visions (83–90), the first relating the judgment of the world in the flood of Noah, and the second the history of the world, with special reference to Israel and to the time of the Maccabees. This section concludes with a vision of the Messianic age, which in this part is pictured as a permanent reign of God on earth.

The last part of the book (Chapters 91–108) consists of miscellaneous material, partly historical and partly apocalyptic.

It will be seen that the teaching of the work, precisely because of its composite character, is far from uniform. In some parts the final reign of God is located on this earth, while in others it is pictured as beyond history, in the new heaven and new earth.

The Book of Enoch has the distinction of being quoted in the New Testament (Jude 14 f., which cites Enoch 1:9).

This does not pretend to be an exhaustive account of the apocalyptic literature, but it introduces the reader to the content of the more important writings in the period between the two Testaments. The equally important IV Esdras is not considered here, since it was not written until the latter half of the first century of the Christian era.

C. PALESTINIAN SECTS

It has long been known that in addition to the main currents of Palestinian Judaism there were a number of "sects."

Both Josephus and Philo (as well as the Roman writer, Pliny the Elder) speak of the Essenes, a community of ascetics, concentrated mainly in the Dead Sea area. They maintained a strict observance of the law according to their own interpretation of it, which however was different from that of the Pharisees. The whole subject of the Essenes has been placed in a new light by the discovery of the Dead Sea Scrolls (see below).

Josephus speaks of a fourth philosophy (*sic*: he is using a term which will appeal to his Hellenistic readers), though he does not tell us what it is. The common theory is that he was speaking of the Zealots, who figure in the synoptic gospels. These were the militant nationalists, who sought to overthrow the hated rule of Rome and to re-establish an independent Jewish state by force of arms. Outbreaks of rebellion occurred from time to time, beginning with that of Judas the Gaulonite in A.D. 6 (see Acts 5:37): the war of A.D. 66–70 represents the climax, and the revolt of Bar Cochba in A.D. 132 the final desperate attempt. Doctrinally, there was no significant difference between the Zealots and the Pharisees: both groups were concerned to uphold the purity of the law against foreign accretions. The real difference was one of method. The Pharisees were quietists: they discouraged the use of force, much as they sympathized with the Zealots' aims.

At least one of the followers of Jesus was a Zealot, namely Simon the Canaanite or "Zealot." It is possible that others were sympathetic to their ideals and even in some cases their methods. Judas Iscariot and the two sons of Zebedee (sons of thunder!) may have been attracted to both aims and methods, while Simon Peter, judging from the conception of Messiahship which he propounded at Caesarea Philippi, may have shared some of their aims. Jesus himself seems to have exercised a peculiar fascination over some of these people and to have constantly shaped his program in conscious rejection of theirs.

D. THE DAMASCUS COVENANTERS

In 1896 there was discovered in the ruins of a "Genizah" in Cairo, that is, a room in a synagogue where worn-out copies of sacred writings were deposited, a manuscript which came to be known variously as the "Damascus Document," "Zadokite Work," or "Fragments of a Zadokite Work." It is the product of a group which called itself the "people of the New Covenant," which at some date apparently migrated from Judea to Damascus under the leadership of a teacher called the "Star" (from Numbers 24:17). The exact date of the document and the history of this community were much debated between 1896 and 1947. Various dates between 170 B.C. and the end of the second century A.D. were suggested, while a few contended that the documents were a medieval forgery. But the discovery of another copy of the same document at Qumran and its obvious affinities with the other Qumran literature has placed the problem of the *Damascus Document* in an entirely new light.

E. THE QUMRAN COMMUNITY

So we come to the Dead Sea Scrolls themselves. The romantic story of their accidental discovery in 1947 and of the subsequent discoveries in the same area since that date has been frequently told and need not be repeated here. The bulk of the main documents is reliably translated by Millar Burrows in *The Dead Sea Scrolls* (1955). A more complete, though not always reliable, translation of the material is in *The Scriptures of the Dead Sea Sect* by Theodore H. Gaster (1947). An authoritative account by an expert working in the field is to be found in *The Ancient Library of Qumran* by F. M. Cross, Jr. (1958). The layman will find a simple but reliable account in *A Guide to the Scrolls* by R. P. C. Hanson, A. R. C. Leaney, and J. Posen (1958). There are other accounts, some of them much more colorful and exciting, which however sometimes lack that scholarly caution which at this stage particularly should be observed in the treatment of the subject. Nor are we here concerned with the manuscripts or fragments of biblical and apocryphal and known pseudepigraphal works, the importance of which lies mainly in the textual field. We shall here confine our attention to four fairly complete documents from Cave I at Qumran on the northwestern edge of the Dead Sea, and to the light they throw on the beliefs and practices of the sect, particularly in relation to the study of Judaism between the two Testaments and to the origins of New Testament Christianity. These four documents are:

> The Habakkuk Commentary
> The Manual of Discipline
> The War of the Sons of Light and
> the Sons of Darkness
> The Thanksgiving Psalms

It is also quite certain that the Damascus Document mentioned above belongs to the same group of writings. There is also the archaeological evidence of the ruined community center of Qumran, close to the cave of the original discoveries.

These documents reveal the existence of a community with its own distinctive beliefs and way of life. Its founder was a "teacher of righteousness," who was considered a fresh and inspired interpreter of the original revelation in the Old Covenant. Under his guidance a group of Jews had separated themselves from what they said was "the habitation of perverse men to go into the wilderness to prepare the way of the Lord." The chosen wilderness was by the Dead Sea, where they studied their scripture intensively, wrote commentaries upon it, held all their property in common, lived together under a rigorous discipline while awaiting the end time, when God's universal rule would be established under the leadership of the royal messiah from the line of David and of the priestly messiah from the line of Aaron. Like the early Christians they believed themselves to be members of the New Covenant; in ideal they were the "poor in spirit" who followed the way (cf. Acts 9:2) under the authority of twelve laymen.

Like the apocalyptists, with whom in some respects they had close affinities, the covenanters believed that the world was characterized by a provisional dualism of good and evil, of light and darkness which throughout history have been in conflict. When God created the world he made two warring spirits, the spirit of truth and the spirit of lying (cf. I John 4:1-6), the latter being the Prince of Darkness, Satan. All men are predestined, as it were, to live under one of these spirits; hence all men can be divided into two groups, the children of light and the children of darkness. But the two worlds, as in the teaching of the apocalyptists, were not coeternal. The world of darkness came as a rebellion against the world of light, and was destined one day to perish. Thus we find certain affinities with later Gnosticism, but also certain differences which are even more important—differences which the Qumran sect shares with early Christianity. For like both the Old and the New Testaments, the Qumran sect believed in one holy and righteous God.

Two scholars, whose views received considerable attention in the press, went so far as to argue that the teacher of righteousness was actually regarded as Messiah, that he suffered death at the hands of the wicked priest, that he had risen again from the dead, and that he was expected to come again as Messiah at the end. It is doubtful whether the champions of this theory could have evolved it without the help of the New Testament! For it rests upon a forced and unnatural interpretation of the texts. There is no doubt whatever that both the royal and priestly messiahs of the covenanters were totally distinct figures from the teacher of righteousness.

It is perhaps possible that the teacher of righteousness was regarded as the suffering servant along the lines of Isaiah 53. This is by no means certain, but if it was, his sufferings were interpreted as those of a martyr, atoning in value insofar as the deaths of all martyrs were atoning (a doctrine which arose in connection with the Maccabean martyrs) but not redemptive in the decisive way that the sufferings of Jesus are regarded as redemptive in the New Testament. The teacher was not the agent of redemption, whether during his earthly life or at a second coming. He was what he was called—a teacher, offering a new interpretation of the Mosaic revelation, to be observed by the true remnant in preparation for the end. True, both Christianity and the Qumran community speak of the New Covenant. But for the Qumran sect, this is a covenant of law and promise, rather than the covenant of an already inaugurated redemption.

The Qumran community organized its common life along lines which suggest certain features of the later Christian organization. The Damascus Document speaks of officials known as "visitors" or "assessors," the exact verbal equivalent of the New Testament *episcopoi* or "bishops" (A.V.). But the distinctively Christian apostle, the bearer of witness to an already inaugurated redemption, is conspicuously lacking.

One of the salient features of their common life was the practice of ritual washings, for the performance of which they installed an elaborate system of water supply in their monastery. In addition to daily rites of purification, they practiced a baptism of initiation. There were also common meals in which bread and wine were used and which were regarded as anticipations of the Messianic banquet. These practices are striking adumbrations of the two gospel sacraments. But, in accordance with the sect's general theological trends, these rites are dominated by the "not yet" to the exclusion of the "already." They look forward, not both backward and forward, as do the Christian sacraments.

If there was any direct link between the Qumran movement and the early Church, that link must have been John the Baptist (see below). But even if positive proof were forthcoming of such a connection, New Testament Christianity is no mere continuation of the Qumran movement. It has a wholly new understanding of redemption centered upon Jesus as the agent through whom it has been inaugurated, an understanding which vitally transforms all the other points of similarity with the people of the Dead Sea Scrolls.

The history of the Qumran sect is difficult to trace from the scrolls. There are all sorts of vague historical allusions in the texts, but it is extremely difficult to pin them down to the known facts of history. Most likely it originated as a schism during the Hasmonaean period, perhaps not later than the reign of Alexander Jannaeus (see above). Like the other great movements within contemporary Judaism, it was an outcome of the great spiritual revival which began under the Chasidim. Were they identical with the Essenes (see above)? Of their general affinity with them there can be no question, though there are certain differences. Many scholars, possibly the majority, have no hesitation in accepting their complete identification. Perhaps, however, it would be safer to say that they were one branch within the Essene movement.

To sum up, we may safely say that the Qumran covenanters were one of the several streams within first-century Judaism which made their contribution to New Testament Christianity. Their discovery has illuminated several aspects of primitive Christianity whose antecedents were previously difficult to trace, and which led scholars to look for precedents outside Judaism. They provided some of the ideas (whether directly or indirectly) and some of the customs which enabled the early Church to formulate its witness and obedient response to the act of God in Christ. But they do not and cannot undermine the uniqueness of that act.

F. JOHN THE BAPTIST AND JESUS OF NAZARETH

From a purely historical point of view it would be more appropriate to consider the movement initiated by John the Baptist as part of first-century Judaism and therefore as part of the inter-Testamental period, rather than as the first part of the New Testament. Such a purely historical survey might also include the ministry of Jesus. For Christianity, properly speaking, does not begin until after the death of Jesus, by which the New Covenant was believed to be inaugurated. From the theological point of view, however, the act of God which culminates in the death and resurrection begins with the outpouring of the Spirit upon Jesus at his baptism by John. John is the "beginning of the gospel," and the apostolic witness to the act of God in Christ begins with firsthand testimony to John the Baptist (Acts 1:22). We prefer therefore to treat the ministry of Jesus as the opening of the New Testament, as the prelude to the Christian gospel, rather than as the epilogue of the inter-Testamental period.

Yet it must be borne in mind that historically it is to the inter-Testamental period that both John and Jesus belong. For neither of them springs out of the blue, nor even directly from the Old Testament, but precisely from the interpretation and understanding of the Old Testament tradition which grew up in the period between the two Testaments. Thus a whole host of concepts appear in their teaching which cannot be explained solely from the Old Testament, but require a knowledge of the inter-Testamental development for their understanding.

That is true of such concepts as the kingdom or reign of God, the age to come, the Son of man (possibly, see above), Holy Spirit (as a phenomenon of the age to come), New Covenant, etc. This is what makes the study of the inter-Testamental period so important for the student of the New Testament. A bridge is needed from the Old Testament to the New, and of that bridge the presence of the Apocrypha in the Bibles on Anglican lecterns is a fitting symbol and reminder.

As regards John the Baptist, it is becoming increasingly probable that he was in some sense a "breakaway" from Qumran. Luke's statement that he "was in the wilderness till the day of his manifestation to Israel" (Luke 1:80) suggests that he was actually brought up as a boy in the community. The scrolls give evidence that the community cared for and trained children in this way. John's choice of the Jordan as the scene of his activity tallies with his having left the nearby Qumran. His teaching about the Coming Age and his practice of water baptism can be understood as growing out of Qumran theology and practice. But there are significant differences, which justify our regarding him as a definite breakaway. Unlike the Qumraners, he is not content to sit inside the "monastery" cultivating his spiritual life in preparation for the end, admitting any who care to knock on the door, but not caring whether they come or not. Rather, John is missionary-minded. He goes out and challenges men publicly to repent in preparation for the Coming Age. Nor is this repentance expressed in an enclosed community life: rather it must take place in the workaday world where men are (see Luke 3:10–14). More than this, it has been suggested that John actually looked for the coming of *two* Messiahs, like the Qumraners (see above, p. 238). One Messiah would be the Strong One (Mark 1:8), who would baptize with fire (Matthew 3:11 paragraph). This, it is suggested, is the same as the Qumraners' Messiah of David, the military figure. The other Messiah would baptize with Spirit (ibid.). This figure would be the Qumraners' Messiah of Aaron, the priestly figure. Christian tradition will then have identified both Messiahs with Jesus, combining them into one. About himself John was very reticent, but his striking dress (Mark 1:6) is clear proof that he cast himself in a pro-phetic role. He would seem to have regarded himself definitely as the Messianic Prophet who, in some forms of the Qumran expectation, was to precede the coming Messiahs. It is thus understandable how on the one hand Christian tradition came to see in him the forerunner of Jesus, while on the other hand later disciples of John himself came to regard him as the bearer of a gnostic type of Revelation (see below, p. 389).

G. HELLENISTIC JUDAISM

There are however two bridges from the Old Testament to the New. The first is Palestinian Judaism, which leads to Jesus and the earliest Church. The second is Hellenistic Judaism, which leads to pre-Pauline Hellenistic Christianity and to Paul himself. The chief center of this type of Judaism was in Alexan-dria in Egypt.

Since Jewish settlers in foreign lands adopted the language of their new country, it was necessary to translate the Hebrew scriptures into Greek. This translation was produced gradually to meet the needs of synagogue worship, the Pentateuch being first translated somewhere in the middle of the third century B.C. The difficulties involved in translating the scriptures from Hebrew into Greek are feelingly described by the grandson of Jesus, son of Sirach, in his preface to the Greek version of Ecclesiasticus:

> For things originally spoken in Hebrew have not the same force in them when they are translated into another tongue: and not only these, but the law itself, and the prophecies, and the rest of the books, have no small dif-ference, when they are spoken in their original language.
> (E.R.V.)

The kind of problem posed for the translator is well illustrated by the attempt to render into Greek a word like *kabod*, the Hebrew word for "glory." This is a purely biblical concept, and there was no already existing word for it in Greek. The Septuagint translators decided to use the Greek word *doxa*. Now in Plato's writings the noun *doxa*, which derives from a verb meaning "to seem" or "appear," is used to denote that which seems to be, "opinion," as opposed to that which is, "reality." In more popular usage it was used to express other people's *opinions* about a man, hence his "reputation." It was this popular meaning which suggested to the Septuagint translators the possibility of using it to render *kabod*, "glory." The result was that it came to mean almost the exact opposite of what it had meant in Plato. It also lost something of the dynamic quality of the original Hebrew, which denoted God's presence in action, and became more static in meaning.

Scholars have naturally debated the extent to which the Old Testament suffered by being translated into Greek. Is the whole biblical revelation thereby transposed into a non-Hebraic, essentially Hellenistic key? Sometimes this was bound to happen. For instance, the sacred name Yahweh was translated *Kyrios*, the common word for "cult deity." This did not necessarily imply that Yahweh was just another of the "lords many" of the Greco-Roman world. Yet some of the pagan associations of *Kyrios* were inevitably carried over, as can be seen from the ease with which Greek-speaking Christians adopted it as a title for the exalted Jesus. A transference of the name Yahweh to Jesus would have been unthinkable.

On the whole, however, as the instance of *doxa* shows, it was the Greek words rather than the Hebraic meanings which suffered. Greek words were violently twisted in order to convey the biblical revelation, and thus the foundations were laid for New Testament Greek, a Greek which has suffered a further violent twist in order to convey the proclamation of the act of God in Christ. Our forefathers were not so far from the truth when they spoke of the "language of the Holy Ghost."

Nevertheless the way in which the Jews of the dispersion held and practiced their faith was bound to diverge from the way it was held and practiced in the homeland. To begin with, it was impossible to observe the law with the meticulous regard for detail which was possible in Palestine, at least in Pharisaic circles. There the dominant impulse was toward elaboration in order to bring every moment of life under the control of the law. In the dispersion, however, the opposite tendency was at work, namely the desire to reduce the law's demands to a minimum in order to mitigate the inconveniences arising from its observation in a pagan environment. Thus, in effect, three points, circumcision, the Sabbath, and the abstention from pork, became the distinguishing marks of the Jew abroad. While they held fast to the ethical prescriptions of the law— and it was their high standard of morality which favorably impressed their pagan neighbors and attracted them to Judaism more than anything else—they tended to fill in the blanks not covered by the precepts of the law by adopting the manners and customs of their neighbors. Moreover, where Jewish morality coincided in spirit or precept with the best of pagan morality, they tended to present their ethical teaching, especially in the instruction of proselytes, in the language and forms of Hellenistic moral teaching. Thus we find such unbiblical words as "virtue," and the four cardinal virtues—justice, prudence, temperance, and fortitude—adopted as commonplaces of Hellenistic Jewish ethics, together with the "household codes," indicating the duties of family life.

Nor was theology unaffected. In addition to their high standard of morality, the Jews of the dispersion were noted among their neighbors for their monotheism, their belief in one God. It was a time when the more serious-minded in the Gentile world were generally dissatisfied with the old anthropomorphic polytheism of the city-state cults. Men were looking either to the more spiritual cult deities, or, in philosophical circles, for a genuinely spiritual monotheism. Thus Hellenistic Judaism enjoyed a favorable environment, not only for the preservation, but also for the propagation, of its faith in the one God. It was therefore not surprising that Greek-speaking Jews took over not only the ethical notions, but also some of the theological notions of their philosophical contemporaries. They adopted Stoic arguments against polytheism and idolatry and their "proofs" for the existence of God. They began to think about what God was in himself, and to speak of his attributes, thus moving away from the biblical conviction that God could be known only in his actions.

As the foregoing paragraphs have hinted, Hellenistic Judaism became a missionary religion. The statement in Matthew 23:15:

> . . . you traverse sea and land to make a single proselyte . . . (R.S.V.)

may be an exaggeration, as far as Palestine is concerned, but it was certainly true of the dispersion. This missionary expansion, as we have already had occasion to note, accounts in part at any rate for the enormous number of Jews scattered about in the Roman Empire. But the Jewish mission to the Gentiles was hampered by several impediments. While it appealed to the lower classes and to women in the upper classes of society, it made little appeal to the educated. This no doubt accounts for the limited clientèle Paul found for the Christian mission when he came to Corinth:

> For consider your call, brethren; not many of you were wise according to worldly standards, not many were powerful, not many were of noble birth. *I Corinthians* 1:26 (R.S.V.)

The chief obstacle to conversions was the requirement of circumcision and the observance of the ceremonial law, even in its minimized form. Consequently many remained on the fringe of Judaism, accepting its faith in the one God, and endeavoring to live up to its moral standards, but hesitating to take the final plunge and become full members of the Jewish community. These are the "God-fearers" of the New Testament, who provided a fertile soil for conversions to the Christian gospel.

We are fortunate in possessing a considerable body of Alexandrian Jewish literature, which has been carefully preserved, not by the Jews, but by the later Christian Church of that city. Since rabbinic Judaism became normative after the fall of Jerusalem in A.D. 70, the Jews themselves suppressed the literary monuments of Hellenistic Judaism and left it all to the

Christians. They even prepared new translations of the Old Testament in Greek, since the Septuagint had become a Christian book. The Apocrypha, as part of the Septuagint, was likewise left to the Christians, as well as the non-biblical literature.

The principal survivals of Alexandrian Judaism are the Book of Wisdom and the voluminous writings of Philo. The purpose of this literature was twofold. First, it was to keep the Jews loyal to their faith amid the subtle and all-pervading temptations, intellectual, moral, and religious, of the pagan world. The method adopted was to restate the biblical faith in terms congenial to the Gentile environment. The second purpose was to refute pagan arguments against Judaism and to commend the Jewish religion to the Gentiles as a reasonable faith. To this literature we must now pay brief attention.

It is generally agreed that the so-called Wisdom of Solomon, one of the chief writings in the Apocrypha, was originally written in Greek. That means that it could not have been written, as it purports to be, by King Solomon. The author was most likely an Alexandrian Jew writing in the first half of the first century B.C., though some authorities would date his work later. The book falls into two main sections:

CHAPTERS 1–9: These chapters set forth wisdom as the way of salvation and its rejection as the way to perdition. Chapters 6–9 describe wisdom as she is in herself.

CHAPTERS 10–19: A recital of Israel's history, showing how wisdom had been her guide throughout, causing Israel to prosper and her enemies to fall.

It is much debated whether the author of Wisdom had a firsthand acquaintance with Greek philosophy and, if so, to what extent it had penetrated his thought. His conception of wisdom is itself clearly a combination of Old Testament and Greek ideas. He starts with wisdom as she is depicted in the Book of Proverbs, especially in Chapter 8 of that work. Here wisdom means God engaged in creation and in the direction of the redemptive history. Wisdom is an aspect of God's being in action. This mainly poetical concept the author of the Book of Wisdom elevates to a quasi-personified reality, distinguishable, though not distinct in being, from God himself (Wisdom 7:25 f.). The ancestry of this line of thought is mainly Platonic. But to it the author further adds the Stoic conception of the Logos (literally, "word"; here, "reason") which is at once the divine reason within man, enabling him to acquire knowledge of the physical constitution of the world and its ways (Wisdom 7:15 ff.) and guiding him in his moral life (9:9b–13), and at the same time the principle of coherence immanent in the material universe (1:7; 7:24–27). From Platonism, whether or not he had a direct acquaintance with Plato's writings, he derives three notions concerning the soul: its pre-existence; its incorporeal nature; and its immortality (3:1 ff.; 9:15 f.). He also regards it as "weighed down" by the body in a manner reminiscent of the Orphic and Pythagorean doctrine of the body as the soul's tomb:

> For a corruptible body weigheth down the soul,
> And the earthly frame lieth heavy on a mind that is full
>   of cares.   9:15 (E.R.V.)

An Old Testament writer could hardly have written this, for it assumes that the soul belongs to a higher order of being than the body.

The Book of Wisdom is important for the New Testament scholar. St. Paul was clearly familiar with it, for there are a number of striking echoes of its language in the early chapters of Romans. Paul found particularly helpful on his missionary labors its apologetic against idolatry and its attack on pagan immorality. Further, its "liberal" approach to the wisdom of the Greeks laid the foundation for the Alexandrian synthesis between biblical and Greek thought which reached its full flower in Origen, one of the greatest of the Church fathers. And its developed concept of wisdom provided the tools for Christological definition in the period of the great councils of the early Church.

The other outstanding writer of Alexandrian Judaism is Philo, who flourished in the first half of the first century A.D.

The bulk of his writings, some thirty-eight volumes, consists of commentaries on the Pentateuch. They are written to support the thesis that the Mosaic revelation contains in revealed and perfected form the philosophy and ethics of the best of Gentile thought. To achieve this end, he took over a method of interpreting ancient documents which had been worked out earlier by secular scholars at Alexandria and employed by them to refine the crudities of Homeric and other early mythology. This method was known as allegorical interpretation. While not denying the literal, historical sense of scripture, Philo discovers a hidden, more philosophical meaning in the text. For example, the patriarchs become types of various virtues, the migration of Abraham an allegory of the pilgrimage of man's soul. Philo borrowed ideas from a variety of sources—from Platonism and Stoicism, and from the rather vague religiosity current in the mystery religions, and, as some hold, from early forms of Gnosticism.

It is difficult to decide which element was constitutive for Philo's thinking. Was his theology fundamentally Jewish or Greek? He really desires to be loyal to the biblical revelation, but at times he slips almost unconsciously into unbiblical ways of thought. For example, he conceives God's transcendence not so much in terms of *action*—as a God who judges and saves, yet whose judgment and salvation are always beyond us and ahead of us—as in terms of *essence*—as a God whose being consists of a kind of supernatural "stuff," above and beyond all that we can know in this world. His exposition of I AM THAT I AM, "He who is" very easily slides into "that which is," the impersonal reality behind all phenomena. Yet on the whole these are probably no more than momentary lapses. God, then, is above and beyond his creation, utterly transcendent and unknowable. Yet he communicates with it, and does so by a series of mediators or principles of mediation. These mediators represent a curious amalgam of Jewish, Platonic, and Stoic notions. There are the angels of the Old Testament and Judaism. There are the demons of popular Greek lore, the "forces" of Stoicism and the "ideas" of Plato. Presiding over them all as the chief mediatorial principle is the Logos (see above), who here takes over most of the functions exterior to man which are performed by wisdom in the Book of Wisdom. Philo preferred the concept of Logos to wisdom because Logos was masculine and wisdom (Sophia) feminine. The Logos was the first being created by God and was then used by him as the agent in creating the rest of the universe. It pervades matter as the source of its coherence and order. Man has a dual nature. Philo knew of the two stories of creation in Genesis 1–2 long before the nineteenth century critics! Genesis 1 relates the creation of the heavenly man or "mind," Genesis 2 the bodily aspect of man. The heavenly man dwells immanently in the earthly man, imparting to human beings an element of divinity. Man's chief end is to know God. Here Philo exhibits a mystical strain derived from the welter of contemporary oriental and Hellenistic religiosity. By his mind or reason man can however know only that God *is* and know what are his attributes, chiefly in the form of what he is not. The authentic knowledge of God as he is in himself is conveyed only in moments of intense mystical awareness of metaphysical reality. All this sounds very unbiblical. Yet the conception of the word of God, implying a personal I-thou relationship between God and man is also found, and here Philo is true to the Old Testament.

On the whole it would be true to say that Philo attempted more than he could achieve. He sought to construct a synthesis between the Hebraic tradition and the best of non-biblical philosophy and piety. He bequeathed his task to the Christian Platonists of Alexandria, who were as successful in achieving the synthesis he sought as it is humanly possible to be.

Is Philo himself a bridge between the Old Testament and the New? Traces of his influence have been sought in the Pauline writings, and more definitely in the epistle to the Hebrews and in the Johannine literature. Whether such influence is proven is another matter. The utmost we can say for certain is that some of Philo's ideas were not peculiar to himself but were generally current in the Hellenistic synagogues. Christian missionaries in the dispersion were bound to come to terms with them. On the whole, however, the differences between the Hellenistic Christianity of the New Testament and Philo's thought are more important and significant than the similarities.

H. JOSEPHUS

The Jewish historian Josephus was born in Jerusalem in A.D. 37 or 38, but since he wrote in Greek mainly for Gentile readers and sought to commend Judaism to them along Hellenistic Jewish lines, he belongs to Hellenistic rather than Palestinian Judaism. His method of doing so was by writing history rather than by philosophical or religious argument.

His two main works, *The Jewish War* (seven volumes written shortly after the fall of Jerusalem in A.D. 70) and *The Jewish Antiquities* (the history of the Jews from the creation to the eve of the Jewish war) serve this apologetic purpose. He sought to present the history of the Jews in as favorable a light as possible, to demonstrate that in earlier times they had been held in great esteem and allowed religious freedom. Although chronologically he is contemporaneous with the New Testament writings, he serves as a bridge from the Old Testament to the New because he enables us to fill in much of the background of the inter-Testamental period. For the rise of Christianity itself he has little or nothing to tell us. In *Antiquities* 18:5 he corroborates the fact of John the Baptist's execution by Herod Antipas, and tells us that this took place in the fortress of Machaerus. Another long passage in 18:3, together with numerous passages in the Slavonic version of *The Jewish War*, purports to give accounts of Jesus. All of this material however is undoubtedly the result of Christian interpolation, and quite valueless. But there is one passage (*Antiquities* 20:9) which relates the execution of James, the brother of the Lord, and says explicitly that he was "the brother of Jesus, said to be the Christ." Many scholars have suspected that this reference to Jesus was also a Christian interpolation. Yet the phrase "said to be" is not quite the way in which Christians would have spoken of their master. In our view this is a genuine reference, and therefore Josephus does at least show an awareness that our Lord was a historical personage, who had a brother.

This must conclude our brief survey of the period between the two Testaments. It is largely the story of a great spiritual ferment which began at the time of the Maccabean revolt. The movement thus released however soon broke up, and the fragments moved in different directions. Consequently its achievements were largely sterile. Yet it was out of the same spiritual ferment that, humanly speaking, Christianity also arose, and with the person of Jesus, interpreted as the decisive act of God, the new religion was able to give coherence to the genuine insights of the various streams in that spiritual ferment. Or, to change the metaphor, the Judaism of the inter-Testamental period provided the seed bed in which the gospel was planted and in which it could thrive in its early days as a tender plant.

PART IV

THE NEW TESTAMENT

CHAPTER I

IN THE BEGINNING WAS THE WORD

What is "basic Christianity"? The man in the street would give various answers to this question. Some would say it was just the simple teaching of Jesus. Some would say it was the Sermon on the Mount. Some define it explicitly as the two great commandments, love of God and love of the neighbor. Some would define it philosophically as the fatherhood of God and the brotherhood of man. In one way or another all these definitions come to pretty much the same thing. For them all, the Christian religion means the religion of Jesus, the religion he believed, taught, and practiced. Hand in hand with this attitude there always goes the further assumption that this originally simple religion of Jesus was, very soon after his day, overlaid and obscured by a religion *about* Jesus. A simple piety and ethic were overlaid by a complicated doctrine of salvation, together with an ecclesiastical organization and a sacramental system. These superstructures may have been valuable in their day, for they secured the preservation of the simple basic religion. But modern scholarship, it is thought, has enabled us to strip away the superstructure and recover the primitive simplicity.

Fifty years ago such a position could claim the support of the best contemporary scholarship. But as so often happens in other spheres, the man in the street has been left far behind by the advance of scholarship. More recent academic study of the New Testament has demonstrated that this conception of basic Christianity is a figment of the imagination. Christianity began as a *proclamation,* an announcement by certain men in Palestine about A.D. 30 that a particular event, or rather series of events, which had recently transpired, was the act of God—not just an act of God, but the final, decisive act of God for us men and our salvation. Jesus had been sent by God into the world, at a particular time and particular place, into the Jewish world which was looking precisely for such an event. His death on Calvary was not just an ordinary human martyrdom, the heroic death of one who died for his beliefs rather than capitulate to his enemies, but the act in and through which God had made available the forgiveness of sins and thus brought men back to a normal relationship with himself. God had raised this Jesus from the dead and thus inaugurated that new age for which the Jews had hoped. After the resurrection, Jesus had appeared as risen to his followers. These appearances brought home to them that the events they had witnessed, the life and death of Jesus, were the great act of God by which man had been redeemed. Thus, to the original disciples, the interpretation which they ascribed to that series of events was not one which they had thought out for themselves. It was one which had forced itself upon them from outside through the resurrection experiences. Moreover this interpretation of the event was not just an external piece of information communicated to them certainly, but leaving them otherwise just as they were. For, as they put it, the risen Lord had imparted to them his "Spirit." The Spirit was not some kind of supernatural substance. It was rather God acting upon them immediately, directly, and in a quite final way and making available for them the whole content of the salvation which the event had inaugurated. Moreover, this direct acting of God enabled them to proclaim to their contemporaries the event with its significance, so that they, too, might accept it as something done for them and, by thus accepting it, appropriate the blessings flowing from it for themselves—or, as the disciples themselves expressed it, "receive the Holy Spirit." Those who accepted the proclamation and "received the Spirit" were thus brought into an already existing community. As the Acts of the Apostles significantly expresses it, they "were added"—that is to say, God placed them in an already existing community, the community of the last days.

Such was the nature of the earliest proclamation as it is recorded for us in the early chapters of Acts. But surely, the man in the street objects, the author of Acts is already writing from the standpoint of a somewhat later age, when the original religion of Jesus had been transformed into a religion about him. Such an objection however can no longer stand the scrutiny of scholarship. To begin with, scholars have shown that the speeches in the early part of Acts (St. Peter's sermon at Pentecost, and even more strikingly the speech in Chapter 3) are clearly Greek translations of an Aramaic original, that is to say, of the language actually spoken by the earliest Christians at Jerusalem. Thus they can hardly be dismissed as the free compositions of a later Greek-speaking Christian: the author must have derived them from some primitive source. That is not to say that they represent the exact words Peter said on those particular occasions. But they do represent the type of thing Peter and his associates did proclaim. A second point to be noticed is that the presentation of the earliest Christian message in these chapters tallies remarkably with the sort of basic preaching which St. Paul takes for granted in his letters to the churches. To this basic message Paul himself refers, moreover, as something he had "received" from others who were Christians before him (I Corinthians 15:3), and whose content he checked with the original apostles on a visit to Jerusalem, not, be it noted, soon after his conversion, but after many years' absence in the mission field, when he had had every opportunity to develop in his own peculiar direction (Galatians 2:1–10). The basic message follows this pattern:

> *Jesus of Nazareth,*
> *born of the seed of David,*
> *died,*
> *was buried:*
> *God raised him the third day*
> *and exalted him to his right hand*
> *as Messiah, Lord and Son of God*

until he comes as Judge and Savior.
In all this God has fulfilled his promises in Scripture
and inaugurated the Age to Come.
The apostles are witnesses of these things,
and offer to those who accept their message
baptism for the remission of sins
and the gift of the Holy Spirit.

The same presentation of Jesus and his history as the redemptive act of God underlies every one of the New Testament writings. The four gospels are really no more than expansions of this primitive outline of the event and its significance. The Acts of the Apostles is the account of how this preaching established the Christian community throughout the Mediterranean lands until finally it reached the capital of the Roman Empire itself. The epistles are expositions of the doctrinal and ethical implications of the gospel message, written in order to deal with the practical problems of thinking and living which had arisen in the communities founded by that same preaching. Dr. A. M. Hunter was not far off the point when he wrote: "In the beginning was the kerygma" (*The Unity of the New Testament,* 1943, p. 22: "kerygma" is the Greek word for the Christian gospel message, the proclamation of the redemptive act of God in Jesus Christ). Present-day American scholarship does not always take kindly to this. Leading New Testament scholars here are still anxious to stress the "varieties of New Testament religion." There is of course much truth in this position. Not only are there varieties in the doctrinal and ethical superstructures which the various writers in the New Testament erect upon the common basis—we need only compare the Pauline epistles with the pastorals or still more with the epistle of St. James to see this, or again the presentation of St. Matthew's gospel with that of St. John. What is more to the point is that there are also varieties in the presentation of the basic formula itself. For instance, St. Paul attaches to the mention of the death of Jesus the interpretative addition that it happened "for our sins" (I Corinthians 15:3), a feature notably absent from the speeches in Acts, while on the other hand the latter ascribe an importance to the life of Jesus before the crucifixion which is notoriously absent from Paul. Despite these varieties of formulation, however, the basic import of the proclamation is everywhere the same. It may be summed up in the words: "God was in Christ." Jesus—his person, and the series of events in which he was engaged—is the redemptive act of God.

It is worth noting that the primitive formulations of the basic Christian message contain in embryo all those features which the man in the street would like to dismiss as later accretions to the original simple gospel. Primarily, the earliest Christian message is a religion about Jesus, not a reproduction of his religion. It is definitely a gospel of salvation, not a system of teaching on piety and ethics, ultimately detachable from the person of Jesus, even if originally started by him. An integral part of the proclamation is the apostles themselves as witnesses of the event, a feature which contains in embryo the later insistence that the ministry is an integral part of the gospel. For however we explain the relation of the Church's ministry to the apostles, it certainly exists to perpetuate their witness to the event of Jesus Christ. And in the proclamation of the work of the Holy Spirit in the community we have the germ of the later articulated "sacramental system," as it is sometimes, though not altogether felicitously, called. Next, since the proclamation is the underlying basis of the whole New Testament, and since also it appeals to the Old Testament as well ("according to the scriptures"), it involves the acceptance of the whole Bible, both Old Testament and New, as an integral part of the Christian religion. Finally, the apostolic preaching is a summary remarkably like the early Christian creeds. Thus it will be seen that the preaching of the earliest apostles contains in embryo all those features which the man in the street so often regards as accretions and perversions of basic Christianity, those four features which, as the Church sees it, delineate the content of Christianity: the scriptures of the Old and New Testaments, the creeds as summaries and safeguards of the Christian faith, the two gospel sacraments, and the ministry. All these features are present in embryonic form in the earliest Christianity.

CHAPTER II

JESUS

A. INTRODUCTORY

Until quite recently, critical scholarship, both radical and conservative, has approached the gospels on the assumption that their primary purpose was to provide a historical account of the life of Jesus. Conservative scholars stressed the reliability of these as based directly or indirectly upon eyewitness accounts. Radical scholars distinguished between primary and secondary sources, and by a process of critical reconstruction sought to lay bare what they considered to be the original, authentic tradition about Jesus. The pendulum has now swung full circle. The gospels, we are now told, are completely "kerygmatic" in character. That is to say, they are written, not to record history, whether for information or entertainment, but to proclaim the good news of God's saving act in Christ. They are written "from faith to faith." They are written to serve the purposes of church life. It is useless to try to cut back behind the evangelical witness in the hope of rediscovering a "Jesus of history." In the gospels we can hear but the whisper of his voice and trace but the outskirts of his ways. Other scholars are discovering in the gospels elaborate symbolical patterns so artificially constructed that the question of their historicity is never so much as raised. If these views are correct, the gospels can be safely used, not as evidence for what Jesus said and did, but only as evidence for the beliefs of the Church at the time when they were written.

There is much truth in this. The primary purpose of the gospels is undoubtedly not historical or biographical, but to evoke faith. The explicit statement of the fourth gospel: "These things are written, that ye might believe that Jesus is the Christ, the Son of God; and that believing ye might have life in his name" (John 20:31) applies equally to the other three. But the pendulum has swung too far. The dilemma is not a true one. It is not really a question of either-or, *either* history *or* proclamation. As is so often the case, it is a question of both-and: *both* history *and* proclamation. The proclamation involves an interpretation precisely of history, and the gospel material consists of historical traditions shaped and molded so as to convey the proclamation. It is quite legitimate to use the methods of historical and literary criticism which were forged during the liberal period in order to reconstruct the underlying history. It is not only legitimate: it is also imperative to do so. For if the Christian proclamation involves an interpretation of a particular history, we have a right to know what that particular history was. This does not mean that our reconstruction of the history will prove that the gospel's interpretation of that history is true. The truth of the Christian proclamation is always a matter for personal decision for those who hear it proclaimed in the Church. But at least we have a right to be assured that the decision we are invited to make is wholly consonant with the character of that history, and not an imposition upon it. After all, we might be invited to make an act of faith in the saving significance of the history of Humpty Dumpty, and in view of the nature of his particular history that would be an entirely arbitrary demand. What we want to know and have a right to know is whether the original history, so far as we can recover it, occurred *within a similar frame of reference* to that in which it is placed in the Church's proclamation. We shall not expect the frame of reference to be identical. After all, when we seek to go back to the history of Jesus we are seeking to penetrate behind the great forty days, behind the Easter experience which convinced the disciples that the history of Jesus was the revelation and redemptive act of God. After the first Easter, they inevitably and rightly read the previous history in the light of the new insight into its meaning which Easter had forced upon them, and all the accounts of Jesus are inevitably and rightly colored by that insight. The task of the historian is to penetrate behind that insight and to lay bare the course of the history as it was actually happening. This is a hazardous and delicate task, and many would deny its feasibility. But the nettle must be grasped.

In the ensuing attempted reconstruction of the history of Jesus certain critical assumptions will be made. The first three gospels stand in a complicated literary relationship to one another, so that they cannot be accepted as three independent witnesses. The Markan gospel is the earliest of the three, probably written shortly before A.D. 70 and certainly not earlier than A.D. 65. Both Matthew and Luke are expansions of Mark, or possibly of an earlier and slightly different form of our canonical Mark, of which the canonical Mark is, like Matthew and Luke, an expansion, though less extensive than these. Matthew and Luke both used a further source or sources in addition to Mark, consisting of a collection or collections almost exclusively of sayings of Jesus. This material is conveniently designated "Q" (German, *Quelle*, source), though the writer prefers to speak of the "Q material" to avoid giving the impression that it was all derived from one written document now lost. Any attempt to date this material is mere guesswork. Some would place it as early as A.D. 50. Since Mark knew some of it, i.e., those parts in which Mark and Q overlap, that much at least will be earlier than Mark, that is, earlier than A.D. 65–70. But it is most improbable that Mark knew the rest of Q; it is difficult to suppose, for example, that he would have deliberately omitted such purple passages as the Lord's Prayer or the Beatitudes. It would seem that the Q material grew up by gradual additions and was current in different, though overlapping, forms in the various local churches. So we conclude that the rest of the Q material was not available to Mark when he wrote, and will therefore assume that these collections of sayings were becoming generally available just about the time when Mark himself put pen to paper. This is quite plausible, since the impulse to literary activity would have come when the original eyewitnesses were beginning to die and when an interval seemed certain between their deaths and the return of the Lord. St. Peter, for example, was almost certainly martyred at Rome in A.D. 64. In addition to Mark and the Q material, both Matthew and Luke also had available special material of their own unknown to either of the other two synoptic writers. We designate this the "special Matthaean" and the "special Lukan" material respectively, thus avoiding the impression that it was necessarily derived from written documents. Thus the synoptic gospels actually provide us with four sources of evidence for the life of Jesus and his teaching. Of these Mark and the Q material must have been fixed in written form at an earlier period than the special Matthaean and special Lukan material. Mark and the Q material will therefore be treated as primary sources, and special Matthaean and special Lukan as confirmatory evidence. This is not to say that the presence of sayings or deeds of Jesus in either of the primary strata is *ipso facto* a guarantee of their historical accuracy. Both collections are the outcome of a process of development in oral transmission, and the laws governing the development of oral tradition have to be rigorously applied.

Lastly, there is the question of the fourth gospel. This is here regarded as the product of a post-apostolic Christian writing toward the end of the first century. The discourses, though they undoubtedly enshrine traditional sayings of Jesus comparable to those found in the Q material, are as they stand the composition of the evangelist, or, as some now think, brought over by him from an extraneous source. Very little therefore of the discourse material can be used as evidence for the teaching of Jesus. But the narrative material in the fourth gospel appears to be derived from a body of oral tradition similar to that contained in the basic strata of the synoptic gospels. Some of it appears to be quite primitive and may well be used to supplement, and even on occasion to correct, the evidence found in the other gospels.

We shall eschew any attempt to write a connected life of Jesus. Since the basic material of the gospels consisted, in the stage of oral transmission, of isolated episodes originally detached from one another, such a procedure would be impossible. All we can say is that the broad outline of St. Mark's gospel, viz., that Jesus' ministry began with his baptism by John at the Jordan and that after this he proceeded to teach and to preach and to heal in Galilee, that he gathered around him an inner circle of followers and finally transferred his activity to Jerusalem, where, at the instance of the Jewish authorities he was executed by the Romans on the charge of being a revolutionary Messianic pretender, is substantially correct, since it is corroborated by the earliest preaching as we find it recorded in the Acts of the Apostles. Beyond that, each separate episode and each saying and parable has to be considered on its own merits, and its original setting is in each case a matter for discussion.

The layman might at first feel appalled to think that our knowledge of the historical Jesus is so uncertain, and that he is apparently so dependent on the verdicts of the experts, who in any case disagree so much among themselves as to which words of Jesus and stories about him are authentic. But the situation is not really as bad as that. Behind the words of Jesus and the memories about him—even behind those words and memories whose authenticity is doubtful—there shines forth a self-authenticating portrait of a real person in all his human uniqueness, an impression which is accessible alike to the layman and to the expert, to believer and non-believer. No reader of the gospel story can fail to be impressed by Jesus' humble submission to the will of God on the one hand, and his mastery of all situations on the other; by his penetrating discernment of human motives and his authoritative demand of radical obedience on the one hand, and his gracious, forgiving acceptance of sinners on the other. There is nothing, either in the Messianic hopes of pre-Christian Judaism or in the later Messianic beliefs of the early Christian Church, to account for this portrait. It is characterized by an originality and freshness which are beyond the power of invention. Here is something that the layman can hold onto quite apart from the vagaries of critical scholarship, for it is a portrait unaffected by the authenticity of any particular saying or story. Such an encounter with the historical Jesus is of course not the same as Christian faith in him. Even Caiaphas, Herod, and Pontius Pilate encountered him in this way. Christian faith is still a matter of decision—either this Man is God's redemptive act, or he is not. Nor is the historical Jesus the object of our faith. That object is the Risen Christ preached by the Church. But the Risen Christ is in continuity with the historical Jesus, and it is the historical Jesus which makes the Risen Christ not just an abstraction, but clothes him with flesh and blood.

B. THE PROCLAMATION OF JESUS

The earliest Church proclaimed that God had acted directly and decisively in Jesus. Jesus also had a proclamation. But it was understandably different from that of the earliest Church. He proclaimed, not that God *had* acted decisively, but that he *was in process of* acting and was *about* to act decisively:

> The time is fulfilled,
>   and the reign of God has drawn nigh;
> repent, and believe in the good news.
>
> *Mark* 1:15

Jesus shared a common world outlook with his contemporaries. He thought in terms, not so much of two worlds—a higher, spiritual world and a lower, material one—but of two ages—this age, and the age to come. This present age is under the thrall of the powers of evil, who exercise a qualified sovereignty beneath the absolute rule of God. There will however be a final denouement, when God will defeat these powers of evil and inaugurate the age to come, his own unquestioned and unqualified *de facto* reign in a new heaven and a new earth. It is in the context of this world view that the proclamation of Jesus is to be understood. But there is a new, distinctive feature in his proclamation. The reign of God is not just something looked for in the future. It is already "at hand": it has already "drawn nigh." It is impending—more than that, although lying in the imminent future, it is already impinging on the present, already operative in advance, just as in the twilight before the dawn the sun, though not yet risen, is already making its appearance felt. The Markan summary quoted above is probably due to the evangelist himself, though his formulation is taken from the actual recorded words of Jesus elsewhere in the basic strata (compare Matthew 10:7 and Luke 10:9, from the Q material). In the Markan summary Jesus does not link the drawing nigh of the reign of God explicitly with his own emergence and proclamation. But it is clear that Jesus saw precisely in his own proclamation the first sign of this dawning act of God. The proclamation was inaugurated by his own baptism in Jordan at the hands of John. "The law and the prophets were until John: *since that time* the reign of God is proclaimed" (Luke 16:16; cf. Matthew 11:12–13, which is probably the original form of this saying, though the Lukan form is here quoted as it brings out the original import of the saying more clearly). If the account of the descent of the Spirit of God upon Jesus at his baptism ultimately rests on the personal testimony of Jesus himself, we should see precisely in that descent of the Spirit (which is essentially a part of the Jewish hope concerning the last times) the point at which the future reign of God began to impinge upon history. From that point, as Jesus proclaims it, God is laying bare his holy arm to inaugurate his reign. This does not however mean that now the reign of God has actually begun in the fullest sense. It has drawn nigh, so near that it is already operative in advance. That energy of God which in a decisive act will assert his sovereign reign is already at work in the preaching of Jesus. But the decisive intervention still lies in the future.

The announcement of the coming reign of God demands a radical decision: "Repent, and believe in the good news." "Follow me." This is a demand for a complete reorientation of a man's life, an unreserved commitment of himself to the future act of God. Men had hoped that they might themselves engineer the reign of God by a scrupulous observance of the Jewish law or by taking military action and driving out the Romans. They had thought the reign of God a matter for apocalyptic dreams, and not a force already to be reckoned with in the present. Now they must do a rightabout-turn.

This demand for a radical decision is reinforced by a series of parables, each of which is intended to challenge the hearers with the necessity of a drastic decision. Many of these parables have been handed down in the oral tradition with no indication of the original context in which they were first uttered, and in the course of transmission have been given a new and different application. A common tendency was to reapply them in order to inculcate some ethical or religious lesson needed in the life of the Church. But by applying the laws by which oral tradition develops it is often possible to recover the original form and purport of these parables and to fit them tentatively into a setting in the historical ministry of Jesus. We can then see that the purpose of these parables was not to convey some rather obvious religious or moral lesson of a purely general character, but to provide a prophetic comment on the challenge of a concrete situation in the ministry of Jesus. They reveal what it is God is doing in the ministry of Jesus and challenge men to accept or reject it.

Take for instance the well-known parable of the sower. This has been transformed into an allegory about the different ways in which converts to the missionary church turned out after their conversion (Mark 4:14–20). Originally, however, it contained one point, and one point only: the contrast between the wastage during the sowing and the abundance of the harvest. That men reject the message of the coming reign of God will not preclude its coming. The assumption is that the ministry is the period of the sowing: the harvest is the still future decisive coming of the reign of God.

The parable of the seed growing secretly (Mark 4:26–29), by contrast, seems to have survived more or less in its original form. Perhaps that is why Matthew and Luke did not use it: it did not readily lend itself to reapplication to their own contemporary situations. This parable suggests that the activity of Jesus is like the secret growth before the harvest. It is the preliminary activity of God which presages the manifest establishment of his reign. The parable contains both a warn-

ing and an encouragement. It warns followers of Jesus against
taking matters into their own hands, like the zealots, in order
to expedite the coming of the reign. They must, like the farmer,
be content to wait. It encourages them to hope that the apparent insignificance of what Jesus is doing is nevertheless
the ushering in of that reign.

The situation presupposed by the twin parables of the mus-
tard seed and the leaven is similar (Mark 4:30–33 and parallels, Matthew 13:33 = Luke 13:20–21 [Q material]). Ob-
scure beginnings can lead to mighty issues, and the ministry
of Jesus, for all its apparent insignificance, is the sign of the
coming of the reign.

The parable of the fig tree (Mark 13:28–29) interprets the
ministry of Jesus in a similar vein. It is like the springtime,
when the sprouting of the leaves contains the promise of impending summer. So, too, the little parabolic sayings about the
cloud and the south wind (Luke 12:54–56; cf. Matthew
16:2–3). The cloud has appeared in the sky: the shower is
imminent. The south wind is rising, and at any moment there
will be scorching heat. So in the ministry of Jesus, God is at
work in a preliminary way, preparing to inaugurate his reign.

Several of Jesus' parables are concerned with the seeking
and saving of that which was lost. Pre-eminent among these
are the three parables in Luke 15: the lost sheep, the lost coin,
and the prodigal son. In Jesus' proclamation of the dawning
reign of God, in his fraternizing with the outcast, the publicans
and sinners, who were more receptive to his message than the
respectable, God is actively seeking and saving those who are
lost and gathering them for his kingdom. Here is a condemnation of the self-righteousness of the scribes and Pharisees.

Sometimes the urgency of the decision is reinforced with a
challenge to drastic action: Let the dead bury their dead! No
man putting his hand to the plough and looking back is fit for
the kingdom of God. If your hand offends you, cut it off; it is
better to enter into life with one hand rather than having two
hands to be cast into eternal fire. Like a merchant discovering
a goodly pearl or a hidden treasure, who sells all he has to
gain the prize, so must men surrender every obstacle to ac-

ceptance of the good news. Other parables contain the warning that soon it will be too late. Among these are the parable of the ten virgins (Matthew 25:1–12) and the parable of the waiting servants (Luke 12:35–40). It is easy to see how the Church later took up these parables and reinterpreted them as warnings to be prepared for the second coming of the Lord. Originally their future reference was to the impending crisis of the coming reign of God.

C. THE DEMAND OF RADICAL OBEDIENCE

Decision to accept Jesus' message involves total commitment to the demands of God. Men's lives must be put entirely at God's disposal. God's demand brooks no qualifications: "Ye have heard that it was said to them of old time . . . but I say unto you . . ." There is no area of life which is immune from the demand of obedience, no moment when the disciple has done all that the Lord requires of him so that he can have a little time off for himself. Every moment, whether it be filled with outward action or only inward thought and desire, is claimed by God. This radical ethic cannot be divorced from the proclamation of the coming reign of God: it is an integral part of that proclamation. It is difficult not to agree with Dr. Albert Schweitzer when he designates the ethics of Jesus as "interim ethics," for this is precisely what they were—the demand of God for the interval between Jesus' proclamation and the consummation of God's redemptive purpose. This radical ethic is summed up in the demand: "Thou shalt love the Lord thy God with all thy heart, and with all thy soul, and with all thy mind; and thou shalt love thy neighbor as thyself." Jesus does not offer a complete system of ethics. He propounds no list of ideals or virtues which a man can go away and cultivate by himself. What he offers is a series of illustrations of what the demand of God involves in concrete circumstances.

D. JESUS' TEACHING ABOUT GOD

This section deals with Jesus' "theology" in the proper sense of the word, i.e., his doctrine of God. Jesus shared many of the assumptions of his contemporaries. Thus he assumed that the God who acts in the affairs of men is also the God who created and who sustains the world and all that is therein. Note the order: it is not that he begins by contemplating the world and deduces from its structure the fact of its creation by a personal deity. He offers no "proofs" for the existence of God. Rather, having encountered him in the immediacy of his redemptive action, he knows him to be the same God who is behind all that happens in nature—the God who clothes the grass, who arrays the flowers, who feeds the birds of the air; the God who orders the common round of daily life, at home, on the farm, in the market place, and on the battlefield. That is why human activities in these spheres serve as parables for what God is now doing in bringing about his reign. It is the same God who is at work in both spheres.

With Judaism, too, Jesus shares the assumption that God is a God who has acted in Israel's past history. It is untrue to say that the God of Jesus is concerned only with the individual and his existential experience, that Jesus "dehistorized" the notion of God. God for him is the God of Abraham, Isaac, and Jacob (Mark 12:26), the God of Moses (Mark 1:44 etc.), who led his people out of Egypt in the exodus and gave them the law, the God of David (Mark 2:25), the God who sent the prophets throughout Israel's history (Mark 12:1–9).

This is not however to say that Jesus simply reasserted the beliefs of his contemporaries. It would be truer to say that while the formal structure of his "theology" was that of his contemporaries, its inner content was something fresh and novel. Later Judaism had pushed God further and further from direct contact with man, had made him more and more "transcendent." If God intervened in human life at all it was through various intermediaries, through his angels, his Spirit, his wisdom, or his word. Jesus however, convinced as he is that God is breaking through and causing his reign to dawn, strikes a new note of immediacy in the presence of God. God is near, is present, is acting, in his demand of obedience and in his offer of salvation. This sense of the nearness of God Jesus expresses by calling him "Father." This is no general universal doctrine of the Fatherhood of God, as the older liberals maintained. It is rather expressive of a unique relationship with God in which Jesus knows himself to stand. That is why Jesus dared to call him, as no other Jew had ever dared, by the intimate address, Abba (Mark 14:36), a term otherwise restricted to one's earthly father. Those who accept Jesus' message may indeed be admitted to the privilege of calling God "Father" as Jesus did (Luke 11:2). But it is always a privilege and always on condition that they have accepted Jesus' message, and thereby have entered into a new relationship with God. Moreover, Jesus' relationship with God as Father is always prior to that of others. It is never "our common Father," but always "my Father and your Father" (cf. John 20:17).

E. THE WORKS OF HEALING

The proclamation of God's dawning reign was accompanied by healings and exorcisms. That Jesus did actually perform such actions is beyond all reasonable doubt. In the course of oral transmission some of the actions ascribed to him have been exaggerated, and some of the popular legends of local wonder-workers (like the story of the Gadarene swine) got attached to him. But that does not alter the fact that Jesus did actually perform such healings. His contemporaries clearly understood that there was a difference between John the Baptist and Jesus in this respect, for "John did no miracle," and none was ever ascribed to him—a circumstance which shows that it was not inevitable for a tradition of miracles to gather round a religious leader. That is not to say that we can be sure that any par-

ticular healing recorded in the gospels actually occurred. Each
case must be decided on its own merits. The important question for the reader of the gospels to ask is not: How can the
miracles be scientifically explained? but: What significance did
Jesus attach to them? Traditional orthodoxy, as in Paley's *Evi-
dences*, regarded the miracles as "proofs" of Christ's divinity.
But such an answer is framed in quite non-biblical categories.
The New Testament never speaks of the "divinity" of Jesus as
a kind of metaphysical, abstract quality. Nor do the gospels
treat the miracles as proofs in a legalistic sense. The liberal answer was that Jesus performed the miracles out of human compassion. Now the motive of compassion is certainly present in
the gospels. We read in our Bibles at Mark 1:41 that Jesus
had compassion on the leper. In Mark 6:34 and 8:2 Jesus has
compassion on the multitude before he feeds them. The later
strata tend to multiply such references to the compassion
(Matthew 20:34, Luke 7:13), and it is possible that the original reading in Mark 1:41 was "was angry" and not "was moved
with compassion." So the emphasis on Jesus' compassion is surprisingly slight. If we are to find the real significance of the
healings in the mind of Jesus, we must look elsewhere. Fortunately, the Q material provides two comments of Jesus on this
very subject. The first is to be found in Matthew 11:2–5:

> Now when John had heard in prison the works of
> Christ, he sent two of his disciples and said unto him:
> Art thou he that should come, or do we look for an-
> other? Jesus answered and said unto them:
> Go and shew John again those things which ye do
> hear and see:
>> The blind receive their sight
>> and the lame walk,
>> the lepers are cleansed,
>> and the deaf hear,
>> the dead are raised up,
>> and the poor have the gospel preached to them.

At first sight Jesus' reply appears to be no more than a summary of what he was doing. Closer examination however re-

veals that his reply is carefully couched in the language of Isaiah 35 and 61. These chapters give descriptions of the signs which are to precede the decisive act of God in redeeming his people. In other words, Jesus interprets his healings precisely as signs of the dawning reign of God.

The second passage which brings out clearly Jesus' own interpretation of his miracles is the so-called "Beelzebub Controversy" in Luke 11:17-22 = Matthew 12:25-29. This culminates in the pronouncement:

> If I by the finger [Matthew: Spirit] of God cast out devils, then is the kingdom of God come upon you.

There are two points to be noted here. First, it is generally agreed in view of St. Luke's special interest in the Holy Spirit, and the unlikelihood that he should have suppressed such a reference in the source before him, that Matthew's "by the Spirit" is secondary and Luke's "by the finger" is original. Now this striking anthropomorphism is perhaps best understood as a subtle allusion to the use of the same phrase in Exodus 8:19. Confronted by the plagues which Moses is inflicting on the recalcitrant Pharaoh and his people, the Egyptian magicians complain that the disasters which have befallen their land are due to the "finger" of God. The plagues of Egypt were preliminary demonstrations of power leading up to the final denouement of the exodus itself. Hence by assigning his exorcisms to the "finger" of God, Jesus is interpreting them as preliminary encounters with the powers of evil which, as the plagues prepared the way for the exodus, are ushering in the reign of God. The exorcisms are the preliminary binding of the "strong man" so that his house can be spoiled (see Mark 3:27 and note how our other primary source agrees in the interpretation of the exorcisms). Second, the exorcisms are a sign that the reign of God has "come upon" men. This means that the reign of God, which, as we have seen, is to be inaugurated by a decisive event in the future, is already making itself felt in the present.

Such, then, is Jesus' own interpretation of the meaning of his healings and exorcisms. They are neither proofs of his transcendental origin nor simple humanitarian acts of compassion: they are signs of the coming reign of God.

F. THE CROSS

But Jesus' mission, as he himself conceived it, was not exhausted when he had proclaimed the coming reign of God and performed signs of its impending advent. It was not enough to call men and women to follow him and to invite the outcasts of society to sit at meat with him. His mission, as he saw it, extended beyond this preliminary activity to the performance of the decisive event in and through which God would inaugurate his reign.

Our earliest gospel, St. Mark's, indicates a change in the type of teaching delivered by Jesus after Peter's confession at Caesarea Philippi as compared with that before it. Before Caesarea Philippi, Jesus' message was directed to the multitudes: after that point it is directed mainly to the inner circle of the disciples. The content of the teaching also changes. Before Caesarea Philippi it was a proclamation of the impending advent of the reign of God: from this point it becomes an explicit prediction of his own death. Now there are many New Testament scholars who are firmly convinced that this change is due to Mark himself. But since the change comes in the episode of Peter's confession itself (Mark 8:27–33) and is an integral part of that narrative; and since also (as I have argued elsewhere in my *Mission and Achievement of Jesus*, p. 54) the episode of Peter's confession is firmly anchored in the tradition, the notion of a change in the type of Jesus' teaching is not a purely Markan construction. A further difficulty about these predictions of the passion is that some of them are couched in terms which strongly suggest that they are written up in the light of subsequent events. It is hard for instance to resist the conclusion that such a prediction as that in Mark 10:33–34 is not influenced by a knowledge of the details of the passion story:

The Son of man shall be delivered unto the chief priests, and unto the scribes; and they shall condemn him to death, and shall deliver him to the Gentiles: and they shall mock him, and shall scourge him, and shall spit upon him, and shall kill him: and the third day he shall rise again.

Not only does this prediction betray a knowledge of the details of the passion. The terms in which it refers to the resurrection ("he shall rise" instead of "he shall be raised," i.e., by God) also suggests a later hand. On the other hand there are other predictions which are of a purely general character and which do not necessarily betray a knowledge of the passion story. It is possible therefore to shorten our line of defense, and to claim that at least these predictions are authentic. Even this reduced claim however does not satisfy everyone. It is pointed out that all the predictions are confined to one stratum of the gospel material, namely to Mark. The only exception is Luke 17:25, which is probably editorial. More significant, there are no predictions whatever in the Q material. This is a strong argument. But it must be remembered that the Q material is not a gospel: it contains no passion narrative. It contains mainly sayings of Jesus which were used in the instruction of catechumens for membership in the Christian Church. Since therefore it contains no passion narrative, there is no particular reason why it should contain predictions of the passion, for they were irrelevant to its purpose. Mark is in fact the only primary *gospel* we have;[1] that is to say, the only document consisting of a passion narrative prefaced by an outline of Jesus' ministry. Hence the critical argument, while strong, is not decisive. Of course, in the nature of the case it is impossible to achieve complete certainty, but there does seem to be good reason for accepting the authenticity of the purely general predictions. Put together, these predictions run as follows:

---

[1]Holders of the "proto-Luke theory" will disagree. They maintain that there was an earlier form of Luke consisting of Q plus special Lukan material, before the Markan material was added.

(The Son of man) must suffer many things, and be rejected and set at naught, and delivered up into the hands of men, and they shall kill him. (For he came) not to be ministered unto, but to minister, and to give his life a ransom for many.

The language of this cento is throughout colored, not by a knowledge of the details of the passion, but by the description of the fate of the suffering servant in Isaiah 53. It suggests that Jesus conceived his death as a necessity laid upon him in fulfillment of that destiny.

It will be noticed that this is no new idea. The mission of the servant was already present to Jesus' mind from the moment of his baptism, where the voice from heaven strongly recalls the language of Isaiah 42:

Thou art my beloved Son, *in whom I am well pleased.*
Mark 1:11, cf. Isaiah 42:1

His proclamation of the impending reign of God recalls the proclamation of the impending divine intervention which is the burden of the later chapters of Isaiah. Even the word for "has drawn nigh" in his proclamation of God's reign strongly recalls some of those passages, e.g., Isaiah 56:1b:

My salvation is near to come,
and my righteousness is to be revealed.

The teaching of Jesus in the Sermon on the Mount, as Professor William Manson has strikingly shown (*Jesus the Messiah,* 1943, pp. 86 f.) draws upon the description of the servant. The healings and exorcisms as we have seen are interpreted by reference to Isaiah 61. Thus the figure of the servant gives a unity to all that Jesus said and did from the moment of his baptism to the moment of his death upon the cross. Remove that background, and his life breaks up into a series of unrelated fragments.

There are other predictions of a different kind in the special Lukan material. There is, first, a prediction so indirect in character that its authenticity can scarcely be doubted:

I came to cast fire upon the earth;
  and would that it were already kindled!
I have a baptism to be baptized with;
  and how I am constrained until it is accomplished!

Luke 12:49–50

In Mark 10:38 Jesus is again represented as speaking of his death in terms of a baptism. The presence of this idea in two strata of the gospel material strongly suggests that the notion has its roots in a very early tradition, which may quite possibly go back to Jesus himself. Indeed, it fits in perfectly with the argument of the preceding paragraph, that Jesus saw in his baptism by John the call to fulfill the total role of the servant, including that of rejection and suffering.

A second saying in the special Lukan material merits attention:

Go and say to that fox, Behold, I cast out devils and perform cures today and tomorrow, and the third day I am perfected [R.S.V.: finish my course], Howbeit, I must go on my way today and tomorrow and the day following: for it cannot be that a prophet perish out of Jerusalem.

Luke 13:32 f.

Here is a public declaration on Jesus' part that his ministry is not exhausted in the healings and exorcisms which occupied its earlier part. There is a further necessity laid upon him, which includes his dying at Jerusalem. If his prophetic activity was of a peculiar kind, namely to be the prophet of the coming reign of God, it follows that his death as a prophet must be similarly linked to that coming reign. His dying, no less than his preaching, teaching, and healing, must have an intimate connection with the coming reign. What precisely is that connection? To answer this question we must examine the sayings of Jesus at the Last Supper.

For none of the words of Jesus which relate to his death is so clear and explicit as those which he uttered at his final meal with his disciples. Our oldest gospel gives these sayings unencumbered by later liturgical developments:

1. The "bread word": This is my body.
2. The "cup word": This is my blood of the covenant.
3. The "prediction": I will no more drink of the fruit of the vine, until I drink it new in the reign of God.

Of course Jesus would have spoken at much greater length at the meal, and if as Mark holds, that meal was actually the Passover; or if, as is more likely, it was an anticipated Passover, antedating the actual Passover, as St. John holds, by twenty-four hours, Jesus would have delivered a lengthy discourse called the "haggada," in which the elements employed at the Passover celebration were related normally to the events of the exodus. On this occasion however Jesus makes a striking change. He transfers the symbolism of the elements from the exodus to his own death. The three Markan words may thus be best regarded as a summary of the contents of that longer discourse which Jesus had already delivered. The words "body" and "blood," mentioned separately, indicate that it is his *death* which Jesus has specially in view. This death is to be accomplished for the "many," a phrase which recalls what is said of the servant's suffering in Isaiah 53:11-12. This does not mean "for a considerable number" but, in accordance with Semitic idiom, "for all men." The benefits which are to be conferred on all men by Jesus' death are defined as a "covenant." Now the inauguration of the New Covenant was an accepted feature of the coming reign of God since Jeremiah:

> Behold the days come, saith the Lord, that I will make a new covenant with the house of Israel, and with the house of Judah . . .   *Jeremiah 31:31*

We know from the Dead Sea Scrolls what a vital part the idea of the New Covenant played among certain of Jesus' contemporaries. There were those who thought that the New Covenant had already been inaugurated. Jesus however declares that it is his death, his blood, which will inaugurate the expected covenant. Jesus, it seems, had never spoken of the covenant before. It looks like the sudden introduction of an apparently new motif. But the impression is no more than apparent. For it was also part of the Isaianic servant's function to inaugurate the covenant:

> I . . . will . . . give thee for a covenant of the people . . .
> *Isaiah* 42:6

Moreover the idea of the covenant was integrally linked with the idea of the coming reign of God, which as we have seen, was central to the proclamation of Jesus and his conception of his mission. And the connection between the two motifs, covenant and kingdom, is clinched by the saying recorded in Luke 22:29, which may indeed have been the original form of the covenant saying before it got attached to the cup word:

> I appoint unto you a kingdom, even as my Father appointed unto me.

Here the verb translated "appoint" comes from the same root as the Greek word for "covenant," so that we might translate:

> I covenant unto you a kingdom, even as my Father covenanted unto me.

What Jesus "covenants" to his followers at the moment when he consecrates himself to die for them is the reign of God. The same connection of thought appears in the third Markan saying which we have called the "prediction." There is a similar saying in the Lukan tradition of the Last Supper which Luke connects with his first cup:

> I will not drink from the fruit of the vine, until the reign of God comes. *Luke* 22:18

Whichever form, Markan or Lukan, may be the earlier, Jesus here declares his solemn resolve to abstain from partaking of wine until the reign of God be inaugurated. Here is another indication that for him his death is the decisive event which will turn the scales of history, and through which God will inaugurate his reign. It was to this end that Jesus willed deliberately to expose himself to death upon the cross.

G. THE PERSON OF JESUS

We have been careful up to this point to avoid asking directly the question: Who was Jesus? Up to now, all that has been clear is that he appeared among his contemporaries as a prophet and as an unconventional sort of rabbi who, without explicitly announcing himself as such, conceived his mission from start to finish in each of its several aspects in terms of the servant of Isaiah. The gospels however represent Jesus as speaking of himself as "Son of man," while other speakers in the gospel narrative are made to address him as "Son of God," "the Christ," "Son of David," and "Lord." Do any of these titles, all of which are clearly meant to imply Messianic status, have any sanction in the mind of Jesus himself? Was he conscious of being more than a prophet, of being the Messiah of Israel? Did he publicly make such a claim? Or did the later Church, in its confession of faith in him as the redemptive act of God, read back the Christological titles into the tradition? This problem has been a subject for endless debate during the past fifty years or more, and it would be idle to pretend that it has been solved. Let it be said at once that the truth of the Christian confession of faith in Jesus as the redemptive act of God does not rest upon the historicity of Jesus' Messianic consciousness or claims. It was (as we shall see) the resurrection which brought the earliest disciples to this faith, not the teaching which he delivered in his earthly life. And we believe in Jesus as the redemptive act of God because we have made a decision of faith in the apostolic preaching as it is continued in the life of the Church, not because we are persuaded that the Jesus of history claimed to be so. Thus we can approach the subject without undue anxiety as to its outcome.

To begin with, we know next to nothing of Jesus' inner life. To attribute to him a "Messianic consciousness" is to use the gospels as evidence for that which they cannot of their very nature supply. They are not psychological biographies but proclamation. Nor was the Jesus of history concerned publicly to assert any claim to exalted status. He was concerned rather to do a work and to fulfill a mission which he believed to have been laid upon him. Yet of course this sense of mission, which we have deduced from his outward actions and his explicit interpretation of them, involved certain presuppositions about his own personal status.

First, there are certain episodes, such as the baptismal and temptation narratives, the transfiguration and the agony in the garden of Gethsemane which suggest that Jesus regarded himself as standing in a peculiar filial relation to God. This filial relationship is not conceived in terms of metaphysical origin or of exalted status, but of vocation and obedience, a conception of sonship deeply rooted in the Old Testament tradition. Israel was in this sense the son of God (Exodus 4:22b–23a), and as the personal representatives of the nation Israel's kings were likewise sons of God (II Samuel 7:14; Psalm 89:26). Obedience meant for Jesus something more specific: it meant the vocation to fulfill the role of the suffering servant of Isaiah. Jesus never claimed to be either Son of God or suffering servant. It was not a question of claim at all, but a vocation to be fulfilled in obedience.

But did Jesus directly identify himself with the Son of man? The sayings which speak of the future coming of the Son of man do not directly identify Jesus with him, and as a matter of fact the clearest of them expressly distinguishes between Jesus and that figure:

> Whoever is ashamed of me and of my words
> in this adulterous and sinful generation,
> Of him will the Son of man also be ashamed,
> when he comes in the glory of his Father with the
> holy angels.   *Mark 8:38 (R.S.V.)*

Yet this very saying makes it clear that there is an intimate connection between Jesus and the Son of man. Jesus is an earthly figure: he is simply the bearer of the "words"—that is, the proclamation of the impending reign of God. The Son of man, on the other hand, is an exalted figure who "comes" in "glory." Yet it is precisely men's acceptance or rejection of

Jesus' message which will determine their acceptance or rejection by the Son of man at his coming. None of the other sayings which speak of the Son of man as coming in glory need necessarily imply an identification or indeed any close connection between Jesus and the Son of man. Consider for instance the most famous of them all, which occurs in the reply of Jesus to the high priest's question, "Are you the Messiah?":

> I am: and you will see the Son of man sitting at the right hand of Power, and coming with the clouds of heaven.   *Mark 14:62*

This saying *could* imply that the Son of man was a figure quite distinct from Jesus. After all, Jesus was on earth, while the Son of man was to come on the clouds of heaven. There are however other sayings which speak of Jesus *in his ministry* as the Son of man (e.g., Mark 2:10, 2:28; Matthew 8:20 = Luke 9:58 [Q material]), and a further set in Mark which speaks of the Son of man, obviously Jesus himself, as destined to suffer, die, and rise again, these last being the predictions of the passion which we have already discussed in another connection. How then can we reconcile those sayings in which Jesus distinguishes himself from the Son of man with those in which he identifies himself with that figure? This can be done if we suppose that Jesus believed himself to be, not already the Son of man in the full sense—how could he be, since the Son of man was a glorified, heavenly figure, while Jesus was on earth? —but *Son of man designate*. In a hidden way, by anticipation, he is already during his ministry exercising some of the functions of the Son of man. Nevertheless he will not be manifested as such until he has entered upon his glory after his suffering. Jesus' attitude to the title "Son of man" corresponds exactly with his proclamation of the coming reign of God. That reign is still in the future, yet it is already mysteriously active in advance in him. Similarly Jesus is not yet the Son of man, but in him the Son of man that he is to be is already active in advance. And just as it is through his death that the reign of God will be decisively inaugurated, so, too, it is through his death that he himself will be decisively enthroned as the Son of man.

As for the other Messianic titles in the gospel narrative, it is significant that Jesus never uses them directly of himself. When Peter at Caesarea Philippi addressed to him the momentous words: "You are the Christ" (i.e., Messiah, Mark 8:29) his confession receives a surprisingly cool reception. True, our view of that incident is colored by the Matthaean version, in which Peter is duly praised (Matthew 16:17); but Matthew 16:17–19 has been inserted into the Markan account from a different context. Jesus neither accepts nor rejects Peter's confession, but enjoins him to silence and hastens on to speak of his impending sufferings. The implication is that to speak of Jesus as the Christ would be premature. Instead, they must concentrate on the business in hand, which is to go up to Jerusalem for the passion. The way is left open for the confession of Jesus as the Christ or Messiah *after* the passion, but that must come as the spontaneous expression of the Church's faith in the full light of the resurrection. It is as if Jesus must fill the title with distinctive content of his own before it can be safely used of him. Otherwise it could only be misleading, and suggestive, perhaps, of a political revolutionary. In fact, it is probable that that is exactly what Peter meant at Caesarea Philippi. Later, at his trial before the Sanhedrin, Jesus, according to Mark, answers the high priest's, "Are you the Christ?" by a straight "I am." It is possible that the actual answer was not so direct as Mark suggests. Both Matthew and Luke have toned it down. Matthew has, "You have said so," the equivalent of "It's your word, not mine, and it all depends on what you mean by it." Luke prefers a different version, which he has probably derived from his special material. To the question, "Are you the Christ?" which is put by the whole Sanhedrin, not, as in Mark and Matthew, by the high priest, Jesus is made to answer "If I tell you, you will not believe." Then follows a second question, "Are you the Son of God?" (since "Son of God" does not seem to have been a current Jewish title for the Messiah, there is probably Christian coloring here), to which Jesus gives a similar reply to that in Matthew: "You say that I am." There are good reasons for supposing that the qualified reply is nearer to history than Mark's straight affirmation.[2] Even in Mark, however, Jesus hurries on to speak, not of his present status, but of the exaltation of the Son of man in glory, thus implying that the term "Christ" can only be applied in a proper sense to the exalted Son of man, not to Jesus as he was on earth. For that again could only imply that he was a political revolutionary.

There is a similar shelving of the title "Lord." While it seems that Jesus was already addressed as "Lord" in the vocative in a purely honorific sense, where it means little more than our modern English "sir," he did speak in a purely academic debate on the doctrine of Messiahship about the *exalted* Messiah as David's Lord (Mark 12:36). This title, like "the Christ," was not applicable to him during his earthly life, since it could rightly be used only of the exalted Son of man.

This same debate (Mark 12:35 ff.) indicates that Jesus did not accept the title "Son of David" as an adequate designation of the exalted agent of redemption. It is quite possible that he, with the rest of his family, believed himself to be of Davidic descent, but this can have had no important bearing on his conception of his destiny. Certainly, if applied by him during his earthly life it could only create the false impression that he was a political revolutionary.

The upshot of this investigation is that Jesus was not concerned to offer his disciples a ready-made Christology or doctrine of his person. Rather, as we have seen, his purpose was to accomplish a mission: first to proclaim, and then to accomplish the decisive event through which God would inaugurate the reign of God in the age to come. Yet at least it may be said that he provided a *framework of interpretation* in which the Church could later assess and proclaim his achievement. But the meaning and content of the Church's confession would be given by the events themselves, not by any preconceived Jewish doctrine of Messiahship or even by any direct teaching on the part of Jesus.

[2] Since the above was written, O. Cullmann in his *The State in the New Testament* has maintained that Mark mistranslated the original Aramaic, which said: "*You* say so," that is, precisely, "It's your word, not mine."

CHAPTER III

THE EARLIEST CHURCH

A. FROM EASTER TO PENTECOST

The statement that "God raised Jesus from the dead" is most baffling for the historian. Although in form it is the statement of an event, it is not strictly speaking an event in history at all. It is a confession of faith and a proclamation, not a historical report. No one saw Jesus being raised from the dead. What the historian can deal with is the occurrences through which the disciples came to believe that God raised Jesus. These occurrences must be sharply distinguished from the resurrection itself, of which they are only the external and visible signs, or, to adapt Karl Barth's vivid metaphor, the craters left by the explosion. The visible signs in question are the empty tomb and the resurrection appearances. With regard to the empty tomb we cannot be sure how far it goes back in the tradition. If the statement in St. Paul's preaching that he "was buried" is inserted in order to imply that his burial was reversed at the resurrection, the empty tomb must belong to the pre-Pauline tradition. And if Psalm 16 provided one of the testimonies which was used in the earliest preaching ("Thou wilt not let thy Holy One see corruption"), then the empty tomb must be pronounced a very early tradition indeed. Its importance in the Christian testimony however is not so much historical as symbolic. It provides a comment on the resurrection appearances: they are the appearances not simply of one who survived death, as though the appearances were on the level of a spiritualist séance, but of one who has overcome death and reversed its sentence. With regard to the appearances themselves the historian cannot pronounce with regard to their objective validity. But he can be sure that the disciples underwent certain experiences which gave them the conviction that God had raised their master from the dead. Otherwise he is left with an insoluble problem on his hands. Without some intervening "*x*," some additional impact upon the disciples subsequent to the death of Jesus, it is impossible to explain how the earliest disciples were reassembled to proclaim with boldness that Jesus was the redemptive act of God. These Easter experiences did take place, whatever their precise nature and however as men of faith or unbelief we choose to explain them. As historians we may call them visions. If we call them "objective visions," meaning thereby that there was something "at the other end" which caused them, we are venturing beyond the realm of history into the realm of faith. For the "object" here is not susceptible of historical observation.

Nor can the historian adequately reconstruct the course of events between the death of Jesus and the inception of the Christian preaching. He cannot with any degree of certainty assign either time or place to the appearances. Our accounts in the gospels are clearly the result of a long process of divergent oral development. The earliest tradition about the sequence of events is that received by Paul at his conversion within five years of the crucifixion and recorded in I Corinthians 15:3 and verses following. Here a series of appearances is listed as follows:

1. To Peter
2. To the Twelve
3. To 500 brethren
4. To James
5. To all the apostles
. . . .
6. To Paul

Nothing is said of the location of these appearances, whether at Jerusalem or Galilee, and no attempt is made to date them. But the fact that Paul can include among them his experience on the road to Damascus at least shows that they were not in principle confined to one place, and also that they did in principle close with the fifth appearance, Paul's being to one "born out of due time." Nothing appears to be said about Pentecost or the outpouring of the Holy Spirit. It has been attractively suggested that the third appearance to the five hundred brethren was the Pentecost event. Be that as it may, we should not be guided too much by the Lukan chronology of Ascension Day and Pentecost as related in Acts 1–2. The account in John 20 shows that the giving of the Spirit was not a single, unique event confined to Pentecost, for John can place the giving of the Spirit to the Twelve at the second appearance listed by Paul.

We may suggest a tentative reconstruction as follows. In the earliest tradition, before the accounts began to diverge in the process of oral transmission, the resurrection and ascension were regarded as a single indivisible "suprahistorical event." God raised Jesus and exalted him to his right hand, and it was as both risen and exalted that he was apprehended by the disciples in their post-Easter experiences. This series of encounters—which incidentally, as some of the later accounts suggest, may have taken place at their common meals, when they met together and broke bread—had for them a number of consequences.

First, the encounters brought to them the insight that the total event of Jesus, his ministry and death, was the redemptive act of God. This insight did not burst upon them as something entirely new and unprepared for. It did not therefore appear as an arbitrary interpretation imposed upon the facts. For it was already prepared for by the frame of reference in which Jesus had during his life on earth interpreted his mission, i.e., the way in which he had related it to the coming reign of God. Jesus had proclaimed that God was acting preliminarily in his ministry, and that shortly he would act decisively. The resurrection appearances brought home to the disciples that God had in fact so acted decisively in the death of Jesus, that he had in fact inaugurated his reign. For in saying that Jesus had been raised from the dead, the early Church was thereby testifying to its belief that God had done just this. This function of the resurrection as revelation is further attested by those Lukan passages which speak of the risen Jesus as unfolding to his disciples the meaning of scriptures (Luke 24:25–26; 44–46) and as showing them how it was necessary for the Christ to suffer and enter into his glory. The impact of the resurrection encounters revealed to them the place of the history of Jesus in the whole process of God's redemptive purpose.

Second, with this new insight came the impulse to proclaim the event thus apprehended, a feature deeply embedded in the tradition of the resurrection appearances. This aspect of the resurrection appearances is implied in the numerous "missionary charges" which the risen Jesus is made to deliver (Matthew 28:18–20; Mark 16:15–18; Luke 24:47 f.; John 20:22 f., 21:15–17), and is directly attested in Paul's own interpretation of his encounter with the risen Christ on the road to Damascus (Galatians 1:15 f.). As the first recipient of a resurrection appearance, Peter is the primary bearer of the apostolic preaching of Jesus. As such he is the rock on which the Church is built (Matthew 16:18; the original context of this famous saying may well have the resurrection appearance to Peter). Closely associated with him are the rest of the Twelve, with whom Peter received the second appearance. The witness even of later recipients of the resurrection appearances must conform to that of the Twelve, and especially to that of Peter; otherwise it is "in vain" (Galatians 2:2).

A third outcome of the resurrection appearances is what the disciples called the "gift of the Holy Spirit." To them was not only committed the message: their proclamation of it is itself the direct activity of God, and the direct prolongation of his saving act in Christ. The Lukan scheme has conveyed a rather misleading impression, and it is tempting to suppose that each appearance of the risen Christ involved not only the commission to proclaim the good news, but also the empowerment to proclaim it.

Fourth, the resurrection encounters carried with them a sense of incompleteness. The reign of God had indeed been inaugurated, but it had not yet come in its fullness. The earliest

Church expressed this insight by saying that the exalted Jesus would "come again" (Acts 1:11). The resurrection appearances look forward to the "consummation of the age" (Matthew 28:20).

Had Jesus himself expected the final consummation to come immediately after his death? The question is difficult to answer. The passages which speak of the "coming" of the Son of man may imply that he did so, though they give no exact chronology. On the other hand there are passages which suggest that the death of Jesus would inaugurate for the disciples a period characterized by their testimony to the event of redemption and by their suffering and persecution for the gospel's sake. This would imply an interval between the death of Jesus and the final consummation. It was the resurrection which straightened things out for them for the time being. It showed that Jesus had already entered into his glory, but that the reign of God, though inaugurated, had not yet been consummated. They expressed this sense of incompleteness by the (mythological) language of the return or "coming" of Jesus as Son of man.

It is the period from Easter through Pentecost which creates the Christian preaching and determines its pattern, and which therefore creates the Christian community. The preceding history of Jesus is not in itself to be treated as part of the data of New Testament theology, but as its presupposition. It can be taken up and worked into the content of the Christian message only when interpreted in the light of the Easter revelation. For the message of Jesus was that God was *about* to act decisively: the Christian proclamation is that God *has* so acted. This explains the difference between the proclamation of Jesus and that of the earliest Church. It answers the problem which caused so much trouble to scholars during the liberal period and still causes trouble to the man in the street—why was it that the religion of Jesus was replaced by a religion about him? There is, we must frankly and without hesitation admit, a real difference between the two. But the difference was caused, not by the mistaken notions of the earliest disciples, but by the act of God in the revelation of Easter.

B. THE LIFE OF THE EARLIEST CHURCH

It is sometimes maintained that the accent of the earliest Church's preaching lay upon the future; that it proclaimed only the future coming of the Messianic redeemer, just like Judaism; and that the only essential difference was that the Church identified him with Jesus of Nazareth. Then, at a slightly later stage, we are told, it came to be realized that Jesus was already reigning in his exalted state as Messiah. It was only in the later Hellenistic churches that the earthly life of Jesus came to be interpreted as a Messianic life. Then the conceptions of his pre-existence and incarnation were brought in from gnostic sources.

Such a presentation of the development of the Christian proclamation is not really fair to the evidence. The earliest preaching, as we have seen, is probably of the kind attributed to Peter in Acts 3:12-26. In language and conception it possesses a rugged antiquity which makes it difficult to believe that it is a free composition of the author of Luke–Acts. It presents Jesus as the new Moses, glorified by the God of Abraham, Isaac, and Jacob, as the first Moses was. Like the first Moses, too, the new Moses was a "holy and just one" and a "prince." The new Moses has by his work inaugurated "these days," the last times foretold by the whole prophetic succession as an interval for repentance before he returns again. At this point, with the mention of the final consummation, the analogy with the first Moses breaks down, for Moses did not live to lead his people into the Promised Land. Then will come the "times of refreshing," the "rest" in the consummated reign of God corresponding to the entry into Canaan, the "times of the restitution of all things." The new experiences upon which Israel may now enter thus correspond to the experiences of their forefathers when Moses brought them out of Egypt, but before they actually entered Canaan. The decisive act is accomplished: the consummation is still awaited.

Thus even the earliest Christian preaching locates the decisive act of God not in the future, but already in the past. Further, it will be seen that the interpretation which this primitive preaching gives to the person of Jesus is formulated within the same framework as that in which Jesus had conceived his own mission. Jesus had conceived his mission as that of the prophet-servant, who by fulfilling his mission would enter upon the exalted status of the Son of man. Peter's sermon presents him as the one who had now accomplished the mission of the prophet and servant like unto Moses and was as a result now inaugurated as the glorified Son of man. Indeed, since the exodus theme, as we saw in the previous chapter, played a part in Jesus' utterances about his mission, it is tempting to infer that Jesus himself had already combined Deuteronomy 18:15 (the prophet like unto Moses) with the suffering servant of Isaiah. Jesus' own implicit Christology was designed to express what God was in the process of accomplishing, whereas the Christology of the earliest Church asserts what God had already decisively accomplished and what he was shortly to consummate.

The basic pattern of the Church's proclamation is thus already set. The later variations and developments in the preaching are due, not to additions or changes, but to a striving for more adequate expression of the same basic insight: God *was* in Christ. Jesus and his history were the final saving act of God. The first step in the development of Christology is indicated in the other speech of Peter in Acts 2:36:

> God has made him both Lord and Christ, this Jesus whom you crucified.

The earlier speech stated that Jesus was *predestined* to return as Christ: the new insight is that he is already reigning as such. This new insight is probably due to reflection on what was involved in the gift of the Holy Spirit, which receives a much stronger emphasis than in the speech in Chapter 3. If the risen Jesus had given the Spirit to his disciples, he must be already Lord and Christ. The speech of Chapter 2 thus adumbrates a line of thought which through St. Paul is to reach its culmination in the fourth gospel. The offer of the Holy Spirit to those who accept the preaching is not of course new. It is already contained in the statement in Acts 3:26 that "God, having raised up his servant, sent him . . . to bless you"—the content of the "blessing" being the benefits of the redemption, which are precisely equivalent to the gift of the Holy Spirit. This gift is the enjoyment in advance of the "times of refreshing from the presence of the Lord," the blessings of the consummated reign of God.

The Reception of the Message

The earliest preaching contained a challenge to repent. For the Jewish audience this meant that they must readjust their whole attitude to the event of Jesus. They must repudiate the national decision which had rejected him as an impostor and realign themselves with the decision that he was the final, saving act of God. Repentance thus issues in faith—the positive acceptance of Jesus as the act of God. This decision once made, the recipients of the message will be admitted to the blessing which flows from the event (Acts 3:26), or, in the language of Chapter 2, they will receive the Holy Spirit. Was this admission already from the beginning accomplished by baptism in water? Chapter 3—which, as we have seen, is probably the earliest account of the primitive preaching—makes no explicit reference to baptism, but only the speech in Chapter 2 of Acts, which is probably slightly later. We cannot be sure whether it is meant to be implied in Chapter 3 or not. I suggest that Luke has omitted any reference to baptism in Chapter 3 because in the context he has used it for it is not an evangelistic speech, but an explanation of the miracle at the beautiful gate. We therefore see no reason to doubt that baptism was practiced from the very first. How did it originate? Later tradition included a charge to baptize among the commands of the risen Christ (Matthew 28:19; Mark 16:16). We cannot be sure that this was part of the earliest tradition. But Jesus himself had already in his earthly teaching defined the whole range of his ministry, culminating on the cross, as the working out of the implications of his baptism at the hands of John (see above, p. 267). That is why he called his death a "baptism." His gift of the Spirit after the resurrection to his earliest disciples was their baptism, for it was their total immersion in the redemptive event. A similar immersion in the redemptive event must follow for those who received the preaching of the apostles, and it was natural for the earliest Church to take over the outward sign by which Jesus had been initiated into his redemptive work by John the Baptist and whose import Jesus had transformed by his death on the cross. In the tradition of the post-resurrection command to baptize there is this element of truth, that the use of baptism, like the preaching of the gospel message, was the result of the impact of the period from Easter to Pentecost. The act of God in Jesus must not only be proclaimed: men and women must be brought, through the ministry of the first witnesses, into the same intimate relation to it as the first witnesses themselves had enjoyed by their direct contact with Jesus, "beginning from the baptism of John, unto the day when he was taken up."

The Common Life of the Earliest Christians

The author of Luke–Acts summarizes the common life of the earliest Christian community at Jerusalem in the classic words:

> They devoted themselves to the apostles' teaching and fellowship, to the breaking of bread and the prayers.
>
> *Acts 2:42*

The Christian life was centered upon a common worship. First there was the apostles' teaching. As well as the missionary preaching, samples of which are provided by Peter's sermons in Acts 2 and 3, there was regular pastoral preaching at the gatherings of the community of the type which the Hellenistic churches later designated *paraklesis,* that is, exhortation or encouragement. This would involve the application of Old Testament passages to Jesus and his history as the redemptive act of God. Some of the narrative portions of the Old Testament were expounded as types depicting in advance the pattern of God's act in Christ, while some of the prophetic portions would be interpreted as direct predictions of the coming of the redemption in Christ. In fact, there are indications in the New Testament that the earliest Christians gathered together a series of "testimonies," Old Testament passages which were applied to the event of Christ. Another activity undertaken in connection with pastoral preaching was the recollection of episodes from the life of Jesus and the shaping of them as a continued proclamation of the redemption. Thus, for instance, stories of Jesus' healings were recollected and preserved in order to preach to the community that this same Jesus, now risen, was still stretching forth his hand to heal men and women in the life of the Church. For the Church lived entirely upon the "word," that is, upon the proclamation of the event of redemption. That event must be continually proclaimed anew to the community that it might be kept in being precisely as the Church, and not degenerate into a purely human community. Thirdly, the connected narrative of the Lord's passion was constructed and recited in the gatherings of the community: "As often as you eat this bread and drink the cup, you *proclaim the Lord's death* until he comes." (I Corinthians 11:26).

In addition to this pastoral preaching there was also need for direct teaching on points of doctrine and behavior. This teaching was later called by the Greek-speaking churches *didache*. The need for materials led the earliest Christian leaders to collect and preserve the sayings of Jesus to serve as guidance for problems of thought and behavior. Thus, for instance, Christians wanted to know whether, now they had entered the reign of God, they were under obligation to pay taxes to earthly rulers. The story of the tribute money gave the answer: "Render to Caesar the things that are Caesar's, and to God the things that are God's." Or again, how to meet the scribal charge that Jesus could not be Messiah, since the Messiah was the son of David and a political ruler? The episode now recorded in Mark 12:25–37 would deal effectively with this problem.

While the "fellowship" or common life had its focal point

of expression in worship, it was carried into everyday life by the sharing of all things in common, as in the Qumran community. This was not due to any economic theory, nor was it a fixed law. Rather, it was a spontaneous expression of Christian "agape" or love. The sin of Ananias and Sapphira (Acts 5:1–10) was not their refusal to comply with a law, but their attempt to deceive not only the community, but God himself (verse 4). Later on, the changed conditions of life in the Greek cities would lead to the tacit abandonment of this particular expression of communal life without controversy, and the substitution of almsgiving and hospitality as expressions of Christian love.

Then there was the "breaking of the bread." Being Jews, the earliest Christians would naturally begin the chief meal of the day with the breaking of bread. This meal took place in the late afternoon or early evening. The breaking of the bread would be preceded by a prayer in which the name of God was blessed for the gift of daily food. But in the case of the early Christians the thanksgiving would be enriched with elements derived from their earlier table-fellowship with Jesus, and particularly from what he had done at the Last Supper. It would recall not merely the mighty act of God which had brought the Israelites into Canaan and thus enabled them to enjoy the fruits of the land, but the mighty act of God in the passion and resurrection of his servant Jesus, by which they had been brought to enjoy the blessings of the reign of God, shortly to be accomplished by the return of that servant in glory. We are told in Acts 2:46 that the early Christians ate their bread with *gladness* and singleness of heart. The word for "gladness" is almost a technical term for the joy of the age to come. This suggests that the daily common meal was thought to be an anticipation of the day when Jesus would return to consummate the reign of God. Hence the prayer *Maranatha,* "Come, O Lord" (I Corinthians 16:22; cf. Revelation 22:20). Was wine invariably used at the meal? Normal Jewish custom was to drink wine only at festivals and on the eves of Sabbaths (i.e., Friday evenings). But we now know that at Qumran the covenanters used wine at their rehearsals of the Messianic Banquet, and the early Christians may therefore have done likewise. Otherwise we must suppose that they used bread only on weekdays and transferred the use of wine from Friday to Saturday evenings, i.e., to the Lord's day.

C. GREEK-SPEAKING JEWISH CHRISTIANITY

The earliest disciples spoke Aramaic, and they believed that the gospel message need be preached only to Israel. They were not opposed to the admission of Gentiles on principle, but, in accordance with Jewish ideas, believed that such Gentiles as were destined to be saved would be given their chance *after* the return of Christ. This seems to have been the view of Jesus himself (Matthew 8:11 f. = Luke 13:28 f.). Hence for the time being no attempt was made to extend the gospel message to the Gentiles. But the preaching was not confined to Aramaic-speaking Jews. If it did not happen already at Pentecost, as Acts suggests, it was not long after that Greek-speaking Jews were brought into the fold (4:36). Tensions grew up between the two sections, and the Hellenistic section had to be provided with leadership of its own. It is inaccurate and an anachronism to call the Seven "deacons"; not only does Luke refrain from calling them so, but their task turns out to be that of extending the apostolic preaching. Under the creative leadership of Stephen certain new emphases in the Christian preaching were evolved. Stephen's speech in Acts 7 is notable for the new self-consciousness of the Church. The earliest Aramaic-speaking Christians had probably already called themselves the Church, for Matthew 16:18, if not an authentic saying of Jesus, emanates from the earliest community. But they regarded themselves as the true remnant within Judaism, and except for their preaching and distinctive common life, they shared the life of Israel as a whole, particularly the worship of the temple. Stephen and his associates, however, see themselves involved in a radical breach with Israel and particularly with its temple. The Christian community is thus on the way to evolving a quite distinctive life of its own, and the foundations are being laid for the Gentile mission.

NON-PAULINE HELLENISTIC CHRISTIANITY

A. INTRODUCTORY

Thus there grew up, after the dispersion of the Church consequent to the martyrdom of Stephen, a new version of Christianity, distinguishable from the original Palestinian version. Its center was at Antioch and its language Greek. It took over much of the old Palestinian tradition, as we can see from the synoptic gospels. These latter all spring from this Hellenistic milieu so far as their language is concerned, yet reflect, except in the editorial sections, the traditions of the earliest Aramaic-speaking church. The communities of these churches were mixed, containing a nucleus of Greek-speaking Jews, a larger proportion of proselytes (converts to Judaism) and God-fearers (Gentiles interested in Judaism, but uncommitted), and a fringe, perhaps, of immediate ex-pagans. It is natural that Hellenistic Christianity, as well as taking over much of the earliest tradition, also adopted much of the outlook and practice of the Hellenistic synagogue.

Our evidence for this type of Christianity is somewhat meager. The New Testament is overshadowed by the presence within it of no less than fourteen Pauline or near-Pauline writings. There is singularly little material of a Hellenistic character earlier in date than the Pauline writings and therefore indubitably free from Pauline influence. Yet Paul himself, before he launched out on his own individual, creative line, was nurtured precisely in this type of Christianity, and therefore it should be possible, by extracting those parts of his epistles where he appears to be reproducing the presuppositions from which he started and not developing special teaching of his own, to reconstruct something of this pre-Pauline Hellenistic Christianity. It should also be possible to discover something from the synoptic gospels themselves, where the authors are arranging and commenting and editing the Palestinian tradition to meet the needs of the Hellenistic churches, thus molding it to give the gospel each his own particular interpretation. Lastly there are non-Pauline Hellenistic writings later in date than Paul. These include not only some of our canonical documents, such as the non-Johannine catholic epistles (I, II Peter, Hebrews—though this perhaps has one foot in the Pauline camp—together with James and Jude), and writings of the sub-apostolic age which did not find their way into the canon, such as the first epistle of Clement, the epistle of Barnabas, the epistles of Ignatius, and the Didache, or Teaching of the Twelve Apostles. The Johannine literature is left out of account in this reconstruction, since it represents a distinctive development of Hellenistic Christianity parallel to, though later than, the Pauline.

B. ITS PREACHING

In the non-Jewish world Christian preaching could not start, as in a purely Jewish environment, with the Jewish hope and proceed from thence to the direct proclamation of Jesus as the saving act of God in history. It had to begin further back with the preaching of the one God. Fortunately there were predecessors in this field. In its approach to potential converts from the Gentile world the Hellenistic synagogue had already devised an apologetic against idolatry and a defense of monotheism. To do so it drew upon the arguments of "natural theology" which had been elaborated by the Stoic philosophers. The law and order of nature contain a revelation of the one true God and a refutation of polytheism and idolatry:

"We . . . bring you good news, that you should turn from these vain things [i.e., idolatry] to a living God who made the heaven and the earth and the sea and all that is in them . . . he did not leave himself without witness, for he did good and gave you from heaven rains and fruitful seasons, satisfying your hearts with food and gladness.   *Acts 14:15b–17*

A more literary approach, adapted to an intellectual audience, is found in the speech attributed to St. Paul by the author of Luke–Acts during his visit to Athens and the Areopagus:

"Men of Athens, I perceive that in every way you are very religious. For as I passed along, and observed the objects of your worship, I found also an altar with this inscription, 'To an unknown god.' What therefore you worship as unknown, this I proclaim to you. The God who made the world and everything in it, being Lord of heaven and earth, does not live in shrines made by man, nor is he served by human hands, as though he needed anything, since he himself gives to all men life and breath and everything. And he made from one every nation of men to live on all the face of the earth, having determined allotted periods and the boundaries of their habitation, that they should seek God, in the hope that they might feel after him and find him. Yet he is not far from each one of us, for

'In him we live and move and have our being';

as even some of your poets have said,

'For we are indeed his offspring.'

Being then God's offspring, we ought not to think that the Deity is like gold, or silver, or stone, a representation by the art and imagination of man. The times of ignorance God overlooked, but now he commands all men everywhere to repent, because he has fixed a day on which he will judge the world in righteousness by a man whom he has appointed, and of this he has given assurance to all men by raising him from the dead."

Acts 17:22–31 (R.S.V.)

It will be noticed how this speech traverses ground familiar to Stoicism and to Jewish apologetic, no doubt winning the assent of the audience, until it takes a sudden turn at the end, and speaks of the event of redemption, which produced a division among the hearers.

That this was precisely the approach of Paul himself is confirmed by his own words in the epistle to the Romans:

> For what can be known about God is plain to them, because God has shown it to them. Ever since the creation of the world his invisible nature, namely, his eternal power and deity, has been clearly perceived in the things that have been made. *Romans 1:19–20*

—and then there follows a polemic against idolatry. This "natural theology" is of course not an addition to the Christian proclamation. It was already presupposed in the earliest preaching of Jesus as the act of God. For that act was the act of the God who had created the heaven and the earth, and of the God who had directed the previous history of Israel. But for a Gentile audience this requires explicit statement, otherwise they cannot understand that Jesus Christ is the act precisely of *God*, of him who made the heaven and the earth. Thus the proclamation of God as Creator does not spring from cosmological speculation, but from the proclamation of the event of redemption.

Later on—a development most clearly seen in the Pauline and Johannine writings, though the casual way in which Paul introduces it, as well as its presence in the epistle to the Hebrews, suggests that it may be a pre-Pauline development—the creation and the event of Jesus Christ are riveted more closely still by the application to Christ of the wisdom concept. Christ becomes the pre-existent wisdom of God through whom God made heaven and earth. This makes even clearer what was already implicit from the start, namely that it is the Creator-God who acts in the event which is Jesus Christ.

Pagan idolatry was the source of pagan vice (Romans 1:24–32; note the "therefore" in verse 24). Repentance therefore acquires a more specific content in the relation to the moral life than it had had for the Palestinian Jews. It meant, not simply a reassessment of the national crime of Israel in executing its Messiah, but, more concretely, the "renunciation" of pagan vices (see below).

In the proclamation of the event of redemption itself there were necessary changes. The term "Messiah," even in its Greek dress as "Christos," was unintelligible to the Greek world. "Christ" therefore became to all intents and purposes a proper name, thus leading to the familiar "Jesus Christ." The old term "servant," which had been applied to Jesus particularly in relation to his earthly life and passion in the earliest Palestinian tradition (Acts 3:13 R.S.V.), survived only in the stylized archaisms of the liturgy (Acts 4:27 R.S.V., cf. the Didache and the ordination liturgy in Hippolytus). It was generally replaced by the term "Son of God." Thus, according to some scholars, the original Aramaic in the voice at the baptism and transfiguration of Jesus had been "Thou art [or "This is"] my Servant." For the author of Mark, "Son of God" has become the typical designation of Jesus, even in his life on earth. To the Greek convert it would, especially when accompanied by the miracle stories, have conveyed the associations of the "divine man"—a holy figure who in virtue of his holiness was able to work miracles. This would not of course have been the belief of Mark himself: for him Son of God, like all the titles of exaltation, meant the agent of the redemptive act of God. What has happened in effect, however, is that even for the evangelists the exalted status of Jesus, which in the earliest tradition was dated from the resurrection, is now pushed back into the earthly life. Quite naturally and properly that life is now being viewed through the spectacles of the resurrection.

Moreover, the earliest Church, taking its cue from the apocalyptic teaching about the agent of redemption, believed that he had been predestined from the beginning of the world.

Thus, for instance, we read in the earliest speech in Acts of "the Christ *appointed* [literally, foreordained, appointed beforehand] for you." A foreordained messiah pre-existed as it were in the mind of God. This kind of pre-existence is implicit in the tradition from the beginning, and was perhaps even present to the mind of Jesus in his use of the term "Son of man." That of course does not mean that he thought of himself as really and objectively pre-existent before his entry into the world. The passages which suggest that he did are confined to the fourth gospel and are clearly later tradition. What it means is that he conceived his own role as predestined by God. In Hellenistic Christianity however this ideal type of pre-existence is developed into a "real" objective pre-existence.

It is generally held that this step was taken by St. Paul, and that he was led to do so because of his identification of Jesus with the wisdom of God as agent of creation. But while the wisdom motif accounts for the association of Christ with the act of creation as its agent, it seems that it is not in connection with that motif that the idea of "real" pre-existence first enters in, but rather with the notion of Christ as the Son of God. This is clear from a passage which may well be a pre-Pauline formula:

> God sent forth his Son, born of a woman . . .
> *Galatians 4:4*

We suggest therefore that it was pre-Pauline Christianity which first took the step of positing a pre-existence of its Lord, and that it did so in connection with his title of Son of God.

But how did that Church come to take that important step? It has been suggested that the notion of real pre-existence had already been adopted into the Church from Gnostic circles, whose agent of redemption was a really pre-existent figure who became incarnate in the world in order to effect the redemption. There is nothing that need shock us in such a possibility. The Church was looking round for adequate concepts in which to express its basic conviction that "God was in Christ," and everything was grist to its mill. It is this central faith which remains constant, while the expression of it was a matter of trial and, if not of error, then at least a discarding of inadequate concepts and those which proved to be unsuited to the changed environment in which the gospel had to be proclaimed. But the theory of Gnostic provenance appears to break down on chronological grounds. While certain tendencies similar to those which appear in the full-fledged Gnostic systems of the second century were present already in Hellenistic, and, if certain interpretations of the new scrolls from the Qumran caves are to be trusted, even within some types of Palestinian, Judaism, we cannot certainly include the presence of the pre-existent Redeemer among them. Moreover the early Gnostic writing discovered in 1948 and known as the *Gospel of Truth* knows nothing of a pre-existent Redeemer who becomes incarnate. That figure, so far as our present evidence goes, emerges only in second-century Gnosticism, and chronology would favor the view that this idea was taken over from Christianity into Gnosticism, and not vice versa. Rather we must suppose a process of internal development within the Church. It was led to move from the conception of ideal to real pre-existence because it found in this a more adequate expression of its basic faith. If God was present and acting in Christ, then the Godhead as such which was in him must, if it was Godhead at all, be really pre-existent. This will have to be our tentative conclusion for the present. Further knowledge of contemporary Judaism, both Palestinian and Hellenistic, may later enable us to track down more precisely the origin of this important step.

It is frequently maintained that the earliest Church glossed over the death of Jesus and concentrated its attention on the resurrection. Further, eucharistic piety, we are told, centered on the presence of the risen Christ rather than on his death. On this view it was St. Paul who first emphasized the saving significance of the cross, both in his preaching and in his sacramental teaching. But the very early development of the cup word in the institution narrative (this is my blood of the covenant which was shed for many) indicates that to the death of Jesus was ascribed a redemptive significance from the very first. Yet there was undoubtedly in Hellenistic Christianity a shift of emphasis. More stress was laid upon the death of Christ as a sacrifice. The following passages are places where Paul is reproducing traditional formulae of a liturgical character:

Christ, our passover lamb, has been sacrificed.

I Corinthians 5:7

. . . the redemption which is in Christ Jesus, whom God put forth as an expiation in his blood.

Romans 3:24b–25a

Compare also:

Christ loved us, and gave himself for us, a fragrant offering and sacrifice to God. *Ephesians* 5:2

Much prominence is given in the Pauline epistles to the notion that by his death Christ won the decisive victory over the powers of evil. This mythological notion was not a feature of the earliest preaching, and the popular attribution of illness to evil spirits which forms the background of Jesus' exorcisms is of a different order. Yet Paul never develops his own characteristic thinking along these lines, and the probability is that the conception of the demonic powers is something which he held in common with other Greek-speaking Christians. This cosmic dualism has often been ascribed to Gnostic sources, from which they supposedly infiltrated into the Hellenistic synagogues and thence to Hellenistic Christianity. But the Dead Sea Scrolls indicate the presence of such a dualism already in some versions of Palestinian Judaism, and it was probably derived ultimately from Persian rather than from Gnostic sources.

Hellenistic Christianity developed its own missionary vocabulary. The Christian proclamation is called the "gospel," good news. Jesus had already used the verb "to gospel." To the Greco-Roman world the word "euangelion" would mean the proclamation of a ruler (as the King of England is proclaimed publicly in every town and city at the beginning of a new reign). In Christian usage it means the proclamation of the reign of God in Christ. Another new word is "kerygma," or preaching, denoting not the activity of preaching, but the content of the message. The acceptance of and adherence to the Christian message is called "pistis," faith.

The earliest Church was conscious of itself as the community of the last days, the true remnant of Israel, and as we have seen, there was probably already in use a Semitic word for "Church." The Greek-speaking Christians adopted the word "ecclesia" for themselves. This is one of the two terms which were employed in the Greek version of the Old Testament, the Septuagint, for the congregation or people of Israel, the other term being "synagoge." It is easy to see why the Christians did not generally use the other term (an exception is James 2:2). Not only was it too popular among the Jews, but its meaning had become restricted to the local congregation; whereas the Christians needed a word to express their consciousness of being the one holy people of God, of which each separate congregation was a local manifestation.

For the instruction of the new converts the Hellenistic Church took over the patterns of catechetical teaching which had been worked out in the synagogue for the instruction of proselytes. These included, on the negative side, a list of pagan vices to be "renounced" or "put aside," and, on the positive, the duties of the Christian life. Here use was made, as already in the synagogue, of the Stoic "household codes," which were circulated by peddlers in the ancient world, like Old Moore's almanacs today, and which listed the duties of husbands, wives, parents, children, and slaves. Naturally the Church also made use of the sayings of Jesus as their predecessors in Palestine had done (hence the preservation of the Q material in its Greek dress, and the numerous echoes of the sayings of Jesus in the "paraenetic" or ethical sections of the New Testament epistles). It is striking how little there is which is specifically Christian in this ethical teaching. Much of it was to be found in the best of Judaism and even of Stoicism. The distinctiveness of the Christian ethic lay chiefly in its motivation. The Christian life was the expression of gratitude to God for what he had done in Christ: "Be kind to one another, tenderhearted, forgiving one another, *as God in Christ forgave you*" (Ephesians 4:32).

C. ITS SACRAMENTAL LIFE

Both the theology and the practice of baptism underwent a number of changes. For the primitive Church, baptism had been performed in the name of Jesus, and its benefit defined as the remission of sins, and, normally at any rate, the gift of the Holy Spirit. Corresponding to the introduction into the preaching of God as Creator, the baptismal confession and the word of administration was expanded in the Hellenistic churches into the familiar threefold formula: "in the name of the Father, and of the Son, and of the Holy Ghost" (Matthew 28:19; cf. also the Didache). St. Paul can also speak of baptism as a symbolical participation in Christ's death and resurrection, and does so in terms which suggest that the idea was not his, but of others before him ("*Do you not know . . . ?*" in Romans 6:3, to a church he had never visited). Such ideas have been frequently ascribed to the influence of the mystery religions, in whose rites the initiate sacramentally shared the fate of the cult deity. Yet the idea was already implicit in the primitive Christian interpretation of Christ's death as itself a "baptism," and also in the idea of baptizing "in the name of Jesus." There is no need to go to extraneous sources for the notion, though we may suppose that it would have the more readily commended itself to those brought up in the atmosphere of the mystery religions. In any case it was given a moral content strikingly absent from the mystery religions. To die with Christ meant the concrete abandonment of the vices of pagan living; and rising with him, though not to be consummated until Christ's return, meant the day-to-day endeavor to lead the Christian life of obedience. It is commonly supposed that there is at least a trace of influence from the mystery religions in the strange practice of being baptized for the dead, but this passage (I Corinthians 15:29) will be discussed later (see p.

348). It is probable that the rite of baptism was administered with increasing elaboration of ceremony and ritual. We may suppose there was already an explicit renunciation of the pagan vices and a solemn profession of faith, first in Jesus as Lord, and later in the threefold name. Here is the origin of the baptismal creed. Another addition to the rite was a laying on of hands (Hebrews 6:2; cf. Acts 8:17; 19:6), which was associated with the gift of the Holy Spirit. By the time I John was written, the ceremony of anointing had apparently been added as well (see 2:20). These additional ceremonies had no independent significance of their own, but were designed to underline the rich meaning of the immersion in water.

The regular place of worship was still in the homes of the faithful, as indeed it would continue to be until the edict of toleration under the Emperor Constantine in A.D. 313 enabled Christians to build special places of worship. But the liturgical action was progressively emancipated from its primitive setting in the bosom of Jewish domestic piety and took on more of the formality of public worship. This was particularly the case with the first part of the Christian service, which centered upon the ministry of the word. First there would be readings from the scriptures, as in the Jewish synagogue, though the culmination would be the reading of the specifically Christian material, and not of the law. This Christian material would consist of letters from Christian leaders which had reached the congregation, a practice which may have originated in the Pauline churches and spread from there to others. It would also include parts of the material which found its way eventually into our written gospels, especially the passion narrative. After the Jewish model the readings would doubtless be interspersed with psalm singing, which would encourage the Christological interpretation of the psalms so common in the New Testament. This would be followed by a sermon, a "word of exhortation," of which the epistle to the Hebrews is an example. Opportunity would also be given for the exercise of prophecy and even for speaking with tongues. Since the Hellenistic churches could no longer meet, as at Jerusalem, for the daily breaking of the bread, these meetings would be confined to the first day of the week, the Lord's day (I Corinthians 16:2; Acts 20:7; Revelation 1:10). Hence the use of wine became regular on every occasion when the eucharist was celebrated. If the Pauline churches were the first to detach the rite with the bread and cup from the common meal (where the bread was blessed at the beginning and the cup at the end) and thus to telescope the two blessings, other churches must soon have found it advisable to follow suit. Both parts of the eucharist would then precede the common meal, as is probably the case in the Didache.[1] The eucharistic rite of the Hellenistic churches must have been somewhat as follows: after the faithful had saluted one another with a holy kiss and all unworthy or unqualified persons had been excluded ("If any one has no love for the Lord, let him be accursed" I Corinthians 16:22), the "president" would take bread and wine, and recite a prayer of thanksgiving for creation and redemption. A good description of the scene and of the content of the thanksgiving is given in Revelation 4:2–11. The thanksgivings would be followed by a petition "Maranatha," "Our Lord, come!" (I Corinthians 16:22; Revelation 22:20), and conclude, like all Jewish prayers, with a doxology and an amen said by the whole congregation (I Corinthians 14:16). The whole rite is thus fundamentally Jewish in structure and conception. There is no trace of any influence from the mystery religions, except in the notion that the unworthy reception of communion might lead to physical death (I Corinthians 11:30). Even this notion however is fundamentally ethical and not magical. There is no belief that the eucharistized bread and wine are supernatural substances with mysterious potencies of their own. Such a notion does not intrude until the time of St. Cyril of Jerusalem, who in the fourth century began to speak of the consecrated elements as "making your hair stand on end." Rather did the early Church believe in a *real coming* of Christ to his people in and through the *action* of the rite. In response to the recalling of the mighty acts of God in Christ,

---

[1] The Didache, or "Teaching of the Twelve Apostles," is a post-Apostolic document containing a church order.

recited in the eucharistic prayer, God made them present to the congregation.

In the earliest Church the ministry of the word was in the hands or under the control of the apostles. For the Greek-speaking Christians of the Jerusalem Church there was a devised, as we have seen (above, p. 298), a subordinate ministry, to which no specific title was given. Not long after, we find mention of "elders" at Jerusalem (Acts 11:30), an institution doubtless borrowed from the synagogue. In Acts 14:23 we are given the impression that the same form of organization was adopted in the churches of the Pauline mission. From this we would naturally infer that the same type of organization was employed in the pre-Pauline Hellenistic churches. Yet it is often contended that the evolution of the "elders" was a post-Pauline development, and that the references to them in Acts are an anachronism. The chief argument in support of this view is that Paul in most of his epistles appears to ignore any local ministry, and writes to the congregations direct. Moreover, in I Corinthians 12 and Romans 12 (cf. Ephesians 4) he appears to envisage a quite different type of ministry, the free or charismatic ministry, in which everyone in the congregation exercised his spiritual gifts. The truth of the matter is that these passages are not really referring to ministries at all, but to the exercise of functions in the community. In practice the "charismatics" would doubtless have been found mainly among the "elders." Paul indeed refers himself to "those who are over you in the Lord and admonish you" when he writes to the Thessalonians (I Thessalonians 5:12). In writing to the Corinthians (the very epistle which talks so much of charismatics), he says of the house of Stephanus that "they have devoted themselves to the service of the saints" and exhorts the Corinthians to "be subject to such men" (I Corinthians 16:15 f.). And in writing to the Philippians he speaks of "bishops and deacons." So we can scarcely doubt that both the Pauline and pre-Pauline churches were governed in the absence of the apostles by a local committee of "elders" (with which at this time "bishop" was synonymous). We now know that the Qumran community, like the community of the New Covenant at Damascus, had officers called "visitors," "overseers," or, in Greek, "*episcopoi*." Therefore it is much more likely to suppose that this type of organization was already evolved while the nascent Church was still in close contact with its Jewish origins, rather than that it consciously revived a Jewish form of organization after the death of Paul. Still less likely is it that it adopted, as has been suggested, a form of organization from Hellenistic secular life. Both titles, "elders" and "bishops," sprang direct from Judaism. It is natural to suppose that when a church was first founded the founding missionaries appointed elders, while afterwards the elders themselves would be responsible for maintaining their numbers, as in the Jewish synagogues.

D. THE SYNOPTIC GOSPELS

In their present form all three synoptic gospels are the products of the non-Pauline Greek-speaking churches. Attempts have been made from time to time to discover Pauline influences in Mark, and tradition has traced a connection between the Pauline evangel and the third gospel, which it ascribed to Luke, the companion of Paul. But much that has been thought to be Pauline in both these gospels is really common apostolic Christianity. The synoptic gospels consist of three strata. The first is the authentic sayings of Jesus himself, which are translations into Greek from the original Aramaic. These of course are firsthand evidence for the teaching of Jesus, and have been used as such in Chapter II. Then there are the narratives about him, which existed in the form of isolated fragments (pericopae). These took shape in the Aramaic Church, for the most part, and have been used as evidence for the beliefs, interests, and activities of the earliest Aramaic Church in Chapter III. There is a third stratum, which is the work of the Greek-speaking evangelists themselves. This consists of their selection and arrangement of the pericopae and the editorial links which they have provided. This third stratum will now be used to throw further light on the beliefs and interests of the non-Pauline Greek-speaking churches.

1. *Mark*

The major impulse behind the writing of the gospels was to preserve the apostolic witness to Jesus Christ at a time when it was in danger of being lost as a consequence of the decease of the original witnesses. But the gospel writers were more than the editors of a tradition. They were also concerned to interpret it and apply it to the needs of the Church of their day.

The material Mark had at his disposal consisted of a connected passion narrative and a collection of originally isolated episodes from the life of Jesus. There are stories about Jesus, such as the baptism, temptation, transfiguration, triumphal entry, and the cleansing of the temple. There are the so-called pronouncement stories, which culminate in a significant saying of Jesus for the sake of which the whole episode is narrated, such as the story of the tribute money, which culminates in the pronouncement "Render to Caesar." There are miracle stories pure and simple, whose climax is the miraculous action of Jesus, such as the healing of Jairus' daughter. There are parables of Jesus, and aphorisms, such as those collected at the end of Chapter 9. Some of this material had probably been gathered together before Mark. That is why it appears in blocks—conflict stories in Chapters 2:1–3:6 and 11:27–12:37, parables in Chapter 4:1–34, miracle stories in 4:35–5:43.

What is the theology which Mark seeks to inculcate by his arrangement of this material? It is that Jesus is present among men as the hidden Messiah. The acts and teaching of Jesus are a series of epiphanies or manifestations of his exalted status. He appears on earth as the Son of God incognito. But those who penetrate behind the incognito fail to discern it aright. The demons realize that he is the Holy One of God. But they are commanded to silence: it is only after the resurrection that the true meaning of Jesus' exalted status will be perceived. Amazement and wonder are evoked in the crowds, but no genuine comprehension. For them all things are "in parables"—that is to say, they are dark enigmas. But to the chosen disciples it is given to know the mystery of the kingdom of God. Yet even they fail to discern it aright. Peter's confession at Caesarea Philippi is at best only a partial insight, for it ignored the necessity of the cross, and at worst a satanic temptation, for "Christ" could mean a political revolutionary.

From this point is becomes clear that the final epiphany will come only as a result of the cross. The whole ministry thus appears under the guise of a series of preliminary and misunderstood epiphanies, each of which prefigures the final epiphany of the cross and resurrection, which in the person of the centurion leads the Gentile world to confess Jesus as the Son of God, and to a life in the inaugurated reign of God in which the believers witness to him amid persecution and martyrdom and await the final consummation. But even the final denouement is left mysteriously hanging in the air. The risen Christ does not appear to his disciples (Mark 16:9 and following verses of course are not part of the original text, and it is best to assume that Mark deliberately ended his gospel at 16:8), but his reunion with the disciples in Galilee is foretold. The fulfillment of this promise is not recorded because Mark identifies it with the final consummation: the Church is still awaiting that consummation, while the tribulations foretold in Chapter 13 and which precede the return of the exalted Christ take place. Mark's gospel contains a message for a persecuted missionary Church.

2. Matthew

Both Matthew and Luke, by their incorporation of a considerable body of teaching into their gospels, have deviated from Mark's classical pattern, which appears in John. Indeed, one might regard the teaching material as the real content of Matthew, and the Markan narrative as its external framework or scaffolding. The teaching is arranged in five main blocks. The first is the Sermon on the Mount, the new law for the Christian community. The second, in Chapter 10, is the missionary charge, which represents the marching orders of the Church's ministry. The third block (Chapter 13) is the parables of the kingdom, in which kingdom and Church are practically equated. The fourth block is commonly called the "address to the community" (Chapter 18). The fifth block is concerned mainly with the last things and the final consummation (Chapters 23–25). Each of these blocks of teaching concludes with a similar formula: "when Jesus had finished these sayings" (7:28; 11:1; 13:53; 19:1; 26:1). Then follows the narrative of the passion and resurrection, which inaugurates the universal teaching mission of the Church:

> Go therefore, and make disciples of all nations, baptizing them in the name of the Father and of the Son and of the Holy Spirit, teaching them to observe all that I have commanded you.   *Matthew 28:19 f.*

in which "all that I have commanded you" represents the content of the five blocks of material distinguished above. A recent critic has aptly designated St. Matthew's gospel as a "Manual of Discipline," comparable in character and purpose to the recently discovered document of that name among the Qumran scrolls. Thus Matthew, by his arrangement and reinterpretation of traditional material, has brought it up to date to meet the needs of his own age. The saying which he attributes to Jesus in 13:52 fittingly describes his own method and achievement: "Therefore every scribe who has been trained for the kingdom of heaven is like a householder who brings out of his treasure what is new and what is old.

3. Luke

It is impossible to consider St. Luke's gospel apart from its sequel in Acts. Luke writes professedly as a historian, and not only as an evangelist; but it is a *theological* history which he is concerned to present. Jesus Christ represents not the end of history, as in Mark, but the decisive event which set in motion a new period in the history of God's redemptive purpose. This history is the story of what God has done through his Holy

Spirit, who is the initiator of each succeeding step. This work of the Spirit is depicted as it is outlined in Deutero-Isaiah as the work of bringing the good news of God's loving-kindness to the human world, to the poor and needy, of binding up the brokenhearted. It is the Holy Spirit who initiates the entrance of Jesus into the world, through whom this work of the Holy Spirit becomes not a promise but an actualization. The universality of the salvation thus inaugurated is declared in the angelic message to the shepherds:

> Glory to God in the highest, and on earth peace, good will towards men who are the objects of his good pleasure.

The same theme is taken up by the aged Simeon as he holds the infant Jesus in his arms:

> A light for the revelation of the Gentiles.

The revelation is not an abstraction or an idea, but the salvation of God made concrete as an event in the person of Jesus. Jesus himself delineates the same program at the inception of his ministry in his sermon at Nazareth, which Luke has deliberately removed from its Markan position to serve as a frontispiece for the whole ministry of Jesus himself and then of Christ in the Church:

> The Spirit of the Lord is upon me,
> because he has anointed me
> to preach good news to the poor;
> he has sent me to proclaim
> release to the captives,
> and recovering of sight to the blind,
> to set at liberty those who are oppressed,
> to proclaim the acceptable year of the Lord.
>> *Luke 4:18 f.*

The rest of Luke-Acts is the execution of this program. First, Jesus concentrates his message particularly upon the outcast and poor, the needy and the oppressed. Then he associates others with this mission, first the Twelve and then the Seventy, thus prefiguring the Church's later extension of the mission, first by the apostolate, and then by the ministry of the elders. Then Jesus interprets his activity in the three exquisite parables of the lost sheep, the lost coin, and the prodigal son (Chapter 15). In the great movement of God to man, initiated in the ministry of Jesus, God rejoices to seek and save the lost. The same theme is continued in the parable of the Pharisee and the publican (18:9 ff.) and in the story of Jesus and Zacchaeus (19:1 ff.). As for Matthew, so for Luke, Jesus is the second Moses, but it is Moses the prophet and servant and agent of God's redemption rather than Moses the lawgiver who makes his special appeal to Luke. So Jesus goes up to Jerusalem to accomplish his "exodus" (the Greek word for "departure," R.S.V., at 9:31), for it cannot be that a prophet should perish out of Jerusalem (13:33). It is through this event that the universal mission of the Church, prefigured in the ministry of Jesus, is set in motion. The decisive nature of the cross is disclosed in the beautiful little story of the penitent thief (Mark had let them both die railing on Jesus), in whom the need of all mankind is concentrated.

So, the decisive event accomplished, the mission can be extended through the impulse, guidance, and power of the Holy Spirit, which had empowered Jesus himself in his prefigurative ministry, in the witness of the apostolate and the Church:

> Ye shall be my witnesses in Jerusalem and in all Judaea and Samaria, and to the end of the earth.

The rest of Acts portrays the fulfillment of this mission. The author is not really interested in writing the history of the early communities, still less the biographies of the Church's earliest leaders, such as Peter or Paul. One by one he drops his heroes like hot cakes as soon as they have served his purpose. Hence the uselessness of inquiring whether Luke intended to add a third work which should include the martyrdom of Paul. What he is really interested in is bringing the gospel to Rome. When that is done, the Church's mission is in principle complete. Luke then is not an ordinary kind of historian: he is a theological historian. Yet his theology has a profoundly human content. The gospel comes to meet the real needs of the Greco-

Roman world, of the poor, the sick, the outcast, and the women, of the Gentile sunk in superstition, idolatry, and vice. Humanitarianism is not the whole of the gospel, but it is a part of it. Luke never cut his humanitarianism adrift from its theological moorings, nor does his gospel stand alone.

To sum up, therefore, we have not three gospels, but one gospel proclaimed in three different ways. For Mark, Jesus is the Son of God whose power and glory are revealed precisely in his weakness and humiliation, an encouragement for a church in its hour of persecution and tribulation. For Matthew, Jesus is the lawgiver, who has replaced the law of Moses by the new law, and the old Israel who rejected him by the Christian Church. For Luke, Jesus is the universal Savior, who is proclaimed as such to the whole world in its need.

ST. PAUL: THE FIRST THEOLOGIAN

A. CRITICAL PRESUPPOSITIONS

The King James version of the New Testament gives us fourteen epistles of St. Paul. Of these, it is all but universally agreed (outside the Roman Catholic Church, which is officially committed to its Pauline authorship) that Hebrews is not by Paul. Of the rest, the pastorals (I–II Timothy, Titus), at any rate in their present form, are generally thought to be the work of a later hand. This view will be accepted here, though the basic nucleus of II Timothy is assumed to be a genuine farewell letter of Paul written shortly before his martyrdom at Rome. Ephesians is often thought to be the work of an unknown genius and devoted follower of St. Paul, though the present writer must confess that he sees no decisive reason for the rejection of its Pauline authorship, and would prefer to regard it as a circular letter written by Paul to a number of his churches at the end of his life and representing the crown of his theology. In deference to prevailing critical opinion, however, Ephesians will be used only as confirmatory evidence for the Pauline theology exhibited in the indubitably genuine letters. A few critics still reject II Thessalonians and even Colossians. In the opinion of the author these doubts are hypercritical, and these letters will be accepted here as genuine. II Corinthians is assumed to be a composite document, consisting of parts of three different letters written by St. Paul on three different occasions (see below).

The dating of the genuine epistles presents a number of delicate problems, none of which is capable of definitive solution. In particular, the date of Galatians is hotly disputed. Some regard it as the earliest of the epistles, dating it before A.D. 50: others place it anything up to five years after 50. The latter view will be taken here, on the ground that its affinities lie with the other controversial epistles, particularly with the "severe letter" of II Corinthians 10–13. The captivity epistles (Philippians, Colossians, and, if genuine, Ephesians) are sometimes placed in a hypothetical imprisonment at Ephesus ca. A.D. 54–57. This however involves compressing practically the whole of the known correspondence of Paul into these three years, and therefore raises more difficulties than it solves. There is indeed much to be said for placing Philippians here, though on the whole it still seems preferable to place it in the Roman captivity and to regard it as close in time and atmosphere to the genuine parts of II Timothy, on the assumption that there was only one Roman imprisonment. Colossians is markedly different from the controversial epistles and appears to presuppose a development of St. Paul's thought in response to a totally new situation. We therefore prefer to place this also in the Roman captivity, and since Philemon is closely linked with Colossians, it too must be placed here.

This then will be our hypothetical dating of the epistles:[1]

DATE	EPISTLE	PLACE OF WRITING
51	I–II Thessalonians	Corinth
54	II Corinthians 6:11–7:1	Ephesus?
55	I Corinthians	Ephesus
56–57	II Corinthians 10–13	Ephesus
	Galatians	Ephesus
58	II Corinthians 1–9	Macedonia
	Romans 1–15	Corinth
	Romans 16 (to Ephesus)	Corinth

[1] The very different chronological scheme recently proposed by John Knox rests upon an excessively skeptical attitude to Acts.

61–63	Colossians	Rome
	Philemon	Rome
	Ephesians	Rome
64	Philippians	Rome
	II Timothy (the genuine parts)	Rome

B. PAUL THE THEOLOGIAN

The pre-Pauline church had a message. It had a body of catechetical teaching. It had an intense common life centered upon its worship. But it did not have anything in the nature of a thought-out theology. It was Paul who appeared as the first significant thinker of the early Church. He alone of the New Testament writers, so far as we can tell, had had a real theological training. Even if, as some think, that statement in Acts that he had sat at the feet of Gamaliel is unfounded, it is clear from his writings that Paul was familiar with Jewish exegesis of the Old Testament, both rabbinic and Hellenistic. An instance of such familiarity is to be found in I Corinthians 10:4; rabbinic exegesis had concluded that since the rock is mentioned on at least three occasions, it must have traveled around with the Israelites in the wilderness. In speaking of the "Rock which followed them" Paul clearly accepts that interpretation, though he adds that the Rock was Christ. Again Galatians 4:21 uses an allegorical interpretation of Hagar in a Hellenistic fashion. The call to be a rabbinic or Hellenistic Jewish theologian, however, was one that Paul had to surrender and to count but dung for the gospel's sake. He abandoned theology in order to become a missionary. Yet he did not cease to be a theologian. The marks of his training were too deeply imprinted for that. Immersed as he was in the practical problems of a missionary, he still approached these problems with the mind and the techniques of a trained theologian. This means that his theology is not of a systematic character: it is definitely *ad hoc* and occasional, thrown off to meet the concrete situations of the mission field. If he made the sacrifice of an Albert Schweitzer, his work presents the quality of, say, a Bishop Lesslie Newbigin, rather than of a Karl Barth. In seeking therefore to systematize Paul's theology we are inevitably doing violence to the material. But it is a risk which must be taken if we are to see Paul as a whole, and, so long as we recognize the ragged edges without trying to smooth them out, little harm will be done. Paul was indeed too great to be invariably consistent.

C. REDEMPTIVE HISTORY

Where shall we start in an attempt to reduce Paul's theology to some sort of order? Traditional Protestantism has ranged everything under the rubric of justification by faith. We ought not, however, to be misled by the prominence of that doctrine in the two controversial epistles, for in the other nine it is barely mentioned. After all, it was the error of the "Tübingen School" to regard the Paul of Galatians and Romans as the only true Paul, with the consequent rejection or at least questioning of those epistles which failed in their view to reproduce that doctrine. More recently "in Christ" has been taken as the key concept to Paul's thinking. This is far more promising. But the concept "in Christ" is part of a wider scheme. It needs to be balanced by "in Adam." It is part of a whole scheme of *redemptive history,* and it is this conception which brackets together both his theory and his practice, both his labors and his writings, both his missionary work and his theological thinking. Here, in redemptive history, we have the real key to Paul's life and thought.

Paul conceived himself to be the key figure in a vital stretch of God's purpose in history. The gospel had been offered to the Jews and rejected by them. Therefore it must be preached to the Gentiles. When the Gentiles have received it and have been incorporated into the Church, Israel will be provoked to jealousy and change its mind. Israel will then come into the Church, and Christ's return will bring the consummation. All this must happen very shortly. This explains the haste with which Paul rushes around the world. Not that he envisages the complete evangelization of the Gentile world. Rather, it must be done representatively by establishing the gospel at the nodal points of communication in the provinces, and finally at the very center of the empire, at the imperial court itself. The importance Paul attached to the collection of funds for the "saints" at Jerusalem should be understood in the light of this. It was meant as an impressive demonstration of the success of the Gentile mission, to provoke Israel to jealousy and to hasten its repentance and the return of Christ.

But this stage is part of a larger whole, stretching back into the past and forward into the future when God should be all in all. It begins with the creation of the world. Paul was perhaps the first Christian thinker to bring creation explicitly into connection with the redemption. The preaching and catechetical teaching of the pre-Pauline churches had indeed prefaced the event of redemption with the declaration that the God who acted redemptively had also created the world. But Paul goes further, linking the creation with him who was also the agent of redemption. To do this he employed the concept of the divine wisdom. In the Old Testament, wisdom is sometimes personified as the agent through whom God created the world. Thus in Proverbs 8:22 and following verses Wisdom cries:

> The Lord created me at the beginning of his work,
>> the first of his acts of old.
> Ages ago I was set up before the beginning
>> of the earth.

> . . . .

> Before the mountains had been shaped,
>> before the hills, was I brought forth:
> before he had made the earth.

> . . . .

> Then I was beside him like a master workman.
>> *Compare Wisdom 9:9; Ecclesiasticus 24:9*

In such passages wisdom appears as antecedent to all creation, the master workman co-operating with God in the act of creation. It thus acquires a kind of "hypostatization," that is to say, it is distinguishable from the being of God without however being ontologically separate. Such conceptions were widely developed in later Judaism, both in Palestine and in the Diaspora, owing to the increased emphasis on the transcendence of God, and they lay ready to have as tools for St. Paul to express what he had found in his encounter with the event of redemption in Christ. St. Paul transfers just this conception of Wisdom to Christ in Colossians 1:15 and following verses:

> He is the image of the invisible God, the first-born of all creation; for in him all things were created, in heaven and on earth, visible and invisible, whether thrones or dominions or principalities or authorities—all things were created through him and for him. He is before all things, and in him all things hold together.

Nearly all these phrases can be paralleled in the wisdom philosophy of late Judaism. Why does Paul boldly transfer them to Christ? Certainly not from any taste for cosmological speculation. He was a busy missionary, not a speculative philosopher. Rather, it was because of the concrete situation he was faced with at Colossae, where, under the influence of an incipient Gnosticism, extravagant claims were being advanced for other mediatorial principles, principalities and powers (Colossians 2:15) and angels (2:18). But there is more to it than that. Paul rejects the Gnostic speculation because it cuts right across the basic Christian experience. The God whom the Christian community had encountered in Christ was the selfsame God who created the universe. Creation and redemption are both his acts, and redemption is the redemption of that same universe which he had created. Redemption is not redemption *out of* the universe, but redemption *of* the universe. Redemption in Christ is the culmination of the series of God's acts which began with creation.

In creating the universe, God's original purpose was that

man should reflect his image and share his glory. But, as Paul explains in Romans 5:12 and following verses, by a concrete act of disobedience man lost this image and glory, and forfeited the relationship with God to which he had been destined. Adam was doubtless for St. Paul an individual, but as the first individual he included all his posterity. In expounding the consequences of this primal act of disobedience, Paul avails himself of a rough and ready anthropology and psychology, which though it may be totally unscientific, is nonetheless profound. Man is "flesh" as well as "mind" or "spirit." This involves a certain dualism, but not an ultimate one. God is the Creator of both, and the one cannot exist in man without the other. The mind, as St. Paul explains in Romans 7:25, serves as a kind of telephone exchange, apprehending the demand of God and passing on the communication to the flesh. The flesh is morally neutral, not intrinsically evil. It is the instrument by which man acts in the external world. Mind and flesh are animated by "soul," and man in his totality can be called a "soul." Mind and flesh are not individual to each man, but each man partakes of so much mind and flesh, which is bounded off from the rest by the body. "Body" means, in effect, man as organic individuality, almost what we mean by personality. What God intended was that man as mind should receive the communication of his commands, pass them on to man as flesh, and the flesh act in obedience to the communication. Adam's act of disobedience introduced a distortion, however, and the primal act of disobedience involved all his descendants in a state of sin. Sin is more than the concrete wrongdoings of individuals: it is a state of being, a universal condition of man. It is a state of arrogant defiance against the will of God. It is an objective condition independent of man's consciousness of it and sense of responsibility for it. In fact, it becomes an objective power outside of man but controlling him, so that every action he takes is under its control. Every impulse of man, even his intrinsically good impulses, are the impulses of fallen man. The chink in the armor through which sin enters man is the flesh, which though morally neutral is weak and easily surrenders to sin. Hence all behavior "according to the flesh" becomes sinful behavior. This state in turn affects the mind, which becomes the "mind of the flesh" and thereby hostile to God.

We have seen that Paul attributes this state of affairs to Adam's primal act of disobedience. This was the Palestinian answer to the problem of sin. Elsewhere however he employs the Hellenistic Jewish answer (Romans 1:18 ff.). According to this, man was created with the capacity to know God but turned his back on him, worshiping the creature rather than the Creator, or in other words succumbed to idolatry. As a consequence man came under the dominion of the demonic powers of which the idols are the visible expression. Thus there was a corporate turning away of man from the worship of the true God, and that is the origin of sin. These two answers to the problem of the origin of sin are not in the last resort irreconcilable, though St. Paul was not concerned to reconcile them, since he had no intention of building a theological system.

As a consequence of his fallen condition, man comes under the "wrath" of God. That is to say, his relationship to God becomes a perverted one. Instead of basking in the sunshine of God's presence, he is under a cloud and in darkness, cut off from communion with him (Romans 1:18; Colossians 3:6). This state of excommunication from God's presence receives its final seal and ratification in *death*. Death, for St. Paul, is not merely a biological fact, but the seal of man's final separation from God:

> Therefore as sin came into the world through one man and death through sin, and so death spread to all men because all men sinned.   *Romans 5:12*
>
>   Compare also verse 21: sin reigned in death.

Actually, however, death comes to have two distinct though related meanings. Death is the physical end of life. In this sense it is the wages of sin. Yet at the same time it is a condition of man prevailing already during his life. The first sense is the objective seal of the second, a fitting symbol of that final separation from God which is already taking shape during man's life in sin and under God's wrath on earth.

This perverted condition spreads to the whole universe. The whole creation was subjected to "vanity," that is, futility and frustration, and has been groaning and travailing together until now (Romans 8:18 ff.). Man, Paul maintains, has dragged the universe down with him. Can we give this any intelligible meaning today, or must it be jettisoned as outworn mythology? Is the evil we see in the universe around us—nature red in tooth and claw—really to be attributed to man's fall? This much at least may be supposed, that our relation to the natural world had been distorted by our perverted condition, and therefore it appears to us other than it would if our state were "normal."

But man was not left to himself. God continued to communicate his demand to man's mind, and though man was impotent to obey, the communication registered itself in the guilty conscience (Romans 2:15; cf. 1:20). Conscience, for St. Paul, acts only as a judicial faculty after action, not as a legislative faculty before. As a result, man suffers from a fundamental malaise; he can never forget that things are not what they ought to be, and retains the hope that someday the situation will be rectified. But man, even with the law of God written on his heart, is incapable of escaping from the dominion of sin. The rectification can only come from the outside. That is just what God has done, not by one act, but by a series of acts, all of which conform to a consistent pattern and will culminate in a decisive act, the coming of Jesus the Christ. The first act of the series was the call of Abraham, who was selected and given the promise of the seed which would bear God's purpose in history. Abraham was then as good as dead, ninety years old. There was nothing in him on which God could build. It was a fresh, creative act, an act of pure *grace*, to which Abraham could only respond by *faith*, that is, by abandoning every attempt to act himself and allowing God to act upon him. Since there was no precondition in Abraham, since his part was solely a matter of faith, it followed that the call was in principle universal. No one could qualify, only God could create the qualification, and therefore it was implicitly open to all. The call of Abraham might seem to involve a narrowing down of God's purpose, but in ultimate effect it meant the widening out of it to include all men. This pattern of selection for ultimate inclusion repeats itself throughout the history of Israel. In the second generation Ishmael is rejected and Isaac becomes the bearer of the seed, while in the third Jacob and Esau are similarly treated.

There comes now however an event which forms an erratic boulder in the Pauline scheme. It is the giving of the law through Moses. It does indeed belong to the same historical line, for Paul is at pains to stress that it occurred precisely 430 years after the promise to Abraham. But it does not conform to the same pattern. It is not a reinforcement of the promise, but a reinforcement of the condemnation of Adam. It was not given directly, but mediately by the hand of angels (here Paul follows a rabbinic legend). This giving of the law to Israel is not altogether easy to fit in with Paul's other suggestion that there was a general law given to all men in nature, since it causes him to assert that during the period between Adam and Moses there was no law, and therefore no imputed sin. But this is just another indication of the lack of system in his thinking. The law does indeed interrupt the execution of the pattern of salvation through call and response, faith and grace which had been initiated in Abraham, but in the end it subserves the same ultimate purpose. It sharpens the sense of sin and the need for a redeemer. Thus it acts as our "tutor" (R.S.V., "custodian") to bring us to Christ. How the commandment in practice acts as a "custodian" to lead us to Christ is indicated in Romans 7:7–19, which however is one of the most controverted passages of the New Testament. Is this a piece of spiritual autobiography? If so, is St. Paul talking of his experience as a Pharisee under the law, or of his life after he became a Christian? The first alternative seems to be ruled out by the way in which elsewhere St. Paul seems to have been perfectly satisfied with his achievements as a Pharisee. He was, he says, touching the law, blameless, having progressed far beyond his contemporaries in its observance. Since the Reformation, scholars have often been tempted to interpret Paul's experience in the light of Luther's, and this danger should be avoided. It is equally improbable that Paul is talking of his experiences as a Christian. He generally lays so much stress on the blessings of salvation he already enjoys in Christ that it is hard to believe that all Christ had wrought for him was a sharpened sense of frustration, however much that austere possibility may appeal to the "Barthian" mind. Accordingly it is best to take the "I" in this passage as "man under law apart from Christ," that is, primarily, though not exclusively, Israelite man. Sin, man's egotistic impulse, is present before man is confronted with a commandment, "thou shalt not," but is not consciously recognized until the confrontation takes place. Through the law comes the knowledge of sin (Romans 3:20). Paul can even say that the law actually incites to sin (Romans 5:20; cf. Galatians 3:19). This may seem an overstatement, but it is sometimes true to experience. Everyone knows the story of the boy who never thought of stealing the next-door neighbor's apples until his father told him not to. The law therefore reduces man to an impasse: "Wretched man that I am! Who will deliver me from this body of death?" Since the law demands total and radical obedience to the will of God, all men stand under a curse. Israel differs from the rest of mankind in that it bears the promise of ultimate release from the impasse, and also in that through the possession of the Mosaic law and not merely the natural law written on the heart the human predicament is more sharply manifest in Israel. Even these are God's gifts, and Israel has nothing about which to boast.

At this point Paul takes over the proclamation of his predecessors in Christ. In the life of Jesus, culminating in his death and manifested in its redemptive significance through the resurrection, God has now acted decisively to avert the impasse. We see here Paul's special contribution to Christian theology. He brings the Christian message into vital relation with man's innermost predicament. He is the first "existential" theologian. Yet he achieves this without forfeiting the corporate objective elements in the early Christian proclamation and in its church life. He does so by keeping the salvation of the individual within the framework of a redemptive history. The modern "existential" understanding of Paul, though often illuminating on the subjective side of man's appropriation of the event of redemption, fails to do justice to the Pauline synthesis between his new insights and the tradition within which he worked them out.

St. Paul presents the theology of salvation under five main images: redemption, justification, reconciliation, victory, and sacrifice. None of these lines of thought seems to have been his own innovation. All of them were probably taken from the liturgical vocabulary of the Church. But Paul gives to each of them an existential profundity which hitherto they had lacked.

1. *Redemption*

The discovery of papyrus fragments from Egypt in the early decades of this century raised enthusiastic hopes that at last all the problems of early Christian language would be solved. The use of the term "redemption" was found to be common in the papyri in connection with the manumission of slaves. In those days slaves used to acquire their freedom by depositing the sum for the ransom in a temple treasury so that they became nominally slaves of the god, but in effect free. This process was known as "redemption." No doubt this current usage helped early Christian preachers; they were using words already familiar to their hearers (cf. Galatians 4:1–4). But after the first flush of enthusiasm it has become increasingly clear that contemporary secular usage is not the sole or even the main clue to the great New Testament words. The main quarry from which the early Christians drew was in fact the Greek translation of the Old Testament, the Septuagint. But they did not simply take over the Old Testament words: these words received a radical twist in meaning by the impact of the event of Jesus Christ. Now in the Old Testament the words "redeem" and "redemption" are applied to God's mighty act of bringing the Hebrews out of Egypt and constituting them his people (see e.g., Deuteronomy 7:8; I Chronicles 17:21, etc.). The word is again picked up to express the mighty act of God in restoring his people from the Babylonian exile (Isaiah 44:23). This return from Babylon raised high hopes: now at last God would establish his reign on earth. But the return proved a disappointment. The reign of God failed to materialize: Israel was still weak and subject to foreign rule. So the great words which had been used for the return were shelved for the future and became part of Israel's hope. Someday God would redeem his people and establish his reign. It is in this sense that the term is picked up in the gospels. The final redemption is now at hand. Thus the Benedictus announces:

> God . . . has [a prophetic perfect, equivalent to "God will"] visited and redeemed his people. *Luke 1:68*

And in Luke 21:28 we read:

> Now when these things begin to come to pass, look up and raise your heads, because your redemption is drawing near.

Jesus proclaimed the impending advent of the redemption, and the earliest Church doubtless continued his proclamation as it looked for the return of its Lord. But as its insight deepened and as it grew to appreciate what God had already done for them in Christ, it began to see that the redemption had already begun: God *has* redeemed his people. There is no need to suppose that it was St. Paul who first took this step, for it was already implied in the earliest Church's belief that the Holy Spirit had been outpoured as a consequence of Christ's finished work.

Now on this background in redemptive history it becomes clear that for St. Paul it is not the salvation of the individual which is primary, but the reconstitution of the people of God in the last days through the death and resurrection of Christ. The individual is translated into this community through his baptism, but the redeemed community is already there. It is in this setting that the redemption of the individual takes place, not in the non-historical setting of existential experience.

2. Justification

Does justification mean that the individual is made *just*, as etymologically it ought to mean, or does it mean that the individual is *accounted* just? Does St. Paul teach the Catholic doctrine of infused righteousness or the Protestant doctrine of imputed righteousness? In either case, justification is conceived as an individual affair. Once again the term must be set upon the background of the Old Testament. First, we must notice that the phrase "righteousness of God," so prominent in Paul's discussion of justification, denotes not a quality or attribute of God, but his concrete action. It is the event whereby God delivers his people, as, for example, in Second Isaiah in restoring the exiles to their homeland:

> Soon my salvation will come,
> and my deliverance be revealed.
> *Isaiah 56:1*

Here "salvation" and "deliverance" are in synonymous parallelism, as they are again in Isaiah 51:6 and in Psalm 97:2. This salvation is the act whereby God vindicates his people by delivering them from their oppressors. This is the background on which we must understand Paul when he says:

> But now the righteousness of God has been manifested apart from the law . . . the righteousness in Jesus Christ for all who believe.   *Romans 3:21*

The verb "to justify" is used in the Old Testament for the action of God's righteousness, thus understood:

> He is near that justifieth me.
> *Isaiah 50:8* (K.J.V.)

God justifies Israel by vindicating her, restoring her to her own land. To justify therefore, in its most characteristic Old Testament sense, means to vindicate by an act of deliverance. Now in Pauline thought the primary object of God's act of righteousness or vindication is, as in the Old Testament, not the ndividual, but the community:

> [He] was delivered up for *our* trespasses,
> and was raised for *our* justification.
> *Romans 4:25* (K.J.V.)

This last text is especially interesting, for it shows, first, that the use of justification as a term for Christ's work probably does not originate with Paul, since this is most likely a pre-Pauline formula. Second, it suggests that the source of the idea lay in Isaiah 53:11, where it is said of the servant that he will "justify many." The individual is justified, vindicated, or delivered by being brought into the justified, vindicated community, the community which before him lives in a right relation to God. The occasion in which men are transferred into this community is of course baptism (I Corinthians 6:11, where "washed," "sanctified," and "justified" clearly refer to the same occasion).

It is clear, then, that justification cannot mean that a man is "made righteous" in an ethical sense. Rather, he is put into a community where he may grow in righteousness by "becoming what he is." This process is often conveniently referred to as sanctification. This however, as I Corinthians 6:11 shows, is to introduce a distinction of language foreign to St. Paul. Justification and sanctification have already been attained as a present reality in baptism. Yet these are anticipatory realizations of the blessings of the age to come. Justification and sanctification are given in advance of the last day at the moment of baptism; they have to be striven for constantly in ethical endeavor, and will be finally attained only at the consummation. For only then will the Christian "become what he is."

3. Reconciliation

Since man apart from Christ exists under the wrath of God, he is as it were at war with him. He is "estranged and hostile in mind, doing evil deeds." He is in a state of rebellion against God (Colossians 1:21), an enemy of God (Romans 11:28).

This objective condition has however been terminated by the act of God in Christ, and an objective condition of "peace" put in its place:

> . . . while we were enemies we were reconciled to God by the death of his Son. . . .   *Romans 5:10*

> God was in Christ reconciling the world to himself.
> *II Corinthians 5:19*

This does not necessarily mean that by accepting Christ the individual attains peace of heart. Paul the Christian can still say "without were fightings, within were fears." It means that God by his act in Jesus Christ has established a new people constituted no longer by rebellion against God, but by that event itself. This new status may result in "peace" and "joy" in the subjective sense, but that condition is the consequence of the objective status of the new community, not identical with peace in its objective sense.

4. *The Appropriation of Christ's Redeeming Work*

It is through faith, and faith alone, that men appropriate what God has done for them in Christ. It is through faith that men enter the redeemed, justified, and reconciled community. Faith, in Pauline language, is always set in opposition to works. By works Paul means all human activity undertaken to establish for oneself one's righteousness with God. In the moment of faith all such attempts are abandoned, and God is allowed to do for us what we cannot do for ourselves. What that means is seen most clearly in the story of Abraham already discussed above (see p. 329). Is it God who is the object of faith, or is it Christ? St. Paul says both, and both amount to the same thing. For it is through Christ that God acts redemptively toward us. Thus faith is not a disposition of the human soul, regardless of its object. It is directed toward a specific event. The formula "justification by faith" cannot therefore mean a feeling that we are in a state of conversion or bliss. It is rigorously directed toward the redemptive event. It

336

is the event, or rather the act of God in that event, which saves, or justifies, not faith. Faith is the necessary precondition on the human side for the reception of the benefits which flow from the event. Justification by faith is shorthand for "justification through the grace and love of God in the event of Jesus Christ, apprehended by faith."

The event by which we are redeemed, justified, and reconciled is defined as the act of God's *love*. Love is not a timeless quality, or an attitude of benevolence of a quite general kind. Love is event:

> [He] loved me, and gave himself for me.
> *Galatians* 2:20

The New Testament word for this love is *agape*, which expresses the wholly unmotivated, uncaused quality of God's activity towards us in Christ. The classical description of this love is to be found in Romans 5:6 and following verses:

> While we were yet helpless, at the right time Christ died for the ungodly. Why, one will hardly die for a righteous man—though perhaps for a good man one will even dare to die. But God shows his love for us in that while we were yet sinners Christ died for us.

The act of God can also be described as his *grace*. Here is another term which has been much abused in Christian theology and piety. Sometimes it is thought of as a kind of fluid poured into the soul in doses. Sometimes it is thought of as the help of God which in a vague sort of way enables us to be good. But in St. Paul's thought it is quite rigorously bound to the act of God in Christ. It is the unmerited aspect of God's love in that event. It is exhibited concretely in his "sending his Son in the likeness of sinful flesh" (Romans 8:3).

> God sent forth his Son.   *Galatians* 4:4

> He spared not his Son, but delivered him up for us all.
> *Romans* 8:32

The event of Jesus Christ has a double character. On the

one hand it is an act of human obedience wrought out in the historical order. This aspect is particularly stressed in the passage which contrasts the disobedience of Adam with the behavior of the Christ (Romans 5:12–21). Adam is the head not only chronologically first, but also representatively inclusive, of the old, sinful order of humanity. Christ, on the other hand, is the head, in the same representative and inclusive sense, of the new humanity. In the famous passage, Philippians 2:5–8, the obedience of the Christ is again stressed. Here the death of the Christ is the culmination of a whole life of obedience wrought out on the plane of history. On the other hand it is precisely in and through this historical act of obedience that God's grace is exhibited—that is, not only demonstrated as a possibility in human life, but actualized toward mankind. That this should be so is a paradox, only to be discerned in faith.

But the cross in its double aspect is not to be isolated from the resurrection: *"therefore* God has highly exalted him." This does not mean that God steps in at the last minute like the *deus ex machina* in a Greek tragedy, reverses the situation and makes it the exact opposite of what it was. Rather, it means that he sets his seal upon the Son's obedience, declaring and revealing it to be what it is, the exhibition of his own grace. The death and resurrection of Jesus thus form a complex, indissoluble event. It is this total complex we mean when we speak of the event of Jesus Christ. The pre-medieval Church clearly appreciated this Pauline insight in its triumph crucifixes, in which Jesus is portrayed, not naked and suffering, but clothed in majesty and crowned with glory on the cross. St. John's gospel will give even sharper expression to this insight.

We inevitably ask: *how* did the death of Jesus have precisely this redemptive significance? If we hope from St. Paul a cast-iron theory of the atonement we shall be disappointed. What he does offer however is two lines of thought along which faith may try to understand itself. One line is the use of the language of victory, the other the language of sacrifice

5. *Victory*

Paul took over from his predecessors the mythological notion that the universe, including man, was under the thrall of demonic powers, the thrones, principalities, and powers, and that Christ's death was the victory which delivered us from their thrall. This is not new, but Paul brings these powers down to existential level by including among them "sin" and the "law." One feels that it is these powers which really matter: the others are just conventional imagery, often used because heretics asserted that they were equal mediators with Christ. Thus Paul speaks of God's "sending his own Son in the likeness of sinful flesh" (or: "to deal with sin," or: "as a sin-offering") by which God "condemned sin in the flesh" (Romans 8:3). In other words, by invading the enemy-occupied territory (flesh, which was occupied by the enemy, sin) and by refusing himself to come under the power of the enemy, preserving his obedience inviolate to the last, Jesus defeated the enemy. Sin put in its claim against Jesus, as it did against every member of the human race, but this time it went too far. The triumph of Jesus is sealed by the resurrection, in which he emerges victorious from the enemy-occupied territory.

> . . . the death that he died, he died unto sin once, but the life he lives he lives to God.   *Romans 6:10*

This, we may object, may have been true for Jesus himself, but how can it affect our lives? How can his victory be ours, except by its power to inspire imitation? Paul's answer is that Jesus was not just an individual, but the representative Man, the head of a new human race. What happened to him happened potentially to all men in him, and becomes effective in men when in baptism they are "united with him in a death like his" and when the "old self is crucified with him so that the sinful body might be destroyed" (Romans 6:5 f.).

The second new demonic power is the law:

> Christ redeemed us from the curse of the law, having become a curse for us—for it is written, Cursed be everyone who hangs on a tree.   *Galatians 3:13*

Paul's argument may not sound very convincing today, but we should try patiently to follow his meaning before rejecting it out of hand. The law pronounces a curse on those who fail to observe it (Deuteronomy 27:26): it also pronounces a curse on those who are hanged on a tree (Deuteronomy 21:23). Hence, argues Paul, Christ did not deserve the curse, because he kept the law, yet was hanged on a tree and so had to suffer the curse. What happened was that the curse of the law came down upon the head of one who was completely innocent, and in so doing overreached itself. Henceforth it lay impotent, exhausted and defeated. How this can affect the lives of others subsequent to Jesus is indicated in the following verse, Galatians 3:14:

> . . . that in Christ Jesus the blessing of Abraham might come upon the Gentiles, that we might receive the promise of the Spirit through faith.

It is by being "in Christ," that is, in the new humanity of which he is the head, that his victory over the power of the law is shared by us, so that we live by the Spirit and not by the law.

Although Paul here uses mythology, it is mythology brought within the range of Christian experience. Christian devotion has always adored the cross as the nadir of God's condescension to seek and save. Here he stooped to the lowest and most bitter depths of human plight, and in sharing it transformed and overcame it. But apart from our incorporation into the new humanity in Christ, of which he is the head and representative, the whole notion still remains mythological, for it cannot otherwise be brought into vital connection with our lives.

6. Sacrifice

The other line of thought, that of sacrifice, is one in which St. Paul is mainly content to repeat the language of the tradition, particularly that of the liturgical tradition (I Corinthians 11:25) without elaborating it any further. It was the author of Hebrews who made the distinctive contribution along this line (see below). Thus Paul often speaks of the "blood" of Christ in a way which suggests that it is synonymous with his sacrificial death (Romans 5:9; cf. Ephesians 1:7; Colossians 1:20). He also speaks quite vaguely of Christ's death as "a fragrant offering and sacrifice to God" (Ephesians 5:2). It is difficult to read out of these passages any specific theological import. There are however two passages which merit further consideration. The first is:

> For our sake he made him to be sin . . .
> *II Corinthians* 5:21

This may mean that Christ is regarded as a "sin-offering" (one of the recognized categories of Jewish sacrifice since post-exilic times), the purpose of which was to make an atonement for sins of negligence by removing their effects. If this is what is meant in 5:21, and not the simpler sense "to deal with sin," it suggests a line of thought which comes out more explicitly in our second passage, Romans 3:25:

> . . . whom God put forward as an expiation by his blood.

This is a much controverted passage. The word represented by "expiation" could also be "propitiation." Propitiation is an act of man directed toward God with the purpose of rendering God propitious or favorable toward man. Expiation on the other hand is an act directed not toward God but to the sin: the stain of the sin is removed by applying the blood of the victim which removes the stain by its holiness. It is claimed that "propitiation" is a pagan concept, while "expiation" is the Old Testament conception. It is thus contended that St. Paul meant "expiation," in the sense that God did for man what he could not do for himself, namely by the blood of Christ remove the effect, particularly the guilt of sin. Since God is the initiator of the action, he could not be also its object. This fits in quite well with what St. Paul has to say elsewhere about God as the initiator of the Son's mission, and about the Son's death as the act of God's love and grace. Attractive as this view is, it seems to rob Paul's doctrine of the atonement of its

341

profundity and to rationalize Paul's doctrine of the wrath of God. Of course the initiative comes from God. But what he initiates is precisely the propitiation of his own wrath! Man could not do it, so God in his mercy undertakes to do for man what he cannot do for himself. In the person of his Son he undergoes the extreme consequence of man's sin, which is to exist under the wrath of God, to be cut off from God's presence. On this interpretation Romans 3:25 becomes a theological comment on the meaning of the Markan cry from the cross: "My God, my God, why hast thou forsaken me?" For in this cry we see God in the person of his Son enduring precisely that separation from God which is the consequence of sin and which is exactly what is meant by the wrath of God. To speak of "expiation" is to do less than justice to what God has done for us in Christ. So we must hold fast to the traditional conception that, for St. Paul, Christ's death is a *propitiatory* sacrifice initiated by God himself.

7. The Resurrection

We have already noticed how for St. Paul the death and resurrection are linked in indissoluble unity as forming together the event of redemption; Paul may have seen this more clearly than his predecessors. The earliest Church at Jerusalem tended to by-pass the death of Jesus as an unfortunate episode and to hurry on to the resurrection. On the other hand Paul's Greek-speaking predecessors (as witness the eucharistic tradition which Paul received) were perhaps in danger of detaching the death from the resurrection and considering it as the event of redemption apart from the resurrection. Paul holds the two together as a single, indivisible event with two facets.

He has also a surer grasp than his predecessors on the representative nature of the resurrection. Christ rose, not just as an individual, but as the second Adam, the head of the new humanity, the "first fruits of those who have fallen asleep":

> For as in Adam all die,
> so also in Christ shall all be made alive.

> But each in his own order: Christ the first fruits, and
> then at his coming those who belong to Christ.
>
> *I Corinthians 15:22–23*

The resurrection is for St. Paul the inauguration of the process of the last times: it is the beginning of the body of Christ, the Church, which is incorporated into his risen body.

Thus with the resurrection a new phase of redemptive history is inaugurated. Previously the purpose of God had been to select and narrow down his elect until the bearer of his purpose was the one man hanging on the cross on Good Friday. There was the sole representative of Israel, the true Israel who rendered that perfect obedience to the law which Israel failed to show. But on Easter day the true Israel is raised again from the dead, henceforth to include all who by adhering to the redemptive event by faith and baptism are incorporated into that risen body. First comes Peter, the rock on which all others are built, then come the Twelve and the rest of the Jerusalem disciples. Then come the repentant members of Israel, the faithful remnant who turn to Christ. It is at this point that Paul's mission comes in: the result of this is to bring in the Gentiles: this is the stage of redemptive history reached in the Pauline epistles, and of which the writing of the epistles is itself a part.

8. *The Spirit and the Church*

St. Paul took over from his predecessors the concept of the Holy Spirit. From the earliest days, as we have seen, the Church had believed that the Spirit was poured forth upon it, an energetic activity of God in the last days, making possible the distinctive activities of the Christian community. In particular, this energy was displayed concretely in the Church's proclamation of the event of redemption, and in the signs which accompanied and confirmed the message. The Hellenistic Church was particularly inclined to see the work of the Spirit in ecstatic phenomena, such as the speaking with tongues, instead of in the more intelligible utterances of prophecy. It also thought of the Spirit less as an occasional invasion of the energy of God, and more as a kind of supernatural fluid or substance.

St. Paul takes up all these notions of his predecessors, but radically transforms their evaluation. In two passages he draws up lists of the manifestations of the Spirit's activity:

I Corinthians 12:8 ff.:
1. utterance of wisdom
2. utterance of knowledge
3. faith
4. gifts of healing
5. working of miracles
6. prophecy
7. discernment of spirits
8. kinds of tongues
9. interpretation of tongues

I Corinthians 12:28:
1. apostles
2. prophets
3. teachers
4. workers of miracles
5. healers
6. helpers
7. administrators
8. speakers in tongues

There is a rough correspondence between the two lists, and in particular it is noticeable how the speaking with tongues comes at the bottom. How does St. Paul arrive at his scale of values? His criterion is what "builds up" the Church, what fosters its corporate life. Thus prophecy, which, unlike speaking with tongues, is intelligible, builds up the life of the community. Knowledge on the other hand "puffs up." Men start to claim possession of special inside knowledge, which others do not have, and it leads to a sense of superiority and cliquishness. But there is an even more excellent way which Paul is inspired to delineate in the immortal thirteenth chapter of I Corinthians. Love, agape, is the supreme gift of the Spirit which must inform all the other gifts, and without which all the others are useless and futile, since without it they cannot contribute to the building up of the community life. Here is Paul's supreme contribution to the understanding of the Holy Spirit. It is not really new, for the common life of the community was the immediate outcome of Pentecost: what was new was the conscious realization that this common life was the work of the Holy Spirit. Here, indeed, was the permanent substitute for the temporary Christian "communism" of the earliest days. The linking together of love and the Spirit brings together the two facts of Jesus and the Spirit, for the event of Jesus Christ is itself the act of God's love, while the work of the Spirit is the extension of that love in the community:

> . . . God's love has been poured into our hearts through the Holy Spirit which has been given to us.
>
> *Romans* 5:5

Once more it is necessary to underline the corporate conception of the Holy Spirit and of Christian love. The Holy Spirit is not a gift merely to the individual to make him better: it is the energy of God which fosters a common life in a community. And Christian love is not the exercise of individual virtue: it is the intense life of the community in mutual fellowship.

9. *The Church*

It has been impossible to speak of St. Paul's theology of redemption without speaking also of the Church. That is because the Church is itself part of the gospel, part of what God has done in Christ.

When St. Paul speaks of "church" he most commonly means a local congregation: "the church of God which is at Corinth," etc. Later on, he, or a close disciple of his, speaks of the Church as a universal society (Ephesians). It is tempting to suppose that there was a process of addition, that the local communities, at some later stage, federated themselves together as a universal society. But that is far from the truth. "Church" in St. Paul, as indeed from the earliest times, does

345

not really mean a local community, but the one people of God re-created from the Old Israel by God's act in Christ. This being so, there can only be one people of God. But the one people of God manifests itself in local embodiments, each of which can be called a "church," and a number of them "churches." There could only be one embodiment of the one people in any particular place, and in New Testament times there were not a number of competing denominations, each either claiming to be the sole local embodiment of the one true Church, or totally ignoring its relation to a universal society.

It is in connection with his belief that the Church is part of the event of redemption that Paul speaks of it as the body of Christ. For both Paul's doctrine of redemption and his doctrine of the Church rest upon the fundamental conception of Jesus Christ as the head of the new humanity, representing and including the redeemed in himself. Here is the ultimate source of the idea of the body of Christ. No doubt the immediate source of it was eucharistic:

> The bread which we break, is it not a participation in the body of Christ? Because there is one loaf, we who are many are one body, for we all partake of the same loaf.
>
> *I Corinthians* 10:16b–17

St. Paul saw in the eucharist the renewal of the Church's incorporation into the body of the crucified and risen head. Thus the term "body of Christ" is not a sociological one, suggesting that Christians form a corporate society like any other human group, but a Christological one: for it depends on the event of redemption, in which the agent of it is the representative head of the new humanity.

10. *The Sacraments*

The Christian proclamation announces an event in history apprehended as the redemptive act of God. That event is the constitutive factor in the whole life of the Church. It is by drawing men and women into relation and contact with that event that they are drawn into the new life created by the event. This drawing of men and women into the event is a renewal of the event itself, and follows the pattern of the event in that it possesses a double character. On the one hand, the drawing of men and women into the event is a visible occurrence, and on the other hand it is the invisible act of God, apprehended by faith. The visible event takes the form of immersion in water and emergence therefrom. The invisible act of God, which is the renewal and application of the original redemptive act, is the translation of the candidate out of his old existence characterized by sin, which is separation from God, into the new existence which will be finally his, at the consummation, but which is already available to him in advance in the life of the Church from the moment of his initiation. This is the meaning of Paul's exposition of baptism in Romans 6:1–6. Baptism has the same two-sidedness of the original event of redemption: the one side visible, the other perceptible only to faith. Apart from faith, baptism appears as an external human action devoid of theological significance. Moreover, it needs to be constantly renewed in the decision of faith and in the rendering of concrete obedience:

> So you must also consider yourselves dead unto sin, and alive to God in Christ Jesus. Let not sin therefore reign in your mortal bodies.   *Romans 6:11–12*

Notice how all the verbs in this passage are in the subjunctive and future tenses: this shows that for St. Paul the baptismal transaction was not, as in the mystery religions, magical and final, but dependent for its realization in constant moral endeavor and for its consummation only at the end. In I Corinthians 1:17 Paul speaks with apparent deprecation about baptism:

> For Christ did not send me to baptize, but to preach the gospel . . .

This passage however must be read in its context. Paul is denying that there is a mystical power inherent in the minister, binding him to the initiates, as in the mystery religions. Rightly understood, baptism is the decisive moment in the Christian life, and Paul can appeal to it as such. But it is the decisive event only when it is subordinated to the preaching of the gospel, that is, to the act of God in Christ which the gospel proclaims. In I Corinthians 15:29 Paul introduces an idea which at first sight seems very close to those of the mystery religions:

> Otherwise, what do people mean by being baptized on behalf of the dead?

Here Paul seems to sanction, or at least refrains from condemning, the practice of undergoing a second baptism of a vicarious kind on behalf of dead friends and relations. But in view of the immense importance he attached to personal decision this seems incredible. An attractive and simple explanation of the practice is that what was happening was that previously unbaptized people got baptized themselves in the hope of joining their (already baptized) Christian friends and relations at the resurrection. This interpretation fits in perfectly with the general argument of the passage, which is to prove that the Corinthian Christians by their own behavior attest to a belief which in theory they are bent on denying.

Paul speaks of the eucharist only in five passages, all of which are in related chapters of the same epistle (I Corinthians 10:3–4; 10:16–17; 10:21; 11:23–34; 14:16). Had it not been for various practical problems confronting the church at Corinth we should not have had even these references, and critics would have contended that the Pauline churches never knew of the eucharist! This shows how unwarranted such a procedure would be. Indeed, we have already observed that the language in which St. Paul speaks of the death of Christ —blood, redemption, sacrifice, etc.—is rooted in the language of the liturgy. Hence it would be quite wrong to relegate the eucharist to the periphery of Paul's theology.

As I Corinthians 14:6 shows, the eucharist, like the common meals of Judaism, began with the recital of a prayer of thanksgiving. The rubric "Do this in remembrance of me" indicates the content of the thanksgiving: it was a recalling and reciting on what God had done in Christ. In accordance with Jewish notions, such a recalling would evoke from God an act whereby he made what was recalled a present reality. Thus in the eucharist the redemption became a present reality in anticipation of its consummation at the return of Christ. Paul's comment on the rubric is:

> As often as you eat this bread and drink this cup, you proclaim the Lord's death until he comes.
>
> *I Corinthians 11:26*

The event of redemption is rendered present by God as the faithful partake of the hallowed food, and its being present is assured by the Lord's promise: "This is my body . . . this is the new covenant in my blood." These words are to be interpreted in the category of event, rather than of substance. Body and blood are not *things*, but the *event* of Christ's sacrificial death. Hence Paul's comment on the dominical promise:

> The cup of blessing which we bless, is it not a participation in the blood of Christ? The bread which we break, is it not a participation in the body of Christ?[2]
>
> *I Corinthians 10:16 f.* (R.S.V.)

The communion is thus a real participation in the sacrificial death. The ensuing argument of Chapter 10, with its analogy from pagan sacrificial meals, shows that Paul presupposes this. The communion is a real participation in which the sacrifice is not repeated, but brought out of the past into the present.

The interim character of the eucharist, implied in the phrase "until he comes" (I Corinthians 11:26), is stressed in I Corinthians 10:1–4:

> I want you to know, brethren, that our fathers . . . all ate the same supernatural food and all drank the same spiritual drink.

---

[2] The order, cup-bread, is a puzzle. In view of 11:23–25 this cannot have been the order of the Pauline celebration. Why then the change? Perhaps Paul is writing when the blessing of bread and cup has coalesced after the removal of the intervening meal: as a

The manna and the water from the rock are here treated as types of the food and drink of the holy communion. It was the rabbinic doctrine that the Messianic age would reproduce all the features of the exodus. For Paul, who believes the Messianic age to have dawned already, the wanderings of Israel in the wilderness, bounded as they were on the one hand by the exodus and on the other by their entry into the Promised Land, are the type of the Church's existence between the times, between the Messiah's death as the Christian exodus, and the second coming as the entry into the consummated kingdom of God.

Finally, we note a characteristically Pauline emphasis on the corporate significance of the eucharist:

> Because there is one loaf, we who are many are one body, for we all partake of the same loaf.
>
> *I Corinthians 10:17*

Since the bread was the effective sign of the body of Christ, and since all by partaking of that bread partook of the sacrificial event through which the crucified body of Jesus passed, the Christians are thereby incorporated anew into that event.

11. The Person of Christ

We have deliberately left the Pauline teaching about the person of Christ until now, for Christology, in the New Testament, is a confession of faith in what God has done in Jesus, a grateful acknowledgment that he is the event of salvation. We must study the redemption before considering the agent of the redemption. This is especially true of St. Paul's presentation of Christ's person, for his specific insights here derive from his distinctive understanding of the salvation which God has wrought for us in him. That understanding, as we have seen, centers upon the conviction that we are saved, not individually, but corporately, as a human race. Paul's doctrine of the person of Christ expresses just this, as we can see from

---

consequence of this the blessing of both bread and cup would precede the breaking of the bread, as in the later liturgies.

the new slant which he gives to the traditional titles for Jesus which he inherited from his predecessors.

We have already seen (above, p. 305) how the Hellenistic Church before Paul dropped, except in liturgy, the term "Servant" for Jesus, and replaced it by the term "Son," a title which was extended to cover the pre-existence, earthly life, and exalted state of the agent of redemption. Paul takes over this concept and combines it, as we have seen, with the wisdom concept. As the pre-existent Son, Christ is also the agent of creation. But the concept of his sonship is widened to include the redeemed as well. By receiving the Spirit of God, which is also the Spirit of Christ, and granted as the result of his redeeming work, the believers are adopted into the same sonship:

> For all who are led by the Spirit of God are the sons of God. For you did not receive the spirit of slavery again, to fall back into fear, but you received the spirit of sonship. When we cry Abba, Father [the intimate address which no Jew before Jesus ever dared to use in addressing God, Mark 14:36] it is the Spirit himself bearing witness with our spirit that we are children of God, and if children, then heirs, heirs of God and fellow heirs with Christ.
>
> *Romans 8:15–17*

> God sent forth his Son . . . so that we might receive adoption as sons. And because you are sons, God has sent the Spirit of his Son into our hearts, crying, "Abba, Father!" So through God you are no longer a slave, but a son, and if a son then an heir.   *Galatians 4:4–7*

The earliest Church, following the hints of Jesus himself, identified him in his exalted state with the apocalyptic Son of man. But in the Hellenistic churches this term was no longer intelligible, and in the developing gospel tradition it became equivalent to a simple self-designation of Jesus. A good instance of this is Matthew 16:13:

> "Who do men say that the Son of man is?"

eliciting the reply which would be almost tautological in the earliest tradition: "You are the Christ." It is as if the reply to the question "Who am I, the agent of redemption?" were "You are the agent of redemption." The title "Son of man" had obviously become useless as a confession of faith, and as such was dropped. Paul, however, revived its original theological content and put it to constructive use. Avoiding the literal translation, he speaks of Jesus as "man." Jesus is the last, or second, Adam —the second man:

> "The first man, Adam, became a living being"; the last Adam became a life-giving spirit.   *I Corinthians 15:45*

> The first man was from the earth, a man of dust; the second man is from heaven . . . Just as we have borne the image of the man of dust, we shall also bear the image of the man of heaven.   *Ibid., verses 47 ff.*

Thus Paul uses the idea of the Son of man, or man, to express his favorite notion of the close connection between Christ and the redeemed. Similarly in Romans 5 he brings out the contrast between the first and second man and the representative and determinative character of their respective histories:

> For if many died through one man's trespass, much more have the grace of God and the free gift in the grace of that one man Jesus Christ abounded for many. And the free gift is not like the effect of that one man's sin. For the judgment following one trespass brought condemnation, but the free gift following many trespasses brings justification. If, because of one man's trespass, death reigned through that one man, much more will those who receive the abundance of grace and the free gift of righteousness reign in life through the one man Jesus Christ.
> Then as one man's trespass led to condemnation for all men, so one man's act of righteousness leads to acquittal and life for all men. For as by one man's disobedience many were made sinners, so by one man's obedience many will be made righteous.   *Romans 5:15–19*

12. The Consummation

Although Paul had a very high conception—higher it would seem than any of his predecessors, whether Palestinian or Hellenistic—of what Christ had already achieved for us and made available for us in the Church, there is a "not yet" which runs through everything he says about our present Christian status. All the blessings which flow from the event of redemption are only an anticipation, a first installment, a pledge of that which shall be at the consummation:

> "What no eye has seen, nor ear heard,
>   nor the heart of man conceived,
>   what God has prepared for those who love him."
>
> I Corinthians 2:9

Consequently there is a future hope which is not just tacked on at the end of Paul's theology, but colors everything he has to say of what we already have in Christ.

This future hope can be analyzed under two headings, his hope for the universe and his hope for the individual within that universal framework.

The Hope for the Universe

Paul came to hold, if Romans 11:25 is meant to imply a fresh insight, that the rejection of Israel was not final. First, as a result of his own mission, the "full number of the Gentiles" was to be gathered in. Does this mean "all" Gentiles, or the full number of those predestined? His use of "all" in verse 32 seems to imply a universal redemption. But this hardly meant that he expected to cover the whole Gentile world and to be universally successful. Rather, Paul is thinking representatively in a manner strange to our way of thinking. He believes that by planting the gospel in every center of the Roman Empire the Gentiles will be representatively converted.

The next stage is that "all Israel" will be shamed into repentance and finally accept Jesus as its Messiah:

353

A hardening has come upon part of Israel, until the full number of the Gentiles come in, and so all Israel shall be saved.   *Romans 11:25–26a*

But this is not an inevitably determined plan such as could give rise to false security. The Gentiles in particular are warned to note the severity as well as the kindness of God. If he can reject the natural branches after a thousand years or more, he can also reject those who have only recently been grafted in contrary to nature! Paul's plan of future history is not meant as an exact forecast: it is rather an affirmation that God being what he is, his purpose will ultimately triumph. At the same time the individual must make his own response of faith and obedience: otherwise he will be cut off. Here is no easygoing universalism, but a dialectical tension between two apparently contradictory affirmations of faith: one in the ultimate triumph of God's plan of salvation, and the other the urgent requirement of faith and obedience, made urgent by the awful possibility of being cut off.

When the full number of the Gentiles has been gathered in and all Israel has been saved, the cosmic scheme is completed by the return of Christ and the reconciliation of the powers hostile to God. The things in heaven and the things on earth are brought within the sphere of God's redemptive purpose, and all things are summed up in Christ. The last enemy that shall be destroyed is death. According to the scheme outlined in I Corinthians 15 Christ finally hands over the kingdom to the Father, that God may be all in all. Here Paul is using the traditional mythology of the millennium, or thousand years' reign of the Messiah. This shows how little we should try to pin him down to an exact forecast or harmonize the pictures he gives of the end. He uses traditional imagery to express the certainty of God's ultimate triumph.

The Hope for the Individual

Although, as we have seen, the believers already share the future life here and now by accepting the message, by baptism and eucharist, and by their daily endeavor to lead the Christian life, yet the final, decisive moment of resurrection lies in the future. But when will the individual attain to that resurrection? Where Paul speaks unequivocally, he places it, not at the death of the individual, but at the second coming of Christ. Those who die before that coming are "asleep" (I Thessalonians 4:13–15). That is to say, they are in an intermediate condition, no less than those who are still alive, who also exist between the times. They, too, like those who are still in the flesh, are awaiting the resurrection. Like those in the flesh, however, they are still in Jesus, still in his body. But death does bring a change. They are "unclothed" or "naked" (II Corinthians 5:2–4). In other words, they have been divested of the relics of this body of sin and death, which already from the time of their baptism had begun to decay. To this extent, to die is gain (Philippians 1:21) and to depart and be with Christ is far better. For with death the conflict between the flesh and the Spirit comes to an end. But in this intermediate state they have not yet attained to final salvation. For that, the dead must wait until Christ's return (I Thessalonians 4:16), when they will rise before the living, and those who are still alive will be caught up with them to meet the Lord in the air. All, living and departed, will then be clothed upon with the "building from God, a house not made with hands, eternal in the heavens" (II Corinthians 5:1). Here Paul seems to mean something more than an individual resurrection body. The language which he uses to describe it echoes what is said elsewhere about the true temple of God. He seems to mean that at the resurrection the individual's incorporation into Christ will be complete and final. And when he speaks of the "spiritual body" (I Corinthians 15:44), he does not mean a body made up of some supernatural material, but rather a perfect instrument adapted to the perfected communal life in Christ. Then Christ "will change our lowly body to be like his glorious body" (Philippians 3:21).

It is sometimes maintained that St. Paul's ideas about the future life underwent a development. Whereas in the earlier letters (I Thessalonians and I Corinthians) he allowed for an intermediate state, he later assumes (II Corinthians 5 and Philippians 1:21) that the individual will pass straight from this life to his final consummation at death. But II Corinthians 5 shows that he still caters for an intervening period of "nakedness," and elsewhere in Philippians (3:21) he still places the consummation for the individual at the second coming. There can hardly therefore have been any essential change of teaching. Rather, it would seem that Paul is using two not altogether consistent mythological schemes, not as a forecast of the future, but in order to express different things he wants to say about our life in Christ here and now. We know that our life in Christ here and now is not what God means it ultimately to be: it contains a pledge of its ultimate consummation as well as a sense of its incompleteness. Death must also bring us nearer on our road to completion, for then we shall have ceased to be vulnerable to sin, which attacks us through the flesh. Yet at the same time it is not until the whole of the human race, and indeed not until the whole universe has been reconciled to God that our being in Christ can be perfect. We without them cannot be made perfect. Thus we cannot take St. Paul's statements about the future as blueprints of God's plan.

AFTER PAUL

In the non-Pauline churches the period of consolidation after the death of the apostles led to an outburst of literary activity which culminated in the writing of our three synoptic gospels. In the Pauline churches there was a parallel movement, which took the form of collecting, editing, expanding, and, in some cases, adding fresh letters to St. Paul's correspondence with his churches.

A. EPHESIANS

Even if, as we are still inclined to believe, Ephesians was written by St. Paul himself, it represents the first move in this direction. For it sums up the stage in redemptive history which had been reached by the apostle's completed mission. Jew and Gentile have been brought into the one Church:

> But now in Christ Jesus you who were once far off have been brought near in the blood of Christ. For he is our peace, who has made us both one, and has broken down the dividing wall of hostility . . . *Ephesians 2:13 f.*

This concern for the unity of Jew and Gentile in the one Church shows that the letter must have been written, if not during St. Paul's lifetime, then at least not long after. For after the destruction of Jerusalem, Jewish Christianity was virtually isolated, and the main body of the Church became almost exclusively Gentile. A later writer would have taken it for granted that the Gentiles were in the Church, and would not have been interested in their unity with the Jewish members. The epistle is full of the genuine Pauline amazement that the Gentiles (!!) should be in the one body.

But the unity of the Church, though a given fact, is also a constant task. For the unity of the Church is only a fragile anticipation of the final unity when God shall be all in all. It is constantly threatened by human sin, and has constantly to be renewed. There *is* one body and one Spirit, one Lord, one faith, one baptism, one God and Father of us all. These are objective, given facts. But the unity of the Spirit must be "maintained" and built up until we all attain to a subjective unity, the "unity of the faith and of the knowledge of the Son of God, to mature manhood, to the measure of the stature of the fullness of Christ"—and that can never be fully achieved, that remains a constant task, until the final consummation. This unity can be built up only by a constant return to the foundation of the apostles and prophets, that is, to their joint witness to the act of God in Christ. Here is the concern, at the moment when the apostolic generation is dying out, to maintain the apostolicity of the Church. It is a concern which will reach its fulfillment in the establishment of the New Testament canon with the episcopate as its guardians.

B. HEBREWS

This document, though certainly not by Paul, comes from a circle in close touch with the Pauline (13:23: there is no reason to suppose that this verse has been added to give the document a Pauline coloring; it is too faint for that). Hebrews calls itself, not only an epistle, but also a "word of exhortation" (13:22). "Exhortation" is pastoral, as opposed to evangelistic, preaching. It is the kind of sermon, or series of sermons, one would have heard at the ordinary Sunday worship of the church, consisting of expositions of scripture. The writer was evidently a person of almost apostolic authority, for he can address a group of Christians over the heads of their local leaders (13:7, 17). He has heard of the situation in this group and has sent off a copy of some of his recent sermons, because he believes they have a direct bearing on the situation of the group. It is tempting to see in the reference to persecution in 10:32 and verse following an allusion to Nero's famous persecution of Christians at Rome in A.D. 64. The group concerned will then have been in the local Roman church, a fact which is also suggested by the allusion to "those from Italy" in 13:24. It will have been written when the persecution was still a memory, but a receding one. A year around 85 would appear to be indicated.

The Christians are in danger of lapsing, not into Jewish temple worship, as was traditionally supposed, but into indifference. As the Royal Air Force used to say, they are "getting browned off." The cause was their failure to progress to a mature grasp of the Christian faith. So the situation must be met by providing "solid food" (5:14). They must leave the "elementary doctrines of Christ" and "go on to maturity." The solid food is an exposition of Christ as the true high priest. The theme itself is not altogether a novelty, for it lay near to hand in the earliest preaching. On an external level, it was suggested by the early application (perhaps by Jesus himself) of Psalm 110:1 to Christ. Since, according to a well-known rabbinic principle, the citation of one verse implied to application of the succeeding verses to the same subject, Psalm 110:4 was already applicable by implication to Jesus:

Thou art a priest for ever, after the order of Melchizedek.

But there was also a deeper, more inward root in the early preaching. This is that Christ died for our sins, and that his death was the sacrifice inaugurating the new covenant. It is these elementary doctrines which form the basis of the mature teaching here offered.

But the author never loses sight of his hortatory purpose: his doctrinal exposition is subsidiary to the hortatory. He wishes to demonstrate the finality of the event of redemption.

There is no going back upon it: the event took place once and for all, and if believers drift away from faith in it they can never be reinitiated. There is no "second repentance." This does not mean it is impossible to repent of post-baptismal sin: it means that there can be no second initiation for the lapsed. To establish the finality of the redemption, the author makes an elaborate comparison between Christ's high priesthood and that of the Levitical ministry established under Moses, and recorded in the Pentateuch. It is a purely scriptural argument based on the Levitical legislation, and we cannot infer from it either that the temple was still standing or that the group addressed was in danger of returning to temple worship. The author has in mind partly the daily offerings, but chiefly the annual ceremonies of the day of atonement. The Levitical priesthood is at once the pattern for Christ's high priesthood (or rather it is the typical foreshadowing of it) and an imperfect and totally inadequate pattern. It pointed to the end which it was intended to accomplish, but was powerless to accomplish it. That end is defined as access or approach to God, forgiveness of sins, and "perfection," a notion which is not so much ethical as religious and cultic, denoting that perfect communion with God which is the end of worship and life.

Several arguments are adduced to demonstrate the inadequacy of the Levitical ordinances. The high priests were mortal men, so that they must constantly be replaced by successors. They had to offer their sacrifices repeatedly, yearly or daily. They were sinners who needed to offer for themselves as well as for the people. Their offerings consisted of the blood of animals, which could never take away sins but could only deal with technical breaches of the ritual law. Moreover the Old Testament itself contained the promise of a superior priesthood, one which was not Levitical, but "after the order of Melchizedek," whose superiority to the Levitical is deduced, rather curiously and unconvincingly to our modern ways of thinking, from the story of Abraham's payment of tithes to Melchizedek in Genesis 14:17–20. In contrast to this, Christ died only once, and now exercises his high priesthood forever. He was sinless and did not need to offer for himself. What he offered was not the blood of bulls and goats, but his own blood, the offering of the obedience of a perfect will even unto death. As a result he has consecrated for us a new and living way, a new covenant by which we have forgiveness of our sins and access to the presence of God.

How exactly the death of one man, even of a sinless man, can remove our sins, their guilt, and their power, the author does not and probably cannot explain. His conviction is based on the Christian experience in worship, doubtless in eucharistic worship, which knows that in Christ the barrier of sin which prevents access to God is done away with. Of course the "altar" in Hebrews 13:10 is not the later piece of church furniture, but the place where the Church obtains access to the true altar of God's presence is surely in the eucharistic action, to which verse 15 also clearly alludes:

> Through him then let us continually offer up a sacrifice
> of praise to God, that is, the fruit of lips that acknowledge
> his name.

Is the writer of Hebrews a Platonist, who thinks in terms of two worlds, a heavenly and an earthly, in which all visible phenomena are copies of heavenly realities? Has the author abandoned the early Christian dualism of two ages for one of two worlds? Some of his vocabulary has an undoubted Platonic ring:

> e.g.: copy
> heavenly/earthly
> pattern
> greater and more perfect
> not of this creation
> not made with hands

But the similarity to the Platonic scheme is apparent rather than real. To begin with, these antitheses are not applied to the universe generally, but only to the temple and its furniture. It is only these that are copies of heavenly realities. Second, the author of Hebrews bases his dualism directly on the text of scripture, Exodus 25:40, which he quotes at 8:5. Here it is stated that God showed Moses the pattern of the sanctuary he was to construct. On the basis of this verse rabbinic Judaism had already postulated the objective existence in heaven of the pattern tabernacle. Moreover there is a further set of antithetical terms which are *temporal* in character and alien to the Platonic scheme:

> old/new
> first/second
> first/new
> shadow/good things to come

and three other temporal words:

> covenant (an institution of redemptive history)
> at the end of the world
> once for all

It would seem that there is an unresolved tension in the author's thought between two worlds and two ages. He clearly thinks of two worlds, though he does not extend his cosmology to the whole universe, but only to the apparatus and institutions of redemptive history; at the same time he speaks of two ages, in which the second is not only a manifestation on earth in temporal succession to the first, but also remains a reality "up" in heaven. There is however a similar combination between the two worlds and the two ages in Jewish apocalyptic literature. The realities of the age to come are conceived as pre-existent up in heaven and as being manifested on earth at the end. Thus there is the picture of the New Jerusalem coming down out of heaven, a picture which finds its way into the Apocalypse of the New Testament. It is along these lines that the affinities of the author of Hebrews are to be sought, not in Alexandrian Platonism.

There is a second much debated problem, not altogether unrelated to the first. Where precisely does the author locate the sacrifice of Christ? Was it offered once at Calvary, or is it offered eternally in heaven? Is it an event in history at a fixed point of time, or is it suprahistorical? Protestants have generally taken the first view, Catholics including high Anglicans the second.

Both sides can quote passages from Hebrews to support their case. The truth however would seem to lie somewhere between the two views. For the author of Hebrews, Christ's sacrifice was clearly a once-for-all event in history, not an eternal offering in heaven. Every word which speaks of his act of offering is in the past tense (e.g., 9:28; 10:12). And a number of times he stresses that this offering was made "once" or "once for all" (e.g., 9:12, 28; 10:10). The Catholic argument that if Christ is "high priest for ever" he must be perpetually offering himself in heaven is an inference which the author of Hebrews never makes and which flatly contradicts his express statements to which we have just called attention. Yet—and here the conventional Protestant case likewise is at fault—this sacrifice of Christ was not confined to the moment of Calvary. The argument in 10:5–12 makes it clear that the offering of Christ was an extended process, beginning with the moment when he "entered the world" (verse 5) and concluding with the moment when he "sat down at the right hand of God" (verse 12). The offering was the total, indivisible event of his life-death-exaltation.

Yet the author makes it clear that Christ remains a priest "for ever" (6:20, etc.). This cannot, as we have seen, mean that he is perpetually offering himself in heaven. What it does mean will be apparent when we recall that even for the author of Hebrews the offering of sacrifice is not the sole, even if it be the central, function of priesthood. The high priest helps those who are tempted (2:18). He shows sympathy with our weaknesses (4:15) and deals gently with the wayward and ignorant. Most important, he makes continual intercession for his own (7:25). Clearly Christ has plenty to do, as it were, in heaven, quite apart from offering sacrifice, and he does it as high priest. This additional work we might call the "pastoral" side of the priestly function. But the ground and basis of the continued pastoral work in heaven is the once-for-all priestly work of offering. That is why the author of Hebrews brackets both parts, the strictly sacerdotal and the pastoral, the once-for-all work and the continued work in heaven, under the rubric of high priesthood. What the author is trying to say is that God's redemptive act in Jesus Christ is not just an event of past history; it has a perpetual efficacy, and is the ground of our relation to God which is realized in Christian worship. In a mythological language which he derives from the Jewish sacrificial system the author of the Hebrews expresses this conviction by saying that Christ, having offered himself in the event of the cross and ascension, now intercedes for his Church on the strength of that offering, pleading for us and pleading his sacrifice for us. This is exactly the theology expressed in Charles Wesley's eucharistic hymns:

> O thou, before the world began,
> Ordained a sacrifice for man,
> And by th' eternal Spirit made
> An offering in the sinner's stead;
> Our everlasting Priest art thou,
> Pleading thy death for sinners now.
>
> Thy offering still continues new
> Before the Righteous Father's view;
> Thyself the lamb for ever slain,
> Thy Priesthood doth unchanged remain;
> Thy years, O God, can never fail,
> Nor thy blest work within the veil.
>
> *Hymns A. & M., 554*

The imagery is all derived from the Jewish sacrificial system. Many other cultures have known priesthood, and to them it should be possible to make the meaning of Hebrews intelligible. In Christian countries it is only intelligible so long as priesthood is a living reality in the Church. Where the representative priesthood of the ministry, as the concrete, focal point of the priesthood of the whole body, is denied, the final result is the denial of the priesthood of Christ himself, since it has become unintelligible.

C. THE PASTORALS

We should beware of exaggerating the difference between the genuine Pauline epistles and the pastorals. It is just not true to assert that whereas Paul teaches justification by faith, the pastorals teach justification through the sacraments. As we have already seen, there is no antithesis in Pauline teaching between faith and sacraments, but between faith and works. The pastorals' doctrine of salvation is good Paulinism:

> God, who saved us and called us with a holy calling, not in virtue of our works, but in virtue of his own purpose and the grace which he gave us in Christ Jesus.
>
> *II Timothy* 1:9

That does not however mean that they were by Paul. It will be assumed here that II Timothy is an expansion by a later writer of the farewell written by Paul himself, no doubt to Timothy, just before his martyrdom in Rome. The original letter consists of the personal elements, such as 1:1–3 and 4:9–18, but definitely excludes all the passages referring to church order and to heresy. There is very little to suggest that Titus is also an expansion of a personal note of Paul, and nothing whatever in I Timothy. These letters were written to claim the authority of St. Paul for the measures needed to combat an early form of Gnosticism. Such tendencies were already emerging when Paul wrote Colossians. How they originated we do not know, but it is possible that they infiltrated the early Christian churches *via* the Hellenistic synagogues. These "Gnostics" support a false cosmic dualism by misapplying the Old Testament, and express it by an ethic of asceticism. The author's method of combating this teaching is by maintaining the apostolic tradition. This tradition is to be handed on by a ministerial succession:

> . . . what you have heard from me before many witnesses entrust to faithful men who will be able to teach others also. *II Timothy* 2:2

The later pastorals (Titus and I Timothy) give these tradition-bearers the name of "elder" or "bishop." It is gratuitous to assume that the author is innovating. He is rather systematizing the loose arrangement of the Pauline churches which already prevailed during St. Paul's own lifetime (see above, p. 312 f.). Nor is the idea of tradition new. Since the Christian message was testimony to an event, and since others besides the original eyewitnesses had to bear testimony to it, it could hardly be otherwise. Hence the Jewish notion of handing on tradition *via* a line of accredited tradition-bearers found a place in Christianity from the start. Since the apostles were still alive during the first generation, this tradition need only be handed on by them to their converts, and they themselves could constantly remind the churches they founded, when they were in danger of letting the tradition slip or were blind to its implications. This is what the Pauline letters are really doing. But as soon as the apostles begin to disappear from the scene, the problem of perpetuating the tradition becomes important, and the leaders of the local churches begin to assume a new and understandable importance as the means by which the tradition is preserved and passed on intact. It is to just this situation that the pastorals bear witness. Their author stands for stabilization rather than for creative innovation.

D. JAMES

The little epistle of St. James is one of the most disputed writings of the New Testament. Here the division of opinion is not that of radicals versus conservatives, but runs right through the critical camp itself. For some, this is the earliest writing of the New Testament, by James, the Lord's brother, affirming a position which was later controverted by St. Paul in Galatians and Romans. Others regard it as the work of St. James, but written *after* the Romans and designed to refute it. Still others regard it as a later, perhaps much later, pseudonymous document written not so much against Paul's own position as against some of his followers who ignored certain features of their master's teaching and pressed others to their logical conclusion.

Here we assume that James is the product of a Hellenistic Judaism in close touch with Palestinian tradition at a time after Paul. The epistle is not directed against an ultra-Pauline party, for his epigoni approached more nearly to the position of "James" himself, judging by their utterances in the pastorals. Rather, James represents a misreading of Paul's position in Romans, emanating from a time when the Pauline epistles were being collected and circulated even in non-Pauline churches.

The author, then, is engaged in a dispute, as he imagines, with St. Paul, but with a St. Paul whom he does not really understand. Paul had asserted that man was justified by faith alone. It was of course Luther who added the little word "alone" in Romans 3:28, but Hebraic idiom would mean that this was not merely a true exegesis, but also a correct translation. St. James would have interpreted Paul's statement just as Luther did, but unlike Luther he rejects it and seeks to disprove it. This he achieves by using the same part of Old Testament history, the story of Abraham, to prove the exact opposite: "by works is a man justified, and *not by faith only.*"

James, of course, is arguing at cross purposes with Paul. To begin with, the sense he attributed to "faith" is quite different:

> You believe that God is one; you do well. Even the demons believe—and shudder.

Faith for him is intellectual assent to theological propositions, not the moment of passivity in which God is allowed to act upon the helpless sinner. Rightly understood, the Pauline doctrine of justification by faith alone does not exclude the necessity of good works: there is no dichotomy between faith and obedience. For faith brings a man into a relation with God in which obedience becomes a genuine possibility for the first time. Disobedience is actually a falling away from faith. Apart from faith, it is true, works cannot justify, but obedience is the natural and inevitable expression of the relationship which faith is. Again, St. James' idea of justification is not the same as St. Paul's. Paul, with his firm grasp of the benefits we already enjoy in Christ in anticipation of the final consummation, places justification at the beginning of the Christian life. James, whose grasp of life in Christ is deficient when compared with Paul's, places justification at the end of the process. Partly of course, this is a difference in terminology; but it is also partly due to James' failure to grasp what we already have in Christ. This raises the question: Was James really a Christian at all? It is not surprising that many critics have thought that James is really a Jewish work with a few Christian interpolations. Closer examination however reveals that James is much more Christian than appears at first sight. He is the "servant of the Lord Jesus Christ"—he accepts Jesus not only as a man, but as Lord and Christ (cf. 2:1). By a concrete act of choice (no doubt James is thinking of baptism) God has brought men into a relation with the redemptive event and made them heirs of his kingdom. This concrete act is a begetting which makes them the first fruits of his creatures, the advance guard of redeemed humanity (1:18). The faithful are gathered by that act into the "Church," consisting of "brethren" (James 1:2, etc.). It has a ministry of elders who anoint the sick with oil to heal them. In this Church prayer is practiced, and forgiveness of sins is offered. Finally, like other New Testament Christians, James looks forward to the coming of the Lord (5:7), when the salvation inaugurated in baptism shall be consummated and the faithful who persevere will receive the crown of life which the Lord has promised to them that love him. Thus, where James betrays his doctrinal presuppositions, they are those of the redemptive history such as we find in the rest of the New Testament. But the bulk of the epistle consists of ethical exhortation, though it must never be forgotten that this is set in a pattern of redemptive history. Moreover the content of the ethical teaching is derived from the pattern of catechetical teaching which was used by the Hellenistic churches generally for the instruction of candidates for baptism, and like that teaching draws upon traditions of the sayings of Jesus such as we find in the Q material in the gospels. All this has to be remembered in an assessment of James. It is as un-reasonable to expect the full doctrinal aspect of the Christian message in James as it is to expect a passion narrative in Q. We cannot therefore use James as evidence of a non-redemptive, purely ethical version of the gospel, or as evidence of the "simple" gospel as it was before Paul. James is avowedly teaching (didache) and not proclamation—though it clearly presupposes the proclamation. Thus James does not give us the whole of Christianity. What it presupposes is found elsewhere in the New Testament. Yet it has an important place in the canon, for it supplies a necessary corrective to a one-sided appreciation of Pauline theology. Some ages in church history have needed the Pauline message to recall it from an excessive emphasis on "works," whether ecclesiastical and monastic asceticism or liberal and humanitarian activism. Other ages have needed to be recalled from a formal orthodoxy to the true conception of faith, to a realization that faith without works is dead. For some ages the epistle of St. James has been an epistle of straw. But other ages before and since Luther have needed it as a priceless pearl.

E. I PETER

The so-called first epistle of Peter can hardly have come from the pen of the apostle himself: its good Greek and Pauline doctrine militate against the traditional view. Most American critics desire to place it quite late, largely because of the references to persecution, which are thought to tally with the situation in Asia Minor described by the Younger Pliny in his well-known letter to the Emperor Trajan (c. A.D. 112). But we do not know enough about persecution in the first century to preclude an early date. Apart from this, all the critical problems are sufficiently accounted for if we take the epistle at its face value and assume that it was written by Silvanus with the authority of St. Peter behind him (5:12). Perhaps Paul has already suffered martyrdom, and Silvanus has undertaken to write to the churches of Asia Minor from Rome ("Babylon" in 5:13 is most likely a cryptogram for Rome). No longer having the authority of Paul behind him, he seeks instead the *imprimatur* of Peter.

The first part of the letter, from 1:3 down to 4:12, contains material from what looks like a baptismal homily. Note the constantly recurring motifs from the pattern of catechetical teaching, such as is found in the Pauline epistles and in James:

    1:13: gird up your minds . . .
     2:1: put away . . .
    2:11: abstain from . . .
    2:13: be subject . . .
     3:1: be submissive . . .
2:18–3:7: servants . . . wives . . . husbands

Note also the direct references to baptism:

    1:3: born anew . . .
  1:18: You know that you were ransomed from the futile
        ways inherited from your fathers . . .
  1:22: having purified your souls . . .
  1:23: born again . . .
   2:2: newborn babes . . .
 2:10: now you have received mercy
 2:10: Once you were no people but now you are God's
        people; once you had not received mercy but now
        you have received mercy
        [N.B. the repeated antithetical parallelism in this
        last quotation suggests that this actually comes
        from a baptismal hymn of Semitic origin.]
 3:21: Baptism . . . now saves you, not as a removal of
        dirt from the body but as an appeal to God for
        a clear conscience, through the resurrection of
        Jesus Christ.

By baptism the converts have been admitted to the priestly people of God:

And like living stones be yourselves built into a spiritual

house, to be a holy priesthood, to offer spiritual sacrifices acceptable to God through Jesus Christ (2:5)

But you are a chosen race, a royal priesthood, God's own people, that you may declare the wonderful deeds of him who called you out of darkness into his marvelous light. (2:9)

The baptized have been brought into a liturgical community, whose focal point of existence is the offering of the sacrifice of thanksgiving, the great eucharistic prayer which recites before God the mighty acts of redemption. But this offering is the focal point of a total existence: their life must be holy (1:15 f.), a holiness which expresses itself in the concrete behavior of daily life as delineated in the ethical injunctions of this epistle.

The author transforms this baptismal homily into an encyclical letter by prefacing an address (1:1 ff.) to the Pauline churches of Asia Minor and by adding an appended exhortation (4:13–5:14) to stand fast in face of persecution which may break out in Asia Minor as it has already broken out in Rome. While it would be injudicious to use this epistle as evidence for St. Peter's own theological position, it gives an interesting view of common sub-apostolic Christianity of a non-Palestinian type which has learned something from St. Paul but lacks his depths and his own special interests. Thus we find the Pauline catchword "in Christ" but without the depths of Paul's corporate understanding of the redemption. The Christology also lacks the developments we find in Paul, e.g., Christ as the wisdom of God and agent of creation. Does the author believe in Christ's pre-existence? In 1:20 he writes:

He was destined before the foundation of the world but was made manifest at the end of the times for your sake.

"Destined" is precisely the primitive form of the pre-existence doctrine (see above, pp. 306, 307), ideal rather than real, in the mind of God rather than objective. This is perhaps the strongest evidence of Petrine affinity, and in any case it is the strongest argument against a second-century dating. It is also perhaps significant that the author never speaks of Jesus by the characteristically Hellenistic title "Son of God." His Christology moves within the primitive framework, with its conception of Jesus, predestined as Son of man in the mind of God, servant of the Lord in his incarnate life, manifest Son of man from the moment of the resurrection, and to return again as Son of man at the end. The Christology at any rate is thoroughly Petrine.

F. JUDE

The typical problems of the sub-apostolic age were, first, the combating of false teaching of a Gnostic type; second, the preservation of the apostolic tradition in face of this danger; third, the delay in the return of Christ; and, fourth, persecution.

Jude, like the pastorals, is concerned with the first and second of these problems. The author, whoever he may have been, and whenever he may have written, is not a creative thinker. Here he stands in marked contrast to the author of the Johannine literature, which is dealing with a parallel situation. His method is that of a party politician in an election campaign—to call his opponents names (verses 4, 8, 10, 12 f., 16, 18 ff.). Then he cites a number of Old Testament examples of dire judgment and examples thereof from the apocalyptic Book of Enoch (9:14), threatening his opponents with the like damnation. Unlike the author of the pastorals, who has a practical end in view—that of establishing a systematized ministry of tradition-bearers—all Jude can offer is exhortation: the recipients are "earnestly to contend for the faith that was once delivered to the saints." They are to "build themselves up on their most holy faith." Phrases like these excite the irritation, not only of our liberal but also of our neo-orthodox scholars, bent as they are on emphasizing the "varieties of New Testament religion." Such objections fail to do justice to the unity which underlies the variety. There *was* a faith once delivered to the saints, not indeed (and here the liberals and neo-orthodox are perfectly right) the whole articulated system of Catholic dogma, but faith in Jesus as the redemptive event and act of God, by which our salvation has been inaugurated and is to be consummated. This faith is found in all the strata of the New Testament, from the earliest sermons in Acts to the Johannine literature. The author redeems the vitriolic quality of his polemics by these fine phrases about New Testament faith, and by the noble doxology with which his pamphlet concludes (verses 24–25).

G. II PETER

Hardly a scholar outside the Roman communion maintains the Petrine authorship of II Peter. For one thing the author "lays it on too thick." He calls himself "*Simon* Peter" (1:1). He claims to be a witness of the transfiguration (1:16–18). He speaks patronizingly of "our brother Paul," and parades his own claim to be an apostle. But he betrays himself by his obvious dependence on the synoptic gospels for the details of the transfiguration, and by his evident knowledge of the Pauline corpus (3:16), which was by now known as "scripture," that is, accepted as canonical. All this suggests a date later than that of the early apostolic fathers, and A.D. 150 could hardly be too early.

The author is wrestling with the third problem of the sub-apostolic age, the delay in the return of Christ. Where is the promise of his coming? Ever since the fathers fell asleep all things have continued as they were from the beginning of creation. The Johannine literature is wrestling among other things with the same problem, but, unlike II Peter, in a highly theological and constructive way. II Peter's method, while not creative, is interesting. He will not abandon the hope of the return of Christ. Indeed, he reiterates it in all its stark crudity by lifting almost bodily the apocalyptic passages from Jude, where however, as we have seen, they are employed for the quite different purpose of threatening false teachers. And then II Peter plays his trump card:

> With the Lord one day is as a thousand years, and a thousand years as one day. The Lord is not slow about his promise as some count slowness.   3:8b–9a

God's time scheme is so different from ours (Psalm 90:4). The primitive belief in an impending event of the exalted Christ may thus retain all its pristine urgency.

THE JOHANNINE LITERATURE

A. THE APOCALYPSE

Traditionally, the Johannine literature includes the Book of Revelation, the Gospel according to St. John, and the first, second, and third epistles of John. Most scholars today would assign the Apocalypse to a different author from the rest of the Johannine literature. While the gospel is written in part in Greek which bears a marked Semitic coloring, the evangelist shows, where he writes on his own, that he can write very good Greek. The seer however writes in such execrable Greek (including even grammatical solecisms) that we might describe it as "refugee," the kind of language spoken by an elderly emigree banished to a foreign land and forced to acquire late in life a new tongue which he has never succeeded in mastering. Perhaps he had fled from Jerusalem after its destruction in A.D. 70 and settled at Ephesus. Yet there are also striking affinities with the fourth gospel. Both have favorite phrases, such as "keep the commandments." Both draw on a common stock of Old Testament testimonies (e.g., "They shall look upon him whom they have pierced," from Zechariah 12:10, cited in John 19:37 and Revelation 1:7). In some ways they are poles apart. The seer frankly accepts the crudest pictures of the end from Jewish apocalyptic. The extent to which he consciously regards them as symbolic is problematical, but since the inner core of the work appears to present the same series of events under a number of different images, it is likely that he meant much of it to be taken symbolically. By contrast, the author of the fourth gospel, while deliberately retaining the future hope as the ultimate rounding off of the process of re-demptive history (e.g., 5:28 f.), is so convinced of the decisive-ness of the salvation already inaugurated that he tends to minimize the other aspect of the "not yet." It may of course be objected that the same author passed through two phases in his thinking and that the gospel represents its ultimate out-come. But such a view raises further problems as to the nature of the theology of the gospel as a whole. If that theology can come to rest finally (and there are at present signs that it may) in a Palestinian environment, it might conceivably be possible to reopen the question of the affinity between the Apocalypse and the gospel. But that time is not yet.

The Apocalypse is the product of a very concrete situation, and is written directly to cope with it. The author, exiled in a time of persecution from his own church (1:9), sees a vision on the Lord's day and is bidden to report it to the seven churches of Asia Minor. He prefaces the report with a letter for each of the seven churches in turn. In these letters he deals with the local variations in the over-all situation.

The central core of the book (4:1–22:5) defies analysis. The series of visions of the final denouement of history are inextricably confused. Basically, of course, the apocalyptic scheme is simple enough. First, there was to come the period of the Messianic woes, then the reign of Antichrist, then the coming of the Messiah, with (as here) or without a thousand years' reign on earth, and then the final consummation with the new heaven and new earth. But the author has probably, as we suggested above, presented the same series of events under a number of different images.

Did the author actually see all these visions in detail? Or did he have a single vision, the exact content of which we can no longer discover but which may be fairly represented in the opening chapter, and did he then expand it with conventional apocalyptic imagery which he quarried from his predecessors, Old Testament, Judaic, and Christian? The latter suggestion would seem most likely. Another strong ingredient is the litur-gical material. It is as if the author, cut off from the Church's worship on the Lord's day, meditates upon its offering of praise and thanksgiving which is counterpart of the heavenly liturgy. We have found the same line of thought in Hebrews, whose connection with the apocalyptic world view has already been suggested. Hence the visions open with a scene which reproduced in heaven the setting of primitive Christian worship. God the Father is seated on the throne, like the president at the eucharist, the four and twenty elders are seated in a semicircle on either side, like the elders of the local church; the four living creatures correspond to the deacons, and the great liturgical prayer includes the Sanctus (Chapter 4). More liturgical material is to be found at 5:9–10, 12, 13b; 7:12; 11:17; 15:3b; 19:1–8. Also reflected is the belief that in the eucharist Christ comes in anticipation of his final coming:

> Amen. Come, Lord Jesus.

This is the same prayer as the Maranatha of I Corinthians 16:22. Compare also:

> I will come . . . and sup with him, and he with me.
>
> 3:20

This liturgical concern is an important psychological clue to the seer's mental processes. It is as he meditates on a Sunday morning on the liturgy of his home church that its true significance for the times in which he lives dawns upon him: it is the anticipation of the final consummation, and thus provides the springboard for the apocalyptic drama which the work unfolds:

> Thou art coming, at thy table
> We are witnesses for this;
> While remembering hearts thou meetest
> In communion clearest, sweetest,
> Earnest of our coming bliss,
> Shewing not thy death alone,
> And thy love exceeding great,
> But thy coming and thy Throne,
> All for which we long and wait.
>
> *Hymns A. & M.,*
> *Standard Edition, 203*

The Apocalypse has suffered alike from its would-be friends and its foes. Its friends have too often taken it as a blueprint forecast of the later historical crises in which they themselves have lived. The intention of the author was not however to forecast the downfall of Hitler, Stalin, or any of the later tyrants of history. He was speaking of the Roman Empire. The Roman Empire did collapse, but only after three more centuries, not immediately as he thought. And when it did collapse, it was succeeded, not by the end, but by further cycles of history. Yet the book has a permanent significance. It is wholly legitimate to deduce from its understanding of history certain principles of wider application for each succeeding crisis in history.

Its foes too have treated the Apocalypse badly. Both in the ancient Church and in the modern, voices have been raised against the inclusion of the Revelation in the New Testament. It has been stigmatized as sub-Christian because of its insistence on the wrath of God and everlasting hell-fire, and above all because of the vindictive attitude toward the Church's persecutors, so patently at variance with the Sermon on the Mount.

The latter point we readily concede. The author, understandably and humanly in his own situation, does fall short of true Christian charity, which extends even to the enemy. But so have other Christians before and since, and it is good to be reminded that even the inspired writers of the New Testament were after all men of flesh and blood. Nor need we complain, since we have the Sermon on the Mount with which to correct Revelation 6:10. Yet perhaps this is not the whole story. The author's cry, "How long?" proceeds not from a mere impatient lust for vengeance, but from a heartfelt self-identification with the purpose of God, imperfectly expressed, no doubt, but in essence identical with the prayer, "Thy kingdom come." With regard to the wrath of God and hell-fire, it is to be observed that the author is at one with the rest of the New Testament, even with the teaching of our Lord himself. Separation from God (or is it the anguish and misery in his presence which springs from unrepented sin?) is always a grim reality and an ultimate, final possibility. Yet the Apocalypse does not seek to frighten men into repentance by the threat of hell-fire, nor does it claim to know in advance who is destined to its flames. It is thus far removed from the corybantic effusions of the gospel halls.

We have to remember that the Revelation is *part* of the canon, not the whole of it. No more than any other New Testament writing does it claim to enshrine the whole apostolic witness to the event of Jesus Christ. Even the epistle to the Romans needs the corrective of James. But to justify its place in the canon the Apocalypse must have something distinctive and positive to offer. Has it? We have already suggested that it provides the principles for a Christian understanding of history. And it shows that the liturgy is not something whose significance is confined to the four walls of the sanctuary or to the individual human soul. It is at once the revelation and the acceleration of the whole cosmic drama which is history. It is its revelation, for here Christ comes as the King he will be, disclosing the temporary character of all human government and the final triumph of his redemptive purpose. It is its acceleration, for in the liturgy men and women are already taken up into a foretaste of that beatitude which is to be finally theirs.

B. THE FOURTH GOSPEL AND THE JOHANNINE EPISTLES

Of all New Testament problems the Johannine problem is the most intractable. James, which is also problematical, remains one of the peripheral New Testament writings. Johannine Christianity, not only because of its bulk, but also because of its own intrinsic quality, is central. For, together with the Pauline writings, it represents one of the two creative achievements of New Testament theology. Hence the problem cannot be ignored.

The problem revolves round three main issues, none of

which can be discussed in detachment from the other two. First, there is the problem of authorship, second, the affinities of the author's thought, and, third, its interpretation.

1. *Authorship*

Tradition is very strong, almost unanimous from the end of the second century, that the fourth gospel was written by St. John, the beloved disciple, son of Zebedee, and that he was the author at least of the first epistle, together with the Apocalypse (though early tradition is by no means unanimous on this last point). Since the early part of the last century, however, critics have questioned and rejected the traditional authorship. They have pointed to the historical discrepancies between the fourth and the synoptic gospels (the latter were taken to be earlier and therefore, especially in the case of Mark, more historical). If Mark was what it seemed to be, the memoirs of the apostle Peter, how could John also be apostolic? For the Johannine Jesus commutes between Galilee and Jerusalem, whereas the Markan Jesus spends his time wholly in Galilee until his final visit to Jerusalem for the passion. The Johannine Jesus delivers lengthy discourses, written in the same style as that of the evangelist himself (see the editorial sections 3:16–21, 31–36). Consequently there would be a Johannine problem even if we did not possess the synoptics. The Jesus of the synoptics, on the other hand, delivers vivid parables and oracular sayings. The content of his message, in the synoptics, is the approach of God's reign; in the fourth gospel it is his own advent, already as revealer and redeemer. The Johannine Jesus declares his Messiahship from the outset and is openly acknowledged as such. The synoptic Jesus adopts a very equivocal attitude toward the question of his Messiahship, to say the least. The thought world of the fourth evangelist appears to be Hellenistic and mystical, that of the synoptics Palestinian and concrete. The traditional view of the authorship was far less unanimous than its supporters had assumed. Most vulnerable was its lateness, not before A.D. 180. Previous writers who might have been expected to mention the gospel fail to do so and are strangely silent about its existence, even where they appear to echo its thought. Moreover, the earliest witnesses to the fourth gospel are the second-century Gnostics. There is also some evidence to suggest that John bar Zebedee suffered an early martyrdom.

Defenders of the tradition were undaunted. They not only upheld the external tradition against the arguments mentioned above, but pointed to a whole series of internal factors which showed, as classically formulated in Westcott's famous "concentric proof," that the gospel was the work of a Jew, a Palestinian Jew, an eyewitness, an apostle, John the son of Zebedee himself. An awkward corollary, which the conservatives tended to shirk, was that if this was so, John must be more historical than Mark.

During the present century there has been considerable modification of the conservative defense, though in Britain there are still a number of reputable scholars who maintain substantially Westcott's position, and many who from the pulpit still quote sayings of the Johannine Christ as irrefragable evidence for his teaching. This modified conservatism has discovered another John, the Elder, a second generation disciple of John bar Zebedee at Ephesus. John bar Zebedee was responsible for the authentic factual elements, and John the Elder for the discourses, though these were to some extent at least based on the witness of John bar Zebedee and the teaching of Jesus. Meanwhile, on the critical side, our whole attitude to the synoptic tradition, and especially to Mark, has changed. We now see that Mark is not just straightforward history, but a string of originally isolated fragments arranged in such a way as to provide a theological interpretation of Jesus, no less than the fourth gospel. The synoptic gospels, no less than John, were written that men might believe that Jesus is the Christ, the Son of God; and that, believing, they might have life in his name. On the other hand, there has also been on the critical side an increasing disposition to recognize the value of some at least of the historical traditions in the fourth gospel. Thus there has been at any rate a partial *rapprochement* between the conservative and critical positions. But a final conclusion about authorship must be deferred until we have considered other aspects of the problem.

2. Affinities of Thought

Is "John" a Palestinian Jewish, Hellenistic Jewish, or purely Hellenistic thinker? And with which stream in these various types of thought is he to be connected? This is perhaps the most thorny of all the Johannine problems.

The case for Palestinian affinity rests upon two lines of argument, linguistic and theological. While it would be an exaggeration to claim as some have done that John is simply a translation from Aramaic, it is clear that the language has a high degree of Semitic coloring. This is true both of the narrative portions and of the discourse material. In the narrative, for instance, the sentences frequently *begin* with the verb, the subject following (e.g., 1:45 reads, not "Philip finds Nathanael," but "finds Philip Nathanael"). In the discourses we find frequent examples of Hebraic poetical forms; for instance, 6:35 exhibits synonymous parallelism. These facts must be taken seriously.

Much more has been learned during the present century about rabbinic Judaism. Many sayings of the rabbis have been studied, and some throw considerable light on sayings in the fourth gospel. For instance, almost every statement made in the Prologue (John 1:1–14) can be paralleled by what the rabbinic writers say about the Torah, or Law of God, considered as God's revelation of himself. The statement "Abraham saw my day and was glad" (8:56) becomes intelligible when we read the rabbinic statement that Abraham was granted a vision of all the days to come, including that of the Messiah. Beyond all doubt, the author was closely acquainted with this type of thought. Yet there is much, too, which finds no parallel in the rabbinic writings. Clearly, this is not an exhaustive clue.

A far more comprehensive explanation of the fourth gospel's affinities is offered on the Hellenistic side, namely, Gnosticism. Gnosticism was traditionally the name given to certain second-century deviations opposed by such orthodox fathers as

Irenaeus and Epiphanius. Of later years, however, it has come to be used in a much wider sense, to denote a syncretistic religious philosophy, antedating Christianity and influencing it from quite early days as it had influenced Hellenistic Judaism before it. It is a movement which crystallized itself in a number of differing schools of thought, all of which however exhibit the same fundamental outlook. Its basis was a dualistic view of the world. There was an upper world, eternal, real, and good, and a lower world, temporal, unreal, and evil. The upper world was the sphere of mind, the lower of matter. Man belonged to both orders. Human souls had pre-existed in the upper world, and it was their misfortune to have been allied with human, material, and evil bodies. Creation was in fact a fall. But man was offered deliverance from this fallen state already in this life. This could be achieved by the acquisition of "knowledge" (*gnosis*), which was brought down from the upper world by a heavenly redeemer, who came down into the lower world in a sort of pseudo-incarnation. This knowledge consisted of information concerning the upper world. Those who received the revelation were delivered from the bondage of the material body and recovered the immortality which was theirs before creation. Thus their return to the upper world was assured at death.

John, it is claimed, was deeply influenced by this scheme of thought, and sought to restate the Christian gospel in terms of it by transferring it to the event of Jesus Christ. The discourse material of the fourth gospel, from the prologue onward is simply the adaptation of actual Gnostic material. It is admitted that there are crucial differences between the Gnostic systems and Johannine theology. For John, the redeemer is a real historical figure of the recent past, whose incarnation was a reality, not an appearance. This redeemer could be weary (4:7) and hungry (4:31); he could weep (11:35) and suffer thirst (19:28 cf. 4:7). Finally, he died a death whose physical reality was attested by the water and blood which flowed from his side (19:34). The content of the revelation is different. It is not a body of factual information about the upper world, but—simply the revealer himself, a person. Response to the revelation is not just predetermined fate, dependent upon whether one is a person of the right sort, with the divine spark of heavenly mind, but a matter of free, personal decision, although paradoxically it is predestined. And the state of salvation manifests itself differently, in personal love and obedience, rather than in the selfish enjoyment of knowledge, with a consequent sense of superiority over other mortals.

It will be seen that the appeal to Gnostic affinities does not undermine our confidence in the uniqueness and Christian character of the fourth gospel. In fact, it strengthens that confidence. If we question this explanation, we do so on historical grounds, not because we feel it destroys the value of the gospel. The real trouble about this solution is that nearly all the evidence which we have about it comes from the second century onward, from such writings as the Odes of Solomon, the recently discovered Jung Codex, the Hermetic, Manichean, and Mandaean writings. That such tendencies were already apparent within Judaism is indeed shown by Philo, and within Christianity by Colossians and the pastorals. So we cannot simply write off Gnosticism as a purely post-Christian phenomenon. What we cannot say for certainty is what this pre-Christian Gnosticism contained, since it is impossible to distinguish what second-century and later Gnosticism borrowed from the Johannine writings, and what the Johannine writings borrowed from pre-Christian Gnosticism. This is pre-eminently true of the figure of the Gnostic redeemer. The newly discovered Jung Codex contains a document which shows that even as late as *circa* 150 there was no heavenly redeemer in that particular form of Gnosticism. In fact it would seem that this figure is a Christian importation into later Gnosticism.

Another difficulty is that in the form in which it is generally stated, the Gnostic argument places John on the side of Hellenism or Hellenistic Judaism, and does insufficient justice to his undoubted Palestinian affinities. There are some critics who feel that the Dead Sea Scrolls offer a solution of our difficulty. These show that many Gnostic features were already present in at least one type of first-century Palestinian Judaism. A number of striking parallels between the fourth gospel and the new documents have turned up. First, there is the dualism: in both the Qumran writings and the fourth gospel this dualism is both ethical and monotheistic, not metaphysical as in the Gnostic systems proper. Such terms as "spirit of truth" and "spirit of error," "sons of light" and "sons of darkness," "to do the truth" are common to both Qumran and Johannine literature. Enthusiasts have jumped to the conclusion that the author of the fourth gospel had been a member of the Qumran community, or was at least familiar with their writings, and that here at last we have the clue to the riddle of Johannine Christianity. Such a conclusion would take us far beyond the present state of the evidence. This much at least may be said, however, that first-century Palestinian Judaism was a far richer, more complex affair than we had guessed (cf. also the Testament of the Twelve Patriarchs, which also exhibits remarkable affinities with John) and that somewhere here must have been the matrix in which the thought of the fourth gospel took shape. This however is only a possibility, not an assured result, but it may at least indicate the line that critical opinion will increasingly follow in the next decade or so. At the same time we do well to pay heed to Hoskyns' warning: "the (Fourth) Gospel refuses to come to rest in any haven provided by historical . . . analysis." That is because the dominant factor is neither Palestinian nor Hellenistic, but Christian. Whatever the basic framework, it has been violently distorted to proclaim the event of salvation in Jesus Christ.

3. *Literary and Oral Sources*

Once the traditional view of the authorship had been abandoned, the question of sources naturally came up for debate. For a long period the possibility of a literary relationship between John and all the synoptics was canvassed. Later, opinion seemed to settle down in favor of the use of Mark only. Now an increasing number of scholars, on good grounds, believe that John used none of the synoptic gospels. Rather, he is drawing on a tradition parallel to but independent of the synoptic.

Following recent suggestions, we may distinguish three classes of material: (a) a "sign" source, which included the basic narrative material of Chapters 1–12, (b) a series of revelation discourses, (c) a passion narrative; (c) may be a continuation of (a). It is (b) which is most problematical. Was this taken over from some kind of Gnostic or Jewish sectarian source, possibly liturgical? Was it taken from a previous Christian source? Or was it composed by the evangelist himself? Quite possibly the right answer is a combination of all three.

4. Authorship—Final Conclusion

The Palestinian affinities of the author do not in themselves vindicate the traditional authorship. Rather, the author seems to stand at the end of a process of oral tradition in a manner similar to Mark. If we feel able to square this with the traditional authorship, we must still maintain that the gospel is the interpretation of a tradition, not a straightforward historical account. That an eyewitness should have given such an interpretation is not beyond the bounds of possibility, since ancient methods of writing history were so different from ours. On the whole, however, it is better to assume that the author is a Christian of the second generation, but one who, as Hoskyns has suggested, was "so created by the apostolic witness that he was veritably carried across into their company." It is in this sense that we must interpret the fourth gospel's patent claim to apostolicity: "*We* have beheld his glory": "That which . . . we have heard, which we have seen with our eyes, which we have looked upon, and touched with our hands . . ." (I John 1:1).

5. The Johannine Writings—An Interpretation

Assuming, with most scholars, that the first epistle and the fourth gospel are by the same hand, we may find in the epistle a glimpse of the situation in which Johannine Christianity took shape. Certain deviationist leaders had split away from the churches over which the writer had oversight:

> They went out from us, but they were not of us; for if they had been of us, they would have continued with us; but they went out, that it might be plain that they all are not of us.   *I John 2:19*

These secessionists denied that Jesus was the Christ (2:22), which probably means that though they believed in a Christ or redeemer, they did not identify him with the man Jesus; they denied his coming in the flesh (4:3). They asserted that he came by water only, not by water and blood (5:6). In other words they were Docetists who denied the reality of the incarnation, perhaps believing that the Christ-spirit descended on the man Jesus at his baptism (hence the reference to water in 5:6) but withdrew from him before the crucifixion (cf. "not by blood" in 5:6).

The author of the Johannine literature realizes that it is not enough to call his opponents names, like the author of Jude, nor even to organize machinery for the perpetuation of the tradition, as in the pastorals. The only effective reply will be a theological one of constructive restatement. For there was point in what the secessionists were trying to do: they were trying to find the right vocabulary in which to proclaim the gospel to the Hellenistic world. This vocabulary was to be found in Gnosticism. But like so many who have attempted at restatement since, they were in danger of throwing out the baby with the bath water, of undermining the event of redemption itself. John therefore sets himself to use their language, insofar as it is sanctioned by the Old Testament and Jewish tradition, not in order to jettison or undermine, but to proclaim the event of redemption.

The theme of the fourth gospel is that revelation, the self-disclosure of God to man, is to be found in the man Jesus, and in him alone. He alone possesses the prerogatives and attributes which the Gnostic secessionists would offer to their unreal redeemer. The gospel opens with a hymn of revelation, the prologue. That this is a Christian adaptation of a pre-Christian

Gnostic hymn to a revealer is a plausible suggestion, borne out by the rhythmical character of these verses, which enables us to distinguish between the hymn and the evangelist's comment:

> In the beginning was the Word,
>   and the Word was with God,
> And the Word was God.
>   He was in the beginning with God.
>
> All things were made through him,
>   and without him nothing was made.
> That which has been made was life in him,
>   and the life was the light of men.
>
> The light shines in the darkness
>   and the darkness has not overcome it.

(NOTE: There was a man sent from God, whose name was John. He came for a testimony, to bear witness to the light, that all might believe through him. He was not that light, but came to bear witness to the light.)

He was the true light
  which enlightens every (man) coming into the world

He was in the world, and the world was made through him, yet the world knew him not.

He came to his own
  and his own received him not

But to all who received him
  he gave power to become children of God.

(NOTE: [that is] to those who believe on his name, who were born, not of blood, nor of the will of the flesh, nor of the will of man, but of God.)

> And the Word became flesh,
>   and dwelt among us
> And we have beheld his glory,

> glory as of the only Son from the Father,
>> Full of grace and truth.

(NOTE: John bore witness to him and cried, "This was he of whom I said, 'He who comes after me ranks before me, for he was before me!'")

> And from his fullness have we all received,
>> grace upon grace.

(NOTE: For the law was given through Moses; grace and truth came through Jesus Christ.)

> No one has ever seen God:
>> the only God,
> who is in the bosom of the Father,
>> he has made him known.

The prologue asserts that Jesus, and not other claimants, particularly, for some reason, not John the Baptist, was the revelation of God. Why John the Baptist? Had the secessionists gone over to a John-the-Baptist sect which had erected a whole system of Gnostic beliefs upon him? The existence of a Baptist group at Ephesus is attested in Acts 19. Here is an attractive speculation, but it lacks proof. The revelation of Jesus is disclosed in his "flesh," that is to say, in the whole observable history of Jesus, not only the moment of the incarnation, or Bethlehem, but the whole history culminating in Calvary and to be recorded in the gospel. That flesh, that history is the "word" or revelation of God. But the history of Jesus is seen as revelation only in the light of the resurrection. Hence the whole gospel will be written under the signature of the resurrection. It is not a straightforward history of Jesus, for that would be flesh, and would profit nothing, but history rewritten in the light of the resurrection. The Christ who speaks in the fourth gospel is the risen Christ. The Christ who acts in the signs is performing pointers to what his work will be in his death and resurrection and in the life of the Church as the risen Lord. This may seem an arbitrary way of treating history, but as a matter of fact all history involves interpretation in the light of its subsequent outcome. If for instance we were to describe the history of Germany from 1933 to 1939, we could do so properly only in the light of what happened on September 1, 1939, namely as a series of steps toward Hitler's conquest of Europe. Before that date it seemed that that history was a series of attempts to redress the injustices of the Treaty of Versailles, but to describe it as such today would be wholly wrong. The same holds good of the history of Jesus. A sound-track film would describe the preaching, healings, exorcisms, and tragic outcome of a prophet. But that would be just "flesh," not word. The resurrection however discloses this history to be the redemptive act of God. The process of rewriting began already in the synoptic gospels, and in the oral tradition before them. In John however the original history has become completely impregnated with the interpretation. Thus, while in one sense, in the purely past-historical sense, the synoptic gospels are nearer to history, in a higher sense—that is, on the level of significance—the fourth gospel is the truest to history. It describes the history of Jesus as faith came to know it after the resurrection. It proclaims the flesh of Jesus to be what it is, the word of God.

Hence the prologue, which shows that this same word that became incarnate in Jesus is the word through whom God made the universe, is not just a piece of cosmological speculation, but the evangelist's way of saying that the God who reveals himself is none other than God himself, none other than the Creator. The God in Jesus is not an intermediary being, but:

> God's presence and his very self,
> And essence all divine.

Jesus is the Creator-God-directly-acting-in-history. The second half of the prologue, from verse 5 onward, indicates the two possible responses to the revelation. Many of his "own," that is, mankind, rejected him, but some received him and were given the privilege of rebirth from above. Here is one of the dominant themes of the gospel—the division of those who accept and those who reject the revelation.

The rest of the chapter is often regarded simply as a review of the Messianic titles. But it is more. John and his disciples are made to give their testimony to Jesus as the revelation, and in that testimony their function is exhausted. This subserves the same apologetic deprecation of the Baptist which we detected in the prologue.

Then, after this introductory chapter, which presents Jesus and him alone as the revelation of God, there follows the so-called Book of Signs (Chapters 2–12), of which traditionally there are seven:

TABLE A: 1. Cana of Galilee, 2:1–12
2. The nobleman's son, 4:47–54
3. The pool of Bethesda, 5:1–16
4. The feeding of the five thousand, 6:1–14
5. The walking on the water, 6:15–21
6. Siloam, 9:1–7
7. Lazarus, 11:1–44

All these episodes seem to be derived from the evangelist's sign source (see above, p. 386). There are other episodes of a narrative character which may also have been derived from that source:

TABLE B: 1. The cleansing of the temple, 2:13–16
2. Nicodemus, 3:1–12
3. The Samaritan woman, 4:1–42 (*but heavily interlarded with the evangelist's dialogue material*)
4. Peter's confession, 6:66–71
5. Jesus at the feast of the tabernacles, 7–8 (*again heavily interlarded*)
6. Jesus at the feast of the dedication 10:22–23; 40–42
7. The Sanhedrin meeting, 11:47–54
8. The anointing at Bethany, 12:1–9
9. The triumphal entry, 12:12–19
10. The Greeks at the feast, 12:20–22

The evangelist's method is to take these signs from his source and to rearrange them in the order he requires. For example, the cleansing of the temple seems to have been shifted from a point immediately after Table B.9 (i.e., after the triumphal entry) to a point immediately after Table A.1 (i.e., immediately after the marriage of Cana of Galilee). Two reasons lead to this suggestion. First, in all the other gospels (Matthew, Mark, and Luke), the cleansing of the temple is firmly fixed at a point after the triumphal entry and therefore at the end, not at the beginning, of the ministry. Second, A.2, the nobleman's son, is expressly called the *"second* sign," whereas, as it now appears in the fourth gospel, it is actually the *third*, following A.1 and B.1. This slip in enumeration can be easily explained if in the author's source A.2 *was* the second sign, following immediately after A.1. The dislocation will then have been caused by inserting B.1 between A.1 and A.2. No doubt there has also been a process of selection, since there are references to other signs not recorded (e.g., 2:23; 3:2; etc., and the explicit statement in 20:30). The evangelist's method is to select and arrange such signs as he needs and to farce them with dialogues or discourses. Sometimes, as in the case of Cana of Galilee, the only addition is a brief editorial remark; sometimes it is a brief dialogue, as in the cleansing of the temple, plus an editorial comment. The fullest and most characteristic form however is where the sign provides the springboard for an extended dialogue or discourse. Thus we get:

1. Dialogue on rebirth (3:1–21) attached the pronouncement in verse 3
2. Speech of John the Baptist (3:25–36) annexed to incident of John and his disciples
3. Dialogue on the water of life (4:9–15) and worship in the Messianic age (4:20–26), together with dialogue with the disciples on the Christian mission (4:35–38), annexed to the Samaritan woman
4. Debate on Jesus' authority (5:17–47), annexed to the sign of the pool of Bethesda
5. Discourse and interpolated dialogue on the bread of

life (6:31–65), annexed to the feeding of the five thousand

6. Discourse on Messiahship (7:16–52; 8:12–59), annexed to feast of the tabernacles

7. Trial scene, a dialogue annexed to the healing of the blind man at Siloam, and expressing theme of judgment (9:8–41)

8. Discourse on Good Shepherd, no narrative setting (10)

9. Dialogue in the Lazarus episode (11)

10. Dialogue on necessity of the passion, annexed to the Greeks at the feast (12:3–36)

11. Concluding summary of teaching in the Book of Signs (12:37–50)

Such an analysis shows how imperfectly the plan of this part of the gospel is carried out. One would expect an orderly succession of episodes with dialogues or discourses attached. Instead, some episodes have a minimum of interpretative addition, others have an excess (e.g., Chapters 7–8) and one discourse floats in mid-air without an episode of its own. It is not surprising that many have undertaken extensive rearrangements of the text. But there are as many proposals for such rearrangement as there are advocates, and an objective test for them has as yet to be offered. So it is best to assume that the gospel is in an unfinished state, the result perhaps of gradual composition over a number of years, and broken off possibly by old age or death, then given out to the world by the author's disciples in the final shape it had reached (21:24).

Is there any progression of thought in the discourses? To some extent there is, though we must avoid imposing a pattern of our own on an ostensibly unfinished work. After the first and introductory chapter there follows a series of events and discourses intended to outline in advance the significance of Jesus' finished work. Thus Cana of Galilee indicates that the old Jewish order of purifying is to be replaced by the new and final purification. Then comes the cleansing of the temple: the old order of purification replaced, there will follow a new order of worship, in which the temple at Jerusalem is replaced by the temple of Christ's body. In Chapter 3 entrance to this new order is secured by a rebirth or birth from above through the Spirit. This introduces one of the salient themes or plots of the gospel, the process by which the new order of the Spirit is made available to the new community. Jesus himself is first endowed with a plenary inspiration of this Spirit (1:23 f.; 3:34). Men require to be initiated into this life in the Spirit by a rebirth from God (3:8), but the Spirit is "not yet," not until after Jesus has performed the decisive event by which it is released, i.e., his death, by which he is glorified (7:39). Later, and only in the context of the impending passion, does Jesus speak at length of the Spirit which the Father will send as a consequence of his own "going away," that is to say once more, his death. Then, when that decisive event has been accomplished, the risen Christ breathes the Spirit into his own (20:22) to fulfill the mission of the Paraclete as outlined in the farewell discourses.

In Chapter 4 further light is thrown on the new order to be constituted by Christ's work of revelation and redemption. The new temple having been established, there will be a new order of worship, "in spirit and in truth." This does not simply mean that the Church's worship will be one of sincerity of heart and consequent independence of set forms. It means, rather, worship offered to God in and through the event of Jesus Christ, who is himself the truth, i.e., the faithfulness of God to his redemptive purpose, and who by the event releases the "Spirit," not the spirit of man, but the extension of the redemptive work of Christ.

The dominant theme of the discourse in Chapter 5 is the new life to which men are to be raised by the saving death of Christ. The healing at Siloam had taken place on the Sabbath day, which was the type of the "rest that remaineth to the people of God" in the age to come. This chapter is also important because it exhibits the future quality of the new life: it is not a timeless, mystical state, but a present anticipation of a life which will be fully realized at the final consummation:

Do not marvel at this; for the hour is coming when all who are in the tombs will hear his voice and come forth; those who have done good, to the resurrection of life and those who have done evil, to the resurrection of judgment.

5:28 f.

So far from being a crude survival of primitive teaching about the end, it is such verses as these which give point to the other, more spiritualized teaching about the realization of the end already here and now. The same tension between the "already" and the "not yet" is exhibited in the next chapter, 6. This resumes the theme of worship in the new age. In this worship there is, if it is offered in spirit and in truth, a feeding on the bread of life, typified by the manna of the exodus. The living bread is the person and event of Christ. It is by constantly assimilating this person and event that men and women enjoy already here and now that life of the age to come which will not be theirs in the fullest sense until the consummation. Hence the constant reiteration of "I will raise him up at the last day." This bread from heaven is now available because it is flesh and blood, which means the life of the Redeemer made available through his sacrifice. At first sight it looks as though there is a transition in verse 52 or 54 from purely spiritual language about the bread of heaven to the crude materialism of the flesh and blood. Some scholars have even gone so far as to suggest that the materialism is from the hand of an ecclesiastical redactor. It is not however a violent transition but a clearer definition of meaning. The movement from bread to flesh and blood is the same movement which we find in the other discourses which speak of a preliminary "not yet" which can only become an "already" in the event of the cross. The bread of heaven can only be made available if it be flesh and blood, that is to say, if it pass through sacrificial death. No doubt it is the sacramental usage which suggested the terminology, but the sacrament is not his immediate concern. Rather, it is the event of Jesus Christ in its totality, which includes not only the coming down of the bread from heaven (the incarnation), but also the flesh and blood (the sacrificial death).

395

The background of Chapter 7 is the feast of the tabernacles. Many themes jostle one another in the discourse material. There is the theme of healing on the Sabbath, which is carried over from Chapter 5, and makes plausible though not imperative the rearrangement of these chapters in the order 5, 7, 6, (but see above, p. 393). There is the Christological theme of Jesus' origin, whether it be an observable historico-geographical origin in Bethlehem or a mysterious origin which can only be described as a "sending" from One who is above history and geography. This theme shows the evangelist's familiarity with Jewish speculations about the Messiah. There was a current notion that the Messiah was concealed somewhere on earth and that he would emerge from his hiding place only at the end. Then comes the theme most immediately suggested by the feast of tabernacles (verses 37 ff.), on the last day of which a libation was poured out in the temple. Jesus is made to declare himself, his person and history, which culminates in his death, as the source of the "Spirit," which the water used in the ceremony suggests. These themes are drawn together by the overshadowing event of the cross, which here appears in twofold aspect: on the one hand it is the Jews' rejection of the Revealer, and on the other hand the event through which the saving revelation is to be made available to man.

In Chapter 8 various themes again jostle one another. Like the previous chapter, it consists of discussions between Jesus and the Jews. As before, the cross dominates the discussion (verses 20–22; 28, 37, 40, 44). Again the Jews, in rejecting and killing the Revealer, are providing the occasion for the event which will be their judgment and the salvation of the believers. There is further discussion of the authority of Jesus, why his words and deeds are indeed the act of God. His words and deeds are this because they rest upon his sending from above (verse 23). This throws further light on the event of the cross: because it is the act of the Son's obedience to the mission of the Father it is the act of God himself. Finally, the paradoxical nature of the cross as the act of God is demonstrated by the discussion about Abraham, which leads to the tremendous pronouncement: "Before Abraham was, I am" (verse 58). The life and death of Jesus is the veritable act of God who was before all history, and particularly before the redemptive history of Israel.

Chapter 9 presents Jesus as the light of the world. As such, he brings a crisis, a sifting among men: that those who do not see might see; and that those who see may become blind (verse 39). There is further discussion about the transcendent origin of the event and person of Jesus (verses 4, 17, 29–33, 36–38; 39). The shadow of the approaching passion lies less heavily over this chapter, but it is hinted at in the words: "*As long* as I am in the world, I am the light of the world." He will be taken away, and *because* he will be taken away, he is the light of the world. And there is still the hostility of the Jews to remind us of the cross.

Chapter 10 is chiefly about the good shepherd. The good shepherd is what he is because he lays down his life for the sheep (verses 11, 15). Thus the image illuminates the meaning of the cross. There are other sheep who must be brought into the fold. Here is the first appearance of a theme which will reappear in Chapter 12 in the episode of the Greeks at the feast—that the cross is to inaugurate the world-wide mission of the Church. During that mission there will be the constant danger of false teachers (we recall the situation of I John) to which the whole Johannine theology was developed as a response. The false teachers are such because they fail to relate their converts to the event of redemption.

Chapter 11 returns to the theme of the resurrection already introduced in Chapter 5. But it also rivets this theme more clearly to the cross. The raising of Lazarus itself provides the direct occasion for the Sanhedrin's decision to get rid of Jesus (the connection between the two is of course theological, not historical: the ultimate reason why the Jews condemned Jesus is because he came to bring redemption). This may be worse history than Mark's account, which makes the decision of the Sanhedrin consequent upon the cleansing of the temple, but it is profounder theology.

Chapter 12 brings together three episodes to demonstrate

the universality of the redemption inaugurated by the cross. At the anointing we are told that the house was filled with the odor of the ointment, symbolizing the filling of the world with the fragrance of the gospel (cf. II Corinthians 2:14–16). The triumphal entry is used to symbolize the universality of the response to the event of Jesus Christ. It evokes the scandalized comment of the Pharisees: "Look, the whole world has gone after him." Finally, there is the scene of the Greeks at the feast, which culminates in the pronouncement: "I, when I be lifted up from the earth, will draw all men to myself" (verse 32), a typical Johannine *double-entendre*, referring both to his lifting up on the cross and his exaltation into heaven, which manifests the true significance of the cross.

Thus the first part of the gospel is designed to offer, not so much a progression of thought, as a series of different approaches to the same topic, the event of the cross, illuminating it from many different angles. The ground of the evangelist's concern with this event is not simply that it occurred in past history, or even that he seeks to evoke an understanding of it considered as an event in past history. Rather, it is because the event of Jesus Christ is perpetually made a present reality in the life of the Church: in its preaching of the gospel message, in its administration of the two sacraments, in its conflict with false teaching, and in its witness to the truth. But the event thus perpetuated still awaits final consummation at the end. As the "not yet" of the ministry points to an "already" of the cross, so the cross inaugurates a new "not yet" which becomes an "already" only at the final consummation.

6. *The Farewell Discourses*

If the shadow of the cross looms large over the whole of the ministry up to Chapter 12, that is even truer of the next chapters, 13–17. Here speaks, not the Jesus who will suffer, but the Christ who has suffered: "Be of good cheer, *I have overcome the world*." The Church has shown a true insight by using these chapters as the quarry for its liturgical gospels in the period between Easter and Pentecost.

These discourses are notorious for the disorderly arrangement of the material. One theme after another (e.g., mutual indwelling, the Paraclete, and petitionary prayer) is introduced, dropped, and later resumed. Then there is the curious cry at the end of Chapter 14, "Rise, let us go hence," suggesting the conclusion of the discourse but followed by two further chapters of discourse covering much the same ground as before. Here is a wonderful opportunity for rearranging the text! It is more likely however that this is another sign of the unfinished state of the gospel. Chapter 14 and Chapters 15 and 16 may represent two alternative drafts of the farewell discourse which the evangelist designed eventually to fuse together. Also we have to remember the mental processes of John. As the first epistle already shows, he tends to think round a subject. Instead of advancing in an orderly manner and building up an argument step by step, he takes up a theme, examines it from a number of different aspects, and returns to his starting point—almost, but not quite, for there is a perceptible deepening of apprehension. It is a method of thinking which has aptly been described as "spiral."

We have seen that the "ideal" pattern of the fourth gospel, though it is not consistently carried through, is that a sign or work of Jesus should be followed by a discourse or dialogue. This same pattern persists in the section we are now considering. For the farewell discourses are really an extended commentary on the foot washing.[1] Like the other incidents, this episode is almost certainly derived from the tradition. Another version of the same tradition is to be found at Luke 22:24–27. In its original setting, as indicated by the Lukan version, as well as by the saying in John 13:14, it was intended as an example in humility directed against the strife of the disciples as to who should be the greatest. The fourth evangelist however has reinterpreted it as a sign of the event of redemption in its totality. He prefaces the narrative with the declaration: "Je-

[1] May it be that the discourse material in Chapters 13–14 was intended to go with the foot washing, while the alternative, Chapters 15–16, beginning as they do with the allegory of the vine, were intended to go with the narrative of the institution of the eucharist?

sus, knowing that the Father had given all things into his hand, and that he had come from God and was going to God . . ." It is to symbolize this coming from God and going to God that the foot washing is related. Jesus had come forth from God: he had divested himself of the glory which he had had with the Father before the world was made (17:5). So he lays aside his garments. But the incarnation does not exhaust the divine act: it is the prelude to an even greater self-emptying. So Jesus washes the disciples' feet, thus symbolizing the purification from sin which is to be wrought by the shedding of his blood. Then he resumes his garments and sits down again, thus symbolizing the resumption of his glory. The foot washing is the most perspicuous of all the signs, but, like them all, its meaning is not perceived until the event to which it points is accomplished: "What I am doing, you do not know now, but afterward you will understand." The farewell discourses then follow as a disclosure, as it were, from the other side of the event.

It is curious that St. John does not relate the institution of the eucharist. There is no reason to attribute this to any anti- or non-sacramental tendency on his part. Rather, just as the transfiguration is, as it were, spread all over the earlier part of the ministry without being directly related, so the whole meaning of the institution is spread over Chapters 13–17.[2] For in the institution of the eucharist as related by the synoptists Jesus initiates his disciples into the meaning of his death: it will inaugurate the new covenant in the reign of God. John achieves the same purpose more thoroughly by the discourses which follow the foot washing.

Do the farewell discourses add anything new or represent any advance in thought? They are certainly not a mere repetition of what was said in Chapters 1–12. If the earlier part of the gospel represents the *public* proclamation of the event of redemption, the middle part, Chapters 13–17, disclose the *inner* meaning of that event in the life of the Church. Here the act of God in Christ is interpreted as the event which sets

[2] For another possibility, see above, p. 399, footnote.

in motion a community marked by an intense common life of Christian love (13:34–35). It is a life of mutual indwelling: the Father dwells in the Son and the Son in the Father; the disciples dwell in the Son and through dwelling in him dwell in the Father. This love and mutual indwelling however are not meant to be taken in a mystical sense. They are expressed in concrete obedience to the will of God. The Son dwells in the Father by laying down his life; the Christians manifest their indwelling in God through Christ by keeping the commandments of God (14:15; 15:10 ff., etc.). Specifically, these commandments are that they should "bear fruit," that is, to bear witness to the act of God in Christ and secure the adhesion of converts to it, and that they should love one another. In fulfillment of its mission, the Church will undergo persecution and suffering, being hated by the world like its Master (15:18–21; 16:1–3). Meanwhile, it will be necesssary for the Church to "ask" for the divine assistance, and since such asking will be in the "name" of the Son, that is, linked to the execution of God's redemptive purpose, it will be answered (14:13; 15:7; 16:23, 30). In this connection, great prominence is given to the work of the Holy Spirit (14:16–18; 14:26; 15:26; 16:7–10; 16:13–14). First, we note that the mission of the Spirit is directly consequent upon the Son's "going to the Father." It is the event of his exaltation, in the double Johannine sense of the word, which releases to the Church the gift of the Spirit. He is sent by the Son (16:7) or by the Father in the Son's name (14:26). Thus the Spirit is no independent religious phenomenon, but rigorously controlled by God's act in Christ, perpetuating that act in the Church's witness to it (15:16; 16:8–11) and in its inner apprehension of its meaning, and bringing to remembrance the words of Jesus (16:13–14). The fourth gospel itself is a product of the Spirit's work: the words of Jesus are brought to remembrance and their deeper meaning disclosed (16:12), the deeper meaning which could not be apprehended until the event itself had fully occurred. But such knowledge is never an addition to the original revelation: "he will take *what is mine* and declare it to you." The Spirit will also disclose the "things to come," such as we find in the Apocalypse, a further indication that the Apocalypse belongs to the same school as the gospel.

The question naturally arises: what has become of the return of Christ at the end of the world? It seems to have been dissolved completely in the resurrection appearances ("I will see you again," 16:22) and in the coming of the Paraclete ("I will come to you" in 14:18b is almost synonymous with "he will give you another Counselor" in verse 16). Moreover, this coming of the Counselor will "be" with the disciples "for ever" (14:16). It would however be wrong to conclude that the whole idea of the second coming is eliminated. As elsewhere in the New Testament there is a tension in the function of the Spirit. On the one hand he points back to the decisive event of Jesus Christ. On the other hand he also points forward to the "things to come." As the Apocalypse shows, the "things to come" are none other than the final consummation. This aspect of the "not yet" is more clearly expressed in the high priestly prayer which contemplates the final union of Christ with his own in heaven after the period of their witness on earth:

> Father, I desire that they also, whom thou hast given me, be with me where I am, to behold my glory which thou hast given me.   17:24

This expresses the same hope which St. Paul has expressed in the cruder traditional language in I Thessalonians 4:16. John has "demythologized" the second coming; but he has not *eliminated* what it stands for, he has *interpreted* it. He thus preserves the authentic New Testament tension between the "already" and the "not yet."

7. The Passion Narrative

In Chapter 18 the evangelist embarks upon the narration of the passion. John's version, while often parallel to the Markan and particularly to the special Lukan versions, is actually dependent upon a special tradition of its own, which enables us to correct or supplement the other accounts at a number of points. Thus the passion takes place on the eve of the Passover, which is much more plausible than the Markan chronology, which places the Last Supper, trials, and crucifixion on the actual feast day itself. The examination before Annas is a plausible correction, for it was more likely a preliminary examination than a trial, and we know from Josephus that he was at that time the power behind the high priestly throne. The dialogue with Pilate about Jesus' kingship is plausible, apart from the introduction of the specifically Johannine motif of witness to the truth. The episode of the Mother of the Lord, the breaking of the legs of the two thieves, and the incident of the water and the blood appear to rest on tradition, rather than upon deliberately concocted symbolism.

For the most part, the evangelist is content to let the narrative speak for itself. Only at one or two points does he venture to offer distinctive theological comment, the definition of Jesus' kingship in terms of witness to the truth and the cry, "It is finished." These two insertions serve to tie up the passion narrative with the preceding discourse material. The discourses had exhibited Jesus as the truth of God. But what is truth? It is not a series of propositions about God or the heavenly world. It is the faithfulness of God to his redemptive purpose, and is disclosed in the giving up of his Son to the cross. "It is finished" proclaims that the redemptive event, foreshadowed and interpreted in the earlier part of the gospel, has now been accomplished.

8. *The Resurrection*

Since the death of Jesus is itself the glorifying and exaltation of the Redeemer, and the going of the Son to the Father, it has been felt that there is no logical place for the resurrection narratives and that they are merely a concession to tradition. But this is a complete misconception. So far from being otiose, the resurrection appearances are intended precisely to reveal the meaning of the cross, to exhibit it as the lifting up of Jesus, his going to the Father, and his glorifying. The cross is not visible as such apart from the revelation conveyed in the Easter event. It is the Easter event which discloses the true significance of the cross, and it is only in the light of the Easter event that the words and deeds of Jesus are perceived in their true meaning. Hence the constant reiteration throughout the gospel of the fact that the apostolic apprehension of their meaning was "not yet," a "not yet" which becomes an "already" only at the resurrection (1:51; 2:22; 3:12; 12:16). Hence, too, the various sayings about the Paraclete, who will come only after the resurrection to recall what Jesus has said and done and to disclose its meaning.

Thus all the words and works of Jesus as recorded in the fourth gospel presuppose the revelation contained in the resurrection. Without it there would be no fourth gospel, just as there would be no synoptic gospels either. Only so could the Church proclaim that Jesus was the Christ, the Son of God, that, believing, men might have life in his name.

CHAPTER VIII

EPILOGUE: THE UNITY OF THE NEW TESTAMENT

That the twenty-seven books of the New Testament exhibit a considerable variety, no one will deny. But it is equally important, as we have seen, to appreciate their underlying unity. For it is precisely in its unity that the authority of the New Testament lies. That unity lies in its testimony to Jesus Christ, in whom God wrought the decisive act of redemption which the Church now enjoys, and to whose completion it looks forward in the final consummation. And it is this testimony to that act which is preserved for the Church in the New Testament and which thus becomes the touchstone and source of its preaching. In all twenty-seven books the one event shines forth in its kaleidoscopic impact upon the Church of the apostolic age. All the New Testament documents witness to that act as the inauguration of the process of redemption, but all of them equally bear witness to the "not yet"—it still awaits its ultimate consummation. It is the faithful preservation of this witness in tension that gives the New Testament both its unity and its apostolic authority. In some writings more emphasis is placed on the "already." That is pre-eminently the case with the fourth gospel. In others the primary emphasis is on the "not yet." That is notably the case with the earlier Pauline writings and the Apocalypse. But never—unless we are prepared to resort to the butcher's knife and postulate the nefarious hand of an ecclesiastical redactor—do we find the tension completely eliminated in favor of either side. It is surely significant, too, that the two extremes appear either in the same author (St. Paul) or in the same school (the Johannine literature). There *was* a faith once delivered to the saints, the faith in Jesus Christ who came and will come: Jesus, in whom we have salvation already, and in whom our salvation will be consummated.

INDEX OF BIBLICAL REFERENCES

OLD TESTAMENT

Genesis

1–11	13, 48–61	11:4	60
1:1–2:3	47, 50–51	11:10	47
1:26	92	11:10–27	47
1:26–31	51	11:27	47
1:27	54	11:31	61
2:4	47	12	67
2:4–7	52	12:2–3	69
2:4–25	50, 52	12:3	61, 65
2:16, 17, 18, 23	52	13	66
3	54–58	13:13	66
3:6, 7	57	14	66
3:7, 21	60	14:17–20	360
3:14, 15	58	15	62, 72, 88
3:20	55	15:6	73
3:22–24	56	15:7–21	68
4:17	60	16	67
4:18–24	60	17	69, 72, 88
4:23, 24	59	18	66
5	47	18:18	65
5:1	47	19	66
6:1–4	234	22:18	65
6:9	47	25:12, 19	47
8:22	59	26:4	65
9:2–6	51	28:14	65
9:6	58	29–31	63
9:11–17	60	30:31	81
9:20, 21	60	31	86
10	47, 60	36:1	47
10:1	47	37–50	13
11:1–9	60	37:2	47
		45:5	66
		49	32

Exodus

1:11	77
2–4	77
3:10	22
4:22b–23a	282
4:31	78
5–11	78
8:15	79
8:19	274
12–13	78, 96
12:39	78
12:40	77
14:4, 18	79
14:10–12	80
14:14	79
14:21	79
14:25	79
15:1–8	79
15:14–18	79
15:23–26	80
16:3	80
17–26	85
17:2, 3	80
19:18	85
19–24	72, 84, 86
19:5–6	87
20	87, 89
20:2	9–10, 74
20:23–23:33	87
21–23	91
24	96
24:7	32, 87
25–31	47
25–40	84
25:16	89
25:40	362
30:22–32	115
32–34	85
34:14	89
34:27	32
35–40	47
40:9–15	115

Leviticus

8:10–13, 30	115
17–26	85, 91
19:18	76, 85, 101, 153

25:8–17	107
25:23	107

Numbers

1–10	86
11	80
11–14	85
12	80
15–19	86
20–21	84
20–25	85
22–24	32
24:17	236
26–36	86

Deuteronomy

1:5	100
4:13	89
4:35	101
4:44	100
5:22	100
6:4–5	76, 101
6:5	89
6:20–25	74
7:8	332
9	82
9:1–6	109
9:4–6	71
10:14–22	75
12–26	91
17:14–20	116
18:15	294
21:23	340
26:5–9	9
26:5–10	74
27:26	340
30:11–14	29
30:15 ff.	102

Joshua

24:8–10	84
24:13	103

Judges

1	104
2:3	111
5	32

Judges (*cont'd*)			
7	108	19–20	132
21:25	111	21–25	122
		22	36
I Samuel		22–23	100, 132
4	114	24	134
4:4	89	24:18	165
8:11–17	114		
13:19–21	114	**I Chronicles**	
18:1–3	82	1–9	137
24:6, 10	116	10 ff.	139
26:9–23	116	17:21	332
II Samuel		**II Chronicles**	
1:17 ff.	118	12:15	139
3:6 ff.	117	20:34	139
7	124	26:22	139
7:14	116, 282	32:32	139
11–12	116, 118		
		Ezra	
I Kings		7–10	142
1–11	122	7:6	142
2:5–6	117	7:12–26	142
3:12	123	7:14, 25	37
4:29–34	190		
5	81	**Nehemiah**	
8	125	1–7	141
9:11	81	8:1–8	36
10	123	8–10	142
10:20	123	12	141
10:23	126	13	141
11:6	127		
16:28–II Kings 11	127	**Job**	
17–II Kings 11	122	2:10	197
18:17	129	7	198
18:19	129	10:8	199
19:18	129	12:2, 5	200
21	116, 130	13:2–12	200
		13:4	200
II Kings		16:19	201
12	127	19:25	201
14:25	180	28	196, 198
14:25, 28	152	31	197
15–20	122	41	202
17	131	42:1–6	203
18–20	131, 158		
18:5	131	**Psalms**	
		2	119

Psalms (*cont'd*)		11:9 ff.	205
2:7	116		
3	185	Isaiah	
16	287	1:16–17, 19–20	160
18	119	2:5–6	160
22	184	5	160
23	187–90	6	159
29	185	6:8	22
29:1	187	7	159
35	186	9:2, 6	162
41	186	9:8–10:4	160
41:13	184	9:11	120
45	119	10:5 ff.	110
50	175	10:5–6	161
72	119	11:1–9	162
89	119	11:6–9	51
89:26	282	40:1–11	175
90:4	374	40:12 ff.	175
98:2	334	40:22–23, 25	28
101	119	41:24	176
105	10	42:1	277
106:7–13	83	42:1–7	177
106:13–33	84	42:6	280
109	185	44:23	333
110	119, 291	44:26–28	158
110:1	291, 359	45:1 ff.	176
110:4	359	49:6	177
136	83	50:8	334
150	184	51:6	334
		52:15	177
Proverbs		53	120, 177, 178, 239, 277
8	194	53:11	335
8:22	194, 325	53:11–12	279
10:12	193	56:1	334
15:20	192	56:16	277
16:8	192	66:1	174
17:1	193	66:1–2	277
18:7	193		
19:6	193	Jeremiah	
22:17–24:22	192	1	165
23:13–14	192	1:5, 7	22
24:28–29	192	2:2	84
		2:11–13	166
Ecclesiastes		2:27	93
2:13	203	5:12	19
3:11–14	204	5:30–31	167
3:16–21	204	7	167

Jeremiah (*cont'd*)		Joel	
9:23–24	166	2:12–14, 28–29	179
15:10	166		
17:17	166	Amos	
18:18	190	3:2	71
20:7	166	5:14–15	154
21	169	5:18	152
23:6	120	5:21	154
26	167	5:21–27	153
27–29	169	6:13	151
31:31	279	7:10–17	152
31:31–34	173	9:13–15	51
31:33–34	96		
33:15–16	120	Micah	
36	168	5:4	120
37:11 ff.	169	6:8	162
38	169		
38:14 ff.	169	Habakkuk	
52	165	1:11	164
		2:4	164
Ezekiel			
3:8	172	Zephaniah	
3:17	171	1:12	19
3:26–27	171		
6:7, 10	172	Haggai	
14:14, 20	197	2:23	120
37:14	173		
37:21–28	120	Zechariah	
44:4 ff.	172	3	196
		4	120
Daniel		9:10	120
7:13	291	12:10	375
Hosea		Wisdom	
1:2	157	1:7	248
1:4	131	3:1 ff.	248
4:6	155	7:15 ff.	248
4:11–19	155	7:24–27	248
4:17	155	7:25 f.	248
5:4	155	9:9	325
7:8	155	9:9b–13	248
7:11	155	9:15 f.	248
8:7	155		
11	156	Ecclesiasticus	
11:1–7	74, 93	24:9	325
14:4	156	44:1–15	229
		44:16–49:16	229

Ecclesiasticus (*cont'd*)		I Maccabees	
50	229	1:1–9	217
51:23, 25	228	1:10–2:70	217
		3:1–9:22	217
Enoch		9:23–12	217
1:9	235	13–16	217
9:14	372	16:23 f.	218
Malachi			
4:2	179		

NEW TESTAMENT

Matthew		1:11	277
3:11	242	1:15	266
7:28	317	1:41	273
8:11 f.	299	1:44	271
8:20	283	2:1–3:6	315
10:7	267	2:10	283
11:1	317	2:23 ff.	229
11:2–5	273	2:25	271
11:12–13	267	2:28	283
12:25–29	274	3:27	274
13:33	269	4:1–34	315
13:52	317	4:14–20	268
13:53	317	4:26–29	268
16:2–3	269	4:30–33	269
16:13	351	4:35–5:43	315
16:17–19	284	6:34	273
16:18	290, 299	8:2	273
19:1	317	8:27–33	275
20:34	273	8:29	284
22:34–40	101	8:38	282
23:15	246	10:33–34	275
25:1–11	291	10:38	278
25:1–12	270	11:27–12:37	315
26:1	317	12:1–9	271
28:18–20	290	12:25–37	297
28:19	295	12:26	271
28:19 ff.	310, 317	12:35 ff.	285
28:20	291	12:36	285
		13:28–29	269
Mark		14:36	272
1:6	243	14:62	283, 291
1:8	242	16:9	316

Mark (*cont'd*)

16:15–18	290
16:16	295
16:19	120

Luke

1:68	333
1:80	242
3:1	221
3:10–14	242
4:18 f.	318
7:13	273
9:31	319
9:58	283
10:9	267
10:25–37	76
11:2	272
11:17–22	274
12:6	53
12:35–40	270, 291
12:49–50	278
12:54–56	269
13:20–21	269
13:28 f.	299
13:32 f.	278
13:33	319
15	269, 319
16:16	267
17:25	276
18:9 ff.	319
19:1 ff.	319
21:28	333
22:18	280
22:24–27	399
22:29	280
24:25–26	290
24:44–46	290
24:47 f.	290

John

1:1–14	382
1:23 f.	394
1:45	382
1:51	404
2:1–12	391
2:13–16	391
2:22	387, 404

3	394
3:1–12	391
3:1–21	392
3:8	394
3:12	404
3:16–21	380
3:25–36	392
3:31–36	380
3:34	394
4	394
4:1–42	391
4:3	387
4:7	383
4:9–15	392
4:20–26	392
4:31	383
4:35–38	392
4:47–54	391
5	394
5:1–16	391
5:6	387
5:17–47	392
5:28 f.	376, 395
6:1–14	391
6:15–21	391
6:31–65	393
6:35	382
6:52, 54	395
6:66–71	391
7	396
7:16–52	393
7:37 ff.	396
7:39	394
8	391, 396
8:12–59	393
8:20–22, 28, 37, 40, 44	396
8:23, 58	397
8:56	382
9:1–7	391
9:4, 17, 29–33, 36–38, 39	397
9:8–41	393
10	393
10:11, 15	397
10:22–23, 40–42	391
11	393
11:1–44	391

John (cont'd)

11:35	383
11:47–54	391
12:1–9	391
12:3–36	393
12:12–19	391
12:16	404
12:20–22	391
12:32	398
12:37–50	393
13–17	398–400
13:14	399
13:34–35	401
14:13	401
14:15	401
14:16–18, 18b, 26	401
15:7	401
15:10 ff.	401
15:16, 18–21, 26	401
16	399
16:1–3, 7–10, 8–11, 12, 13–14, 22, 23, 30	401
16:22	402
17:5	400
17:24	402
18	402
18:31	224, 225
19:28	383
19:34	383
19:37	375
20	289
20:17	272
20:22	394
20:22 f.	290
20:31	262
21:15–17	290
21:24	393

Acts

1:11	291
1:22	241
1:26	107
2	223
2:33–36	120
2:36	294
2:42	296
2:46	298

3:12–26	293
3:13	305
3:26	294, 295
4:27	305
4:36	299
5:1–10	297
5:37	235
7	224, 299
8:17	311
8:34	177
9:2	238
9:6, 15	22
10:6	311
11:30	313
13:16	112
13:23	112
14:15b–17	303
14:23	313
15	72
17:22–31	304
17:24–25	175
19	389
19:6	311
20:7	312

Romans

1:18 ff.	328
1:19–20	304
1:20	329
1:24–32	305
2:15	329
3:20	331
3:21	334
3:24b–25a	308
3:25	341, 342
3:28	367
4:3, 9, 27	67
4:25	335
5:5	345
5:6	337
5:9	341
5:10	336
5:12	327, 328
5:12–21	338
5:15–19	352
5:20	331
6:1–6	347

Romans (*cont'd*)

6:3	310
6:5 f.	339
6:10	339
6:11–12	347
7:7–19	330
7:25	327
8:3	337
8:15–17	351
8:18 ff.	329
8:32 f.	337
10:2 f.	230
11:25–26a	354
11:28	335
11:32	353
12	313

I Corinthians

1:17	347
1:26	246
2:9	353
2:12–13	25
5:7	96, 308
6:11	335
10:1–4	349
10:3–4	348
10:4	323
10:16b–17	346
10:16–17, 21	348
10:17	350
10:21	348
11:23–25	349 fn.
11:23–26	96
11:23–34	348
11:25	340
11:26	297, 349
11:30	312
12	313
12:8 ff.	344
12:28	344
13:12	29
14:6	348
14:16	312, 348
15	354
15:3	257, 258, 288
15:20	348
15:21–22	61

15:22–23	343
15:29	310
15:44	355
15:45, 47 ff.	352
16:2	312
16:15 f.	313
16:22	298, 312, 377

II Corinthians

2:14–16	398
5	356
5:1	355
5:2–4	355
5:19	336
5:21	341
10–13	322
11:2	94

Galatians

1:15 f.	290
2:1–10	257
2:2	290
2:20	337
3:6	67
3:13	339
3:14	340
3:19	331
4:1–4	332
4:4	306, 337
4:4–7	351
4:21	323

Ephesians

1:7	341
2:13 f.	357
4	313
4:32	310
5:2	308, 341

Philippians

1:21	355, 356
2:5–8	338
3:21	355, 356

Colossians

1:15 ff.	326
1:20	341
1:21	335

Colossians (*cont'd*)
2:15, 18 — 326
3:6 — 328

I Thessalonians
4:13–15 — 355
4:16 — 355, 402
5:12 — 313

II Timothy
1:1–3 — 365
1:19 — 365
2:2 — 365
4:9–18 — 365

Hebrews
2:18 — 363
4:15 — 363
5:14 — 359
6:2 — 311
6:20 — 363
7:25 — 363
8:5 — 362
9:12, 28 — 363
10:5–10, 12 — 363
10:10, 12 — 363
10:32 — 359
13:7, 17 — 359
13:10 — 361
13:15 — 361
13:22 — 358
13:23 — 40, 358
13:24 — 359

James
1:2, 18 — 368
2:1 — 368
2:2 — 309
2:19 — 367
5:7 — 368

I Peter
1:1 ff. — 371
1:3 — 370
1:13 — 370
1:15 f. — 371

1:18, 22, 23 — 370
1:20 — 371
2:1 — 370
2:2, 10 — 370
2:5, 9 — 371
2:11, 13 — 370
2:18–3:7 — 370
3:1 — 370
3:21 — 370
4:13–5:14 — 371
5:12 — 369
5:13 — 370

II Peter
1:1, 16–18 — 373
3:8b–9a — 374
3:16 — 373

I John
1:1 — 386
1:1–18 — 366–69
2:19 — 387
4:1–6 — 238

Jude
4, 8, 10, 12 f., 16,
18 ff. — 372
14 f. — 235
24–25 — 373

Revelation
1:7 — 375
1:9 — 376
1:10 — 312
3:20 — 377
4:1–22:5 — 376
4:2–11 — 312
5:9–10, 12, 13b — 377
6:10 — 378
7:12 — 377
11:17 — 377
15:3b — 377
19:1–8 — 377
19:7 — 94
22:20 — 298, 312

INDEX OF NAMES

Aaron, 77
Abel, 59
Abner, 117
Abraham, 33, 47, 48, 62–73, 88, 329–30
Absalom, 185
Achan, 108
Adam, 47, 48, 55, 327, 338
Agur, 191
Ahab, King, 116, 122, 127–30
Ahaz, 116
Ai, 105
Albright, W. F., 5
Alexandra. *See* Salome.
Amenemope, Wisdom of, 192
Amos, 71, 122, 151–55, 156, 180
Ananias, 297
Anath, 20
Anathoth, 169
Antioch, 112
Antiochus Epiphanes, 209
Antiochus the Great, 223
Antipas, 220, 221, 251, 266
Antipater, 220
Apsu, 49
Aquinas, Thomas, 26
Aramaeans, 62
Archelaus, 220–21
Areopagus, 303
Aristobulus, King, 219
Ashtoreth, 20
Athanasius, 41
Athens, 303

Baal, 20, 49, 129
Balaam, 32, 85
Bar Cochba, 235
Barnabas, 302

Barth, Karl, 287
Baruch, 168, 233
Bathsheba, 116, 118
Bedouins, 76
Beelzebub Controversy, 274
Bethel, 105, 152
Beth ha-midrash, 228
Bildad, 199
Book of Signs, 391
Brunner, Emil, 25
Burrows, Millar, 237

Caesarea Philippi, 236, 284, 316
Caiaphas, 266
Cain, 59, 60
Canaan, 8, 10, 49, 61, 63, 64–65, 103, 108, 110
Canon, 31, 211–12
Carchemish, 168
Celsus, 69
Charles, R. H., 232
Chasidim, 219, 240
Chronicler, the, 36, 137 ff.
Clement, 302
Colossae, 326
Constantine, Emperor, 311
Cross, F. M., 237
Cullmann, O., 285 fn.
Cyril, St., 312
Cyrus the Persian, 174, 176, 177

Damascus, 128, 152, 236
Damascus Document, 236–37, 238, 239
Daniel, 38–39
Darwin, Charles, 20
David, 9, 34, 35, 82, 105, 112–13, 116, 117–19, 126, 138, 185, 186, 190

417

Dead Sea Scrolls, 5, 6, 37, 157, 209–12, 235, 237, 279, 308, 384
Debir, 105
Deborah, 32
Diaspora, 326
Didache, 302, 305, 310, 312, 369
Docetists, 387

Ebal Mountains, 103
Ebenezer, 114
Eden, 52, 55, 56
Edom, 105, 178
Eli, 167
Eliezer of Damascus, 62
Elihu, 201
Elijah, 78, 127, 129–30, 150
Eliphaz, 198
Elisha, 78, 127, 130, 150
Elohist, 35
Enlil, 20
Enoch, 233
Ephesus, 322, 375, 389
Ephraim, 155, 156
Epiphanius, 383
Esau, 47
Essenes, 210–11, 231, 235, 240
"E" stratum, 35
Eve, 47, 48, 55
Ezra, 36, 142–45, 182, 211, 233

Frank, Erich, 26 fn.

Gad, 233
Galilee, 105, 219, 231
Gamaliel, 323
Gaster, Theodore H., 237
Gerizim Mountains, 103
Gibeon, 106
Gideon, 108
Gilgamesh Epic, 55
Gnosticism, 307, 326, 381, 382–85
Gomer, 157

Habakkuk, 164

Hagar, 67, 323
Haggai, 140, 141, 179
Hamath, 128
Hammurabi, King, 91
Hanson, R. P. C., 237
Haran, 62, 63, 133
Hazor, 105, 106
Hebron, 106
Herod the Great, 12, 202, 221, 251, 260, 266
Hezekiah, King, 131–32, 139, 158, 168, 191, 192
Hippolytus, 305
Hiram, King, 81, 124
Hiroshima, 110
Hoskyns, 385, 386
Hunter, A. M., 258
Hyrcanus, John, 218, 219
Hyrcanus II, 219

Iddo, 139
Idumea, 218, 220
Ignatius, 302
Iran, 133
Irenaeus, 383
Isaac, 47, 62, 63
Isaiah, 116, 122, 132, 151, 157–62, 167, 174–78
Iscariot, Judas, 236
Ishmael, 47
Ishtar, 20
Issachar, 233

"J," 33, 34
Jacob, 32, 47, 62, 63, 73, 81, 86
Jairus, 315
James, 251, 266–69
Jannaeus, Alexander, 219, 240
"JE," 35, 36
Jehoiachin, King, 170
Jehoiakim, 116
Jehu, 130, 139
Jeremiah, 116, 134, 144, 159, 163, 164–70, 173, 194
Jeremias, Joachim, 291
Jeroboam, 127
Jeroboam II, 151, 180

Jericho, 105, 106
Jerusalem, 35, 122, 133, 138, 139, 141, 158, 162, 167, 168, 219, 223
Jezebel, 122, 127–30
Joab, 117
Job, 196–203
Joel, 179
John bar Zebedee, 381
John Mark. *See* Mark.
John the Baptist, 182, 240, 241–43, 251, 265, 295, 389
John the Elder, 381
Jonah, 179–81
Jonathan, 82, 117, 118
Joseph, 63, 65–66, 233
Josephus, 218, 227, 235, 251–52, 403
Joshua, 33, 103, 106, 107, 110
Josiah, King, 100, 132–34, 163, 167
Judas the Gaulonite, 235
Jung Codex, 384

Kadesh-Barnea, 84, 85
Kerygma, 258
Khirbet Qumran, 37
Know, John, 322 fn.

Laban, 63, 81, 86
Lachish, 105
Lamech, 59
Leaney, A. R. C., 237
Lemuel, King, 191
Leontopolis, 218
Levi, 77, 79, 138
Leviathan, 49, 202
Logos, the, 248, 249–50
Lot, 66
Luther, Martin, 164, 367
Lydia, 223

Maccabaeus, Jonathan, 217
Maccabaeus, Judas, 217
Maccabaeus, Simon, 217, 218
Manson, William, 277
Marduk, 49

Mariamne, 220
Medes, 133
Megiddo, 125, 134
Melchizedek, order of, 359, 360
Mencken, H. L., 4
Mendenhall, George E., 88, 89, 90
Merneptah, Pharaoh, 104
Miriam, 32
Mishnah, 227
Moab, 85, 105
Moses, 21–22, 32, 33, 76, 77, 78, 90, 96, 99–100, 103, 233
Mount Carmel, 129–30
Mount Horeb. *See* Mount Sinai.
Mount Sinai, 8, 13, 32, 33, 72, 84, 88, 96, 101

Naboth, 116, 130
Nahum, 163
Nathan, 116
Nebuchadnezzar, 134, 140, 168
Necho, Pharaoh, 133, 134
Nehemiah, 141
Nero, Emperor, 359
Newbigin, Lesslie, 324
Nineveh, 133, 163, 180, 181
Noah, 47

Obadiah, 178
Odes of Solomon, 384
Omri, 127–28
Origin, 249

Paley, 273
Paul, 22, 25–26, 40, 67, 112, 144, 164, 227, 246, 248, 257, 258–59, 288–89, 290, 301, 303–4, 306, 307–8, 310, 313, 331 ff.
Peter, 236, 290, 293–94, 296
Pharisees, 219, 231, 236
Philip, 220
Philistines, 114
Philo, 235, 248–51, 384
Phoenicians, 110
Phrygia, 223

Pisidia, 112
Plato, 33, 244, 248
Platonism, 248, 362
Pliny the Elder, 235
Pliny the Younger, 369
Pompey, 219, 223
Pontius Pilate, 12, 221, 266, 403
Posen, J., 237

Qarqar, 128
"Q" material, 41, 263–64, 267, 269, 273, 276, 283, 309, 368, 369
Qumran community, 38–39, 219, 231–32, 233, 236, 237–41, 242, 298, 385. *See also* Dead Sea Scrolls; Essenes.

Rachel, 63

Sadducees, 219
Salome, 219
Samaria, 128, 218
Samuel, 114–15, 117, 167
Sanhedrin, 224, 225, 284
Sapphira, 297
Sarah, 63, 67
Satan, 196–97, 238
Saul, King, 82, 112, 114, 116, 117, 118, 185
Schweitzer, Albert, 270, 324
Semites, 47, 61
Shalmaneser, 128
Shear-jashub, 161
Sheba, Queen of, 123
Shechem, 100, 103, 106, 107
Shem, 61
Shemaiah, 139
Shiloh, 106, 113, 167
Sidon, 110, 128
Silvanus, 369
Simon the Canaanite, 236
Sirach, 228–29
Smith, William Robertson, 71
Solomon, 33, 34, 81, 114, 119, 122, 123–27, 190–91, 203, 247
Sophia, 250
"Star," the, 236
Stephen, 224, 299, 301
Stoicism, 245, 248, 249, 302, 309
Strabo, 223

Talmud, 145, 213
Testament of the Twelve Patriarchs, 231, 233–34, 385
Thebes, 77
Tiamat, 49
Tillich, Professor, 21, 28
Torah, 142, 229
Trajan, Emperor, 369
Tübingen School, 324
Tyre, 110, 128, 129

Uriah, 118
Uzziah, King, 139

Wadi Murabba'at, 210
Westcott, 381
Wesley, Charles, 364
Wilson, Edmund, 5
Wisdom of Sirach, 228–29

Xerxes, King, 208

Yahweh, 244
Yahwist, the, 33, 34, 35
Yehud, 140

Zacchaeus, 319
Zadokite Work, 236–37
Zealots, 235–36
Zebedee, 236
Zechariah, 140, 141, 179
Zedekiah, King, 116, 169
Zephaniah, 163
Zeribbabel, 120, 140, 179
Zeus, 209
Ziggurat, 60
Zophar, 198, 199

ANCHOR BOOKS

RELIGION

AFRICAN RELIGIONS AND PHILOSOPHY—John S. Mbiti, A754

THE AMERICAN PURITANS—Perry Miller, ed., A80

THE AMERICAN TRANSCENDENTALISTS—Perry Miller, ed., A119

AQUINAS: A Collection of Critical Essays—Anthony Kenny, ed., AP8

ARCHAEOLOGY AND THE RELIGION OF ISRAEL—William Foxwell Albright, A696

THE BIBLE FOR STUDENTS OF LITERATURE AND ART—G. B. Harrison, ed., A394

THE BIBLICAL ARCHAEOLOGIST READER, Volume III—Edward F. Campbell and David Noel Freedman, ed., A250c

THE BIRTH OF CIVILIZATION IN THE NEAR EAST—Henri Frankfort, A89

THE BOOK OF THE ACTS OF GOD: Contemporary Scholarship Interprets the Bible—G. Ernest Wright and Reginald H. Fuller, A222

CHANGING MAN: The Threat and the Promise—Kyle Haseldon and Philip Hefner, ed., A700

THE COSMOLOGICAL ARGUMENTS: A Spectrum of Opinion—Donald R. Burrill, ed., A586

CRITIQUE OF RELIGION AND PHILOSOPHY—Walter Kaufmann, A252

THE DEAD SEA SCRIPTURES—Theodor H. Gaster, trans., A378

THE DEVIL IN MASSACHUSETTS: A Modern Enquiry into the Salem Witch Trials—Marion Starkey, A682

THE DOGMA OF CHRIST AND OTHER ESSAYS ON RELIGION, PSYCHOLOGY AND CULTURE—Erich Fromm, A500

THE EASTERN ORTHODOX CHURCH: Its Thought and Life—Ernest Benz, A332

EITHER/OR, Volume I, II—Søren Kierkegaard, A181a, b

ESSAYS ON OLD TESTAMENT HISTORY AND RELIGION—Albrecht Alt; R. A. Wilson, trans., A544

EVANGELICAL THEOLOGY: An Introduction—Karl Barth, A408

EVOLUTION AND CHRISTIAN HOPE: Man's Concept of the Future from the Early Fathers to Teilhard de Chardin—Ernst Benz, A607

FACE OF THE ANCIENT ORIENT—Sabatino Moscati, A289

THE FAITH OF A HERETIC—Walter Kaufmann, A336

FIVE STAGES OF GREEK RELIGION—Gilbert Murray, A51

FOUR EXISTENTIALIST THEOLOGIANS: A Reader from the Work of Jacques Maritain, Nicholas Berdyaev, Martin Buber, and Paul Tillich—Will Herberg, ed., A141

FROM FERTILITY CULT TO WORSHIP: A Reassessment for the Modern Church of the Worship of Ancient Israel—Walter Harrelson, A713

FROM RITUAL TO ROMANCE: An Account of the Holy Grail from Ancient Ritual to Christian Symbol—Jessie L. Weston, A125

15Ab

FROM THE STONE AGE TO CHRISTIANITY: Monotheism and the Historical Process—William Foxwell Albright, second edition with new introduction, A100

THE FUTURE OF AN ILLUSION—Sigmund Freud; W. D. Robson-Scott, trans.; revised by James Strachey, A381

THE GATHERING STORM IN THE CHURCHES: The Widening Gap Between Clergy and Laymen—Jeffrey K. Hadden, A712

THE HEATHENS—William Howells, N19

IN PRAISE OF KRISHNA: Songs from the Bengali—Denise Levertov and Edward C. Dimock, Jr., trans.; Anju Chaudhuri, illus., A545

INVITATION TO THE NEW TESTAMENT: A Guide to Its Main Witnesses—W. D. Davies, AO13

ISLAM—Fazlur Rahman, A641

ISSUES IN AMERICAN PROTESTANTISM: A Documentary History from the Puritans to the Present—Robert L. Ferm, ed., A650

JOHN CALVIN: Selections from His Writings—John Dillenberger, ed., A751

MAGIC, SCIENCE AND RELIGION and Other Essays—Bronislaw Malinowski, intro. by Robert Redfield, A23

MAKER OF HEAVEN AND EARTH—Langdon Gilkey, A442

THE MAKING OF A COUNTER CULTURE—Theodore Roszak, A697

MAN IN THE MODERN AGE—Karl Jaspers, A101

MARTIN LUTHER: Selections from His Writings—John Dillenberger, ed., A271

MONT-SAINT-MICHEL AND CHARTRES—Henry Adams, A166

MOVEMENT AND REVOLUTION: A Conversation on American Radicalism—Peter L. Berger and Richard J. Neuhaus, A726

MY PEOPLE IS THE ENEMY—William Stringfellow, A489

MYTHOLOGIES OF THE ANCIENT WORLD—Samuel Noah Kramer, ed., A229

THE OCHRE ROBE—Agehananda Bharati, A776

THE ONTOLOGICAL ARGUMENT FROM ST. ANSELM TO CONTEMPORARY PHILOSOPHERS—Alvin Plantinga, ed., intro. by Richard Taylor, A435

THE PROMETHEUS PROJECT: Mankind's Search for Long-Range Goals—Gerald Feinberg, A683

PROTESTANT-CATHOLIC-JEW: An Essay in American Religious Sociology—Will Herberg, A195

PSYCHEDELICS: The Uses and Implications of Hallucinogenic Drugs—Bernard Aaronson and Humphry Osmond, A736

THE PSYCHOLOGY OF NIRVANA—Rune E. A. Johansson, A728

THE RELIGIONS OF MANKIND: Their Origins and Development—Hans-Joachim Schoeps; Richard and Clara Winston, trans., A621

THE RELIGIOUS FACTOR—Gerhard Lenski, A331

A RUMOR OF ANGELS: Modern Society and the Rediscovery of the Supernatural—Peter L. Berger, A715

THE SACRED CANOPY: Elements of a Sociological Theory of Religion—Peter L. Berger, A658

RELIGION (cont'd)

THE SUFIS—Idries Shah, A765

THE TANTRIC TRADITION—Agehananda Bharati, A745

THE THREE JEWELS: An Introduction to Modern Buddhism—Bhikshu Sangharakshita (Stavira), A763

THREE WAYS OF THOUGHT IN ANCIENT CHINA—Arthur Waley, A75

TWO SOURCES OF MORALITY AND RELIGION—Henri Bergson, A28

VARIETIES OF UNBELIEF—Martin E. Marty, A491

WORLD OF THE BUDDHA: A Reader—From the Three Baskets to Modern Zen—Lucien Stryk, ed., A615

ZEN: Poems, Prayers, Sermons, Anecdotes, Interviews—Lucien Stryk and Takashi Ikemoto, trans. and eds., A485

ZEN BUDDHISM: Selected Writings of D. T. Suzuki—William Barrett, ed., A90

ZEN FLESH, ZEN BONES: A Collection of Zen and Pre-Zen Writings—Paul Reps, ed., A233